# TITAN

# TITAN

## The Art of British Power in the Age of Revolution and Napoleon

William R. Nester

UNIVERSITY OF OKLAHOMA PRESS | NORMAN

Library of Congress Cataloging-in-Publication Data

Names: Nester, William R., 1956– author.
Title: Titan : the art of British power in the age of revolution and Napoleon / William R. Nester.
Description: Norman : University of Oklahoma Press, 2016. | Includes bibliographical references and index.
Identifiers: LCCN 2015043545 | ISBN 978-0-8061-5205-9 (hardcover : alk. paper)
Subjects: LCSH: Great Britain—Politics and government—1789–1820. | Great Britain—Foreign relations—1789–1820. | Napoleonic Wars, 1800–1815—Participation, British. | France—History—Revolution, 1789–1799.
Classification: LCC DA520 .N38 2016 | DDC 940.2/7—dc23
LC record available at http://lccn.loc.gov/2015043545

The paper in this book meets the guidelines for permanence and durability of the Committee on Production Guidelines for Book Longevity of the Council on Library Resources, Inc. ∞



1 2 3 4 5 6 7 8 9 10

Interior layout and composition: Alcorn Publication Design

A fleet of British ships of war are the best negotiators in Europe, they always speak to be understood and generally gain their point.

Horatio Nelson

Let peace continue for five years and we shall again look any Power in Europe in the face.

William Pitt

All my efforts to make a majority of this House of Commons understand the subject have been fruitless . . . They can be embarked in a war from motives of passion, but they cannot be made to comprehend a case in which the most valuable interests of the country are at stake.

William Pitt

To desire war without reflection, to be unreasonably elated with success, and to be still more unreasonably depressed by difficulties, and to call for peace with an impatience which makes suitable terms unattainable, are the established maxims and the regular progress of the popular mind in this country.

William Grenville

From the intercourse of commerce . . . [Britain] will in some measure participate in the growth of other nations.

William Pitt

The Constitution of Great Britain is sufficient to pervade the whole world.

William Grenville

All modern wars are a contention of the purse.

Henry Dundas

We can be but precariously safe as long as there is no safety for the rest of Europe.

George Canning

We shall proceed upon the principle that any nation of Europe that starts up with a determination to oppose a power which . . . is the common enemy of all nations . . . whatever may be the existing political relations of that nation with Great Britain, becomes instantly our ally.

George Canning

I know not whether I can do it in one sentence; but in one word I can tell him that it is Security. But it is also more than this: it is Security against a danger, the greatest that never existed in any past period of society.

William Pitt

Security may be urged by every nation with equal propriety as the pretext for continuing expensive and ruinous wars.

Charles Tierney

# Contents

# Illustrations

## FIGURES

## MAPS



## TABLES

# Preface

The French Revolution posed one of history's greatest challenges to an existing international system and to British national security.[1] This was not immediately evident to most Britons, who viewed the astonishing political reforms in Paris during the summer of 1789 as reminiscent of their own Glorious Revolution, which had a century earlier transformed their government from an absolute into a constitutional monarchy. This initial sympathy was reinforced by the belief that France's threat to its neighbors, especially Britain, would diminish as the restrictions on its monarch's powers grew. Prime Minister William Pitt was the most prominent voice welcoming France's revolution for inaugurating a new age of peace, prosperity, and freedom.[2]

But the revolution was soon locked in a vicious cycle of fear, hatred, and violence with counterrevolutionary forces in France and other European states. Most French leaders eventually reasoned that their revolution would survive only if they destroyed the foreign monarchies that opposed them and planted in the ruins republican governments dedicated to the ideals of liberty, equality, and fraternity. France went to war against Austria, Prussia, and their minor allies in April 1792, and against Britain, Spain, and Holland less than a year later.

Britain warred against France nearly nonstop for the next twenty-two years. During that time, British leaders devised, funded, and struggled to lead seven coalitions first against France's revolutionary, then against its Napoleonic government. Eventually those efforts crushed France and established a system of European great power relations that prevented another world war for nearly a century. An exploration of British policies from 1789 to 1815 offers fascinating insights into how statesmen and generals struggle to master the art of power in a complex, prolonged global struggle.

How is this struggle for mastery best understood? Two great nineteenth-century writers and thinkers asserted polar-opposite views of history and, thus, power. For Ralph Waldo Emerson, history was the biography of great men. For Leo Tolstoy "great" men were the helpless and deluded puppets of historical forces that they barely understood, let alone controlled.[3]

These views, of course, complement rather than contradict each other. At times, leadership is crucial. Imagine how different that era's history would read had William Pitt, Horatio Nelson, and Arthur Wellesley never lived or lived in obscurity. Yet, more often than not, these men and countless others in positions of power were the prisoners rather than the masters of bewildering bureaucratic, political, economic, psychological, sociological, technological, ideological, and international forces. *Titan* explores the art of British power during the age of revolution and Napoleon through the full span of possible insights.[4]

# Maps

The Low Countries Front. 

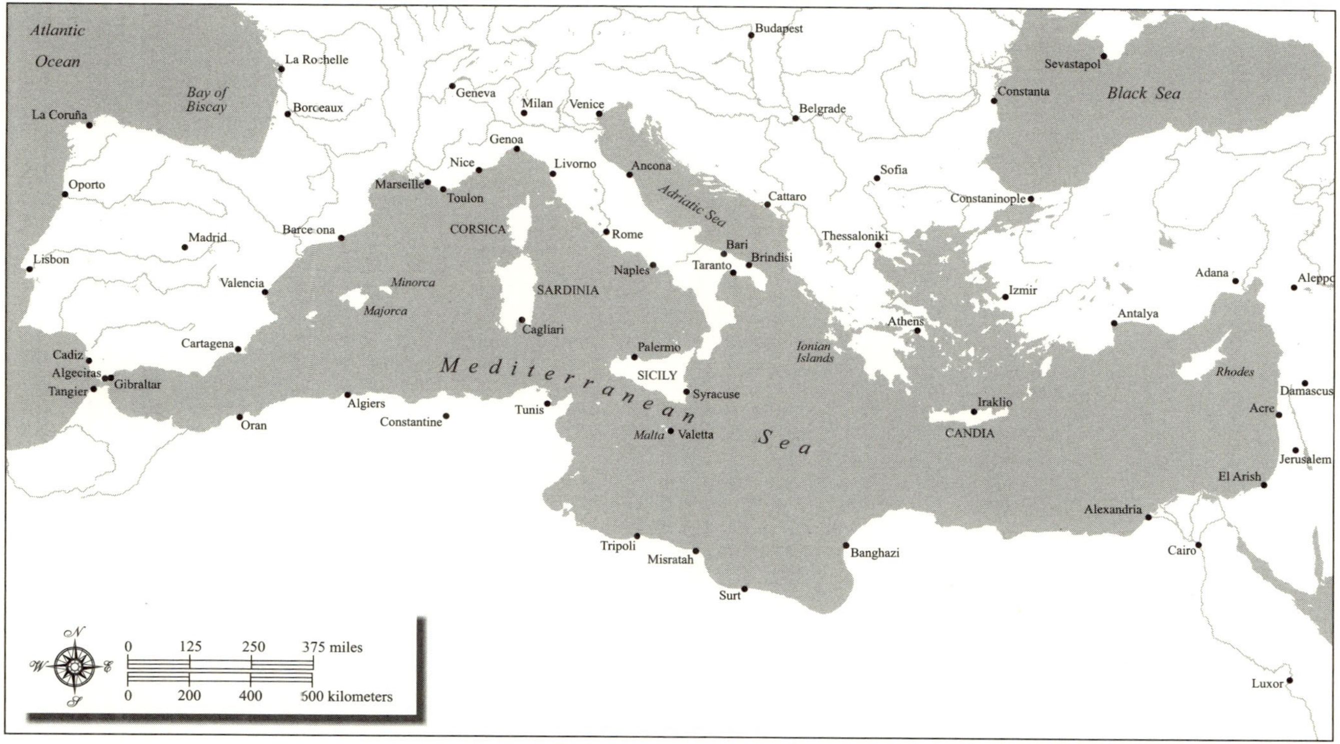
Atlantic Ocean
Bay of Biscay
La Coruña
Oporto
Lisbon
Madrid
Cadiz
Algeciras
Tangier
Gibraltar
Cartagena
Valencia
Barce ona
La Ro:helle
Borceaux
Geneva
Milan
Venice
Genoa
Nice
Marseille
Toulon
Livorno
CORSICA
SARDINIA
Cagliari
Minorca
Majorca
Rome
Ancona
Adriatic Sea
Naples
Bari
Taranto
Brindisi
Cattaro
Budapest
Belgrade
Sofia
Thessaloniki
Constaninople
Constanta
Sevastapol
Black Sea
Izmir
Athens
Ionian Islands
Palermo
SICILY
Syracuse
Malta
Valetta
Mediterranean Sea
Oran
Algiers
Constantine
Tunis
Tripoli
Misratah
Surt
Banghazi
Iraklio
CANDIA
Antalya
Adana
Aleppo
Rhodes
Damascus
Acre
Jerusalem
El Arish
Alexandria
Cairo
Luxor
0 125 250 375 miles
0 200 400 500 kilometers

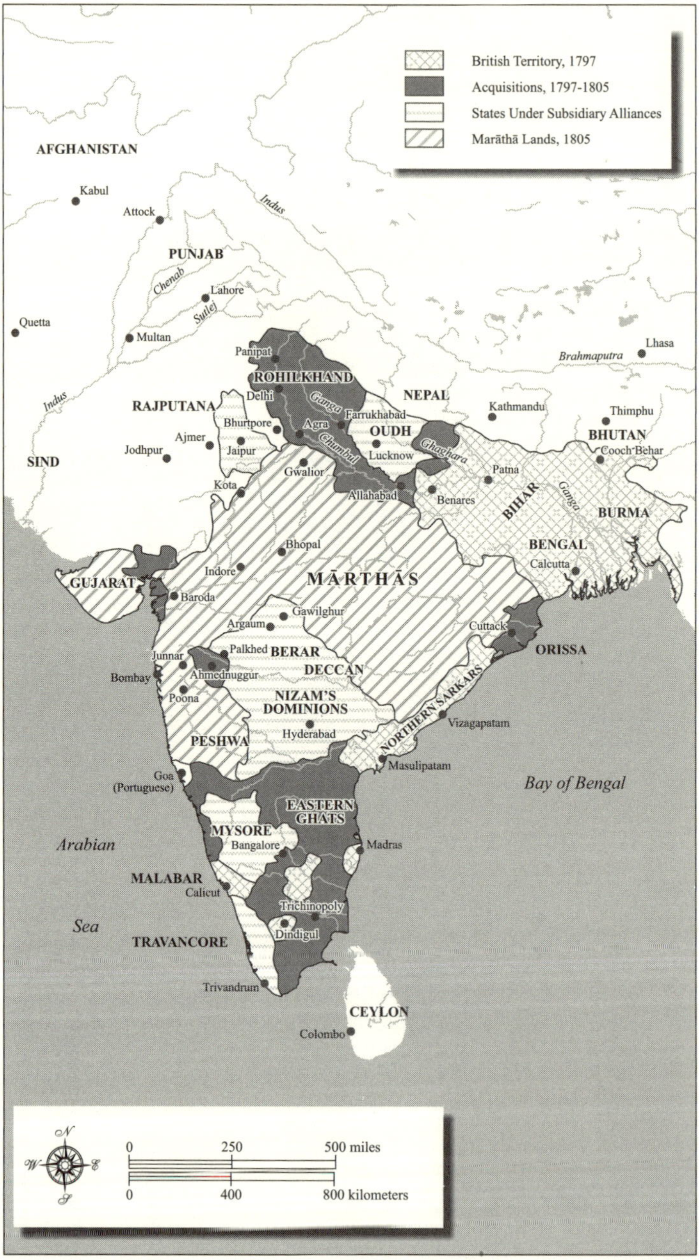


The India Front. 

The Peninsula Front. 

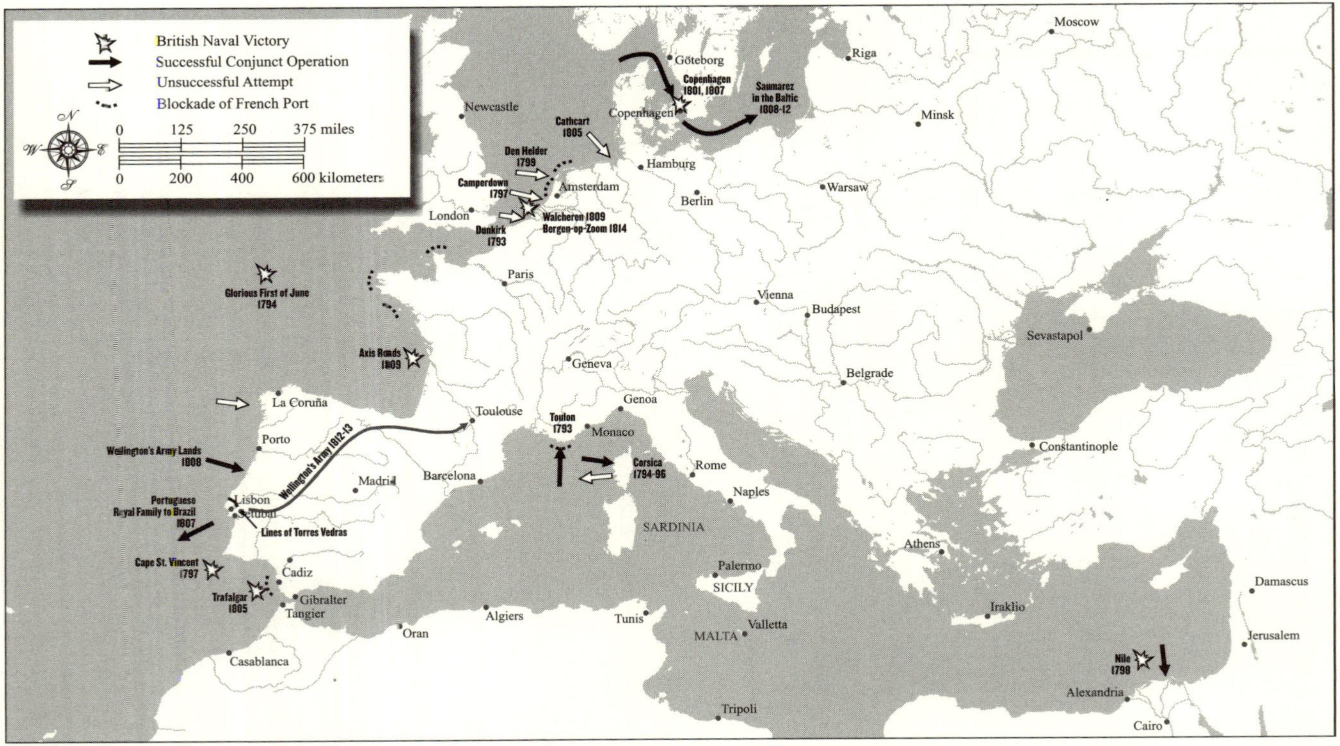


The European and Mediterranean Frcnt, 1812–1814. 

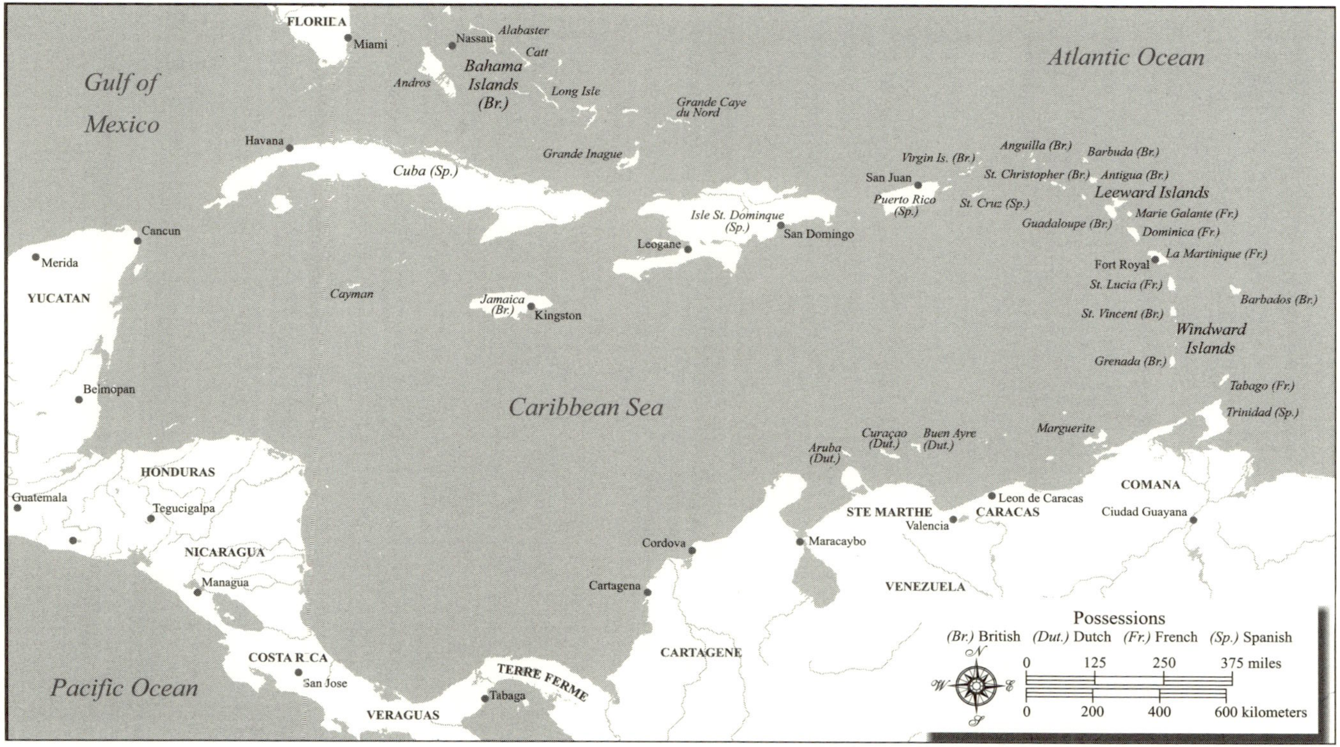


The Caribbean Front. Copyright © 2016 by the University of Oklahoma Press. All rights reserved.

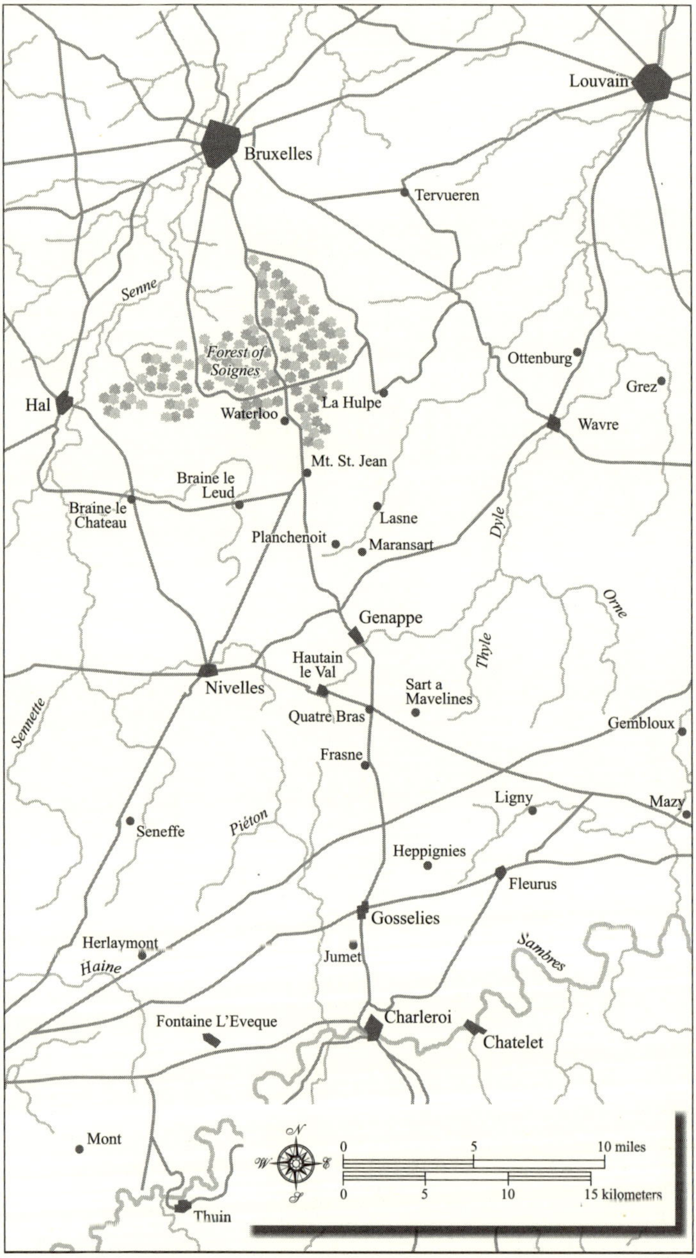


The Waterloo Campaign Front, 1815. 

# TITAN

CHAPTER 1

# The Art of British Power

Power involves doing what one can to get what one wants.[1] Politics and power are distinct but inseparable. Politics happens when two or more individuals or groups are in conflict. Power is the means that each uses to defend or enhance its interests in its conflicts. Since politics is integral to life, the exercise of power is an art that all people struggle to master, although few do.

So what, then, is that elusive but essential art of power? Two and a half millennia ago, Chinese general and philosopher Sun Tzu identified timeless principles of power.[2] Although Sun Tzu explained the art of power in war, his principles apply to any conflict. Knowledge is the key—one must know the interests, values, aspirations, strengths, weaknesses, and psyches of one's enemies, one's allies, one's potential enemies, one's potential allies, and, above all, oneself. All of that knowledge will reveal the nature of the conflict and how best to prevail.

As such, the art of power is easier said than done. People tend to mistake their beliefs for knowledge, and beliefs are often no more than wishful thinking. The worse one's ignorance and delusions, the worse one's exercise of power. Among the most common reasons for power's poor exercise is a failure to know one's limits. Power is relative. Ultimately power is measured by how much one gets of what one wants. Those who reach even relatively modest goals are more powerful than those whose ambitions exceed their abilities. Another reason is a failure to distinguish appropriate from inappropriate power. Power has been explained in many ways, but the best explanation distinguishes among hard, soft, and smart power. Hard power is physical, soft power is psychological, and smart power is the selection and assertion of those elements of available hard and soft power necessary to prevail.

The challenges of mastering the art of power are magnified for sovereign governments ruling numerous diverse, complex, competing groups of people amid rival nation-states. Ideally, there is a virtuous relationship among national interests, policies, and power whereby each reinforces the others. Political actors wield appropriate powers according to appropriate policies to defend or enhance national interests. One constant national interest is to amass more power to defend or enhance all the other national interests. Here again, all this is much easier said than done.

Governments vary greatly in their ability to understand, let alone tap and assert, potential sources of power. Nation-states themselves are composed of a myriad of institutional, legal, and cultural components that in most cases emerged haphazardly over time in response to crises. Somehow leaders must transcend the tunnel vision of the bureaucrats, politicians, interest groups, editors, and the public at home, and the generals, admirals, diplomats, and spies in the field. Perceiving the common good in the midst of multiple competing interests, of course, is an enormous challenge under the best of circumstances.

A chicken-and-egg relationship exists between political and military power, succinctly expressed by Charles Tilley: "War made the state and the state made war."[3] Such mutual reinforcement certainly characterized the development of European states from the Renaissance to the mid-twentieth century, and the United States from World War II through the Global War on Terror and beyond. Yet, starting in the late nineteenth century, one might say that welfare also made the state and the state also made welfare. Regardless, by 1792 related advances in administration, finance, and technology enhanced the power of European states not just to wage war but to better deal with an array of other challenges. Wars pressured states to adopt these innovations sooner rather than later.[4]

War is power's ultimate assertion and clearest measure, as it forces governments to grapple with and pay the consequences for responding to a series of vital questions. First, is the war worth fighting? If so, then how is it best fought? The answers come from knowing the ends and means of oneself and one's enemy. History records a seemingly endless parade of governments failing to perform this elementary task of power. A frequent reason for this is ignoring the reality that money is hard power's literal and figurative bottom line, what historian John Brewer aptly called "the sinews of power."[5] Pasty-faced clerks and bookkeepers in dimly lighted counting rooms and warehouses are as important to national power as ruddy-faced, brawny soldiers in the field and sailors at sea. Yet money itself is not power unless it is invested in ways that protect or enhance national interests. Governments often squander potential economic power as senselessly as they do military power.

Governments are just as likely to misunderstand and thus misapply or neglect the exercise of soft or psychological power. Soft power must be believed to exist. People act on what they think is true. So manipulating the beliefs of oneself and others in one's favor is crucial to the art of power. For instance, one's reputation can enhance or diminish one's power. Potential aggressors tend to bully those perceived to be weak and bow before those perceived to be strong. Thus a reputation for toughness can be self fulfilling if it deters challengers. But here too the art of soft power can be tricky. All too many people mistake hubris for confidence, snobbery for sophistication, glorification for patriotism, and tyranny for leadership, and so undermine rather than advance themselves.

Nationalism, or a people's mass emotional belief in their common legacy, language, values, institutions, interests, and aspirations, is a relatively new source of power in history.[6] Nationalism and war are often dynamically linked, with one promoting the other. Indeed, one could say that in the modern world nations make wars and wars make nations. The reason is at once simple and profound. Identity is as much about what one is not as what one is. People define themselves within one group opposed to other groups; the worse the antagonisms with other groups, the stronger one's identity. Eric Hobsbawn nicely expressed that phenomena: "There is no more effective way of bonding together the disparate sections of restless peoples than to unite them against outsiders."[7]

The American and French revolutions revealed just how powerful nationalism can be. People believed so fervently in their nation that they were willing to kill and die not just to defend but even to glorify it. Yet, for monarchs, a dilemma was embedded in trying to conjure up nationalism—it appeared intertwined with a liberalism that championed natural rights and representative government. They sought to harness nationalism's power after gingerly detaching it from liberalism. No one was more adept at that than Napoleon.

State building and nation building are related but distinct processes, with the latter far more daunting than the former. State building involves expanding, transforming, and creating institutions, laws, and practices that better promote the dynamic between security and prosperity. Nation building is about converting often disparate identities into a common identity within and sometimes beyond the realm. The result is known as a nation-state. Yet nation-state building never truly ends. National identities change, and the state adapts to new problems with new institutions and policies. A nation-state's power to get what its leaders want is grounded crucially if not exclusively on how well "the state" works and how much "the people" identity with their "nation."[8]

A nation-state's hard and soft power is, of course, relative to that of others in the same conflict. The more nation-states that are involved, the tougher the challenge for each government to calculate the distribution of power and manipulate it in its favor. Since each conflict is unique, a past winning strategy might be disastrous if asserted in the present. A fundamental question that governments face is whether to go it alone or form or join a coalition. If the decision is to seek allies, should one join (bandwagon) or oppose (counterbalance) the side that seems more powerful? Ideology can be decisive. One tends to join those of a like mind against those of the opposite, yet history is filled with other national interests trumping ideology. In a complex world, there is no magic formula. Henry Kissinger explained that "the effectiveness of diplomacy depends on elements transcending it; in part on the domestic structure of the states comprising the international order, in part on their power relationship."[9]

## British Interests, Policies, and Powers

For centuries British leaders tended to believe that their realm had no permanent friends, only permanent interests, and that survival is any state's number-one enduring interest, which in turn determines one's enemies and allies from one existential threat to the next. Like most truisms, these are more catchy than true. In reality, national interests are dynamically related to one's shifting friends and foes, and thus can and do change with time. As for survival, for nine centuries after the Norman conquest of 1066, the British Isles did not face a serious threat of being invaded, let alone vanquished, until 1940, not even in 1216, 1779, or 1805, although perhaps in 1588.[10]

Nonetheless, centuries of acting on these beliefs fostered a distinct set of British interests, powers, and policies. From 1509 to 1763, a series of governments in London more or less transformed the realm from a peripheral into a great power. National interests expanded with the English, then British, empire until they girdled the world. In this transformation, aggressive trade and colonization policies backed by military force were crucial. In a virtual circle of power, revenues from foreign trade and colonies paid for the navy and army that protected the British Isles and its swelling foreign trade and colonies. All along, no interest was more vital than thwarting any one great power or alliance from dominating Europe.

A key reason why these policies worked was that they usually included appropriate and parsimonious measures of soft and hard power, and thus smart power. By 1789, policy makers could see only a handful of truly vital strategic spots worth fighting for around the globe, including the Low Countries, Hanover, Gibraltar, the Copenhagen strait, Cape Horn, Jamaica and other West Indian sugar islands, and Bengal for its saltpeter.

Of these, the oldest tripwire for shifting from diplomacy to war was a threat to the Low Countries, the Dutch and Austrian Netherlands spreading across the lower Scheldt, Meuse, and Rhine Rivers draining into the North Sea. Of the two countries, the Dutch Netherlands or United Provinces was more vital economically and strategically. Although the British and Dutch were perennial trade rivals that occasionally warred against each other, Whitehall had helped the Netherlands win independence from Spain and repeatedly fought to prevent its conquest by France. Then there was Hanover, whose fate would have elicited shrugs were it not the latest royal dynasty's ancestral home. Since George I took the British throne in 1714, the king was also Hanover's elector, a duty that entangled the realm in central Europe's politics and, inevitably, wars, and thus diverted and often squandered British power.

Aside from being obsessed with the fate of its trade, colonies, the Low Countries, and Hanover, British foreign policy shared essential elements with other states on the continent. A security dilemma trapped European states—the measures each took to protect itself at once threatened others. These threatened states naturally took similar measures, believing that they had no choice in the matter. The appearance of weakness seemed to invite aggression. The dilemma was that there was little peace in strength. As states raced to mass more arms and allies, they made war more likely. This drove diplomacy from one crisis of brinksmanship to the next. Although diplomats resolved many of these crises, by cruel necessity governments were either preparing for, waging, or recovering from war. As a result, threats arose much more from miscalculation than design.

The "classic balance of power system" dominated Europe from the 1648 Peace of Westphalia to the French Revolution's eruption in 1789. For nearly a century and a half, concrete interests like filling vacant thrones or snipping off bits of territory from one's neighbors rather than abstract ideals like which version of Christianity should prevail determined diplomacy. Shorn of ideological motives, statesmen followed the timeless maxim "The enemy of my enemy is my friend." One's ally in one war was often one's enemy in the next. Weaker states tended to act on their common interest in allying against stronger states that might diminish or outright conquer them. During that century and a half, Britain naturally played off different sides against each other and backed the weaker. George Canning, who would list foreign secretary and prime minister among his numerous government posts, explained why: "We can be but precariously safe as long as there is no safety for the rest of Europe."[11]

A new age began with the French Revolution. For the next quarter century, the related ideologies of liberalism and nationalism were diplomatic wild cards, complicating and at times outright confounding the "enemy of my enemy is my friend" maxim. Nonetheless the traditional orientation of British foreign policy persisted. With France firmly in mind, Canning explained: "We shall proceed upon the principle that any nation of Europe that starts up with a determination to oppose a power which, whether professing insidious peace or declaring open war, is the common enemy of all nations . . . [and] whatever may be the existing political relations of that nation with Great Britain, becomes instantly our ally."[12]

## The Power of the Nation-State

Essential to any country's power is the nature of the government that rules it. The key is how effective or "smart" the political system is in letting its leaders swiftly select and assert appropriate resources of hard and soft power to thwart threats, seize opportunities, alleviate chronic problems, and forestall future challenges, all in the name of national interests.

The nation-state "Great Britain" is the most enduring result of English imperialism. It took several centuries for England to subdue and engulf its neighbors into one state. England and Wales joined their parliaments in two stages by Acts of Union in 1536 and 1543. In 1603 the thrones of England and Scotland joined when Scotland's King James VI became England's James I. Great Britain finally emerged in 1707, when a third Act of Union created the United Kingdom of England, Wales, and Scotland. To realize that end, the founders took three vital steps, two substantive and one symbolic. The Scots dissolved their parliament for seats in England's parliament, and gave up their currency for what was thereafter known as the British pound sterling. Two national flags became one, with the crosses of England's St. George and Scotland's St. Andrew superimposed on a blue field; the new flag soon became popularly known as the Union Jack. Even then Great Britain was not complete. The next decisive territorial and institutional stage came in 1800, with an Act of Union whereby Britain's parliament absorbed that of Ireland.[13]

Forging this state was prolonged and challenging enough. The process of morphing English, Welsh, Scots, and Irish into "Britons" was far more complex and, inevitably, incomplete. Wars against common enemies were vital in transforming identities and loyalties by inspiring in each subsequent generation greater meaning in a shared flag, tongue, coin, government, army, navy, and market. As important was the reality that the English not only far outnumbered but diluted with commerce, settlements, and language the "Celtic fringe" of Welsh, Scots, and Irish that they were trying to blend into Britons. Fouling this process was the harsh political, economic, and social bigotry by the Anglican majority against "dissident" Protestant sects and Catholics.[14]

Vital to the process of developing a nation-state was the debate among political philosophers over what Britain was and what it could or should be. Although most seventeenth- and eighteenth-century thinkers supported the notion of Great Britain as a national identity, they clashed sharply over how power should be distributed in the state. Tories propounded an absolute monarchy, with parliament acting mostly as a rubber-stamp assembly for the king's will. Whigs championed a constitutional monarchy, with the bulk of power in parliament. The divisions within each camp were often as sharp as those between them.[15]

Yet, regardless of which version they advocated, Britons were largely united in lauding their government as superior to all others. Home Secretary William Grenville captured that prevailing view with this exuberant assurance to King George III: "The Constitution of Great Britain is sufficient to pervade the whole world."[16] Setting aside the question of its universal appeal, a more fundamental problem stalked, and still stalks, Britain's constitution: where is it? Unlike virtually all other peoples, the British never got around to composing a formal blueprint for government. Britain's "constitution" is a hodge-podge of documents, principles, practices, and institutions that emerged from nearly a millennium of political struggles. In spite of this, during the eighteenth century, a dynamic equilibrium of power symbolically prevailed among institutions in three different sites—Westminster,

Whitehall, and Windsor. The political system's essence, however, was the relationship between the parliament and the monarchy.

To assist the king, an assembly of the realm's most powerful nobles existed throughout the various Anglo-Saxon and Norman dynasties. The origins of the modern parliament, however, is perhaps best dated to 1215, when a coterie of nobles forced King John to sign the Magna Carta, which acknowledged their rights and powers, including being consulted on crucial political matters. Parliament was an unicameral institution until 1341, when its wealthy commoners began meeting separately from the nobles and bishops. After Parliament's move into Westminster Palace in 1548, the House of Lords met in the White Chamber and the House of Commons in the chapel. By 1780 there were 232 lords, also known as peers, of whom 26 were bishops, three were royal dukes, and the rest held an array of titles. The number of secular lords rose sharply over the next three decades as Prime Minister William Pitt sought to build a majority in the House of Lords as solid as his majority in the House of Commons. In all, George III added 119 lords, most handpicked by the prime minister, during Pitt's eighteen years in power. By 1800, the House of Commons had 558 members, with 489 from England, 45 from Scotland, and 24 from Wales. Two members came from each of the forty counties. The universities of Oxford and Cambridge each had two members. Then there were 203 cities and boroughs with 403 members split among them. After Britain and Ireland united in 1801, the House of Commons took in a hundred Irish parliamentarians, bringing the total to 658.[17]

After the 1688 Glorious Revolution, Parliament met annually for several months, with members called to convene any time from November to January. While debates and votes on laws, resolutions, and petitions were the core of each house's business, members mostly worked in committees that dealt with particular issues. Most bills began in the Commons, with either house able to amend and pass a bill received from the other side. When this happened, it was passed back for the other house's approval.

Power in the houses differed in two ways. All financial bills originated in the Commons and were usually passed by the Lords with little debate. The House of Lords acted as the supreme court when its law lords ruled on controversial lower court decisions. Style also differed. The Lords personified dignity and decorum. In sharp contrast, Commons sessions were often raucous, with frequent calls for order. Cheers and jeers frequently disrupted speakers and often flummoxed those more easily distracted. These distinctions have persisted through today.

No organized parties then existed, only vague, shifting, and overlapping affiliations of politicians sharing similar outlooks or interests.[18] The clearest divide was between those who backed the cabinet and those in the opposition. The names Whig and Tory, originally terms of opprobrium, arose in the late seventeenth century to designate the philosophical divide over whether the monarchy or Parliament should harbor the bulk of sovereignty; Tories favored the former and Whigs the latter. But for much of the eighteenth century, everyone was more or less a Whig, although the more progressive distinguished themselves as New Whigs from the more conservative Old Whigs. By the era's end, the Old Whigs were known as Tories, and later in the early nineteenth century the New Whigs became Liberals.

Rather than parties, factions prevailed, formed around rich and charismatic leaders who shared prestige and patronage with their followers. After the king tapped a prime minister, he struggled to cut deals with other faction leaders to forge a governing coalition that represented a parliamentary majority. Even then that did not ensure support on every issue. For instance, after a swelling chorus of protests against his brinksmanship policy with Russia in 1791, William Pitt lamented: "All my efforts to make a majority of this House of Commons understand the subject have been fruitless. . . . They can be embarked in a war from motives of passion, but they cannot be made to comprehend a case in which the most valuable interests of the country are at stake."[19]

Clubs reflected and shaped the split between the government and the opposition.[20] Charles Fox began the slow process of party formation when he founded the Whig Club in 1784. White's Club was the most prominent of those that supported the king and his cabinet, and Brook's Club was the hangout for the Prince of Wales, Fox, and their cronies. William Pitt, however, was an introvert who avoided socializing with those he did not know well even if they were political allies; he and his intimates gathered at Goostree's Club. No matter where they met, amid the often boisterous eating, drinking, and gambling, faction leaders and their followers forged strategies, struck deals, rewarded loyalty, and punished betrayal.

The 1716 Septennial Act required elections to be held at least every seven years, but the king and prime minister could dissolve Parliament and call for elections at any time.[21] Elections were hastily run affairs. Voting began days after Parliament's dissolution, giving potential opponents little time to mount a challenge. Even more formidable was the landed gentry's entrenched power in the House of Commons. New, prosperous, and rapidly growing cities like Birmingham, Manchester, Leeds, and Sheffield were not even represented. As late as 1812, three of four members still reaped most of their wealth from the land, while only one in four derived their income from being a merchant, lawyer, manufacturer, or member of some other profession. Further bolstering the gentry's power was the reality that around one in five members of the Commons was the son of a peer in the Lords. Given the overwhelming odds in its favor, it is not surprising that the sitting government won each of the six national elections—1796, 1820, 1806, 1807, and 1812—held between 1789 and 1815.[22]

During this era, property and religious restrictions permitted only about fifteen of a hundred British adult males to vote, while perhaps only one in one hundred could afford to run for Parliament. The eligibility to vote and run for office varied enormously. There were two types of constituencies, counties and boroughs. The counties were less elitist; property owners with an annual rental value of forty or more shillings held the right to vote. Religion was as powerful a barrier as property to voting and running for office. The 1661 Corporation Act forced all municipal officers to take an oath to the Church of England, and the Test Acts of 1673 and 1678 expanded the oath to all civil and military officers. The oath specifically barred Catholics from power, but also discriminated against "dissidents" from non-Anglican Protestant sects. Although the penalties of these harsh laws were suspended by the 1727 Indemnity Act that was thereafter annually renewed, the official discrimination persisted.

All forty counties and nearly all boroughs each had two delegates that went to the two top vote-holders or those first "past the post." The boroughs varied widely in their number of constituents, with the largest holding thousands and the smallest of the "rotten" or "pocket" boroughs, Sarum, with seven. Then as now, running for office was expensive; costs tended to rise with a district's number of voters.

Elections were generally decided not by one's political philosophy or principled stand on the issues but on how much largess one could dispense to local power brokers, who then did what they could to deliver the vote of their own clients. The secret ballot did not exist. Voting was a very public and often intimidating affair, as bully boys from each candidate loomed near polling places, cajoling and mocking, or beckoning with hot food and hard drink, or discreetly pressing coins into the palms of coy fence-sitters.

The worst irregularities were in the boroughs. At least half of them went to the highest bidder, with average prices ranging from £3,000 to £4,000 during the era. Faction leaders brought many a promising young politician into parliament by buying him an open "rotten" borough. Many a "nabob" who made a fortune in India began a political career in England by purchasing a borough.[23]

Winning elections were expensive enough, but maintaining a parliamentarian's lifestyle with a home, servants, and array of other expenses in London was a financial challenge for all but the richest members. Members did not receive a salary, so they had to make money any way that they could get away with. Among the advantages of being tapped for a cabinet post was receiving a salary and, for the top portfolios, a place to live.

Two familiar institutions of Britain's government—the prime minister and his residence—coalesced during William Pitt's nearly two decades in power. The term "prime minister" gradually edged aside "first" or "chief" minister to designate the man who forged and led a parliamentary majority that empowered him to form a government. This position, however, was not yet a separate and formal post but instead was usually if not always bestowed by the king upon the first lord of the treasury. The row of houses called Downing Street was built in the 1730s, and soon George II designated Number 10 to be the first lord of the treasury's abode.

William Pitt explained and realized his conception of the prime minister's duties and powers: "There should be an avowed and real minister possessing the chief weight in council and the principal place in the confidence of the King. In that respect there can be no rivalry or division of power. That power must rest in the person generally called the First Minister; and that minister ought . . . to prevail."[24]

The prime minister drew his cabinet from both houses of Parliament and beyond. He generally chose members from the prominent factions in either house. This was no easy task, given the amorphous nature of the era's political allegiances. Complicating this was the prime minister's need to get the king's approval for a proposed minister before tapping him for the post.

The prime minister thus was the first among equals in a cabinet that took "collective responsibility" for their decisions to the king and country. Yet the entire cabinet rarely met, and then usually to ratify previously made decisions. Fox noted that the cabinet meetings gave "the members an opportunity of consulting with each other and stating their ideas reciprocally on points connected with their several departments, but with no intention of communicating the result to his Majesty."[25]

The prime minister worked with the relevant ministers for devising or adjusting policies that dealt with their respective and often overlapping duties. During the Age of Revolution and Napoleon, an "inner cabinet" of four positions dominated policy, the first lord of the treasury, the secretary of state for foreign affairs, the secretary of state for war, and the home secretary, responsible not just for domestic security but also all colonial affairs except for India. Despite their vast duties, each secretary had only a dozen or so assistants to immediately help him.

The British state extended far beyond London. Each of the forty counties and couple of hundred cities and towns had its own government. A lord lieutenant, appointed by the king, headed each county and appointed the justices of the peace that upheld law and order and rendered justice on most petty crimes or civil disputes. A mayor, aldermen, and councilors ran each city and town. Few of those charged with administering the law knew much about it, although many did ground their decisions on an intuitive sense of justice.

Overlapping local governments were 15,000 Anglican parishes, each with its own pastor and vestrymen whose duties included dealing with local political along with religious matters. They appointed the constables, fed and sheltered the homeless, and repaired the roads and bridges.[26] The Church of England enjoyed a steady stream of income, since the law forced everyone to tithe it whether or not they attended.

Two deep-rooted forces in the political system ate away at British power. Nothing drains national power worse than corruption, the diversion of public resources for private gain. It does so by transforming money, skill, and time from productive to wasteful ends. Corruption, like power, is relative, and a nation's threshold of how much corruption it tolerates changes with time. Britain's threshold was especially high during the eighteenth and early nineteenth centuries.[27] The line between public duties and private interests was hazy in the era's political culture, and services, offices, and votes went to the highest bidders. Payoffs were endemic to politicians and bureaucrats. Supplicants to officials often had to pay an under-the-table "fee" for an audience and much more for any favor. The king, prime minister, and other cabinet ministers had varying appointment powers, which they tended shamelessly to distribute to their friends and allies, and many were outright sinecures. For instance, in 1792 George III awarded William Pitt the post of Lord Warden of the Cinque Ports, an anachronistic office dating to the Norman Conquest and now simply a conduit for bestowing income to and eliciting loyalty from the recipient.

There was another voracious leech on British power. Literally lording it over everyone else were the aristocrats, who numbered less than one of a thousand Britons but owned perhaps one of four acres by 1800.[28] The four hundred or so families preserved their wealth, power, and status by marrying among themselves and ensuring that only one child, ideally the firstborn son, inherited the land. The male aristocrats enjoyed more than sprawling palaces, blooded horses, parliamentary seats, and officer's commissions. Most boys attended lower schools like Winchester, Eton, Harrow, or Westminster, then the University of Oxford or Cambridge, and finally enjoyed the finishing educational and sybarite touches of a Grand Tour of Europe's cultural highlights that often took years to complete. Most emerged fluent in

French, proficient in Greek and Latin, conversant in history, the fine arts, and the natural sciences, and insufferably snobbish to their lessers. Those not in Parliament or the military could devote themselves full time to managing their estates and indulging in such diversions as balls, gambling, fox hunts, and the waters at Bath. Despite or perhaps because of their incredible riches, many lived far beyond their means and fell deeper into debt. Worst of all, most aristocrats not only resented but resisted the efforts of upstart parvenus like merchants, entrepreneurs, and financiers to realize their own dreams of wealth, power, and prestige.[29]

## The Power of the Royals

The aristocracy's aristocracy, of course, was the royal family. In his book *The Rights of Man,* Thomas Paine asked many sharp-edged questions and gave even more cutting replies, none more so than those concerning kingship: "What is this metaphor called a crown, or rather what is a monarchy? Is it a thing or a name or a fraud? . . . It appears to be a something going much out of fashion, falling into ridicule, and rejected in some countries both as unnecessary and expensive."[30]

Although the British king was a "constitutional monarch" beholden to parliament and the law, he was no figurehead.[31] He peaked not one but two pyramids of related power, the government and the Church of England. His powers, however, mostly depended on his ability to persuade other powerful men through some mix of reason, emotion, appointment, and payback. His most potent weapon was his Civil List, or the yearly allowance he received to fund his court and government, but which he also tapped to buy votes in both houses of parliament. As for the royal seat of power, over the centuries the court had moved from the Tower of London to Westminster Palace to Whitehall Palace to, most recently, St. James Palace, along with Windsor Castle a day's coach ride westward. Reinforcing the king's institutional and legal powers were the throne, scepter, rituals, and all the other regalia of power rooted in a thousand or more years of history that virtually every Briton instinctively bowed before.

Nonetheless, although the king appointed his cabinet's members, the bulk of power lay with them rather than him. It was the ministers who debated the issues, devised policies and laws, and then, with the king's approval, had the appropriate institutions implement them. While the king might confer with the prime minister each week or so, he often met daily with his Privy Council, composed of a half dozen or so trusted advisers picked from the realm's most powerful noble families. The Privy Council issued the king's edicts and Orders in Council, but only after consulting with the cabinet and receiving its approval.

The king opened each parliamentary session with a speech that addressed the prevailing issues and strongly hinted how he wanted them resolved. The speech was usually written in close consultation with his Privy Council and prime minister. For support in parliament, the king naturally relied more on the House of Lords than the House of Commons. In the Lords, the bloc of conservative peers, known as the Crown Party, voted either enthusiastically or reluctantly as he wished. From 1760 to 1800, King George III shamelessly swelled his party's ranks by creating 197 new peers. With the same means he dominated Ireland's parliament by appointing 135 of the 240 peers in its House of Lords.[32]

Theoretically, the monarch could veto any bill or other official act of parliament. In practice, Queen Anne cast the last formal veto in 1708. Yet the ruler retained the power of imposing an unofficial veto simply by declaring his or her royal will on the matter. A cabinet could override that "will" only with its own unanimity backed by nearly everyone in Parliament.

An essential element of the royal family's power kept Britain politically entangled in the heart of Europe. The king was also the elector of Hanover, the royal family's ancestral home. This title came with a small army of 17,000 troops and a seat on the Holy Roman Empire's council of nine electors. George III declared that "I certainly feel myself as warmly and zealously attached to my Electoral Dominions as any sovereign can be and never will part with them but with my life."[33]

As with any other position, the throne's actual power depended on who filled it. George III was the king for sixty years, from 1760 to 1820, the realm's third longest reign after Victoria and Elizabeth II.[34]

War accompanied most of his reign. He mounted the throne at age twenty-two in October 1760, toward the victorious end of the Seven Years' War, and reigned during America's War of Independence and the first five of the seven coalitions that Britain forged against France from 1793 to 1815. Although Parliament declared him insane in January 1811 and passed the crown's duties to the crown prince, George III remained officially the king until he died in January 1820.

At his coronation, George issued this crowd-pleasing declaration: "Born and educated in this country, I glory in the name of Britain, and the peculiar happiness of my life will ever consist in promoting the welfare of a people whose loyalty and warm affection to me I consider as the greatest and most permanent security of my throne."[35] The affection of Britons for their new king was genuine and widespread. Yet, while his then youth and amiability certainly explained much of his initial popularity, events far beyond his control also mattered. Britain conquered Canada in 1760 and over the next three years defeated French and Spanish fleets and armies elsewhere. By the 1763 Treaty of Paris, Britain took Canada from France, East and West Florida from Spain, and the West Indian islands of Grenada and the Grenadines. His popularity declined with time, nose-diving during the disastrous war that led to American independence. He survived assassination attempts in 1795 and 1800 and one thwarted plot in 1802.

Although still reviled in America, George III had many redeeming qualities. He was a devoted husband to Sophia Charlotte of Mecklinburg-Strelitz, whom he married in 1761 and with whom he sired fifteen children, nine boys and six girls. In addition to his family, he loved music, astronomy, hunting, horticulture, reading, and theater. Unlike most royals, he spurned adultery, gambling, and drinking to excess. His official letters reveal him to be knowledgeable about the world and devoted to his duties. He offered this insight into his values: "My mind is not of a nature to be guided by the object of obtaining a little applause. . . . Rectitude of conduct is my sole aim."[36] He insisted that "I have no other view in life than to the best of my judgment to fulfill my duty."[37]

Then there was his downside. With time he grew more petty, obstinate, intolerant, vindictive, and self-righteous. He came to loathe and condemn as disloyal those who differed with him. This dark side of George's character at times inflicted grievous harm on British power. When faced with the prospect of a cabinet that included several opposition leaders whom he detested, he declared: "I would rather lose the Crown I now wear than bear the ignominy of possessing it under their shackles."[38] Several times during his reign, his hatred obstructed the formation of a cabinet that would have united all the major factions in a truly national government during wartime. The worst dynamic between George's character and the government's policy determined the fate of the British Empire. Among history's most intriguing questions is what if George III had accepted rather than rejected the Olive Branch Petition that he received from Congress in October 1775. In it the Americans requested reforms, most importantly representation in parliament, not independence. Had he granted that wish, America might still be part of the British Commonwealth.

The king's oath on taking the throne officially defined his duties and powers. George III was inflexibly committed to upholding every tenet of the oath, especially the one barring Catholics from political power or even civil rights. He angrily rejected bills in 1787, 1789, 1790, and 1801 that would have alleviated some of the repression suffered by Catholics.

George III was determined to rule actively rather than preside passively over Britain and its empire. He wanted to be his own prime minister and insisted that the monarch was the ultimate commander in chief: "The king must be understood as reserving to himself at all times the undoubted right of deciding on the measures which may be proposed to him respecting the military service and the administration of it, both with reference to the prerogatives of the Crown, and the nature and expediency of the measures themselves."[39]

Madness first afflicted him in October 1788 and persisted until February 1789, when lucidity suddenly reemerged. While the king's subjects cheered his recovery, thereafter the fear lingered that the madness would recur. This fear was realized several times over the next twenty-three years until insanity permanently engulfed him in 1811. The image of a drooling, ranting, leering monarch was unsettling to anyone, especially those who sought a heroic image of Britain. It is now known that the king's madness came from porphyria, a condition in which toxic chemicals surge and overwhelm one's nervous system. This disease ran in the king's Hanoverian line and was among a litany of genetic defects that festered among Europe's inbred nobility.[40]

The man who served as regent until his father's death and then became George IV hardly had the makings of a model monarch.[41] Most Britons condemned and some admired him for his insatiable womanizing, gambling, eating, and drinking. While he seduced or paid for the charms of countless women, one was his life's love. Maria Anne Fitzherbert must have had some extraordinary talents either despite or because of her two divorces. George secretly married her in December 1785, and in doing so he violated two laws. The 1701 Act of Settlement forbade a royal marriage with a Catholic. The 1772 Royal Marriage Act prevented any royal from marrying before age twenty-five without the blessing of the king and parliament. And all along his debts soared, no matter how much money he was able to finagle from public and private sources. When he became a legal adult at age twenty-one in 1783, he received the small palace known as Carlton House with its scores of servants, an annual £62,000 pension, and £29,000 to pay off some of the interest on his debts. Over the next three years alone, he racked up £370,000 in more spending, of which £250,000 was borrowed and mostly would never be paid off. George was a liberal and enjoyed talking politics during drinking and wenching bouts with Charles Fox and his fellow debauchees.[42]

For all this, George III openly despised his firstborn son. He acted on his contempt by refusing to confer on him the title of general while granting high army or naval ranks to his younger sons who lived to adulthood: Frederick, Duke of York; William, Duke of Clarence; Edward, Duke of Kent; Ernest, Duke of Cumberland; and Adolphus, Duke of Cambridge. Indeed, in a stunning act of nepotism, George named York the army's commander in chief.

## The Power of the Press and Public

For British power, it mattered little if George III was mad or lucid, or if the profligate Prince of Wales backed the opposition or government.[43] Yet the fact that we know so much about the foibles of this era's royals and other prominent public figures spotlights two essential related pillars of British power—the press and the public. In this chicken-and-egg dynamic, an increasingly literate, informed public received and demanded more to read, especially works that explored national problems and what to do about them. Publishers yearly churned out scores of daily and weekly newspapers, hundreds of books, and thousands of pamphlets and broadsides. Of the nation's most prominent newspapers, the *Morning Chronicle* and the *World* generally supported the government, while the *Morning Post* backed the opposition. Even then, Britain had tabloids like the *Sun* and the *True Briton* that peddled sensationalism. Cartoons mercilessly lampooned those in power, including the royals.[44]

All this in turn inspired a growing portion of the public to get involved in politics whether or not they were legally entitled to do so. By the late eighteenth century in Britain, a reform movement composed of an array of interest groups and outspoken, progressive personalities emerged with a very long list of proposals.[45]

Britain was far from being a liberal democracy practicing one-person, one-vote, due process, and equal rights guaranteed to all. Instead the realm was a quasi-authoritarian state, with its unwritten constitution; rights guaranteed and franchise limited to Anglicans; blatant discrimination against all other religions such as Dissenter Protestants, Catholics, and Jews; and loyalty expected of all subjects to the king and all that he symbolized. Although the 1689 Toleration Act permitted Trinitarian Protestant Dissenters to worship privately, they still had to tithe the Anglican Church. A similar "emancipation" for Unitarians and Catholics lay a century and a half in the future.

Theoretically all Britons enjoyed certain rights regardless of their religion or income, including trial by a jury of their peers; habeas corpus, or the ability to be freed from custody unless a formal charge was issued; the sanctity of one's property; and the expression of grievances through petition to those in power. In practice, the ability to exercise these rights varied sharply depending on how much money, connections, prejudices, and conflicts of interest were involved, while the government at times outright suspended those rights in the name of national security.

Freedom of the press was hardly absolute. Those who published political tracts and cartoons did so at the peril of being prosecuted for libel or even sedition. Years of persecution plagued John Wilkes, a liberal parliamentarian, who lambasted the cabinet and king in his newspaper, the *North Briton.* Whitehall finally cracked down in April 1763, after his issue Number 45 derided the Treaty of Paris that ended the Seven Years' War. He fled to Paris ahead of an arrest warrant for seditious libel. The liberal opposition rallied to his cause, and his constituents reelected him three times to defy a parliamentary majority that expelled and forbade him from returning.

In all, "the people" held a latent power that they might assert at critical periods, usually by excessive enthusiasm for or rage against an event, policy, or law. When this happened, those in power found themselves struggling to lead rather than be led. William Grenville, who spent a couple of decades in the cabinet, explained this mass psychology: "To desire war without reflection, to be unreasonably elated with success, and to be still more unreasonably depressed by difficulties, and to call for peace with an impatience which makes suitable terms unattainable, are the established maxims and the regular progress of the popular mind in this country."[46]

The American Revolutionary War politicized countless Britons, otherwise apathetic to the doings of those in power. The war dragged on, year after year, with no end in sight as the toll in death and debt soared, and the popularity and prestige of the king and cabinet plummeted. This emboldened more parliamentarians, merchants, and humanitarians to speak out against the war, which then provoked enraged government backers to denounce their "disloyalty."[47]

These swelling animosities erupted into violence in the spring of 1780, although the war was not the direct cause. In April, prominent liberals formed the Society for Constitutional Information as a watchdog organization that exposed and protested government corruption, incompetence, and repression. Their first coup was to win a vote of 233 to 215 in the House of Commons to investigate the king's Civil List, which Parliament had increased to £900,000 in 1777. Although the Civil List was supposed to underwrite the daily expenses of the monarchy and government, the king diverted a portion of the money to buy votes from parliamentarians and favorable articles from newspaper editors.

This provoked a vicious reaction from conservatives. While they could not justify the corruption revealed by parliament's investigation of the Civil List, they did find an easier wedge issue with which to assault liberals. The liberal-sponsored Catholic Relief Acts of 1772, 1774, and 1778 had eased some of the worst government repression of property rights, education, and worship imposed on people of that faith. These reforms enraged conservatives, who insisted that Catholics were entitled only to repression. In June 1780, Lord George Gordon, who headed the Protestant Association, presented to Parliament a petition to repeal these reforms. When a majority rejected his petition, he mobilized a mass demonstration in the streets that turned violent.

These battles between liberals and conservatives were mere skirmishes compared to the mass protests, violence, arrests, and repression during the Age of Revolution and Napoleon that lay ahead.

## The Power of the Economy

If Britain or any country has an enduring national interest, it is not survival but the creation and distribution of wealth. Money is power's literal and figurative bottom line. No state then enjoyed greater power to raise money by taxing and borrowing than Britain.[48] Indeed, this financial clout was so vast that Britain was the arsenal of monarchy for not one but seven coalitions against France from 1793 to 1815.

Where did all the money come from? In the late eighteenth century, Britain's economy was transformed by an industrial revolution fueled by symbiotic advances in agriculture, trade, finance, management, technology, transportation, manufacturing, urbanization, and literacy.[49] This economic superpower let Britain increasingly espouse free trade for all. Prime Minister Pitt expressed the liberal ideal version of Britain's role in international trade: "From the intercourse of commerce . . . [Britain] will in some measure participate in the growth of other nations . . . The rude wants of countries emerging from barbarism and the artificial and increasing demands of luxury and refinement, will equally open up new sources of treasure, and new fields of exertion in every state of society, and in the remotest quarters of the globe. It is this principal . . . which . . . maintains . . . successive improvement in the general course of the world."[50]

If Pitt and other free trade advocates actually believed these platitudes, they did so by ignoring their own nation's experience. The British government could preach liberalism because for centuries it had practiced mercantilism, which historically has been the superior strategy for creating and distributing wealth. The free trade ideals first extensively expressed by Adam Smith in his 1776 tome, *An Inquiry into the Wealth of Nations*, only work for those countries, industries, or businesses that are already ahead. Once Britain enjoyed a clear and widening technological, manufacturing, financial, and corporate lead, it could afford to entice strong and bully weak states into reciprocal market-opening deals.

Like other governments, Britain's recognized and acted upon a simple truth—that a country made money when it exported more than it imported and lost money when it imported more than it exported. Whitehall wielded several strategies to maximize national profit. One was to grant monopolies to companies to colonize and exploit foreign lands or capture foreign markets. Another was to impose high tariffs on imports or outright ban some products from other countries or its own colonies to protect domestic industries. A third was to encourage the development of new technologies and industries by offering patents and subsidies. For instance, to regulate food prices and supplies, the Corn Laws prevented the export of grain when the price of wheat reached forty-four shillings for a quarter ton or eight bushels. Finally, the Navigation Acts forced ever more trade to be carried in British vessels. When Britain went to war in 1793, 16,300 vessels were registered across the empire. Over the next three years, that number rose past 17,000 despite 3 percent losses to enemy warships and privateers.

The numbers increased because ship owners sought protection in the convoy system that Whitehall organized in 1793 and made mandatory in 1798.[51]

These mercantilist policies fostered a virtual cycle of ever greater national power. The government reaped more taxes and tariffs, then invested this money in ways that enhanced key industries that created wealth and the military that protected the expanding volume of exports and number of colonies. In a March 1798 report, Secretary at War Henry Dundas elaborated that dynamic among trade, wealth, and power: "The prosperity of this country knows no bounds, unless . . . its industry and commercial enterprise shall outrun the extension of its foreign markets."[52]

An agrarian revolution led and literally fed the industrial revolution. Growing productivity for crops and livestock starting in the seventeenth century swelled the population that supplied the demand for more soldiers, sailors, miners, and factory workers in the eighteenth century. Farmers gradually produced more as they adapted the innovations in plows, plowing, seeds, seed drills, grafts, crop rotation, new crops, husbandry, fertilizer, breeding, and drainage introduced by Jethro Tull, Turnip Townsend, Robert Bakewell, and other tinkerers. Scientific farming was popularized by the government's Board of Agriculture and through such publications as *Farmers' Journal* and *Farmer's Magazine*. This transformation was accelerated by the enclosure movement, whereby landlords replaced peasants with livestock. Many of these men, deprived of their homes, ended up working in a mine, factory, ship, or regiment.

Scarcity inspired innovation. As Britons clearcut their forests for ships, buildings, charcoal, and firewood, wood prices soared. Fortunately, there was a previously scarce alternative that became increasingly abundant. Steam power was first harnessed to fuel pumps, which drained water from mines that dug coal from deep seams. This partly alleviated the wood shortage as cheap coal replaced wood in hearths and forges. The substitution of higher-temperature coke smelting for charcoal forged higher-quality iron and steel.

Success bred success. Investors poured money into an increasingly diverse array of ventures and thus transformed one industry

**Table 1. Population (in Millions) of the Great and Middle Powers**

| | 1700 | 1750 | 1800 |
|---|---|---|---|
| Britain | 9.0 | 10.5 | 16.0 |
| France | 19.0 | 21.5 | 28.0 |
| Austria | 8.0 | 18.0 | 28.0 |
| Prussia | 2.0 | 6.0 | 9.5 |
| Russia | 17.5 | 20.0 | 37.0 |
| Spain | 6.0 | 9.0 | 11.0 |
| Sweden | — | 1.7 | 2.3 |
| Netherlands | 1.8 | 1.9 | 2.0 |
| United States | — | 2.0 | 4.0 |

Source: Kennedy, *Rise and Fall of the Great Powers*, 99.

after another from small-scale cottage into large-scale factory production that caused output to soar and prices to plummet. No industry's productivity advanced faster than textiles; British factories produced £1.2 million worth of cloth in 1760, £6.5 million in 1780, and £51.6 million in 1800![53]

Urbanization at once stimulated and was stimulated by the agrarian, manufacturing, financial, and trade revolutions. Only the Netherlands had a larger portion of urban dwellers. By 1800, about one of four Britons lived in cities with 10,000 or more inhabitants. London's population alone was 765,000, with 134,300 people crowding the core and 630,700 sprawling across the suburbs.[54]

The relative size of a country's population can be critical for national power; the more numerous a people, the larger its number of potential consumers, producers, soldiers, and sailors. The 1801 census counted about 8,893,000 Britons in England and Wales, a further 1,608,000 in Scotland, and perhaps 4,700,000 in Ireland, which made it Europe's third most populous realm after France and Russia, with about 28,000,000 subjects each.[55] The relative quality of a people, however, enhances national power far more than sheer numbers. For instance, literacy and wealth are dynamically related. In the proportion who could read and write, Britons trailed only Americans and Dutch.

As Britain's economy expanded, business power became increasingly entangled with political power. Practitioners of the art of national power were hardly confined to politicians, generals, and naval captains. The heads of huge mercantile and financial firms played vital behind-the-scenes roles in shaping government policies toward issues that directly affected them, and at times outright determined what was or was not done. The trouble is, of course, that delegating public policy to private interests can be a risky business for national interests.

## The Power of the Purse

Military and financial power are inseparable, as Secretary at War Henry Dundas explained: "All modern wars are a contention of the purse."[56] Preparing for, waging, or recovering from war was every government's primary duty during that era. The British government's budgets reflected these harsh geopolitical realities. From 1688 to 1815, 80 percent of the budget was earmarked for the army, navy, mercenaries, allies, or debt incurred by these expenses.[57]

Calculating the costs and benefits of war versus peace is at once the most crucial and daunting art of power. War is a budget buster. Many a country lost a war that its government believed it could win or won a war only to lose the subsequent peace by bankrupting itself. For instance, the French Revolution would never have erupted in 1789 had Louis XVI spurned Foreign Minister Vergennes's advice in 1777 to ally with the American rebels against the British empire. Doing so forced the king a dozen years later to convene the Estates General to approve sweeping fiscal measures that might forestall his realm's financial collapse. What happened instead was an increasingly radical revolution and eventually war that lasted nearly a quarter century.

Although wars also swelled Britain's national debt, Whitehall capitalized on periods of peace and prosperity to lighten the burden. During the Seven Years' War, which actually lasted from 1754 to 1763, the national debt nearly doubled, from £75 million to £134 million. During the subsequent dozen years of peace, the debt fell to £128 million in 1774, then soared again during the American Revolutionary War, itself provoked partly from the tax increases the crown imposed on the colonists. By 1783, Britain's national debt stood at £243 million. Over the next decade, Prime Minister Pitt's policy of spending cuts and tax hikes reduced Britain's national debt to £232 million when the nation once again went to war against France.

Unlike France, Britain had the power to pay for its debt because it was far better at taxing and borrowing revenue. A tax is any device that raises money for the state that does not have to be paid back. Britain's tax system was more efficient because the government directly collected it rather than farming it out to private businesses as in most other states. This led to more accountability, transparency, and thus trust in the system, so people tended to pay rather than evade. No great power had a higher tax rate than Britain during the Age of Revolution and Napoleon, when it reached 35 percent of the economy. Direct taxes included those imposed on the amount of one's land, hearths, windows, and closets, while indirect taxes included duties on imports and excises on British-made goods, to name the most prominent. By 1790, 75 percent of taxes were indirect. Whitehall's relative fiscal responsibility let it fill the inevitable gap between revenues and expenses by borrowing money from domestic and foreign financiers at interest rates far lower than those paid by the other great powers. The Bank of England, founded as a stock company in 1694, provided the most reliable source of low-interest loans.

## The Power of the Army and Navy

Britain ultimately vanquished France in the nearly nonstop fighting from 1793 to 1815, much as it had won every war that it fought between 1689 and 1815, except America's War of Independence.[58] After that war, in 1783, national morale quite possibly reached the lowest point in British history. Over the preceding eight years, the Americans, eventually backed by the French, Spanish, and Dutch, won independence by inflicting a series of humiliating military defeats on Britain. Under the subsequent peace treaties with those nations, Britain lost not only the thirteen rebellious American colonies but West and East Florida to

Spain. Chancellor of the Exchequer William Pitt expressed in February 1783 the prevailing gloom among Britons for their nation's future that "the visions of her power and pre-eminence are passed away."[59]

That defeat's onus weighed most heavily on the army's shoulders. Although the redcoats and their German and Loyalist auxiliaries won more battles than they lost, this mattered little, given the surrender of armies at Saratoga and Yorktown to America's "rabble in arms," as the British sneeringly called them, and worsened the already leery feelings most Britons harbored toward the "thin red line" on land that backed the "wooden walls" at sea that deterred and at times defeated would be invaders.

Among the unique aspects of Britain as a great power was the prevailing aversion to a standing army. Britons justified this fear by pointing to the military dictatorship of Oliver Cromwell and his New Model Army from 1649 to 1660. This aversion was actually a vital source of national power because it checked the growth of an army that drained scarce resources, potentially threatened liberties at home, and provoked ruinous wars overseas. William Pulteney, first Earl of Bath, succinctly explained what most Britons were eager to avoid: "The Army causes Taxes, the Taxes cause Discontents, and the Discontents are Alledged to make an Army necessary. Thus you go in a circle."[60] Of course, Britons enjoyed the luxury of a bare-bones army because they lived securely on an island realm as long as the Royal Navy mastered the surrounding seas.

The downside of the aversion to a standing army was that military amateurs rather than professionals were mostly in charge. Officer commissions below the rank of colonel were bought rather than earned; the higher the rank, the higher the price. Training was on the job, since no officer schools then existed. The king appointed generals and was so generous in handing out these political plums that the army grew increasingly ponderous beneath their weight, peaking in 1813 with 5 field marshals, 223 lieutenant generals, and 224 major generals; the seniority system exacerbated the stultifying problem of having far too many chiefs. The commander-in-chief was not a permanent post but was reestablished during wartime, and it usually went to someone noted more for his royal connections than his military prowess. Of the army's commanders-in-chief during the era, Frederick Augustus, Duke of York and the king's second son, dominated the office from 1795 to 1809 and from 1811 to 1827, while generals Jeffrey Amherst and David Dundas served brief respective two-year stints of 1793 to 1795 and 1809 to 1811. Although the title conferred far more status than power, none of these men brought luster to the role and York made a mess whenever he led an army into the field.

A Byzantine bureaucracy exacerbated the amateurism. The secretary at war was not a cabinet member but a second-tier official who led the War Office and worked mostly with the Paymaster General to budget and distribute money to the regiments to cover their costs. Prime Minister Pitt established the portfolio of secretary at war in 1794, to act as a policy maker and to help coordinate army and navy efforts. Then there was the adjutant general for discipline and equipment and the quartermaster general for housing or encamping the troops. Among the Treasury Department's many duties were buying and shipping provisions to the soldiers. Separate from the army was the Ordnance Board, with the crucial tasks of training gunners, engineers, and cartographers at the Royal Military Artificers College at Woolwich and either ordering from private manufacturers or producing artillery, firearms, munitions, wagons, tools, and other equipment, as well as uniforms, and distributing them to the army and navy, which competed fiercely for these resources. Transportation was in private hands; the Transport Board hired captains with crews and vessels to convey troops and supplies at sea and teamsters with wagons, carts, and draft animals to convey supplies on land. Neither transportation source came cheap, and prices rose with Whitehall's increasing demands. For instance, an 1805 report found that sending 20,000 infantry and 2,000 cavalry from Britain to Hanover required respectively 30,000 and 16,000 tons of shipping.[61] At times the Admiralty Board pared costs by stripping warships of their cannons and munitions and using them for transports. This maze of overlapping institutions and officials often frustrated and at times infuriated most of the army's ranks. Hugh Percy, Duke of Northumberland, expressed the prevailing dismay: "What alas are we to expect when lawyers are allowed to think themselves Generals, and plan our military operations?"[62]

So when Whitehall mobilized for war in 1793, the army faced not just a foreign enemy but a tarnished legacy, skeptical public, and bureaucratic hobbles.[63] The redcoats did not overcome these handicaps anytime soon, for the triumphs of Wellington on the Iberian Peninsula and at Waterloo lay far ahead. In between were fifteen or so years of numerous abysmal defeats, long stretches of inaction, and a handful of minor victories.

Just filling the army's ranks was a Herculean struggle. Each regiment was responsible for keeping itself at full strength. Desertion and death, with disease claiming ten times more lives than battle, kept a regiment's recruiting teams constantly on the prowl. Finding enough willing and able men was tough enough in peacetime and increasingly difficult as Whitehall established more new regiments to war against France. Enlistment bounties, known as "the king's shilling" and issued by a sergeant in the local pub, enticed many a man, usually in his cups. Invited for a pint or two, countless men found that they had unwittingly enlisted after nearly swallowing a shilling the sergeant had deposited in a frothy mug and thrust into his eager hand. He could back out within twenty-four hours provided that he gave back that shilling, which was usually consumed in another round for his newfound mates. Otherwise he was ushered before a magistrate to swear an oath to join the king's service. Few sober men enlisted for the pay. Privates received thirty shillings a month, about one-quarter the average laborer's wage. Soldiers never actually palmed all those coins, as the army made deductions or stoppages for uniforms, equipment, and food. Only very desperate men indeed, refugees from poverty or the law, found the army an appealing berth. As Arthur Wellesley, Duke of Wellington, notoriously remarked, the British army was "composed of the scum of the earth," and he marveled that "we should have made them the fine fellows they are."[64]

Backing the army were militia and fencibles. Every able-bodied man from the age of eighteen to forty-five had to be in his parish's militia company. Whitehall could call on parishes to hold drafts and send those with unlucky numbers to the regulars. Draftees could evade service by finding a substitute or paying a fine. Fencibles were an intermediary force between regulars and militia. Joining exempted one from the militia and possibly being drafted into the regulars.[65] Auxiliary troops like engineers, miners, sappers, and medics were, however, limited in numbers and abilities compared to their French counterparts.

Then there were mercenaries. No great power relied on foreign soldiers more than Britain, with the proportion peaking at one in eight in 1813. Very good reasons underlay this policy. It was actually cheaper and quicker to rent foreign regiments than to raise new redcoat regiments. Not only were the direct costs of British troops greater, but the indirect costs of diverting healthy men from the economy undercut the nation's wealth and, thus, power. In addition, the foreign troops were seasoned, disciplined professionals, while in contrast, it takes months to recruit, train, and equip a new regiment, and it can take years for the soldiers to acquire the skills to march, camp, and fight effectively together.[66] Finally, when the war ended, the mercenaries were paid off and sent home. Disbanding British regiments was more complex; while the soldiers could be transferred to under-strength regiments, the officers suddenly found themselves holding expensive commissions and no immediate prospects of a post or sale.

Nearly all foreign regiments came from small German principalities, with those from the king's ancestral homeland of Hanover usually the first to be hired. After the French overran Hanover in 1803, Whitehall organized the King's German Legion for volunteers from Hanover and other German states. In 1809 Portugal's government designated Wellington the generalissimo for all Portuguese troops. Wellington assigned British officers to train and command Portuguese regiments, which were integrated into brigades usually with one Portuguese and two British regiments. With time the Portuguese equaled the British as first-rate soldiers. Although Spain's government grudgingly designated Wellington its generalissimo in 1812, Spanish pride and corruption kept the British from achieving similar results with them.

Given all the challenges of finding and keeping volunteers, how could Britain compete with revolutionary France with its levée en masse and slogan "Every citizen a soldier and every soldier a citizen"? Actually Whitehall swiftly raised huge numbers of troops, with the ranks soaring threefold from 38,945 men, including 34,262 infantry and 4,681 cavalry in 1793, to 129,262 men, including 100,452 infantry and 28,810 cavalry in 1795.[67] The trouble was that the invasion threat forced Whitehall to keep most troops in the British Isles to defend the realm.

With fewer soldiers, British armies, unlike those of the other great powers, were built with divisions rather than corps, with usually two brigades making a division and three regiments a brigade. It was only in 1813 that Wellington massed enough troops to organize his army into corps of three or so divisions. Most regiments had only one battalion of eight "line" or regular companies and two "flank" companies, one of lights and the other of grenadiers. Light infantry were usually the battalion's most energetic men and best shots and were deployed before the other companies to skirmish with the enemy. Grenadiers were usually the battalion's strongest and largest soldiers and often led attacks. At times a general would combine his army's flank companies into temporary light and grenadier battalions. Although permanent grenadier regiments had existed for over a century, the first light infantry regiments were established in 1803. Ideally a company numbered a hundred men but usually fielded far fewer, as recruits fell behind attrition. Training mostly involved learning how to properly maneuver and handle muskets. In all these developments, the British emulated earlier French innovations. While the standard infantryman's jacket remained red, trousers were switched from white to gray in 1812. Grenadiers continued to sport bearskin hats throughout the era, while the line and light infantry gave up their tricorn hats for shakos in 1800. Starting in 1809, highlander regiments began exchanging their plaid kilts for plaid trousers and their bonnets for shakos.

Soldiers spent little time practicing shooting. Smoothbore muskets were inaccurate beyond a score or so yards and were the deadliest when fired by massed men at other massed men at short ranges. During the late eighteenth century, a few regiments each raised a riflemen company. The first battalion of riflemen emerged in 1797 as the Sixtieth Regiment's Fifth Battalion. The first regiment of riflemen, the Ninety-fifth, which eventually reached three battalions, was established in 1800. Riflemen were generally deployed as skirmishers, who picked off the enemy but avoided close combat since their short-barreled Baker rifles could not mount bayonets. They wore green rather than red coats, and depending on the regiment, either green or gray trousers.

The cavalry was split between "heavy" dragoon and "light" hussar regiments, with the former sporting carbines and pistols along with swords, while the latter brandished slender curved sabers. British horsemen were renowned for their skills and bravery but criticized for their lack of cohesion in battle. Wellington famously blistered them "for galloping at everything, and their galloping back as fast they gallop on the enemy. They never consider their situation and never think of manoevering before an enemy." He tried and failed to get his cavalry commanders to wield this simple but effective tactic: "All cavalry should charge in two lines, of which one should be in reserve."[68]

Artillerymen received the best training, since cannons and howitzers demanded the most technical and team skills. Although gunners, like infantry, were organized in battalions, they were usually dispersed in companies or batteries of 120 men, five cannons, and a howitzer. Artillery was divided between huge "siege" cannons to batter enemy fortifications and two types of "field" cannons, "foot" and, starting in 1793, "horse." Cannons were designated by the weight of the ball they fired, howitzers by the width of their bores; with their higher trajectory, howitzers were better deployed firing explosive shells over walls while cannons fired balls or canister directly at the enemy. For cannons, 24- or 18-pounders were the most common siege guns; 6-pounders prevailed among the foot artillery through 1812, and 9-pounders thereafter; horse artillery galloped into action trailing 3-pounders. Throughout the era, the 5 1/2-inch howitzer remained the standard for foot artillery. Introduced in 1807, Congreve rockets were bombs that weighed from twelve to thirty-two pounds and were fired along a pole twenty-four feet long; they proved to be more effective at large targets like fortresses and cities than at troops. Until 1794, the Ordnance Board hired civilians as teamsters to get the guns, caissons, and horses to the battlefield, where the gunners took over; thereafter soldiers composed the Corps of Drivers. Gunners and teamsters wore blue rather than red coats.

Britons generally celebrated their navy as much as they scorned their army. The navy's war record was as exemplary as the army's was blemished, and it reached unsurpassed heights during the wars against

France from 1793 to 1815. Yet the navy faced its own shortcomings and challenges.[69]

Like the army's, the navy's bureaucracy was cumbersome, with a range of uneven overlapping peaks rather than one bureaucratic mountain with an apex. The first lord of the admiralty and his staff of twenty-nine officers presided over, rather than ruled, this vast realm. Boards dealt with overlapping issues like pay, provisions, equipment, dockyards, rope yards, hospitals, and recruitment. For instance, the Admiralty placed orders with the Navy Board for ships, the Recruiting Board for sailors, the Ordnance Board for cannons and munitions, and the Victualling Board for food and drink. Paying for all this was a separate bureaucracy, the treasury of the navy, that complied a budget and submitted it to the paymaster general.

The Royal Navy suffered from an acute Achilles' heel. Virtually all the materials for constructing vessels came from foreign sources. The most critical ingredient was wood. Just one 74-gun warship demanded three thousand loads of timber culled from fifty-seven acres of forest![70] Centuries of the navy's voracious needs combined with civilian demand for lumber and firewood to deforest the British Isles. Shipbuilders increasingly depended on Canada, Scandinavia, and Russia for the massive oak trees to carve up for a vessel's frame and planks, and tall straight pines for masts. Likewise, the British scoured overseas markets for flax for canvas, hemp for rope, and copper to sheath ship bottoms, while demand annually outstripped domestic supply for the hundreds of tons of iron that was pounded or cast into scores of products from nails to cannons. In every war the imperative to secure the array of natural resources that literally kept the Royal Navy afloat dictated much of Whitehall's diplomatic and naval strategy.

Without constant repairs and copper bottoms that thwarted sea worms, wooden ships lasted only a half dozen or so years before they were good for nothing but prison hulks or scrap. To overhaul its vessels, the navy had huge dockyards at Portsmouth, Plymouth, Sheerness, and Chatham in Britain, and overseas at Gibraltar; Halifax, Nova Scotia; English Harbor, Antigua; Port Royal, Jamaica; and smaller facilities at Bombay, Madras, and Calcutta in India. At each port, the royal dockyards were the largest industrial complexes, with those in Britain employing thousands of workers organized in hundreds of related tasks.

A lesser technical weakness afflicted the Royal Navy. French and Spanish warships tended to be better designed, with sleeker lines that made them relatively more swift and easier to maneuver. The British made up for that with superior seamanship. The trouble was finding enough seamen.

The Royal Navy's demand for sailors invariably fell far short of the willing supply. Recruitment was tough enough in peacetime and a Sisyphean labor in wartime. Losses from disease, desertion, discharge, and battle eliminated an average 10,000 or so sailors each war year, with scurvy, malaria, and yellow fever the worst scourges. Relatively few men volunteered. The choice between stretching one's hammock on a warship or merchant ship was a no-brainer; a seamen earned about twenty-five shillings a month in the navy and ten times that on a private vessel. Atop that was the navy's far harsher discipline. Navy recruiters did hold out the distinct possibility of prize money, although sailors shared only a tiny sliver of what the officers pocketed, with usually half taken by the captain. The Royal Navy notoriously filled the fleet's empty hammocks by dispatching press gangs that kidnapped able-bodied men and forced them to serve; those who resisted were beaten until they submitted.

These weaknesses aside, the Royal Navy enjoyed overwhelming superiority in hard and soft power. The most obvious advantage was in sheer numbers of vessels. Warships were rated by the number of cannons that they carried. Ships of the line comprised four types: first rates of 100 guns or more on three decks, second rates of 80 to 99 guns on three decks, third rates of 64 to 89 guns on two decks, and fourth rates of 50 to 63 guns on two decks. Frigates were either two-deck warships of fifth rates with 40 to 49 guns or single-deck sixth-rates with 20 to 39 guns. Seventh rate sloops carried 12 to 20 guns. In each category, the Royal Navy enjoyed a wide lead in numbers over France's navy, the world's second largest.

Then there was the soft side of naval power. Superior diet was among the many reasons why Britain ruled the seas; food consumed one-quarter of the navy's budget. The most vital item was fruit juice.

In 1781 Admiral George Rodney permitted his fleet's head doctor, Gilbert Blaine, to test the anecdote that lemon juice prevented scurvy, the vitamin C deficiency that rotted and infected gums and vital organs until the victim was bedridden or died. The results were astonishing—scurvy killed not a man during the test. Blaine tirelessly pressured the Royal Navy to end scurvy by mixing lemon or other fruit juices with the rum ration. The Admiralty soon advised the practice but did not require it until 1795. Thereafter, "limeys" were healthier than sailors of other nations, at least at sea. As for malaria and yellow fever, in 1787 Dr. Leonard Gillespie began testing whether cinchona, or Peruvian tree bark, could prevent or treat those dreaded diseases. The results were so promising that in 1792 the Admiralty required sailors to take two daily doses of what became known as quinine with their grog.

The most vital related reasons for British navy superiority were audacity, tactics, guns, and gunnery. Tactics and technologies are inseparable. British ships of the line usually had longer-range cannons on the lower deck and carronades above. The carronade was a snub-nosed 32-pounder cannon that lived up to its nickname—"the smasher"—at relatively short ranges. Its use forced captains to spread sail and haul rope to maneuver their warships as close as possible to where a broadside of carronades could cripple an enemy vessel. Like lemon juice, the carronade was a new innovation, having been introduced in 1779 during the American Revolutionary War. The carronade's rate of fire was as crucial as its weight. British captains drilled their gunners until they fired twice as fast as French and Spanish crews. Finally, the British developed a sophisticated yet simple flag-signaling system during the early 1780s that gave fleet commanders superior means of directing their captains. All these hard and soft power edges reinforced the long-standing defeatism of French officers who preferred to evade the Royal Navy and preserve their ships to evade another day rather than fight to destroy the enemy's warships. Tactics reflected this mentality, as French captains ordered their gunners to aim at the enemy vessel's masts and rigging to slow its pursuit so that they could escape.

The Royal Navy's aggressive new tactics defied tradition. For a couple of centuries, each navy's fighting instructions forced captains to keep their ships rigidly in line two cable lengths apart as the fleet maneuvered to gain the weather gauge, or upwind, then fire at the enemy's line of ships whether they were sailing in the same or opposite direction. The Admiralty enormously boosted British naval power by abolishing these tactics in 1791, thus freeing captains to steer their vessels as far into harm's way as they dared. No captain was more aggressive than Horatio Nelson in sailing his warships directly at the enemy line to sever it and fire broadsides at vessels on either side. A battle's goal now was to annihilate rather than repulse the enemy.

The Royal Navy could be just as formidable a source of power in diplomacy as in war. As Nelson put it: "A fleet of British ships of war are the best negotiators in Europe, they always speak to be understood and generally gain their point."[71]

## The Power of Covert Operations

Espionage is a vital element of national power at which the British excelled during this era. In January 1793, Whitehall set up the Alien Office to register foreigners in Britain but soon expanded its operations to include spying and other covert actions at home and abroad.[72] To avoid parliamentary oversight, the king funded the Alien Office out of his Civil List. Covert actions did not come cheap, and the Alien Office did not skimp on expenses. For instance, William Wickham, Britain's spymaster in Berne, tapped a £3.6 million account in just the first half of 1800.[73] While the home secretary oversaw the Alien Office's daily activities, the more ambitious, dangerous, sensitive, expensive, and deadly the mission, the more likely the prime minister and foreign secretary worked with him to pull it off.

The Alien Office's foremost duty was to gather, analyze, and share intelligence with those who could best use it. Then as now, spies operated either with or, far more often, without diplomatic cover. They garnered secrets through such ageless techniques as the "three Bs"—bribery, blackmail, and burglary, with the first by far the most common. A few endowed with special gifts mingled pleasure with business, got an earful with pillow talk, and gleaned nuggets of insights from the usually scandalous gossip.

As if this duty was not challenging enough, the Alien Office was also charged with spy catching. Its network of "watchers" shadowed "people of interest," aliens and British subjects alike, and at times searched their residences for incriminating documents when they were away. Feigning radicalism, agents penetrated antiwar and republican groups to learn names, plans, and connections, and at times to provoke riots as excuses for mass arrests and interrogations. Plenty of good information came simply from reading the mail of suspected spies and sympathizers. The Alien Office coordinated its efforts with the Foreign Letter Office, which intercepted, opened, decoded, resealed, and sent on letters between "persons of interest." Wickham expressed the nature of this counterespionage effort this way: "Without bustle, noise or anything that can attract public attention, Government possesses here the most powerful means of observation and information . . . that was ever placed in the hands of a free government."[74]

In this revolutionary era, the battle for hearts and minds at home and abroad was as crucial then as in more recent times. Propagating disinformation was a key covert action. In Britain itself, the Home Office was armed with an annual £5,000 budget that underwrote the founding of the tabloids the *Sun* and *True Briton* in 1792 and influenced other editors to print favorable articles. Overseas agents spread stories that played up the victories of Britain and its allies and downplayed those of their enemies. Year after year the Alien Office sought to convince the French empire's subjects that their "emperor has no clothes" by smuggling Fleet Street's realms of satirical cartoons, poems, and essays into the eager hands of those with a sense of humor and hatred of Napoleon. The Alien Office also enlisted printers to forge tons of French banknotes that were smuggled into the country and distributed to devalue the currency and thus support for the government.[75]

Then there was the rougher stuff. The Alien Office funded, armed, and at times trained groups dedicated to destroying the French Revolution and later Napoleon's regime by any possible means, ideally through mass revolution, but if necessary by terrorism. The object of terrorism is to provoke the targeted government to self-destruct. This can happen when those in power overreact to an attack with harsh repressive measures that alienate ever more people and drive them into the arms of the state's enemies.

Circumstantial evidence links the Alien Office to such "wet operations" as the attempted murder of Napoleon Bonaparte in 1800 and actual murder of Tsar Paul in 1801. If so, then this was most likely authorized not by rogue agents but by those at the very pinnacle of the British government. After becoming the foreign secretary in 1806, liberal leader Charles Fox found to his horror an Alien Office link to an ongoing assassination plot against Napoleon—and then, hoping, for moral and diplomatic reasons, to inspire gratitude in Napoleon that might lead to a peace treaty, he tipped the emperor off to the plot.[76]

No matter how brilliant and daring a spy might be, he is often so focused on his own intrigues that he is blind to his nation's grand strategic needs. William Wickham was just such an operative. Henry Dundas remarked that "I don't think our friend Wickham always recollects that it is not so easy to move an army as it is to write a dispatch."[77]

## The Power of the Empire

Over several centuries a series of governments in London compiled the world's most widespread empire. They did so largely on shoestring budgets.[78] Indeed, the empire's most crucial expansions occurred as private companies capitalized on government grants of monopolies to take over and rule foreign lands and peoples. In peacetime private rather than public funds bore most costs. In wartime this burden shifted to Whitehall, especially for the West Indies.

Yet whether the empire was a net asset or liability for British power is debatable. The colonies were expensive to conquer, develop, run, and defend but overall gained revenues for the government, profits for many businesses, and platforms to seize enemy colonies. Ireland and Canada probably cost more than they reaped, while the Caribbean islands and India generated huge earnings. What is certain is that the empire at once shaped and was shaped by British strategy.

The empire literally and figuratively began in Ireland.[79] England's first overseas colony was just a short sail away. The English began the conquest and exploitation of Ireland and its people in the fifteenth century, and their colonial system peaked in the late eighteenth century. A harsh pyramid of feudal power prevailed. At the pinnacle of the pyramid, representing around 4,753,000 people in 1791 was a tiny Anglican minority of 450,000 people who owned three of every four acres. Nearly all the remaining land was owned by 900,000 or so Scots-Irish Presbyterians. Finally, there were the 3,400,000 Irish Catholics, who were largely landless, poverty stricken, malnourished, and downtrodden.[80]

The political apartheid was just as harsh. A lord-lieutenant, appointed by the king, ran Ireland in harness with Parliament, whose seats were nearly all Anglicans except for a few token Presbyterians. Catholics were forbidden to vote, run for office, and serve on juries. The only options for nearly all able-bodied Catholic men was to spend their lives toiling as serfs or sailors. Catholics were barred from the militia known as the United Volunteers that backed the several understrength regiments stationed in Ireland both to deter and, if necessary, defeat a foreign invasion and/or Irish Catholic uprising. Two recent reforms slightly lightened this suffocating English rule. Westminster permitted Irish wool and glass to be exported directly to any British colony in 1780, and granted autonomy to the Irish parliament in 1782, although the lord-lieutenant still retained his quasi-dictatorial powers. Ireland would be a net drain on British power during the era, as enormous amounts of British troops were deployed there to crush any insurrection and repel any invasion.

The financial jewels in Britain's imperial crown were its West Indian colonies, which produced "white gold" or sugar, along with an array of other valued tropical products like indigo, hardwoods, coffee, cacao, cotton, and fruits.[81] These plantations accounted for around 80 percent of the empire's wealth and 20 percent of British imports. George III explained how vital they were to British power: "If we lose our Sugar Islands it will be impossible to raise money to continue the war."[82] In the late eighteenth century, these colonies held around 50,000 whites, 10,500 free blacks, and 456,000 slaves. With around 250,000 slaves tending plantations, Jamaica produced greater profits for investors and revenues for the crown than the other islands combined, about half, with Barbados second in population, profits, and revenues.[83]

No corner of the British empire was more distant, complex, and politically entangling than India.[84] And no one could have foreseen how powerful the East India Company would become when, in 1600, it got a royal charter to monopolize the realm's trade beyond the Cape of Good Hope, including the Indian subcontinent. Over the next two centuries, the East India Company carved out an empire across swaths of India through diplomacy, trade, and war. By the late eighteenth century, the company ruled the colonies of Bombay, Bengal, and Madras. Twenty-four directors ran this empire through thirteen committees, with the most crucial the Secret Committee, which wielded a vast array of soldiers, sailors, and spies. The company's political power equaled its economic and military power; indeed success in one realm almost invariably led to success in the other. At their headquarters at the East India House in London, the directors devised and implemented plans to reap more profits overseas and more political sway at home, and a portion of all the gold and silver shipped back to London filled the pockets of politicians who backed bills that enhanced the Company's power and opposed bills that diminished it.

The East India Company's monopoly naturally applied only to would-be British rivals. France and the Netherlands each had its own East India Company with its own colonies centered on deepwater ports on the South Asian mainland and islands across the Indian Ocean and adjacent seas. Any war that erupted between Britain, France, or the Netherlands inevitably spread to their East India Companies, although it took a half year or so before word sailed to that distant part of the globe. The worst fighting took place during the Seven Years' War, when the British and French East India Companies mustered armies of nationals and natives against each other. When the fighting ended, Britain's East India Company had conquered nearly all of its rival's holdings. The last French colonies were the small enclaves of Pondicherry, Mahe, and Chandermagore on India's southeast coast and the islands of Reunion, Bourbon, France, Seychelles, and Roderigue, while the Dutch clung to the Cape of Good Hope, Ceylon, and Java.

During the 1790s, the Mahratta Confederacy, Hyderabad, and Mysore posed the only genuine threats to the East India Company. The most dangerous was Mysore, whose ruler, Tipoo, hated the British.

Although General George Cornwallis defeated him in 1792, Tipoo burned with a desire for vengeance and rebuilt his army with the help of French military advisers. He would renew his war against the East India Company and would only be crushed after years of fighting; the British general most responsible for his demise would later be known as the Duke of Wellington.

## The Power of Others

Power is relative. The power to get what one wants depends on the power of one's rivals to get the same things. Thus leaders must calculate and asset their nation's interests and powers in relation to the interests and powers of others involved in the same conflict. This was no easy task in Europe given the array of states, each with its unique interests and powers that inevitably changed, gradually or abruptly.[85]

The threat of war overshadowed any period of European peace and prosperity. When states were not fighting, they were either preparing for or recovering from war, and the psychological reasons for any of these endeavors were usually more compelling than the geopolitical ones. The blatant aggression of one state or alliance rarely caused a war. Instead, a security dilemma ensnared Europe. Each government perceived itself as peaceful and defensive but beset by the imperialistic ambitions of others. Each also believed that strength deterred and weakness invited aggression. As a result, whenever any state for any reason bolstered its army, its fearful neighbors usually launched their own recruitment drives. When any two or more states formed an alliance to counter a perceived threat, those left out hurriedly opened talks to create their own alliance. As tensions rose, war seemed more likely; if war erupted, victory was more likely for the side that mobilized and attacked first. So each country involved in the conflict resolved to be first. The result was a self-fulfilling prophecy. Preparing for war often precipitated the war that most governments hoped to avoid.

In all this, geography gave Britain a crucial edge over its rivals. The British Isles were close enough to the continent for its merchants to enjoy relatively short sailing times to its markets, while they were far enough away to pose a tough challenge for any would-be invaders. As for "the politics of the Continent," George Canning explained that "our true policy has always been not to interfere except in great emergencies and then with a commanding force."[86] More often than not, Britain enjoyed a peace dividend when wars ravaged its neighbors. Britain's economy expanded while vast military expenditures stunted and distorted the economies of its rivals or invaders outright gutted them.

A clear but fluid pecking order shaped European relations, with five great powers, four secondary powers, six tertiary powers, and scores of minor realms that were nothing more than political pawns. The great powers of Britain, France, Austria, Prussia, and Russia had Europe's largest populations and economies, and fielded the largest armies. As for naval power, Britain, France, and Russia had large fleets to protect and expand their empires on distant continents and islands, while those of Austria and Prussia were miniscule because their territory was confined to Europe. Of the great powers, Britain had the smallest army and largest navy. Each great power had allied with or fought against the others numerous times as their respective national interests demanded.

The secondary powers were declining empires that included, in order of military might, Spain, the Ottoman Empire, the Netherlands, and Portugal. The first three fielded both large fleets and armies, and while the Dutch fleet remained formidable, its small army struggled to defend its homeland and colonies. Portugal had a relatively small fleet and army. The secondary powers were often pulled into wars with the great powers either because of conflicts with one or more of them or in hopes of enjoying spoils from being on the winning side when they fought against each other.

The tertiary powers included Sweden, Bavaria, Saxony, Denmark, Sardinia-Piedmont, and the two Sicilies. With small armies and overshadowed by one or more great powers, they were nearly always aggression's victims rather than initiators, and geography rather than manpower was their prime asset. At times powerful states searched for allies among the smaller states if they were strategically located, which gave small states bargaining power. An alliance was always a gamble, but being on the winning side could boost a small state's power. Victory might eliminate a threat posed by a dangerous neighbor, aggrandize one's territory, provide greater access for one's exports to the great power's market, or join in marriage one's ruling family with the great power's dynasty. And this enhanced diplomatic, economic, or dynastic power could, if carefully wielded, beget even more power.

Finally, there was the wild card of European diplomacy. From 1792 to 1815 the United States cast a long shadow, despite its remote location three thousand miles west of Europe's Atlantic shores, miniscule army of a couple of thousand troops, and tiny navy with a few frigates. America was a rising economic power whose merchant ships sailed to the world's most distant ports to jostle with European merchants for markets and profits. It faced more immediate economic and military threats from the British empire in Canada and the Spanish empire in East and West Florida and the Louisiana Territory beyond the Mississippi River. For most of this era, America was neutral and capitalized enormously from its neutrality by selling to all sides, although ever more vessels carrying "contraband" war materials to one side were captured by the other side's warships. The Royal Navy added insult to that injury by stopping American ships and impressing or kidnapping any sailors that they claimed were British. The turning point came in 1807, when a British warship fired on an American warship in American waters. Thereafter the United States took a harder line against those depredations, culminating with Congress's declaration of war against Britain in June 1812.

## Legacy

So what did British leaders do with all this potential hard and soft power?[87] Quite simply, from 1793 to 1815 they made the most of it, although not always smartly and often controversially. Prime Minster William Pitt offered what became a classic response to George Tierney, an opposition leader who demanded that he state in one sentence just what Britain was fighting for: "I know not whether I can do it in one sentence; but in one word I can tell him that it is Security. But it is also more than this: it is Security against a danger, the greatest that never existed in any past period of society."[88] To that Tierney retorted, "Security may be urged by every nation with equal propriety as the pretext for continuing expensive and ruinous wars. [Mr. Pitt] has availed himself of a phrase which undoubtedly sounds well . . . but . . . is only . . . evading a distinct answer to a most important question."[89]

Such were the opposite and irreconcilable visions of the art of British power.

## CHAPTER 2

# Pitt the Younger

Pitt seemed made to glide and to command, even more than to persuade or to convince, the assembly that he addressed.

Nathaniel Wraxall

Mr. Pitt must have felt, and his colleagues must have felt also, that he had such comprehensive talents and power that he was himself essentially the Government in all its Departments—that he could form a Government almost of himself, and each of his colleagues must have felt that Mr. Pitt could do without him, though he could not do without Mr. Pitt.

Spencer Perceval

In the popular imagination, William Pitt personifies this era's politics much as Arthur Wellesley, Duke of Wellington, and Horatio Nelson are the respective faces for war on land and sea. Unfortunately, their renown tends to obscure that era's important, if not as decisive, achievements of many other statesmen, generals, and admirals. Of the three, only Pitt was a boy wonder whose career skyrocketed at a young age. This was apt, since Pitt had a very tough act to follow.

After becoming prime minister in 1757, his father and namesake, who decades later became known as William Pitt the Elder to distinguish him from his illustrious progeny, led Britain to victory during the Seven Years' War, with Canada and much of India among the spoils. He politely declined King George III's offer of a title to reward those achievements, preferring to stay in the House of Commons, where he exercised power, to being kicked upstairs to the House of Lords, where he would be less influential. He finally yielded in 1766 to become Earl of Chatham, hoping that the sinecure might pay off some of his mountainous debts. In his later years, the elder Pitt was as eager to appease American complaints about British injustices as he had been ruthless in crushing French power. During America's War of Independence, he was a mostly lone voice for compromise and peace with the Americans.

For reasons that are lost, William Pitt the elder withheld his name from his first son and conferred it on his second, who was born at Hayes Place in Kent on May 28, 1757.[1] The lad spent a happy, luxurious childhood there with its twenty-eight bedrooms, score or so servants, and surrounding hundreds of bucolic acres. He had two older sisters and a brother, and, eventually, a younger brother to play with.

The younger Pitt's mother was Hester of the politically powerful Grenville family. She either spurned or was denied marriage offers until she joined hands with William Pitt when she was thirty-three. Her husband had delayed matrimony even longer; he was forty-six when he finally succumbed to the social and political pressure to have a wife and family.

Few children have had such flamboyant and conflicting heritages. Pitt's most meticulous biographer describes his paternal lineage as displaying "an imperious and often quarrelsome temper, extravagant behavior and emotion, a marked inability to understand other people, and a fundamental simplicity which sometimes gave its possessors a surprisingly sweet and winning charm." In contrast to the Pitts, whose "energies were fitful and unpredictable," the Grenvilles "were methodical, uncreative, and cultivated. The Pitts dissipated their strength as a family; the Grenvilles concentrated theirs . . . Both were immensely proud. But where the Pitts were moved by a fierce sense of individuality, the Grenville pride was a collective affair, cold and dense and withdrawn." The younger William was much more a Grenville than a Pitt in character, appearance, and interests.[2] He did share at least one dominant trait with his father. One biographer maintains that the "Pitts were unstable, sometimes to the extent of derangement," noting that one of the elder Pitt siblings "died in an asylum, and at least two more were mentally disturbed."[3] While neither the elder nor younger William Pitt descended into madness, both could be erratic in their behavior.

Physically Pitt was a slender, sickly, and ever taller youth, eventually rising to over six feet. He had thick auburn hair that had turned steel gray by his late thirties, large brown eyes that bore sharply into the eyes of others, a long pointed nose, and an ever more florid face. With time excessive eating and drinking combined with a dearth of exercise to swell his once lanky frame with corpulence.

Pitt was homeschooled until he entered Pembroke College of Cambridge University at age fourteen. The prodigy took his degree after six years of learning and joy with the tight circle of friends he nurtured there. His father's death in 1778 briefly disrupted his studies as the family struggled to settle the estate, but in 1780 he finally left Cambridge to study law at Lincoln's Inn in London.

Given Pitt's namesake, gifts, education, and interests, a political career was inevitable. He first tried to enter the House of Commons by running for one of Cambridge University's two seats in 1780 but lost in a five-man race. Friends got him elected to the rotten borough of Appleby, in northern England. He was just twenty-one when he entered the House of Commons on January 23, 1781. He squeezed into that crowded chamber amidst such luminaries as Charles Fox, Edmund Burke, and Richard Sheridan. This dazzling company inspired rather than daunted him. Pitt's maiden speech on February 26, 1781, was extremely well received. The *Parliamentary Register* gushed that "his voice is rich and striking, full of melody and force; his manner easy and elegant; his language beautiful and luxuriant . . . not unworthy of his immortal parent."[4]

Pitt was a rare type of politician, an introvert in an extrovert's profession. Around people that he did not know or trust he was "cold, stiff, and without suavity or amenity. He seemed never to invite approach or to encourage acquaintance, though when addressed he could be polite, communicative, and occasionally gracious. Smiles were not natural to him."[5] His personality changed completely with his friends, far from the maddening crowd and political foes. Starting at Cambridge, he forged warm lasting friendships with a small coterie of young, witty, mostly handsome males with similar values and tastes. In his early political years, his closest friend was William Wilberforce, with whom he graduated from Cambridge and won seats in Parliament. Wilberforce described Pitt as "the wittiest man I ever knew. . . . Others appeared struck by the . . . association of brilliant images; but every possible combination of ideas seemed present to his mind, and he could at once produce whatever he desired . . . Many professed wits were present, but Pitt was the most amusing of the party and the readiest and most apt in the required allusions."[6]

Pitt was an enthusiastic member of Goostree's Club, intimately limited to twenty-five seats. There Pitt could relax and be himself amid the hearty discussions, laughter, gambling, and, especially, drinking. It was a hard-drinking era, and Pitt could knock back tankards of ale and goblets of wine with the best of them. Indeed, Pitt became known as a "three bottle man" for the amount of claret, port, and other libations that he consumed during the long course of the typical supper with his intimidates.[7] As a young man his metabolism burned off those calories, but age slurred and thickened his body.

Part of the paradox of Pitt's life involved money—he could accurately keep the empire's books but not his own. Although he was relentless at imposing fiscal discipline on Britain, privately he was a spendthrift whose personal debts soared year after year. By August 1792 his official annual salary of £10,000 as first lord of the treasury was augmented when King George named him Lord Warden of the Cinque Ports, after Frederick, Lord North's, death left the sinecure vacant. Alas, even this only partly covered his expenses.[8]

In what would become his only foreign trip, Pitt journeyed with Wilberforce and Edward Eliot to France for six memorable weeks in September and October 1783. He was received at Fontainebleau Palace by Louis XVI and Marie Antoinette, had tea with Benjamin Franklin, and was wooed by the wife of Jacques Necker, France's treasury minister, to marry their then seventeen-year-old daughter Germaine, who would achieve fame as the provocative writer and wit, Madame de Stael.

The Neckers were among many ambitious families that hoped to wed a daughter to this swelling titan of British power. They would all be disappointed. Pitt never married. The reason was straightforward enough. Females did not rouse his passions, and he spurned any notion of being trapped in a loveless marriage. The only woman that he was ever close to was his sister Harriot. A friend of the Pitt family once remarked that "twas a pity she was his Sister for no other woman in the World was suited to be his wife."[9] Pitt was devastated when Harriot died of a fever shortly after giving birth to a daughter in 1786.

Throughout his adult life, Pitt was whispered to be "unnaturally" attracted to men, and political cartoons and verses lampooned the alleged tendency. The most blatant smear came in the House of Commons in February 1784, when Richard Sheridan compared Pitt's relationship with King George to that of the openly homosexual Duke of Buckingham with James I. If those accusations were true, the surviving evidence is solely circumstantial. Although he enjoyed surrounding himself with handsome young bachelors like himself, no document clearly links him sexually with any of them.[10]

The American War of Independence dominated Parliament during Pitt's first four years there. He shared his father's views that the Americans should be appeased rather than repressed. As such, he gravitated toward the faction of William Petty Fitzmaurice, Lord Shelburne. Shelburne was highly intelligent, articulate, and knowledgeable, a man of the Enlightenment, and a friend of Benjamin Franklin and antiwar British liberals like Joseph Priestly and Richard Price. He favored compromise, leniency, and autonomy, although not independence, for the Americans. The similar temperaments of Shelburne and Pitt reinforced their American War position. Each masked his shyness and bolstered his authority by being aloof and slightly disdainful in public, and was attracted to this trait in the other. Eventually they would fall out and sever all ties, partly because they were such mirror images.

During his early years in the House of Commons, Pitt was chiefly interested in parliamentary reform. On May 7, 1781, he motioned that a new electoral system be instituted that eliminated the rotten boroughs and other inequities and imposed a truly representative system. His motion lost by 161 to 141 votes.

This was a close vote, given the large if declining conservative majority that adamantly opposed any reforms. Frederick, Lord

North, led the government from 1774 to 1782. His cabinet's policies, approved and strongly insisted upon by George III, were disastrous for British interests and power. These policies provoked the Americans to struggle first for reform and then, after the king rejected their Olive Branch Petition, for independence. After eight years of war, they finally won their struggle, with crucial aid from France, Spain, and the Netherlands, who joined their fight against Britain. As a result, Britain was shorn of its thirteen most prosperous colonies with 2.4 million subjects, and along the way, its national debt skyrocketed from £128 million to £243 million; it was repeatedly fought to a standstill or outright defeated by the Americans; and it suffered the humiliating surrender of two armies, General John Burgoyne with 5,500 troops at Saratoga in October 1777 and Edward Cornwallis with 7,500 troops at Yorktown in October 1781.

It was news of Cornwallis's surrender that convinced most of Parliament and the public that the war was lost. The opposition imposed no-confidence votes against North's government on March 8 and 15, 1782. Although George III reacted defiantly, he finally agreed to North's plea to resign on March 20. The king asked Charles Wentworth, Marquis of Rockingham, to form a government. Rockingham tapped Shelburne to serve as his secretary of state for the Home Department, which included colonial affairs. Rockingham's tenure was short; influenza killed him on July 1. The following day, the king asked Shelburne to head the government. Shelburne tapped Pitt to serve as chancellor of the exchequer on July 13, 1782. There Pitt worked closely with Shelburne, who was first lord of the treasury.

Shelburne's government, however, was also short lived. From the start it was tattered by factions and mounting opposition criticism over how to end the American War. In January 1783, Augustus Keppel, first lord of the admiralty, and Charles Richmond, master general of ordnance, resigned because of irreconcilable differences with Shelburne and most of the cabinet over the peace terms with the Americans, French, and Spaniards. Shelburne failed to find replacements that the king approved and resisted bringing North into his government as the king insisted. The opposition's core now included what became known as the "infamous coalition" of the House of Commons's two largest factions, whose heads, Frederick, Lord North, and Charles Fox, could not have differed more in outlook, lifestyle, and character.[11] Their ambition for power let them paper over those differences, at least for a few months, and they prevailed in no-confidence votes of 224 to 208 and 207 to 190 respectively on February 17 and 23. North and Fox jointly engineered those votes, but they were incapable of divvying up the spoils in a cabinet that each wanted to dominate. Shelburne resigned on February 24.

Britain's humiliating defeat in the American War discredited nearly an entire generation of parliamentary leaders. The king and the old political chiefs searched for young, dynamic politicians who ideally could restore Britain's ravaged finances, empire, and prestige. They believed they had found the perfect candidate in William Pitt.

George III tried to break the stalemate by asking Pitt to be first lord of the treasury and thus prime minister. Pitt politely refused. The deadlock dragged on. On March 20, the king again asked Pitt to form a government, only to receive the same reply. King George then appealed to Pitt's sense of duty and patriotism: "I am much hurt to find you are determined to decline at an hour when those who have any regard for the constitution as established by law ought to stand forth against the most daring and unprincipled faction that the annals of this kingdom ever produced."[12] Pitt not only begged to differ but resigned his post on March 31. The king turned to William Henry Cavendish Bentinck, Duke of Portland, who accepted the post of first lord of the treasury on April 1, while North and Fox each became a secretary of state.

During the nearly nineteen years that North had previously headed the cabinet, George III upheld him not just as a tool of his policies but as a respected friend. These feelings in the king died after North allied with Fox, and thereafter he sought any chance to bring down their government. An opportunity soon arose. On November 18, 1783, Fox presented to the Commons his East India Company bill, designed to break the company's monopoly on trade and power on the subcontinent. Under the bill, Parliament would appoint a board of seven commissioners to oversee the company's operations in India and eight assistants to run the business directly. The East India Company exerted all its related financial and political power to defeat this bill. Pitt led the bill's opposition in the House of Commons, arguing that the East India Company operated legally and profitably according to its charter, The monopoly's most powerful ally was the king, who rallied his loyalists in the House of Lords. As a result, the bill overwhelmingly passed the Commons by 229 to 120, but it died in the Lords by 87 to 79 votes.

King George sought to reward the most articulate voice that backed him in the Commons. On December 18 he again asked Pitt to form a government. This time Pitt accepted. The king then summoned Fox, Portland, and North for a midnight meeting and asked them to resign. They had no choice but to bow to the royal will.

William Pitt was only twenty-four years old when the king entrusted him with national power on December 19, 1783. Most of the time he worked well with George III during his eighteen years in power, especially in dispensing royal largess to as many influential parliamentarians as possible. Yet the strain of governing Britain broke Pitt's self-control several times, most notably in 1805, when he got in a shouting match with the king over who should be the next archbishop of Canterbury. As for the court, his shyness, which he awkwardly masked with stiff formality, made him unpopular. To their mutual relief, he rarely attended the court's glittering levees and soirees.

Pitt soon found the cabinet an unwieldy body for policy making. He preferred debating and deciding policies informally with the ministers directly responsible for an issue. He worked most closely with Henry Dundas and William Grenville, whom he made respectively home secretary and foreign secretary in June 1791. The trio shaped Britain's key policies for the next decade.

Yet that lay ahead. Currently Britain's international power was at a low ebb. The lost war against the Americans, French, and Spaniards caused the nation's debt to soar and prestige to plummet. In July 1784 the king admitted that British statesmen had to realign the nation's ambitions with its reduced abilities: "Till I see this Country in a situation more respectable as to Army, Navy, and Finances, I cannot think anything that may draw us into troubled waters either safe or rational."[13] To those who despaired at the nation's eclipse, Pitt exuded confidence that Britain's restoration of power was just a matter of time and effort: "Let peace continue for five years and we shall again look any Power in Europe in the face."[14]

In all, Pitt swiftly mastered the art of power. In pondering that, Spencer Perceval, who became prime minister in 1809, concluded that Pitt achieved a virtuous cycle between his performance and the deference of his colleagues: "Mr. Pitt must have felt, and his colleagues must have felt also, that he had such comprehensive talents and power that he was himself essentially the Government in all its Departments—that he could form a Government almost of himself, and each of his colleagues must have felt that Mr. Pitt could do without him, though he could not do without Mr. Pitt."[15]

Perhaps no British prime minister has had a more peripatetic lifestyle than Pitt. Although he officially resided at Downing Street, he rented a small house near Putney, and eventually bought Holwood House just two miles from his childhood home of Hayes Place. He also spent numerous nights with Wilberforce at his home near Wimbledon Heath, where Dundas and Grenville also had homes. Pitt made many of his crucial decisions as prime minister during his sojourns at Wimbledon. Dundas recalled that "in transacting the business of the State, in forming our plans &c. we never retired to Office for that purpose. All these matters we discussed & settled either in our morning rides at Wimbledon, or in our evening walks at that place. We were accustomed to walk in the evening from 8 oClock to sometime 10 or Eleven in the Summer season."[16]

Pitt had a distinct way of presiding over Parliament, a method designed to keep order, shape debates, and nurture votes:

> From the instant that Pitt entered the doorway of the House of Commons, he advanced up the floor with a quick and firm step, his head erect and thrown back, looking neither to the right nor to the left, nor favouring with a nod or a glance any of the individuals seated on either side, among whom many . . . would have been gratified even by so slight a mark of attention . . . Pitt seemed made to glide and to command, even more than to persuade or to convince, the assembly that he addressed.[17]

Pitt was among the age's greatest orators, who spoke with depth and eloquence on any pressing issue. His style was as low key, methodical, and rational as the opposition leader, Charles Fox, was flamboyant and emotional. One observer compared their speaking styles: "Mr. Fox had a captivating earnestness of tone and manner; Mr. Pitt was more dignified than earnest. . . . It was an observation of reports in the gallery that it required great exertion to follow Mr. Fox while he was speaking, none to remember what he had said; that it was easy and delightful to follow Mr. Pitt; not so easy to recollect what had delighted them."[18]

This was not the only contrast between the two. Fox was Pitt's polar opposite in tastes, appearance, and views. He was short, stocky, swarthy, rumpled, and often unwashed, yet was highly successful as a womanizer, apparently counting Georgiana, Duchess of Devonshire, among his conquests. Generally he preferred the conveniences of whoremongering, although he paid a heavy price both from his purse and health. At one point he confessed that "I have had one pox and one clap this summer. I believe I am the most unlucky rascal in the universe."[19] The two men did share similar beliefs on at least one vital question—religion. Like Fox, when it came to God, Pitt shifted between agnosticism and deism. Wilberforce recalled that Pitt "tried to reason me out of my convictions, but soon found himself unable to combat their correctness, if Christianity were true. The fact is, he was so absorbed in politics that he had never given himself time for due reflection on religion."[20]

Fox did more than debate Pitt on the issues. Pitt and his cabinet enjoyed a very short honeymoon in office before Fox and his followers opened fire with criticisms. At first their biggest complaint was the relative youth and inexperience of Pitt and his colleagues, who were lampooned for being little more than prodigious eaters and drinkers. But an issue of substance soon arose.[21]

Before becoming prime minister, Pitt had helped defeat Fox's East India Company bill. But the problems that inspired the bill did not go away. Pitt had to devise his own version to address the charges of massive corruption and incompetence against the East India Company. His bill appeared similar but differed substantially from Fox's.

A board of control—including the chancellor of the exchequer, one of the secretaries of state, and four other councilors appointed by the king—would work with the East India Company's directors to manage the business, but the profits were to remain in the latter's hands. The board of directors could recall any official. No official in India could negotiate a treaty or wage war without the king's approval. Ultimately, East India Company officials were subject to Britain's laws and courts. All this seemed progressive enough, but without financial oversight, the directors could continue their massive and blatant purchase of votes in Parliament. Fox rallied his supporters and narrowly killed the bill by 222 votes to 214.

Pitt mulled resigning. King George insisted that he stay. Pitt agreed and mobilized for the next big battle, this one over the annual Mutiny Bill that grants the government emergency powers should they need it for the following year. The deadline was March 25. Fox and his fellow liberals challenged the need for such a bill when the nation was at peace and the economy was expanding, but Pitt prevailed with a majority.

Pitt followed up this victory by dissolving the House of Commons and calling for an election. This time Pitt stood for and won one of Cambridge University's two seats. When Parliament opened on May 18, 1784, although his supporters held a clear majority, Pitt chose to dispute the election results in Westminster, where Fox came in second in a close race against two Pitt supporters for the two seats. This was a risky gamble. Although Fox was Pitt's opposing leader, he was not his nemesis. Trying but failing to overturn his election would embitter him. And that is exactly what happened. In the end, Fox held his seat but was shorn of the goodwill and friendliness that he previously felt toward the young Pitt.

Pitt devoted the rest of the year's Parliament to addressing two looming issues. The first was the steadily worsening fiscal crisis caused by the vast expenditures during the American War. In 1784 the national debt was £243 million and tax revenues merely £13 million, of which £8 million serviced the interest on the debt. Pitt eliminated much of the deficit with a bill that lowered tariffs on imported tea from 119 percent to 25 percent. This actually raised revenues by reducing the incentive to smuggle; most importers now unloaded their tea at official warehouses where the value was assessed and a duty imposed, rather than at secluded coves in the dead of night.[22]

He then submitted a slightly modified version of his India bill, which this time passed by the overwhelming victory of 271 to 60 on August 13, 1784. Henceforth, a board of control composed of the secretary of state, the chancellor of the exchequer, and four privy councilors would oversee the directors, while the king picked the governor-general, governors, military commanders, and other high officials. But then a funny thing happened to all this oversight—the outsiders became insiders. As the outsiders helped run the East India Company, they soon adopted the insider view that the East India Company's interests were synonymous with the nation's interests, and acted accordingly.

This was the last major business before Parliament recessed. Then, after reconvening in January 1785, Pitt presented his colleagues with an even more ambitious agenda. He submitted his parliamentary reform bill, designed to eliminate 36 rotten boroughs and redistribute 72 seats to render the electoral system more representative; to ease that reform, £1 million was budgeted to buy out the power brokers in the rotten boroughs. The final vote was 248 against and 174 for the bill. Vested interests again thwarted a reform that would have greatly enhanced the efficiency and legitimacy of Britain's political system. Leading those fiercely opposed to reform was King George himself, whose ability to buy the votes of parliamentarians would have been sharply curtailed had the bill passed. Despite this defeat, and in defiance of the king's will, Pitt remained committed to reform. Indeed, he let George III know "how much I was personally pledged to Parliamentary Reform on the principles I had publicly explained, which I should support on every seasonable occasion."[23]

Throughout his career Pitt was repeatedly forced to ponder a key political question: "What is it that in truth will give satisfaction and restore permanent tranquility to Ireland?"[24] For him the obvious answer was economic and political reforms that liberated Irish Catholics from most if not all their shackles. Economically, he sought a mutually beneficial relationship between Britain and Ireland. In explaining how he hoped to bring that about, he revealed his understanding of the dynamics of power and one way to master it. The principles that he articulated could have served as guidelines for the rest of the empire:

> It is certainly on general principles desirable . . . that the system of commerce should be arranged as to extend the aggregate wealth of Great Britain and Ireland to its utmost limit, without partiality . . . to one part of the Empire or the other. But for this purpose two things seem fundamentally requisite. One, that Ireland, which will thus gain upon England in relative strength and riches, should proportionally relieve her of the burden [of debt and administration] which she now sustains exclusively. The other, that this increase of strength and riches in Ireland may really prove either a positive addition to that of it to the other, and may not in the end be so much strength taken from ourselves and given to a separate country.[25]

As for political reform, he called for joining Ireland's parliament to Britain's free trade between Britain and Ireland. But his plan threatened the profits and power of too many vested interest groups, and opponents in London and Dublin killed the bill in 1785.

Pitt parted ways with most other reformers with the Corporation and Test Acts. He warned that "were we to yield on this occasion, the fears of the Church of England would be roused, and their apprehensions are not to be treated lightly. It must . . . be conceded . . . that an Established Church is necessary . . . no means can be devised of admitting the moderate part of the dissenters and excluding the violent; the bulwark must be kept up against all."[26] Knowing its fate, he allowed a vote to repeal the act. The bill was decisively defeated by 176 votes to 98.

The American War had not just cost Britain thirteen prosperous colonies. With their vast forests, the Americans enjoyed a comparative advantage in shipbuilding that let American merchants capture an ever larger portion of the carrying trade across the Atlantic Ocean and beyond. Determined to regain British domination of this trade, Pitt got the Navigation Act passed in 1786, forcing British investors to buy only British-made or captured foreign vessels.

This policy backfired. The proportion of bilateral trade carried by American ships rose from about 50 percent in 1790 to 60 percent in 1792 to 95 percent in 1800. Two reasons explain why. First, the bill's practical effect was to raise the cost of buying British-made vessels, so British merchants simply saved money by conveying their goods in American-owned vessels. This became an imperative after Britain went to war and its merchant vessels began to fall prey to French warships and privateers.[27]

India remained a problem, despite the 1785 India Bill. Ever more prominent voices demanded that the king convert India into a crown colony as the public learned appalling revelations about the depth and breadth of the East India Company's corruption, especially by its latest governor general, Warren Hastings. In 1785 Hastings returned from India with £74,000 and rumors that he had acquired much of it illicitly. The House of Commons opened an investigation and eventually voted to impeach him in 1788. The trial sputtered on and off for seven years until Hastings finally won an acquittal in 1795. His victory was pyrrhic: Hastings spent £71,000 defending himself and died the following year.

Pitt tried to purge India's Augean Stables of corruption. In May 1786 he had General George Cornwallis sail for Calcutta to serve as Bengal's governor. Then, in February 1788, he submitted the India Declaratory Bill to tighten the government's oversight. As usual, East India Company officials greased the palms of enough politicians to defeat a law designed to curb their power.

Although the East India Company reaped vast monopoly profits from its realms, it faced rivals elsewhere in the Indian Ocean basin. The Dutch East India Company had colonial enclaves at Cape Town at Africa's southernmost tip, Trincomalee in Ceylon, Rhio on the Malay Peninsula, and various ports on the islands Java and Borneo, and the Celebes and Moluccas, known as the Spice Islands. The Pitt cabinet launched an initiative to forge an oligopoly between the two East India Companies, and as a lure offered a loan to the cash-strapped Dutch version. Although the Dutch East India Company officials were interested, the conflict between stadtholder William V of Orange and the Dutch provinces prevented any deal from being cut.

During this time, many British officials and merchants eyed an even more distant Asia realm, China. The Chinese permitted a trickle of trade through Canton. British traders pressured Whitehall for help in persuading China's government to cut entangling red tape and payoffs to corrupt officials there, force Chinese debtors to pay their British creditors, and open more ports to trade. Spearheading that lobbying was James Cathcart, a former East India Company official and now a member of Parliament. In 1787 the cabinet agreed to dispatch Cathcart to China's imperial court at Beijing and negotiate a trade treaty. Fearing a treaty that ended its monopoly in Asia, the East India Company tried but failed to spike the mission. In December 1787 Cathcart sailed for China but died en route at Malaysia in June 1788. It took nearly a year for word of his demise to reach London and nearly three more years before the next mission set forth, this one led by George, Earl Macartney, who had been a diplomat in Russia and the governor of Madras, then of Bengal. He sailed in September 1792 but failed to interest China's imperial court in trade.

Pitt's most important policy before 1793 was to arrest and begin paying down the soaring national debt. He launched this campaign in a three-hour speech before the House of Commons on May 29, 1786. His bill raised revenues, converted debt into publically traded stocks, and cut spending by streamlining or reorganizing parts of the government; the bill included 2,537 separate resolutions for specific cuts, adjustments, and increases. He followed that bill's passage with another, in February 1787, that united all revenues into one consolidated fund. If all worked out as planned, the government would begin running surpluses in a few years and eliminate the national debt within thirty years. As a result of these measures, Pitt triumphantly announced in May 1788 that revenues exceeded costs and the national debt was £2.5 million lower, while the navy's budget rose by £7 million.[28]

Pitt sought more revenues from more trade with Europe. To this end, he sought free trade deals with France, Spain, the Netherlands, Russia, Prussia, Poland, Portugal, and the Two Sicilies from 1785 to 1792. All but one of these realms spurned any deal that would bring a flood of cheaper-priced and better British-made industrial goods that bankrupted their own industries. The only successful effort was in Paris. In April 1787 George III ratified a treaty with France that promoted trade by lowering barriers; soon revenues swelled with the flow of goods across the Channel.[29]

Tragically, war threatened to destroy this budding, mutually advantageous relationship. Political chaos swept the Netherlands as the Patriot Party deposed stadtholder William V and established a republic. Whitehall sought to undermine the Patriots and bring William and his Orange Party back to power with covert action. Pitt instructed James Harris, Earl of Malmesbury, the minister to the Netherlands, to "endeavor to keep together a party which may act with advantage, both for their own country and for us, on some future day, if it should arise."[30] To this end, Harris received £9,000 in 1786 and an additional £12,000 in 1787. He wielded these funds to influence prominent Dutchmen to put venality before patriotism. The trouble was that the conversions did not come cheap and failed to save the Patriot cause. Harris worried that "if we lose this country, France will acquire what she has always considered as the climax of her power."[31] Pitt upped the ante to £70,000.[32]

In the end, blunt military force prevailed where covert action failed. A crisis erupted in July when Princess Frederika, fed up with her dithering husband William, took matters into her own hands, but she was arrested as she tried to sneak back to the capital, The Hague, and rally Orange supporters against the Patriots who had taken over. She managed to send appeals for military aid to Britain and her brother, Prussian king Frederick William II. Meanwhile, the Patriots asked France to mediate their conflict with the Orange Party. Louis XVI eventually sent word that he would not get involved. As Pitt mobilized the fleet for action, Frederick William massed 20,000 Prussian troops on the Dutch frontier and demanded that the Patriots fully restore William to power. When the Patriots refused, he ordered his army to invade the Netherlands on September 12, 1787. The Prussian troops routed the Patriot forces and placed the stadtholder back on his throne in The Hague on September 20.

Thus did the Prussians advance British interests by advancing their own. And this was just fine with Pitt and his colleagues. To solidify these gains and deter France from any interference, Britain and Prussia signed an alliance in October 1787, and in April 1788 welcomed the Netherlands into what became the Triple Alliance.

This alliance had unintended and, ultimately, tragic consequences. The success of the Dutch Patriots inspired Polish nationalists. In late 1788, Poles under Russian rule rebelled against their masters, and in early 1789 a delegation of Polish rebels appeared in London to lobby Pitt's government for aid. As Poland was well beyond Britain's easternmost sphere of influence on the continent, Whitehall refused to help. Nonetheless, the Poles managed to drive the Russians from their territory by May 1789, and for the next few years, Catherine II's attempts to reconquer her Polish provinces while simultaneously warring against Turkey and Sweden would divert Russian attention from the revolutionary events happening in France.

For several months a crisis at home eclipsed foreign policy concerns. A "madness" now known to be intermittent porphyria seized King George on October 22, 1788.[33] Thereafter for several months he ranted gibberish, had to be force fed, and struck several of his attendants. On February 5, 1789, Pitt submitted to the House of Commons a bill to establish a regency. The bill passed on February 12 and went to the House of Lords on February 16. As the lords debated the bill, the king's madness receded as swiftly and mysteriously as it had appeared.

The restoration of the king's sanity came as a godsend to Pitt and his supporters. If the crown prince became regent, he would have dismissed Pitt and asked his fellow carouser and liberal Charles Fox to form a government. Pitt feared the ruin of Britain's empire with George the regent and Fox the prime minister. During a speech by Fox lauding George, Pitt slapped his thigh and muttered: "I'll un-Whig the gentleman for the rest of his life."[34] With this crisis resolved, Pitt felt that the time was right to act on a promise he had made years earlier.

Slavery was not something that most Britons thought much about. Technically slavery had been illegal in the British Isles since Parliament passed a bill in 1750 that forbade holding humans against their will. A ruling by Lord Chief Justice Mansfield in 1772 clarified that bill's ambiguous wording and freed the small number of slaves still retained by rich families and businesses. While slavery was out of sight and thus out of mind for most Britons, it remained crucial to the imperial economy. Investors reaped enormous wealth from transporting and selling slaves or exploiting slave labor on West Indian plantations. Much of this wealth was garnered by huge mercantile firms in Liverpool, Bristol, and London.

Slavery was certainly on the periphery of Pitt's mind until, in 1785, two forces joined to transform his outlook. First, he read William Paley's *The Principles of Moral and Political Philosophy,* with a chapter that condemned slavery. Then his friend William Wilberforce experienced a revolutionary spiritual awakening: "God almighty has set before me two great objects, the suppression of the slave trade and the reformation of manners."[35] Paley and Wilberforce were hardly the first Britons to believe that slavery was wrong and sought to end it.[36] The Society of Friends, or Quakers, was the first group to do so during a convention at London in 1727. John Wesley, who led the Methodist Great Awakening in the 1730s and 1740s, added ending slavery to a list of goals that true Christians should embrace. But these "dissident" sects had few followers and were barred from Parliament. At best the Quakers and Methodists could raise the awareness of those who attended their sermons or read their tracts.

Thereafter Pitt favored abolishing first the slave trade then slavery itself. Yet this clear moral path was strewn with daunting political obstacles, the most powerful of which were the interest groups that enriched themselves from slavery. West Indian planters formed a well-organized and -endowed effort to spike any abolitionist bills in Parliament. Their most formidable argument was that Britain's economy and security would suffer if it unilaterally abolished slavery while France, Spain, and the Netherlands continued to enrich themselves from the practice. Then there was the question of how to compensate slaveholders for the loss of their property. Finally, they argued that Britain faced far more pressing problems that Parliament should concentrate on confronting. These planters found allies not just in Parliament but in Pitt's cabinet, of which Home Secretary Dundas was the most outspoken, with practical arguments for leaving slavery be. To counter those voices, abolitionists founded the Committee for the Abolition of the Slave Trade in May 1787 and launched their own efforts to lobby Parliament and public opinion.

Pitt finally acted in December 1788, by talking George III's Privy Council into setting up a committee to investigate the slave trade. Then, in May 1789, coincidently the same month that the Estates General convened at Versailles, Pitt moved that the House of Commons establish its own committee to study the issue. Wilberforce bolstered Pitt's efforts with a speech that was celebrated as the most profound of his career. The committees concluded that the slave trade was inhuman and should either be reformed or ended. But proslavery interests worked behind the scenes to vote down the abolitionist bill this year and for years to come.

And all along the struggle in Parliament was overshadowed by revolutionary events unfolding for the liberation of man on the other side of the English Channel.

CHAPTER 3

# The Great Debate, 1789–1792

"All political speculation will now turn to France."
William Eden, Lord Auckland

"The present convulsions of France must sooner or later terminate in general harmony and regular order; and though the fortunate arrangements of such a situation might make her more formidable, it might also render her less obnoxious as a neighbour."
William Pitt

"Tremble all ye oppressors of the world! . . . You cannot now hold the world in darkness . . . Restore to mankind their rights and consent to the correction of abuses, before they and you are destroyed together."
Richard Price

Revolutions involve rapid, systematic change. Political revolutions are as rare as the conditions that breed them are common. It is not enough for a government to become ever more corrupt, inept, and brutal; for the rich to get richer, fewer, and more exploitive of the poor, who get more poverty-stricken, numerous, enraged, and desperate; and usually atop all this for the country to suffer a catastrophic economic collapse or defeat in war. These are just the prerequisites. For a revolution to erupt, let alone stand a chance of succeeding, there must be brilliant, ruthless leaders who champion an ideology that justifies why revolution is essential and inevitable, and who forge the political, military, and social organizations that mobilize the masses to destroy the system that represses and exploits them and, upon its ruins, establish a new system dedicated to righting all wrongs.

All this characterized France for a span of years straddling 1789. The kingdom was disintegrating from an array of widening legal, political, economic, social, and cultural cleavages. Regional differences in taxes, tariffs, weights, and measures sapped France's potential economic power. Eight of ten people were peasants who toiled either for a landlord or their own small plots that barely yielded enough food for them to survive. Only ten cities had more than 50,000 people, of which Paris, with 650,000 people, was by far the largest. Most city dwellers were just as poverty stricken and desperate as most peasants. Perhaps one in five people could be counted among the middle or bourgeois class of shopkeepers, artisans, traders, and lawyers. There was a tiny, very rich class of nonnoble financiers, merchants, and manufacturers. Anywhere from 120,000 to 350,000 people may have held titles of nobility, but most lived modestly, and the aristocratic elite that resided or circulated at Versailles numbered no more than a thousand. Although less than one in a hundred people had taken religious vows, the Catholic Church owned at least a quarter of French land and wealth. Reigning atop this pyramid of political, economic, social, and religious power was Louis XVI, a well-meaning but ignorant, narrow-minded, indecisive, and insecure king.

France faced bankruptcy in 1788. A dozen years earlier, Versailles began aiding and eventually allied with the Americans in their independence war against Britain. But Versailles could not afford its ultimate victory, and the French celebration over inflicting a devastating blow to their traditional enemy faded rapidly as ever more and higher bills came due. This became a crisis in 1788, when an economic depression and bad harvests emptied France's treasury. In desperate need of new revenues, Louis XVI accepted his ministers' advice to convene the Estates General, which last met in 1614, and get it to approve tax increases. The Estates General included equal numbers of clergy, nobles, and commoners.

The king and his ministers convened the Estates General on May 5, 1789, hoping that it would swiftly rubber-stamp new revenues before being dismissed into another prolonged obscurity. This did not happen. The Third Estate, composed of commoners, promoted a wide-ranging reform agenda. Since the three estates had only one vote each, the clergy and nobles blocked those proposals. On June 17 the Third Estate tried to break the deadlock with an unauthorized meeting during which, by a vote of 491 to 89, they declared themselves the National Assembly and invited the nobles and clergy to join them as individuals. Most nobles rejected and most clerics accepted this offer. On June 20 the National Assembly reacted to the king's order to lock them out of their meeting hall by convening on a nearby tennis court and swearing an oath to remain in session until they had transformed France into a constitutional monarchy. What followed was a tense, weeklong standoff with the king, who ordered the National Assembly to disperse and revert to the Estates General. When the reformers persisted in defending their new institution, Louis finally relented, and on June 27 he ordered the nobles and clergy to join the National Assembly.

The unfolding revolution turned violent on July 14. Until then, the liberals had led a series of reforms at Versailles by presenting a united front to the conservatives and grounding their appeals on reason. But this day, reacting to rumors that the king was bringing in foreign troops to crush the liberals, a mob in Paris first took over the arsenal at the Invalides and wielded the stolen arms to capture the Bastille, a castle that had become a symbol of royal repression. For the next several years, violence worsened as moderates and radicals struggled to control the revolution, with the former favoring a constitutional monarchy and the latter a republic. Both, however, voted to abolish feudalism on August 4, issue the Declaration of the Rights of Man and the Citizen on August 26, and nationalize the Catholic Church's property on November 2, 1789.

The French Revolution dominated newspaper stories and countless discussions in pubs and coffeehouses across Britain. Initially most Britons wholeheartedly cheered the dramatic changes.[1] They viewed events at Versailles and in Paris through the prism of their own Glorious

Revolution of 1688, when Parliament and the Church of England vanquished the forces of absolutism and papism. French liberals appeared to be following the same path that Britons had pioneered toward a constitutional monarchy, parliamentary supremacy, and the natural rights of man. A practical reason joined idealism in welcoming the French Revolution: the political convulsions distracted and weakened France from pursuing imperial ambitions and made war less likely. Should the revolution succeed, most Britons believed that a constitutional monarchy would be far less aggressive than the absolute monarchy that it displaced.

Prime Minister William Pitt shared and shaped this prevailing view. In February 1790 he offered the House of Commons this optimistic assessment:

> The present convulsions of France must sooner or later terminate in general harmony and regular order; and though the fortunate arrangements of such a situation might make her more formidable, it might also render her less obnoxious as a neighbour. . . . Whenever the situation of France should become restored, it would prove freedom rightly understood; freedom resulting from good order and good government; and thus circumstanced, France would stand forward as one of the most brilliant Powers in Europe she would enjoy just that kind of liberty which I venerate.[2]

In this opposition leader Charles Fox was in perfect accord. During a House of Commons debate in April 1791, he declared these events across the Channel as "the most stupendous and glorious edifice of liberty, which had been erected on the foundations of human integrity in any time or country."[3]

The French Revolution's initial phase of progressive reforms inspired liberals to champion similar changes in Britain.[4] To these ends, two groups already existed and many more mushroomed during the early 1790s. The Society for Constitutional Information, founded in 1780, renewed its reform efforts. In November 1788 the London Revolution Society was established to commemorate the Glorious Revolution's centennial and in 1789 embraced the French Revolution as a model for Britain. In January 1792, shoemaker Thomas Hardingfounded the London Corresponding Society for the Reform of Parliamentary Representation as an umbrella organization for all the local progressive groups emerging across Britain. Patriots emphasized reform through such varying versions of nationalism as the United Britons, United Englishmen, United Scotsmen, and United Irishmen. All groups denounced the corruption, inequities, discrimination, elitism, and favoritism that permeated British politics, business, and society. They demanded the end of this insiders' game by abolishing the religious and economic restrictions that denied all adult males equal rights to vote and run for office, redrawing electoral district lines to represent similar numbers of constituents, inaugurating secret ballots, and paying parliamentarians.

A growing body of radicals threatened outright revolution if Parliament failed to enact those sweeping reforms.[5] The Unitarian minister Richard Price was the first powerful voice to do so. In his fiery sermon, "A Discourse on the Love of Our Country," published in November 1789, he issued this warning: "Tremble all ye oppressors of the world! . . . You cannot now hold the world in darkness . . . Restore to mankind their rights and consent to the correction of abuses, before they and you are destroyed together."[6] Radicals organized themselves into groups like the London Revolution Society.

One lone prominent voice cut through the initial popular enthusiasm for the French Revolution and warned darkly of the horrors that lay ahead. Edmund Burke was Britain's Cassandra. In a speech before the House of Commons on February 9, 1790, he declared: "The French had shown themselves the ablest architects of ruin that had hitherto existed in the world. In that very short space of time they had completely pulled down . . . their monarchy, their church, their nobility, their law, their revenue, their army, their navy, their commerce, their arts, and their manufactures."[7] Price's sermon and the proliferation of radical groups enraged Burke. He responded by writing a book that sounded the alarm of the French Revolution's potential dangers to British security and European civilization. His *Reflections on the Revolution in France* appeared on November 1, 1790, and sold over 30,000 copies during the next two years.[8]

As a liberal writer, thinker, and activist, Thomas Paine was Edmund Burke's nemesis.[9] His essays had helped inspire the American Revolution, and now he systematically assaulted Burke's arguments in a book called *The Age of Reason*, of which part one appeared in March 1791 and part two in February 1792. The eventual sales of over 200,000 copies are especially impressive, given Whitehall's attempts to intimidate the printers from keeping up with demand. Paine himself left London for Paris in September 1792, after the National Assembly made him an honorary member and French citizen. Paine was brilliant at composing inspiring revolutionary aphorisms such as this one: "The present age will hereafter merit to be called the Age of Reason, and the present generation will appear to the future as the Adam of a new world." He insisted that a revolution's essence was simple enough: "For a nation to love liberty, it is sufficient that she knows it; and to be free, it is sufficient that she wills it."[10]

Although Paine bested Burke as a writer and thinker, the latter's view eventually prevailed politically as the French Revolution became increasingly violent and radical.[11] Conservatives, however, needed time to organize themselves as effectively as liberals. The first step came on March 13, 1790, when a group of prominent London conservatives established the Church and King Club to chorused denunciations of progressive ideas, leaders, and groups. This inspired like-minded men across the country to open their own branches. An increasingly powerful group emerged from a meeting at the Crown and Anchor pub in London on November 20, 1792. Calling themselves the Association for Preserving Liberty and Property against Republicans and Levelers, they called on the silent majority of Britons to raise their voices against those that threatened to engulf the nation in revolution. This inspired tens of thousands of Britons to act. Within a year, over 2,000 Loyal Associations sprang up across Britain, with 150 in London.[12]

The debate over the French Revolution did not clearly affect the June 1790 election, from which Pitt's party emerged with 340 seats to the opposition's 188, along with 29 independents.[13] Relations among the rivals remained largely civil and constructive. Indeed, in the spring of 1791, Pitt and Fox still shared core progressive values and worked constructively together. In April, they jointly sponsored the Catholic

Relief Bill, which granted followers of that faith the right to acquire churches for worship, and upon taking the test oath, to practice law, be appointed to minor local public offices, and be received by the king. The bill passed the Commons without opposition and the Lords with only a slight change in wording.

This limited reform inspired most Irish Presbyterians and Catholics to want more. To promote complete equality, a dozen prominent Presbyterians, including ten merchants, army officers, and a fiery lawyer and writer named Theobald Wolfe Tone, founded the United Irishmen in Belfast in October 1791. As their group's name implied, they welcomed all Irishmen into their group. A branch soon opened in Dublin and included 56 lawyers, 104 merchants, 31 textile manufacturers, 24 doctors, and 30 landowners.[14] Tone soon became the United Irishmen's leader. His book "An Argument on Behalf of the Catholics of Ireland" had appeared anonymously in September 1791 and had inspired the group's creation. It embraced the same agenda as British reform groups of eliminating all property and religious restrictions on adult males twenty-one years and older for owning land and businesses, voting, and running for office; the inequality in population among the electoral districts; and the requirement that non-Anglicans bear oaths and tithes to the Anglican Church. Whitehall's crackdown on reform groups in Britain and Ireland after war erupted with France in February 1793 would radicalize the United Irishmen and eventually lead to a mass rebellion against British rule, and to mass death as the British crushed that rebellion.

Liberals sought to free an even more reviled and exploited people. The ease with which the Catholic Relief Bill passed gave hope to William Wilberforce and his followers that they might enjoy similar success in their crusade to end slavery. Pitt gave his friend the nod. On April 18, 1791, Wilberforce motioned that no more slaves be imported into the West Indies. Pitt and Fox were the most prominent in the chorus backing the motion, and Pitt himself launched a powerful moral attack on Britain and slavery: "The truth was that [with slavery] we stopped the natural progress of civilization; we cut off Africa from improvement; we kept down that Continent in a state of darkness, bondage, ignorance, and blood."[15] But despite these efforts, the slave lobby again trumped the abolitionist lobby. The vote was 163 against and only 88 for Wilberforce's motion.

This defeat energized rather than demoralized the abolitionists. Over the next year they gathered half a million signatures on 519 petitions and submitted them to Parliament. Yet events undercut their efforts. Slaves revolted on Saint Domingue, France's most lucrative sugar island, and planters warned that any talk of liberation might provoke uprisings on Britain's West Indian plantations. Nonetheless, in April 1792 Wilberforce again motioned to end the slave trade, although this time with the word "gradually" inserted. This led to the motion's approval by 193 to 125 votes, while a motion to abolish slavery outright lost by an overwhelming 230 to 80 votes. Eventually a consensus was forged that the slave trade would end in 1800. This deadline would not be realized.[16]

During this time, Britain nearly warred against Spain over who owned North America's Northwest Coast. Captain James Cook had charted the waters and laid claim to this remote territory in 1778. His expedition's reports noted the region's bountiful fur-bearing animals like sea otters and beavers, along with whales along that stretch of ocean. During the 1780s, entrepreneurs sailed to the Northwest Coast to reap that harvest. In 1789 a group of British merchants established a small trading post on Nootka Sound on Vancouver Island's south end. Hearing of this enterprise, Spain's viceroy in Mexico dispatched two warships to eliminate what they believed were trespassers in their empire, and in July 1789 the Spanish captured the fort and vessels, raised their flag above their prizes, and arrested the British interlopers for trial and prison in Mexico.

Whitehall did not informally learn of this act until nearly seven months later, in January 1790. While Pitt and his ministers were still trying to understand that garbled report, they received, on February 10, a formal statement from Spain protesting Britain's intrusions into Spain's empire and demanding that they end forever. This provoked Pitt and his secretaries to issue their own demands.[17] First, Spain must immediately release its British prisoners, along with its vessels, and compensate the British for their losses. Second, Spain must renounce its claim to the region. To back this ultimatum, Pitt had a flotilla readied to sail to that far end of the earth and made sure that the press reported the campaign's preparations.

It took more than two months for Charles IV and his advisers to debate how to respond and then send a formal reply. Meanwhile, Anthony Merry, Britain's minister in Madrid, reported that the Spanish king had authorized a fleet of forty ships of the line to prepare for war. This prompted Pitt and his ministers to mobilize a hundred ships of the line, with a score ordered to attack Spain's colonies in the Caribbean basin.[18] On April 20, 1790, the cabinet mulled over a letter that repeated Madrid's initial demands and categorically rejected those of Whitehall.

With war likely, Pitt tried to emotionally ready the nation with a rousing speech before the House of Commons on May 5. He denounced Spain's Northwest claim as "the most absurd and exorbitant that could well be imagined; a claim . . . which was indefinite in its extent, and which originated in no treaty, or formal establishment of a colony, nor rested on any one of those grounds on which claims of sovereignty, navigation, and commerce usually rested. If that claim were given way to, it must deprive this country of the means of extending its navigation and fishery in the [Pacific] Ocean."[19]

Pitt sent to Madrid a declaration to sign, a declaration in which Spain admitted that it did not possess the region that it claimed, promising to settle the dispute with negotiations, and pledging to release immediately the prisoners and their vessels. In return, Britain would sign a counterdeclaration accepting Spain's declaration. Hand delivering these documents was Alleyne Fitzherbert, who would replace Merry as ambassador.[20]

Pitt won this initial "game of chicken." Learning of Britain's naval preparations, Charles IV had no realistic choice but to yield. Spain was incapable of winning a war alone against Britain. Charles IV had asked Louis XVI to stand with him on the grounds of their long-standing defensive treaty known as the Bourbon Family Compact. Although the French king readily agreed, the National Assembly angrily denounced the pledge and prevented him from acting on it. So, on July 24, 1790, Fitzherbert and Foreign Minister Jose Monino y Redondo, Count Floridablanca, signed, respectively the declaration and counterdeclaration.

The crisis did not end there. The next critical step was to draw the line between the two countries' North American empires. Whitehall's initially insisted that Spain's northernmost boundary in North America was at 31 degrees. This line would have cut off Spain's possessions from just south of San Diego eastward to the Atlantic Ocean and rendered to Britain virtually all of California and New Mexico and most of Texas; Spain would have retained only East and West Florida, and South Texas. Not surprisingly, Charles IV and his government angrily rejected the demand. This, in turn, provoked Whitehall again to rattle its saber. Fitzherbert delivered an ultimatum to Floridablanca on October 12. And again, Spain bowed to Britain's overwhelming power. On October 28, 1790, Floridablanca and Fitzherbert signed a convention whereby Spain permitted the British to exploit and even settle freely on lands beyond Spain's northernmost California settlements.

Pitt and his government had scored a stunning diplomatic coup. Yet this bloodless victory was hardly costless. To prepare forty ships of the line of the ninety-three in port, and join them with thirty-seven ships of the line already at sea cost £3.133 million. Pitt examined the government books, did some calculations, and announced that he could pay the bill within four years with some relatively minor tax increases.[21]

The crisis with Spain was no sooner resolved than a new one arose. If there was a great power that seemed menacing from 1789 to 1792, Britain's foreign policy elite stared far more warily at Russia than it did Spain, let alone France. Joseph Ewart, the British ambassador at Berlin led a growing chorus of voices sounding the alarm over how Russian expansion in the Baltic and Black Sea basins threatened national security.[22] For now these fears were confined to Whitehall's inner sanctums. The press, public, and most parliamentarians were unaware of what was going on and would be stunned when they learned about it.

What followed was one of those hysterias that can afflict a great power's foreign policy. "Groupthink" is a gripping emotional state where everyone, even those with contrary views, conforms to the same view of a situation and how to respond to it. While groupthink can happen any time, the susceptibility heightens with the perception of a threat. Perhaps most striking about such bouts of paranoia is how often they involve symbolic rather than substantive dangers.[23]

Such a psychosis gripped Whitehall after word arrived in January 1791 that the Russians intended to keep the fortress of Ochakov that they had captured from the Turks in 1788. Ochakov's vital strategic importance to Russia and Turkey was undisputed, given its site near the Black Sea mouths of the Bug and Dniester Rivers. The question was its importance to British national security. Pitt convinced his colleagues to share the fear that Russia's occupation of Ochakov imperiled Britain. Those who thought the threat was overblown or outright delusional kept silent or confided their thoughts to close friends. For instance, the ambassador to The Hague, William Eden, Lord Auckland, was far more leery of a potential French than Russian threat but only shared this with a confidant: "If that Russian business could happily be settled we might sit still & look at the French Story like Spectators in a theatre."[24]

The prevailing view confounded any dispassionate analysis. In reality, the security of not just Britain but every European country rose when the Russians expanded southward and eastward. The reason was simple. The more Russian treasure and troops that flowed in those directions, the less were available to expand westward. So, rationally, Whitehall should have cheered rather than condemned Moscow's retention of Ochakov. A stable but tense balance of power between Russia and Turkey in the Black Sea basin diverted minds in St. Petersburg and Constantinople from making mischief elsewhere far closer to the rest of Europe. Oddly, Britain's policy makers then were oblivious to this obvious truth.

Having determined that Russia's occupation of Ochakov threatened Britain's security, the next question was how to thwart it. The answer followed naturally from the assumption. Ochakov was worth fighting over. Britain was ready for war, or at least for a naval war. The fleet was still mobilized for the just-ended Nootka Sound crisis with Spain, so Pitt did not have to go begging to Parliament for more money. Two fleets would attack Russia, one of thirty-six ships of the line and twenty-nine smaller warships in the Baltic, and another of twelve ships of the line and a dozen or so smaller warships in the Black

Sea. Intelligence reports concluded that Russia's military and financial power was stretched to near the snapping point. The most effective time to pressure the Russians to back off was now.

The trouble was that British naval power alone could not prevail. Whitehall needed allies, and the larger the coalition, the greater the chance of success. So in January 1791, Pitt sought to forge an alliance as a vital step before issuing an ultimatum to St. Petersburg. This diplomatic offensive fizzled, as only Prussia agreed to stand with Britain against Russia.[25] But this one ally was enough for the administration to justify forging ahead. On March 15 the foreign secretary sent to Berlin an ultimatum for the British and Prussian ambassadors at St. Petersburg to present to Empress Catherine. George III sent a message to Parliament on March 28, asking its members to vote for an emergency budget to cover the war's opening costs. On March 31, press gangs began rounding up navy "recruits" in ports around the country.

It was then that the press, public, and Parliament's opposition and most backbenchers first learned that their nation might go to war with Russia over a faraway place that most had never before heard of. The result was a political thunderbolt. With his stirring speech before the House of Commons on March 29, Fox acted as the choirmaster for a spectrum of antiwar protests within and beyond Parliament. Simon Vorontsov, Russia's ambassador in London, worked with Fox to mobilize against the cabinet's policy a united front of newspapers and merchants whose profits would suffer from any war. All this encouraged hitherto silent skeptics within the cabinet to speak out. Grenville, Stafford, and Richmond urged Pitt, Leeds, and Chatham, the policy's most fervent advocates, to reconsider. Then Admiral Samuel Hood himself weighed in with his unease at just how his own campaign might end: "How we are to get at [Russia's] fleet I don't see. . . . Narrow seas and no friendly ports are bad things."[26]

Pitt finally gave in to the mounting pressure on April 15, by admitting to his cabinet that the policy had been misguided and offering to resign. His colleagues urged him to stay. Instead Foreign Secretary Leeds fell his on his sword for Pitt, returning his seal of office to the king on April 21. Pitt promptly appointed William Grenville to that vital post and transferred Henry Dundas to the Home Ministry. These three close friends now dominated foreign policy. In the end, the Pitt administration quietly acquiesced to Russia's retention of Ochakov and the region westward to the Dniester River.

With this expansion of Russia's empire secure, Catherine turned her guns westward toward Poland. The partitions of Poland by Russia, Prussia, and Austria in 1793 and 1795 swelled the power of all three relative to that of Britain, and this potentially undermined British national security. Yet Whitehall watched helplessly as this happened and, in doing so, helped abet it. In the summer of 1791, Pitt's government refused Polish requests that it guarantee their new constitution. Grenville expressed the prevailing sentiment: "We have . . . no other concern in the miseries and misfortunes of other countries than what humanity calls for."[27]

Concern rather than apathy toward Poland might have prevailed had not Pitt marched Britain to war's brink with Russia over Ochakov. This raises an inevitable but unanswerable question: What would have been Poland's fate had Whitehall taken as firm a stand against its destruction as it had, at least initially, against Russia's retention of Ochakov? The Pitt government had suffered a humiliating self-inflicted wound by provoking then retreating from the Ochakov crisis. With this behind them, Lord Auckland captured the relief and trepidation with which British policy makers looked abroad: "All political speculation will now turn to France."[28]

CHAPTER 4

# The First Coalition, 1792–1797

"The misfortune of our situation is that we have too many objects to attend to, and our force consequently must be too small at each place."

George III

"The die is cast and if there are fifty sail I will go through them. England badly needs a victory."

John Jervis

Prime Minister William Pitt delivered one of his career's most triumphant and, ultimately, controversial speeches before the House of Commons on February 17, 1792. He addressed the revolutionary effect of his policies on the government's finances, proudly noting that when he took office eight years earlier, the realm faced a soaring national debt and annual deficits for the foreseeable future. His responsible fiscal policies of raising taxes, cutting spending, and battling corruption had transformed chronic deficits into growing surpluses. Interest rates fell as the public sector competed less with the private sector to borrow money. This in turn encouraged entrepreneurs to borrow and invest more, which created and distributed ever more wealth, and generated more government revenues that paid off more of the national debt. He ended his speech with an outburst of optimistic speculation: "We must not count with certainty on a continuance of our present prosperity . . . but unquestionably there never was a time in the history of the world when, from the situation of Europe, we might more reasonably expect fifteen years of peace than we may at the present moment."[1] To his humiliation, he would soon be forced to eat these exuberant words.

## The Road to War

While Britain enjoyed unprecedented prosperity, France's revolutionary leaders got locked into a vicious cycle of extremism, paranoia, threats, and retaliation with Austria and Prussia that eventually led to war.[2] The struggle for power between moderates and radicals tilted sharply to the later following the aborted attempt of the French king and his family to flee to safety in foreign exile on June 20, 1791. The would-be royal refugees got as far as Varennes, a dozen miles from the frontier, when alert national guards arrested and escorted them back to Paris. Fearing for the safety of his sister Marie Antoinette and her family, Austrian emperor Leopold II issued, on July 5, 1791, the Padua Circular, whichcalled on Europe's royal leaders to unite in pressuring France to protect and restore its monarchy. On July 25 Prussian king Frederick William II joined Leopold II in pledging their mutual cooperation to that end.

French radicals pointed to these acts to justify locking Louis XVI and his family in the Temple Prison on August 13 and setting up a tribunal to judge those accused of political crimes on August 17. This in turn inspired a hasty summit between Leopold and Frederick William. During their meeting in Saxony on August 27, they issued the Pillnitz Declaration that again expressed their concern for France's royal family and appealed to all European states to join in protecting them. Vienna and Berlin directly asked Whitehall to sign the Pillnitz Declaration. Pitt and his colleagues agreed that neutrality best served British interests as war on the continent appeared likely, so Whitehall issued this polite but unequivocal reply: "The King has determined not to take any part in supporting or opposing" his fellow monarchs.[3]

France's radicals and moderates debated whether to depose or coopt the king. They finally forged a brittle consensus that, for now, it was better to hold the king as a puppet and hostage than martyr him for their royalist enemies. They released the royal family from the Temple Prison back to the Tuileries Palace. For two years, a committee had been slowly crafting a constitution that stripped the king of his absolute powers and forced him to share power with the 745-seat unicameral Legislative Assembly, formerly called the Constituent Assembly. After approving the constitution in August, the Legislative Assembly presented it to the king. Louis XVI sullenly signed the document on September 13, 1791.

When the Legislative Assembly convened on October 1, the most pressing issue was the worsening foreign threat. Austria and Prussia backed royalist émigrés who vowed to topple the revolutionary regime and were forming regiments of exiles to that end. On November 9, the Legislative Assembly decreed that any émigrés who did not return to France and swear to uphold the new constitution by January 1, 1792, would be condemned to death for treason and have their property confiscated. Louis XVI refused to sign this decree. On November 29 the Legislative Assembly demanded that the king sign an ultimatum that called on Europe's monarchs to outlaw and disperse any counterrevolutionary forces in their realms or else be considered enemies of France. After a couple of weeks discussing with his advisers what to do, on December 14 Louis XVI issued this ultimatum, hoping that it might provoke a war that led to an invasion of France by an allied army that would crush the revolutionaries and restored the monarchy to power.

War appeared inevitable as 1792 dawned. On January 17 Vienna issued orders to expand the army by 40,000 troops. On February 7 Leopold II and Frederick William II signed a treaty of alliance. When Leopold II died on March 1, 1792, he was replaced by his son Francis, then a twenty-four-year-old hothead with no military experience. Together Francis II and Frederick William II called on the other European powers to join them in a crusade to destroy the French Revolution.

Although the Pitt government thoroughly sympathized with the counterrevolutionary forces swelling across the continent, the official position of neutrality prevailed. Ideally, the allies would topple the revolutionary regime later that year. Pitt sought to quiet growing fears in Parliament and the public that Britain might somehow get sucked into a war that virtually no one wanted. Although Pitt enjoyed a crushing majority of 340 members to the opposition's 183, with 29 determined independents and 6 fence sitters, these numbers could shift rapidly against him if he promoted war without a genuine threat to the nation's security. He knew all too well the fate of Frederick, Lord North's, cabinet during the American War—the antiwar movement swelled steadily and eventually drove North's government from office.[4]

Louis XVI and most other royalists secretly welcomed with enormous relief the mounting likelihood that Austria and Prussia would war against France. They shared the optimism in Vienna and Berlin that the professional Austrian and Prussian armies would swiftly rout the revolutionary rabble and march into Paris to destroy the radical regime and restore the absolute monarchy. So with this hope in mind, Louis XVI eagerly backed the Legislative Assembly's declaration of war on April 20, 1792.

France was unprepared for war. Although the army appeared powerful, with its paper strength of 250,000 troops, only 94,700 troops were actually in the ranks.[5] Atop that, the army lost some veteran commanders when, during the summer, Generals Jean-Baptiste Rochambeau and Nicholas Luckner resigned. On August 19 General Gilbert de Lafayette called on the army to follow him to Paris to depose the radicals, but finding himself without support, he had to flee to the enemy lines to escape arrest. By mid-September General Charles François Dumouriez was leading the Army of the Center and General François Christophe Kellermann the Army of the North, guarding respectively eastern and northeastern France, each with paper strengths of about 50,000 troops

Frederick William III and Francis II met at Mainz on July 16, and agreed that Karl Wilhelm, Duke of Brunswick, should command the allied forces. Brunswick himself would lead an army of 42,000 mostly Prussian troops marching west up the Mosel River, while General Karl Josef Clerfait advanced with 56,000 mostly Austrian troops southwest up the Meuse River from the Austrian Netherlands. They would converge in eastern France, then advance to Paris.

At Koblenz, on July 25, Brunswick issued a manifesto warning that the allies would destroy Paris if the revolutionaries harmed the royal family. This enraged rather than intimidated the radicals. On August 10, a mob overran the Tuileries Palace, slaughtered the Swiss Guards, and imprisoned the royal family. Upon learning of that atrocity, Pitt and his cabinet decided on August 17, 1792, to withdraw Britain's envoy in Paris, George, Earl of Gower, both to protect him and protest the French government's increasingly violent policies.[6] On September 2 word reached Paris that the allied army had invaded France and captured Verdun. The mob reacted by slaughtering as many as 1,400 "royalist" prisoners. On September 22 the government, now known as the Convention, abolished the monarchy and established the French Republic, ignorant that two days before the French army had won a decisive victory over the invaders.

The combined 50,000 troops of Kellermann and Dumouriez repelled an attack by Brunswick's 33,000 troops at Valmy in eastern France on September 20. Severely outgunned and nearly out of supplies, Brunswick ordered his army to retreat to Germany. Johann Wolfgang von Goethe, who observed the battle, presciently remarked: "From here and today there begins a new epoch in the history of the world."[7]

France's revolutionary armies followed up Valmy with offensives that spread France to its "natural frontier." General Philippe de Montesquieu led an army that drove the Piedmont-Sardinian army from the region of Savoy and Nice back over the Maritime Alps. General Adam Philippe Custine pushed the Austrians out of the Palatinate and captured Speyer, Worms, Mainz, and Frankfort by late October. Dumouriez routed the Austrians at Jemappes on November 6, marched into Brussels on November 14, and by the month's end completed the conquest of the Austrian Netherlands as his troops occupied Antwerp, Louvain, and Liège.

Revolutionary fervor gripped France's generals, politicians, and public, vividly expressed by Dumouriez's proclamation: "Liberty is triumphant everywhere . . . it will establish itself on every throne, once it has crushed despotism and enlightened the people. . . . This present war will be the last and all tyrants and privileged . . . will be the only victims of this struggle between arbitrary power and reason." The Convention issued on November 19, 1792, the Edict of Fraternity, declaring that "the French nation . . . will grant fraternity and assistance to all peoples who wish to recover their liberty." In other words, the French Revolution would embrace any revolutionary movement that struggled for liberty anywhere. On December 15 the Convention declared that it would impose republican governments on all liberated countries and open for commerce and transportation all rivers to the sea. To this end, revolutionary commissars followed French armies and set up foreign legions to overthrow their governments and transform them into republics; soon there were Belgian, Dutch, German, Swiss, and Savoyard legions. On January 31 the Convention triumphantly declared that "the limits of France are marked out by nature. We shall reach them at their four points, at the ocean, at the Rhine, at the Alps, and at the Pyrenees."[8] Pitt and his colleagues viewed these developments with rising alarm. France's revolution without frontiers most threatened British security in the Low Countries.

On November 19, 1792, Paris declared that henceforth the Scheldt River would be open to navigation, blatantly violating the 1648 Peace of Westphalia that had closed this river to commerce from France. Having overrun the Austrian Netherlands, French troops massed on the borders of the Netherlands and appeared ready to "liberate" the Dutch people.

Although Pitt and his colleagues were desperate to deter this attack, they hoped to do so without rattling sabers too loudly or openly. A bilateral treaty in 1788 committed Britain to defend the Netherlands against invasion. Yet a stern reference to this treaty was not included in a statement, penned on November 13, that Foreign Secretary Grenville fired off to Ambassador Auckland to announce at The Hague. Instead, Britain was committed without "hesitation as to the propriety of . . . assisting the Dutch Republic, as circumstances might require against any attempt to invade its dominions or to disturb its Government."[9] This statement was also printed in British newspapers. When Paris did not reply, Grenville warned on November 29 that British neutrality would end if France did not repudiate its declarations on spreading revolution and opening the Scheldt River. French minister François Chauvelin, now joined by envoy Hugues Maret, met with Grenville and urged him to uphold British neutrality in return for an unofficial understanding rather than public denunciation that France would not assert its declarations. Although this was not good enough for Whitehall, it hesitated to revoke neutrality.

Russian Ambassador Simon Vorontsov asked the Pitt government to ally Britain with Russia, Prussia, Austria, the Netherlands, and as many lesser states as possible to crush revolutionary France once and for all.[10] Grenville demurred and instead called on these other states to join Britain in demanding that the French abandon their conquests, withdraw their armies to their national territory, respect the rights of other sovereign states, and stop fomenting revolution beyond their own borders. If the French failed to do all this, Britain would take "active measures for the purpose of obtaining the ends in view."[11]

While awaiting a reply from those countries, Grenville issued a circular diplomatic note excerpting a Pitt speech declaring that "England never will consent that France shall arrogate the power of annulling at her pleasure and under the pretence of a . . . national right, of which she makes herself the only judge, the political system of Europe, established by solemn treaties, and guaranteed by the consent of all the powers."[12] Instead, Britain was committed to restoring Europe to its pre-1789 borders.

These British statements sobered the French government. Foreign Minister Pierre Lebrun authorized Chauvelin "to declare to Mr. Pitt that the Scheldt would be as good as given up, that the Convention will do away by a revision of its law all the offensive matter contained in the decree of November 19, and that the Executive Council had rejected the offers of Liège and some of the Belgic provinces to incorporate themselves with France."[13]

Any positive effect those promises might have had on Whitehall died with the news that reached London on January 23, 1793. Two days earlier, on January 21, the guillotine's blade had decapitated Louis XVI. Yet even then Pitt's government held back from declaring war. Parliament and the public alike would be far more unified if France was the first to issue that declaration. Instead, on January 24, Grenville informed Chauvelin that he and his mission were persona non grata and were to leave Britain no later than February 1.

War now was just a matter of time. Pitt tried to ready the public for this on February 1, by depicting the nature of the enemy that Britain faced:

> They have explained what that liberty is that they wish to give every nation, and if they will not accept of it voluntarily, they compel them. They take every opportunity to destroy every institution that is most sacred and most valuable in every nation where their armies have made their appearance; and under the name of liberty they have resolved to make every country . . . a province dependent on themselves, through the despotism of Jacobin societies. . . . We see . . . that France has trampled underfoot all law of nations . . . and unless she is stopped in her career, all Europe will soon learn their . . . models of government and principles of liberty from the mouths of French cannons.[14]

The severance of diplomatic relations provoked Paris to promise to "give up Nice, Mainz, Worms, & all conquests on the Rhine. That it would renounce Liège, the Low Countries (provided Great Britain would guaranty their independence), the Scheldt, & contrive the means of detaching Savoy from France."[15] These were extraordinary concessions. Had Pitt's government written them up into a treaty signed by France and all the other great and lesser powers, Europe might have been spared the horrors of the next twenty-two years. But Whitehall rejected this peace offering. As a result, on February 1, 1793, France unanimously declared war on Britain and the Netherlands. It took six days for official word to reach London.

King George III was among those delighted by the news. He reckoned that France's war declaration would "rouze a spirit in this country that I trust will curb the insolence of those despots and be a means of restoring some degree of order to that unprincipled country, whose aim at present is to destroy the foundations of every civilized state."[16] On February 11 he officially declared that Britain was at war with

France. In a speech before the House of Commons the following day, Pitt tried to rally the nation by illuminating just how titanic the struggle was: "It now remains to be seen whether, under Providence, the efforts of a free, brave, loyal, and happy people, aided by their allies, will not be successful in checking the progress of a system, the principles of which, if not opposed, threaten the most fatal consequences to the tranquility of this country, the security of its allies, the good order of every European government, and the happiness of the whole human race."[17]

Pitt spoke nonchalantly of allies because he assumed that uniting with the realms already warring against France would be easy enough. He could not imagine that struggling to forge and sustain what eventually became seven coalitions would be the most frustrating and time-consuming duty for himself and his successors. Yet the only alternative to this Sisyphean labor was to accept peace on French terms, since the other great powers lacked the deep financial pockets to sustain their effort without British aid, and Britain could not defeat France alone. Peace was acceptable only when France no longer threatened to dominate Europe. So the logic both of upholding the power balance and the idea of "the enemy of my enemy is my friend" would determine British foreign policy for the next twenty-two years, just as it had in previous centuries and would for a couple of future centuries.

Following the balance of power demanded discarding other lines of logic that might have led to different policies and thus radically different subsequent readings of history. For instance, around the same time in January 1793 that France's Convention voted to decapitate a man, the monarchs of Prussia and Russia, later joined by Austria's, agreed to dismember a nation. The guillotining of Louis XVI provoked feelings of horror and outrage among Britons, even though their ancestors had similarly executed their own king 143 years earlier. Yet Whitehall did not protest, let alone try to prevent the Second Partition of Poland by Austria, Prussia, and Russia that reduced the realm to a rump state this year, nor did it utter a diplomatic peep when the countries completely devoured Poland two years later. In the minds of Pitt and his cabinet, a greater good justified this silence. Austria and Prussia were already allied with Britain against France, and ideally

Russia could be enticed to join them. In a speech before the House of Commons, Pitt explained the moral dilemma: "Shall we, because a partition was made of Poland, abate that resistance without which we must fall a prey to the destruction leveled at all Europe?"[18]

Whitehall soon cobbled together what became known as the First Coalition. Britain already had a defensive alliance with the Netherlands and Prussia, signed in 1788. Under that treaty, the British and Dutch could ask the Prussians to provide them up to 20,000 and 12,000 troops, respectively, in return for which each country would underwrite their "bread and forage." Foreign Secretary Grenville fired off a flurry of instructions to British diplomats to reactivate that alliance and knit it into a broader coalition with other realms. On March 25 Russia was the first to sign a treaty, then Sardinia on April 25, Spain on May 25, the Two Sicilies on July 12, Prussia on July 14, Austria on August 31, and, finally, Portugal on September 10.

In addition, the British cut deals with several small German states to supply mercenaries, including Hanover for 17,000 troops, Hesse-Cassel for 8,000 troops, Hesse-Darmstadt for 3,000 troops, and Baden for 754 troops.[19] The treaties differed in the tradeoff of cash for soldiers. For instance, Hanover got a much better deal by taking £455,851 for 17,000 troops compared to Baden's £5,013 for a battalion of 754 troops. As the bills reached Parliament, ever more members called for a cap on spending for mercenaries. Pitt agreed and in 1794 got Parliament to appropriate £1,169,000 for foreign troops.[20]

Foreign sovereigns varied in the extravagance of their demands and the haggling skills with which they tried to get them. No one was tougher than Catherine II, who insisted that she could only part with 10,000 troops for nothing less than £600,000. Ambassador Charles Whitworth politely explained that her figure was exorbitant. With a shrug, she turned over the negotiation to Simon Vorontsov, her ambassador in London, and authorized him to halve the price. Even £300,000 was too much for Whitehall, so Grenville had Whitworth inform Catherine that "unless the idea of a subsidy is abandoned, all possibility of a future concert is at an end."[21] That was fine with Catherine, whose armies were either fighting the Turks or threatening the Poles and Swedes, and for this she needed money and plenty of it. As for the

French Revolution, it enhanced rather than threatened Russian interests by distracting Austria, Prussia, and Britain from Catherine's ambitions. To swell this distraction, she signed a treaty with Britain in 1794, but the document simply stated counterrevolutionary principles.

Frederick William II played nearly as hard to get as Catherine. To entice him, Grenville dispatched James Harris, First Earl of Malmesbury, one of Britain's most skilled negotiators. The king bluntly explained that "I have not in my treasure enough to pay the expense of a third campaign."[22] He promised to field 100,000 troops in the spring of 1794 if Britain paid Prussia £2 million. Malmesbury explained that Britain was unable to come close to this figure. The negotiations persisted through 1793 and well into the next year, when their talks were moved to The Hague to include the Dutch in the final deal. On April 19, 1794, Malmesbury and his Prussian counterpart Kurt von Haugwitz signed a treaty whereby Prussia would join 62,400 troops with British and Dutch forces by May 24, in return for a startup fee of £400,000 and monthly payments of £150,000 beginning in April. In a separate treaty signed that same day, Britain and the Netherlands agreed to split the subsidy costs, with London supplying three-fourths and The Hague one-quarter the amount, with their respective startup costs of £300,000 and £100,000, and subsequent £950,000 and £400,000 payments, spread to the year's end. In addition to the money, Prussia was released from its obligations under the 1788 treaty to supply on demand 20,000 and 12,000 troops to Britain and the Netherlands, respectively.[23]

Finally, there was Austria. Chancellor Johann Thugut instructed Ambassador Louis Starhemberg to seek £3 million from Britain, but as a loan rather than a grant, and from banks rather than Whitehall. In May Starhemberg cut a deal with Boyd, Benfield, and Company for issuing £2.5 million of Austrian bonds paying 3 percent and providing a £500,000 loan that Vienna paid over twenty-five years for 10 percent.[24]

Although Pitt was pleased to avoid paying the Austrians public money, he worried about all that private money leaving the country. Yet his hands were legally tied, since no British law prevented such a transaction. All he could do was reject Starhemberg's request that the government back the loan. He then sought to capitalize on this loan by sending to Vienna Thomas Grenville and Henry, Earl of Spencer to ask Francis II to expand his army and devise a common strategy.[25]

The Austrians agreed, but at a stiff price—they now wanted a subsidy from Whitehall and warned that without one Austria would be forced to withdraw from defending the Low Countries. Pitt countered by agreeing to seek Parliament's approval to back the private loan that the Austrians had secured, but refused to make any direct payments. In return, the Austrians had to increase their army fighting in Flanders to 160,000 troops and place it under a British commander. Thugut angrily rejected this notion and fired back a demand for £6 million in return for a 100,000-man Austrian army under Austrian command. After months of debate, Pitt and his inner cabinet agreed to guarantee a £6 million loan in return for a 200,000-man Austrian army. Grenville sent Sir Morton Eden to Vienna with this offer and his credentials as Britain's latest ambassador.[26]

Britain and its allies had pledged themselves to war until they destroyed France's aggressive revolutionary regime and imposed a congenial government. Just how such a government could be identified and set up was left unsaid. Although the refugee Bourbons insisted that they were France's legitimate government, Whitehall refused to endorse them. The Bourbon cause appeared to be a very poor bet. Louis XVII, the actual heir to the French throne, was then only eight years old and imprisoned in the Temple in Paris. He was rumored to be in wretched health and abused by his guards. He had suffered the trauma of losing first his father and then his mother to a guillotine's blade. His oldest uncle, Louis, Comte de Provence and future Louis XVIII, was then in exile with his wife and a small court at a palace in Hamm. This Louis was best known for his gargantuan girth, earned from virtually nonstop eating, and his unsteady waddling during those few times he ventured from the banquet table. On January 28, 1793, Provence proclaimed his dedication to restoring the Bourbons to power in France and asserted himself as his nephew's regent; thereafter he sought official recognition of these claims from Britain and other countries. Third in line to the throne was Louis's younger brother, Charles, comte d'Artois. The future Charles X was as good-looking and vigorous as Louis was indolent and toadlike in appearance, but he carried some heavy political baggage. He had racked up ever-larger debts to finance his insatiable love for gambling and womanizing, interests that made him France's version of Britain's prince regent, the future George IV, although the two failed to bond during their few encounters. This was it in the direct Bourbon line, and of the Bourbon's more prolific collateral branch, the most important person was Louis Joseph, Prince de Condé, who commanded several regiments of exiles then based at Coblenz.

Louis tapped Charles to spearhead the Bourbon campaign for recognition and subsidies from Britain, but Whitehall turned down Charles's request for funds to help underwrite their counterrevolutionary efforts. Charles then sought those funds indirectly from London via St. Petersburg. Whitehall rejected that channel as well. Undaunted, Charles asked permission in April 1792 to visit Britain to make his case in person. Fearing his visit would embarrass all concerned, Whitehall politely pressed him to desist. Artois had run up huge debts during his previous sojourn in London before skipping town to escape his creditors. He might well be sued or arrested if he reappeared, and that would damage the counterrevolutionary cause. Artois stayed away. [27]

Meanwhile, the Bourbons tried to link up with counterrevolutionary groups within France itself. Early in 1793, two separate royalist groups, the Chouans in Brittany and the Vendeans in the lower Loire valley rebelled, and in August groups of moderates and royalists in the lower Rhone joined forces against the radical regime in Paris, and took over Lyons, Marseilles, and Toulon.[28]

Whitehall's Alien Office was also interested in working with rebel groups in and beyond France. The key agents charged with that mission were William Wickham in Berne, Francis Drake in Genoa, and John Trevor in Turin, who wielded an array of means to organize, fund, and launch counterrevolutionary operations. For instance, Wickham helped form the overt Bernese Council, which aided over two hundred exile families, and the Secret Council, which ran agents into France with forged passports and coin-filled purses. Drake and Trevor formed similar groups in their own bailiwicks. Since espionage morphs inevitably into counterespionage, the three devoted enormous efforts trying to nab spies sent by Paris to infiltrate their own groups.

Among the Alien Office's most successful operations was setting up the Institut Philanthropique in Paris. The organization's dedication to alleviating poverty was a perfect front for espionage and counterrevolution, and its resulting network spread through Freemason and Jesuit groups in Paris, Lyons, Bordeaux, Nantes, Vannes, St. Malo, Dunkirk, and Boulogne, and linked with an array of royalist groups, most notably the Chouans and Vendeans. The Institut Philanthropique's English Committee was the direct conduit for agents, money, and instructions coming from the Alien Office, as well as intelligence back to London. Inevitably, Whitehall found itself cooperating with the Bourbons, who were trying to nurture those and other counterrevolutionary groups through their Exterior Agency, charged with both diplomacy and espionage. By the late 1790s, the Alien Office and Exterior Agency were working closely together even while Whitehall refused openly to endorse the Bourbon insistence that they were France's sole legitimate rulers.

## The 1793 Campaigns

Most people in the cabinet and across the country went to war reluctantly. It was a mere decade since Britain had ended its last war in 1783. The military was ill prepared, the army a David to the continent's Goliaths, with only about 14,000 troops in the British Isles and 30,000 scattered across the empire from Canada to the West Indies to India.[29] To overcome this gross disadvantage, Whitehall launched a massive campaign to recruit troops in Britain and mercenaries or allies overseas. In contrast, the navy appeared formidable, with its 115 ships of the line compared to France's 88. The British ships of the line at potential battle stations included 25 in the English Channel, 20 in the Mediterranean, 12 in the West Indies, and 5 in the East Indies. But only about a fifth of the Royal Navy's vessels were ready for action, including 26 ships of the line, 32 frigates, and 34 sloops, while 87 ships of the line and 28 frigates were in severe need of sailors, repair, and provisions.[30]

Britain was as deficient in soft power as it was in hard power. As the nation went to war in 1793, an adjutant general offered this bleak assessment: "There is not a young man in the army that cares a farthing whether his commanding officer approves his conduct or not. His promotion depends not on their smiles or frowns—his friends can give him a thousand pounds with which he goes to the auction room . . . and in a fortnight becomes a captain. Out of the fifteen regiments of cavalry and twenty-six of infantry with which we have here, twenty-one are literally commanded by boys or idiots."[31]

Mustering the military forces of one's nation and allies was, of course, just the first step in waging war. The next was deciding what to do with them. The trouble was that Pitt's closest advisers—Home Secretary Henry Dundas and Foreign Secretary William Grenville—advocated opposite views. Dundas asserted a "colonial" strategy whereby British armadas captured one colony after another of France and its allies until they gave up; Britain could keep the more lucrative conquests while wielding the rest as bargaining chips during peace talks. Grenville insisted that France could only be beaten with a "continental" strategy whereby a large British army worked in harness with allied forces to march on Paris. The two ministers did agree that building and sustaining a coalition underwritten with gold was essential for victory. Seeing merit in both plans, Pitt devised a hybrid strategy from what he believed were each's best elements.[32]

For political and personal reasons, Pitt and his inner circle disdained the one man in the cabinet who had actually been a professional soldier—Charles, Duke of Richmond, now the ordnance general. During the Seven Years' War, he had fought mostly in Germany where he rose to become a major general. Richmond was the cabinet's Cassandra, whose warnings of policies bound to fail were ignored. Early on, he tried explaining to Pitt that

> he was going on much too fast with His Calculations. That men just raised upon paper were not soldiers . . . that I thought it required at least six months . . . assembled in Corps either in Camp or in quarters to make them at all fit for service & even then they would be but very young & raw Soldiers. . . . I particularly represented to Mr. Pitt that . . . His schemes & Ideas were . . . much too vast to be executed within any Thing like the Time He talked of [and] that . . . by undertaking too

> much he would do nothing well. That great & long Preparations were necessary for all Military Services, and He could not too soon fix upon the precise Plan He meant to pursue, determine His force . . . appoint His Commander & fix the time for His operations.[33]

As for strategy, Richmond called for massing the navy and army to invade northwestern France, seize Cherbourg or St. Malo as a supply port, and ally with the region's Chouan and Vendean rebels. This would trap the French in a vise squeezed ever tighter by the British and rebels forces advancing from the west and Austrian and Prussia armies from the east. Eventually the allies would march triumphantly into Paris, topple the regime, and reimpose a Bourbon king on the throne.[34]

The war between Britain and France naturally began at sea but even there took a while to get started. It was not until May, three months after war declarations were issued, that cannon shots were indecisively traded first between a British frigate and a French privateer, then between a British frigate and a French frigate. The French scored the first victory when one of their frigates captured a British sloop, and the first genuine naval battle erupted on June 19, when the frigate HMS *Nymphe,* captained by Edward Pellew, squared off with the French frigate *Cleopatre* in the English Channel; the French commander struck his colors after exchanging broadsides for forty-five minutes. Two days later the *Nymphe* towed the shattered *Cleopatre* into Portsmouth harbor, and five days after that George III knighted Pellew at St. James Palace. The war at sea was off to a glorious dawn that the Royal Navy would sustain for the next twenty-two years.

An emergency rather than choice triggered Grenville's continental strategy. On February 16, 1793, General Dumouriez launched an attack on the Netherlands that threatened to overrun the country. The Hague sent an urgent plea to London for help. The Cabinet swiftly agreed to ship 1,500 Royal Guards to the Netherlands and mobilize a larger force.[35]

Warfare in the Low Countries was a slow, laborious process. The landscape grants enormous benefits to defenders and imposes harsh penalties on attackers, as it is dotted with fortresses and strung together with canals. Generalship in such a theater demands the methodical mind of an engineer rather than the galloping mind of a cavalry commander. The general who commanded Britain's army in Flanders lacked either attribute.

George III committed a blatant act of nepotism when he tapped his second son, Frederick Augustus, Duke of York, for the command.[36] This decision had tragic consequences. York displayed nothing more than mediocrity and often incompetence during this and other campaigns that he was entrusted to lead. Fortunately, a succession of fairly able second-in-commands like Generals Gerard Lake, Ralph Abercromby, and James Murray ensured that York did nothing completely disastrous.

Britain's worst handicap in Flanders was not generalship but manpower. With over 100,000 troops, Dumouriez's army in the region outgunned by a three-to-one ratio York's 34,500-man army, which included 6,500 British, 17,000 German, and 11,000 Dutch troops. While the British took pride in assembling this army, the Austrians and Prussians, unimpressed with the hodgepodge force, were especially scornful that Whitehall had committed so few redcoats to the continent. In contrast, the Prussian army had 46,000 troops, while Austria's army numbered 93,000 troops in Flanders and 38,000 in Alsace.

The Austrians and Prussians not only fielded more men but fought and won more battles. Frederick, Prince of Coburg, launched an offensive in March that routed the French at Liège, Louvain, Aldenhoven, and Neerwinden and recovered most of the Austrian Netherlands. Dumouriez defected in April; self-preservation rather than ideology or gold motivated him to do so: failed generals faced a firing squad. Coburg went on to besiege Valenciennes.

It was then that York entered the fray. Until then he had debated, Hamletlike, what to do. His orders were to capture Dunkirk and to assist Coburg. He could not do both at once. He finally decided to shelve an advance on Dunkirk and instead march to join Coburg at Valenciennes in May. After the fortress capitulated on July 28, Coburg pressured York to commit his forces to a joint campaign to retake the barrier fortresses in the Austrian Netherlands. York asked Whitehall for instructions. A month passed before Pitt's government read the request, debated it, and decided that with most of the Austrian Netherlands retaken, York should capture Dunkirk.

Elsewhere the allies also scored victories. Karl Wilhelm, Duke of Brunswick, led a Prussian army to besiege 18,000 French at Mainz, and forced them to surrender on July 23. A Spanish army fought its way across the frontier and nearly to Perpignan before turning back. In western France, the rebel Chouans in Brittany and the Vendeans in the lower Loire valley gained more ground and tied down more French troops. The city of Lyons and the entire island of Corsica revolted. In Paris itself, the battle for control of the revolution between the moderate Girodins and radical Jacobins was becoming more violent. A crushing defeat of France appeared inevitable as the Coalition now included all four great powers—Britain, Austria, Prussia, and Russia, along with Spain, Portugal, Sardinia-Piedmont, the Two Sicilies, Tuscany, the Papal States, Modena, and Parma. All this prompted Pitt to exclaim in the Commons that "every circumstance concurs to favour the hope of our being able completely to accomplish every object of the war."[37]

Events soon disillusioned Pitt of his ecstatic view that the war was all but won. York and his army finally reached Dunkirk on August 21. Unfortunately, his siege train was far away and would not catch up any time soon. This was not York's fault; he had requested one months earlier. Ordnance Master General Charles, Duke of Richmond, had deliberately delayed approving the requisition order from hatred for York, with whom his family had feuded for years, and out of spite that Pitt and his inner cabinet had rejected his campaign plan. So for now all York could do was encamp his army and zigzag forward trenches whose redoubts would hold the siege guns when they arrived. The French fouled that strategy by opening the sluice gates on the dikes holding back the sea and flooded much of the countryside around York's army. The siege train finally reached Nieuport, the closest harbor to Dunkirk held by the British, and from there was floated by canal toward the siege.

After learning that 45,000 French troops led by General Jean Houchard were marching to attack him and relieve Dunkirk, York fired off a message to Coburg asking for help and deployed his Hanoverian troops at Hondschoete to protect his lines around Dunkirk. At Hondschoete, the Hanoverians repelled the first French attack on September 16, but they were routed and suffered 3,000 casualties during the next assault two days later. As Houchard advanced to inflict the coup de grace, Coburg's army struck him on September 15, and forced the French to retreat. The Committee of Public Safety replaced Houchard with General Jean-Baptiste Jourdan, who massed troops and supplies, then attacked Coburg at Wattignies on October 15 and 16 and forced the Austrians to retreat.

This left York exposed at Dunkirk. During his campaign, he had suffered losses of nearly 10,000 men from disease, desertion, skirmishes, and the battle of Hondschoete. With only 24,500 troops left, he faced being crushed by Jourdan at Dunkirk. He had no rational choice but to withdraw. Unfortunately, he lacked the time to drag off his siege guns, which he ordered spiked and abandoned. In all, Britain's first campaign in the Low Countries had been a debacle. It would not be the last.

In any war with France, a key element of British strategy was to blockade Toulon, France's most important naval base in the Mediterranean. Crowding Toulon's harbor in 1793 were forty-five vessels, including seventeen ships of the line ready for action and five more being prepared. From Spithead, Admiral Samuel Hood set sail with fifteen ships of the line and nine frigates on May 22; the fleet dropped anchor beyond cannon shot of Toulon's coast on July 18. The British were soon joined by a Spanish fleet of twenty-four ships of the line led by Admiral Don Juan de Langara.

An astonishing message to Hood alleviated the tedium of blockade duty on August 23. Two days earlier rebels had taken over Toulon, declared themselves for Louis XVII, and now invited Hood to fight with them against the revolutionary regime. Hood conferred with Langara and together they negotiated an alliance with the rebels. On August 28, a force of 1,500 marines, soldiers, and armed sailors stepped ashore to occupy Toulon and the forts on the surrounding hills.

Pitt was jubilant when he learned on September 13 that Hood's flotilla had captured Toulon, declaring that victory "the most important which could be struck towards the final success of the war."[38] He envisioned Toulon the base of operations for a campaign that first liberated southern France, then marched north up the Rhone River and eventually over into the Seine River valley to converge on Paris, with British, Austrian, Prussian, and other allied troops advancing from the east. He sent orders to York to divert 9,700 British and German troops from his army to Hood, while Grenville issued instructions for his ministers in Vienna, Turin, and Naples to ask their hosts to send as many troops as possible to Toulon. Francis II declined, dismissing the Toulon campaign as a side-show that diverted scarce resources from the vital fronts along the Rhine and in Flanders. However, Ferdinand IV at Naples and Victor Amadeus III at Turin sent what troops they could spare.

Over the next four months, reinforcements swelled the allied army until it peaked with 2,114 British, 1,542 French, 1,584 Piedmontese, 4,832 Neapolitans, 6,846 Spanish, and around 2,000 Sardinian troops.[39] To bolster the alliance, Hood asked Spanish Admiral Frederico Carlos de Gravina to command the land forces. Gravina did so ably until he was wounded on October 27. Hood then gave that command to General Charles O'Hara.[40] Meanwhile, the French government ordered General Jean François Carteaux to organize an army and retake the lower Rhone Valley and adjacent coastline. By early September Carteaux's army had crushed the rebellion in the region and was besieging Toulon; commanding the French army's artillery was Major Napoleon Bonaparte.

Hood's seizure of Toulon in the name of Louis XVII spotlighted a delicate diplomatic issue. Until then Whitehall was careful not to commit itself to the Bourbons. George III tried to clarify Britain's position on October 29, when he proclaimed:

> His Majesty by no means disputes the Right of France to reform its Laws. It never would have been able to employ the Influence of external Force with respect to the particular Forms of Government to be established in an independent Country . . . except in so far as such Interference is . . . essential to the Security and Repose of other Powers. Under these Circumstances,

> He demands from France . . . the Termination of a System of Anarchy, which has no Force but for the Purpose of Mischief. . . . The King demands that some legitimate and stable Government . . . be established, founded on the acknowledged Principles of universal Justice, and capable of maintaining with other Powers . . . Peace. . . . His Majesty invites the Co-operation of the People of France . . . to join the Standard of an hereditary Monarchy . . . in order to unite themselves once more under the Empire of Law, of Morality, and of Religion.[41]

Although in his ringing endorsement of monarchy for France George III did not explicitly endorse reimposing the Bourbons on their former throne, he certainly seemed to imply it. This forced Pitt to explain: "This by no means preludes us from treating with any other form of regular government, if, in the end, any other should be solidly established; but it holds out monarchy as the only force from which we expect any good, and in favour of which we are disposed to enter into concert."[42]

Word reached London in October that Louis, Comte de Provence, was planning to depart his residence at Turin and journey to Toulon, where he intended to rally the French people to the Bourbon cause. This set off the latest cabinet debate over just how far to lean toward the Bourbons without embracing them. They decided to draw the line at Toulon. Grenville fired off instructions to Francis Drake, the British minister at Genoa, to exert all polite efforts to dissuade Provence from undertaking his mission. To Whitehall's relief, Provence never stirred from his cozy palace.[43]

This turned out to been the best decision for all concerned. The allied grip on Toulon weakened steadily as the French massed ever more troops and heavy guns in their siege lines around the city. Hood was increasingly pessimistic over whether he could hold on. Not only were his troops outnumbered but their overall quality was dismal, especially the Spanish and Neapolitan troops. Although he received 3,786 more Neapolitan troops in late November, they merely replaced the over 3,000 troops downed by disease and the hundreds more killed or wounded in the fighting.[44]

It was Napoleon Bonaparte who planned and led a series of attacks on key points in the allied lines. General O'Hara,wounded and captured on November 29, was replaced by General David Dundas, the home secretary's brother. The decisive battle came on December 17, when Bonaparte led his troops to capture Fort Mulgrave, which overshadowed Toulon and its harbor packed with Hood's flotilla.

Hood ordered Toulon evacuated on December 18. That night the surviving troops were withdrawn from the forts and entrenchments to vessels already crowded with nearly 7,500 royalist refugees. Hood had sailors man thirteen French warships and ordered the rest burned, along with warehouses and docks. The fleet sailed from Toulon amid an inferno of burning ships and buildings, and cannon shots from French batteries on the surrounding hills.

Despite this withdrawal, the sojourn of that allied armada under Hood's command in Toulon was a decisive victory. In all, the British sailed away on three French ships of the line, three frigates, and seven corvettes, and destroyed fourteen and damaged eleven warships. France would need years to rebuild this fleet. In doing so, enormous amounts of men, money, and material would be diverted from other vital fronts.[45]

Meanwhile, a plan unfolded to land a British expedition in Brittany to join rebel Chouan and Vendean forces. Whitehall gave the command to Francis Rawdon, Earl of Moira, who was an able general when he fought in the American War. With Britain's military forces spread thin, Moira faced a tough challenge mustering all the 12,000 infantry and 2,000 cavalry that he insisted he needed. After assembling those troops, he had to decide what to do with them. He and his staff debated the merits of capturing St. Malo or Nantes as a base from which to supply and train the rebels and eventually lead them against the French. They finally agreed that St. Malo was easier to reach with supplies, reinforcements, and communications. Moira's expedition sailed on December 1 and for a week hovered off Normandy's coast, fruitlessly trying to contact Chouan forces ashore. Meanwhile, storms battered and disease swept through his flotilla, killing hundreds and sickening thousands. He finally decided to call off the campaign.

Home Secretary Dundas convinced the cabinet to dispatch an expedition under Admiral Alan Gardner and General Cornelius Cuyler to the West Indies to protect Britain's colonies and capture as many French colonies as possible. France's West Indian empire was vulnerable. Struggles had erupted in St. Domingue, Martinique, Guadeloupe, and Tobago among republicans, royalists, and slaves, with free blacks split among those factions. With only small contingents of French troops and warships in the colonies, some groups of planters appealed to the British for help. The expedition seized Tobago in April, and landed a small force at Mole and St. Nicolas, in St. Domingue, France's greatest sugar-producing colony, in September. On the other side of the world, word of the latest war with France did not reach India until late that year. British forces reacted swiftly by seizing Mahe, Chandernagore, Karica, Yanam, and Pondicherry.

By the end of 1793, Pitt and his colleagues could congratulate themselves on how many forces and campaigns they had organized and launched: a British army was operating in the Low Countries; expeditions had picked off French colonies in the West and East Indies; and a British-led allied armada had occupied Toulon and captured or destroyed much of the French fleet before withdrawing. Yet none of those efforts inflicted more than minor damage on France. George III sagely explained why: "The misfortune of our situation is that we have too many objects to attend to, and our force consequently must be too small at each place."[46] British power was limited: the thinner it was spread, the more ineffective it became. Two decades of war would pass before Britain mobilized its resources to the point where, in harness with the allied armies of Russia, Austria, Prussia, Spain, and lesser states, it finally crushed France. Many reasons led that war to last as long as it did, an essential one being that the British and their allies had trouble comprehending the nature of the war they were fighting.

For France's revolutionaries, the only strategy that might defeat its array of foreign and internal enemies was total war or mobilizing all human and material resources of power. The first step came on April 6, 1793, when the Convention set up the twelve-man Committee of Public Safety to gather and direct all necessary means to crushing insurgencies within France. This mission tended to attract the Jacobins, the most ruthless French revolutionaries, who struggled with the moderate Girodins for power. The next and most crucial step came on August 23, 1793, when the Convention declared a "levee en masse":

> From this moment until that in which our enemies shall have been driven from the territory of the Republic, all Frenchmen are permanently requisitioned for service in the armies. The young men shall fight; the married men shall forge weapons and transport supplies; the women will make tents and clothes and will serve in the hospitals; the children will make up old linen into lint; the old men will have themselves carried into the public squares to rouse the courage of the fighting men, to preach the unity of the Republic, and hatred of the King's.[47]

The result was astonishing. The number of French troops tripled from 361,000 in February 1793 to peak at 1,108,300 in September 1794. Previously the most troops ever mobilized was 300,000 under Louis XIV. The production of uniforms, shoes, arms, munitions, provisions, and other vital equipment kept up with the vast expansion of soldiers. For instance, by 1794 French factories were turning out 750 muskets a day, nearly as many as that of all its enemies combined.[48] Finally, on September 5, 1793, the Committee of Public Safety, chaired by Maximilien Robespierre, declared that henceforth "terror" would be the principle weapon in fighting the counterrevolutionaries. The Convention was so impressed with the results that on October 10, 1793, it issued to the Committee of Public Safety the power to direct the war. The Convention then voted on December 4, 1793, to confer upon the Committee of Public Safety all powers of state. The final step in conferring dictatorial powers on the committee came on April 1, 1794, when the Convention replaced the council of ministers with commissions all controlled by Robespierre and his colleagues. Also subordinate to the Committee of Public Safety was the Committee of General Security, which commanded the secret police.

Such was the nature of the regime that Britain was warring against. To fight, let alone defeat, such a enemy demanded an extraordinary and unprecedented mobilization of British power.

## The 1794 Campaigns

A prime minister's duties were wearying enough in peacetime and nearly crushing in wartime. In July 1794 Pitt sought to spread some of the burden by creating a new portfolio for a secretary for war and handing it to his trusted friend Henry Dundas, then home secretary. Dundas objected: "The Idea of a War Minister as a Separate Department . . . cannot exist in this country . . . All modern Wars are a Contention of Purse, and unless some very peculiar Circumstance occurs . . . the Minister for Finance must be the Minister for War."[49] Pitt insisted that the "very peculiar Circumstance" was now. Dundas reluctantly agreed. Pitt's inner war cabinet included Dundas as secretary for war; Secretary at War William Windham (effectively the secretary for war's chief of staff); Foreign Secretary William Grenville; First Lord of the Admiralty George, Earl of Spencer; and Home Secretary William Bentinck.

All along Pitt struggled to keep up British morale amid the widening war and setbacks. In a speech on January 21, 1794, he declared that France's revolutionary regime would eventually self-destruct: "The more monstrous and terrible the system has become, the greater is the probability that it will be speedily overthrown. From the nature of the mind of man, and necessary progress of human affairs, it is impossible that such a system can be of long duration, and surely no event can be looked for more desirable than the destruction of that system, which at present exists to the misery of France and the terror of Europe."[50]

Pitt, of course, was wrong about this. A lasting peace would evade France and the rest of Europe for two more blood-soaked decades. Along the way, one version of despotism would yield to another in Paris. It would also lead to an increasingly repressive government in Britain itself. As the nation's toll in debt and death soared, Whitehall wielded its own version of despotism to fight despotism. The justification was worsening antagonisms between most Britons who backed the government, the war, and the political status quo and the increasingly radicalized minority who opposed all that.[51]

The first step came even before Britain went to war. George III and his ministers concluded that the French Revolution threatened Britain more with ideas than arms. Ever more Britons appeared infected with radical beliefs that imperiled the government and society with revolution. Conservatives feared that, as in France, any attempt to coopt the radicals with reforms would only whet their appetite and demands for more. Revolution could be prevented only by repressing the revolutionaries. This reasoning led the king to issue, on May 21, 1792, the Royal Proclamation against Seditious Writings and Publications, which asserted that "there is not a more indispensable duty in the executive power than to support the civil magistrates in suppressing riots, where it cannot otherwise be effected."[52]

The result was a self-fulfilling prophecy as conservatives initiated a vicious cycle of violence in the belief that they were smothering a revolution.[53] What they did instead was radicalize progressives. In July 1792 a Birmingham mob reacted to a dinner held by liberals to celebrate Bastille Day with three days of rioting that burned three Unitarian churches, a Baptist church, and the homes of twenty-seven progressives, including that of the renowned scientist and outspoken philosopher Joseph Priestly. Although the government had not instigated that attack, George III was among those who reacted with conflicting emotions: "I cannot but feel better pleased that Mr. Priestly is the sufferer for the doctrines that he and his party have instilled and that the people see them in their true light; yet cannot approve of their having employed such atrocious means of showing their discontent."[54]

The political seesaw had shifted sharply from those heady days in the summer of 1789 when virtually all Britons enthusiastically cheered the French Revolution. Doubts grew in the minds of most sympathizers as they learned of the worsening violence, with the most disillusioning the September 1792 massacres and the king's beheading in January 1793. France's war declaration against Britain in February 1793 was the final assault on the consciences for most of those who the revolution had so greatly inspired four years earlier.

Yet a hard core of true believers remained not only unshaken in their zeal for anything France's revolutionaries did, no matter how extreme and violent, but advocated the same sweeping and harsh measures for Britain. Another group of dissidents spurned revolution but fervently opposed the war. Finally, there were the ever more desperate poor, who at times rioted over the skyrocketing prices of food and other necessities.[55]

Whitehall lumped the radicals, pacifists, and paupers together and sought to crush them. The first step came when Pitt got each house of Parliament to organize a secret committee to draft bills and other measures that enhanced the government's counterrevolutionary powers; the members numbered twenty-one and nine, respectively, in Commons and Lords. The first fruit of those committees came on May 23, 1794, when George III signed into law the Habeas Corpus Act, which passed by 146 to 28 votes in the House of Commons and by an overwhelming voice vote in Lords. The act suspended the right not to be imprisoned without formal charges for the rest of that year; Parliament annually renewed that measure for the war's duration.

Although the first of eventually thousands of arrests began shortly after the king's signature dried on the document, Pitt and his cabinet soon despaired that the measure was not powerful enough to thwart the revolutionary threat, as one jury after another acquitted those charged with treason. Clearly Whitehall needed a much more expansive definition of treason.[56]

Parliament obliged in 1795. The Treasonable Practices Act declared treasonous any criticism of the king, the government, or the constitution; it passed the House of Commons by 226 to 45 and the the House of Lords by 66 to 7. The Seditious Meetings Act outlawed any unauthorized meetings of fifty or more people; it passed by 266 to 51 in Commons and by 107 to 18 in Lords. Both acts became law on December 18, 1795.[57] Supporters reassured Britons touchy about their rights that the measures were temporary—in three years a debate would arise over whether to renew them—and besides, those acts would never harm law-abiding Britons, only dangerous radicals who threatened to destroy the nation's liberties and rights.

Not everyone in Parliament accepted the logic that the government had to destroy the people's rights in order to save them. Progressives denounced those repressive measures as "Pitt's gagging bills." In a typically rabble-rousing speech in the House of Commons on November 9, 1795, Opposition leader Charles Fox lamented "that a free constitution is no longer suitable to us . . . [that] of the calamities which this war has occasioned, I state a grievance by petition or make any declaration of my sentiments which I always had a right to do, but which if I now do in a manner that may appear to a magistrate to be seditious, I am to be subjected to penalties which hitherto were unknown to the laws of England."[58]

As the crackdown worsened, most protesters struggled to stay within the tightening vise of ways that they could publicly express their beliefs. When dissidents refused to break the law, the government often broke it for them. Undercover agents turned nonviolent protests violent by smashing windows or heads. This signaled nearby troops or militia to charge the crowd and round up as many protesters as possible for long terms in prison without trial.

The thwarted French invasion of Ireland in 1796 and the Irish revolt of 1798 prompted the king and cabinet to push through a series of laws that further bolstered the government's power and diminished civil rights, including the 1797 Seduction from Duty Act, the more effective 1797 Suppression of the Societies Act, the 1799 Seditious and Treasonable Purposes Act, the 1799 Combination Law, and the 1800 Combination Law. Convictions for over two hundred types of crimes now carried the death penalty. Pitt's so-called "reign of terror" peaked in early 1798, when authorities arrested hundreds of suspects on the charge of treason and imprisoned most of them without trial for up to three years or shipped them to Botany Bay, Australia.

Meanwhile, the war overseas dragged on. After withdrawing from Toulon in mid-December 1793, Admiral Samuel Hood's fleet resumed its blockade of the port. An unforeseen opportunity broke that duty's monotony. Pascal Paoli, the brilliant Corsican rebel leader, wrote George III, asking him for help driving the French from the island. Whitehall dispatched diplomat Gilbert Eliot and two officers to talk with Paoli, assess the viability of his forces, then report to Hood. Although the assessment was bleak, Hood was willing to gamble on Paoli, since the capture of Bastia or Corte on Corsica would serve as a much needed base for his fleet.[59]

Hood launched the campaign at the small port of St. Fiorent on the western side of a mountainous peninsula on Corsica's northern coast. The campaign immediately bogged down when Hood called for the siege of St. Fiorent and General David Dundas, the army commander and secretary for war's younger brother, insisted that he lacked the manpower to do so. Hood fumed, as he had no immediate choice but to yield to Dundas and land a force of his own marines and armed sailors to besiege the town. The man who Hood tapped to command this force would eventually achieve renown as Britain's greatest naval commander.

Horatio Nelson grew up beside the North Sea as the fifth child of a village parson and his wife.[60] He was a slender, short, and sickly boy who, from a young age, longed for adventure sailing the world's oceans. His dream came true in 1771, when his father got him a midshipman's berth on a warship. Thereafter he compensated for his puny stature with seemingly insatiable energy, enthusiasm, and courage. His commanders rewarded his crisp leadership at each post along the way by propelling him to ever higher ones, in just a few years. He rose to lieutenant in 1777; was promoted to captain and received command of his first warship, a twenty-gun brig, in 1779; participated in the siege of Fort San Juan, Honduras, in 1780; was transferred to command a small frigate in 1781, when he ordered an unsuccessful attack on Grand Turk Island; and took command of a larger frigate in 1784. The American War's end landed him and nearly all his colleagues in professional doldrums, and navy budget cutbacks forced him to retire on half pay in 1787. That same year he married Frances Nisbet, whom he had met on the West Indian island of Nevis. France's declaration of war against Britain in February 1793 brought Nelson out of retirement at age thirty-five to command the *Agamemnon*, a sixty-four-gun ship of the line attached to Hood's fleet at Toulon. Nelson was sent to Naples to convey troops from that kingdom to Toulon, and it was there that he first met British ambassador Sir

William Hamilton, then sixty-three years old, and his beautiful twenty-eight-year-old wife, Emma. He was there only six days before all the Neapolitan troops were packed into his flotilla and he sailed back to Toulon. There he could only join his fellow naval captains to observe from the port as the French siege tightened against the allied forces in the surrounding hills and Napoleon Bonaparte's series of carefully planned attacked eventually forced the armada to withdraw. As for Nelson, Hood was impressed with how professionally he captained his warship and the strategic and tactical visions that he propounded. This led Hood to pick Nelson of all his captains to command the naval land forces on Corsica.

Nelson's force was not big enough to invest the St. Fiorent but could merely construct breastworks and batteries on the north side. Before his cannons could open fire, the French troops withdrew over the mountains to Bastia. After garrisoning St. Fiorent, Hood ordered the armada to sail to Bastia. There the clashes of ego and strategy between Hood and Dundas got so bad that the army commander resigned and sailed back to Britain. The next senior officer, Colonel Abraham D'Aubant, was hastily promoted to brigadier general and took command of the soldiers. He too insisted that he lacked enough troops for a proper siege, so again it was Nelson who actually conducted operations mostly by bombarding Bastia from his squadron of warships and batteries ashore. The French surrendered on May 22, 1794, and after garrisoning Bastia, Hood sailed back to blockade Toulon while sending Nelson and his squadron to take the fortress and port of Calvi on Corsica's west coast.

Nelson's squadron dropped anchor beyond range of Calvi's guns on June 17. Nelson led the naval contingent ashore and General Charles Stuart, the soldiers. The two worked well together because Stuart was a bold leader in stark contrast with his timid predecessors, Dundas and D'Aubant. During the siege, which led to Calvi's surrender on August 10, Nelson suffered his first severe wound when a cannonball chipped off a stone fragment that blinded his right eye. Throughout the Corsica campaign, both before and after his wound, Nelson displayed steadfast courage, audacity, and initiative, although ironically it was on land rather than at sea. Amid the campaign, Nelson learned of a naval battle between British and French fleets that he would have loved to have joined.

The battle took place when three separate fleets, two French and one British, collided after sailing from their respective ports to protect convoys. The British fleets escorted ninety-nine vessels into the Atlantic Ocean where they would peel off into smaller groups bound for Newfoundland, the West Indies, and the East Indies. The French convoy sailed on April 11 from Norfolk, Virginia, where the components had gathered after months of purchasing grain and other provisions from other American ports and the West Indies. Richard, Earl Howe, led the Channel fleet of thirty-four ships of the line and fifteen smaller warships from Spithead to sea on May 2, 1794. Three days later, Admiral James Montagu and his six ships of the line and two frigates split off to convoy the West Indian convoy to its destination, while Howe's fleet continued due westward with the rest of the merchant ships. Meanwhile, a fleet of twenty-five French ships of the line commanded by Admiral Louis Thomas de Villaret-Joyeuse and another of five ships of the line under Admiral Joseph-Marie Nielly had sailed respectively from Best and Rochefort to intercept that French convoy in the mid-Atlantic. In mid-May, Nielly's fleet intercepted a score of British merchant vessels sailing from Newfoundland and captured most of them only to lose them a few days later when Montagu's fleet appeared. Meanwhile, the French convoy broke up into three separate flotillas. On May 28, Howe's fleet spotted Villaret-Joyeuse's fleet four hundred miles west of Ushant and closed for action. The battle, which became known as the Battle of the Glorious First of June, raged off and on for the next five days as the British pursued the French toward Brest. Eventually the British sank one, captured six, and severely damaged a half dozen French ships of the line. The victory would have been even more crushing had Howe not called off the pursuit of five demasted French ships being towed by others.[61]

Whitehall sought to capitalize in 1794 on the previous year's gains in the West Indies.[62] Packed aboard Admiral John Jervis's fleet were 7,000 British troops led by General Charles Grey. The armada captured in quick succession Martinique, St. Lucia, Guadeloupe, Marie Galante, and Desiderada. Grey dispatched a force led by General John Whyte to seize Port au Prince, St. Domingue's capital. The cost of those victories was relatively bloodless but nonetheless deadly. A cocktail of diseases like yellow fever, malaria, and dysentery devoured British forces, with 40,000 sailors and soldiers dying within the next two years.

The British campaign in the Low Countries suffered a humiliating defeat in 1794, although Prussia was mostly to blame. King Frederick William II eagerly took British subsidies but refused to send the 62,400-man army led by General Richard von Mollendorf that he had promised to his erstwhile allies, the British and Dutch. Pitt and his ministers fumed in worse frustration at Prussia's deceit. Yet it was not until late September that Grenville warned Berlin that London's subsidies would end unless Mollendorf joined forces with York. When that failed to move the Prussians, Whitehall acted on its threat. In all, the British had paid the Prussians £1,306,495 for nothing.[63]

Meanwhile, York's army sat on the sidelines as French counterattacks defeated other allied forces piecemeal and overran much of the rest of the Low Countries. In this campaign, Arthur Wellesley, then the Thirty-third Regiment's lieutenant colonel, received his baptism of fire and crucial lessons in how not to wage war. That year's decisive battle came at Fleurus on June 25, when General Jean-Baptiste Jourdan's 60,000 troops routed an allied army of 44,000 led by Coburg. This caused York to retreat into Germany all the way to the mouth of the Weser River, where 21,000 surviving troops, of whom half were sick, packed aboard a British flotilla and sailed back to England. The Netherlands' ruler, Stadtholder William V, the Prince of Orange, was among the refugees. The French triumphantly entered Amsterdam on January 20, 1795, and would hold the Netherlands until early 1814.

## The 1795 Campaigns

Defeat appeared inevitable as 1795 dawned. France had overrun the Netherlands. Prussia and Spain seemed poised to abandon the coalition. The national debt and taxes soared higher, with no ceiling in sight. To counter all this, the Pitt government redoubled its efforts to strengthen Austria's commitment to the coalition and bring in a new, powerful member.

In Vienna, Ambassador Morton Eden and Chancellor Johann Thugut haggled for months before they signed, on May 4, 1795, a convention whereby Britain guaranteed a £4,600,000 loan to Austria for fielding 170,000 troops in Germany against France until the year's end. If Austria defaulted, Whitehall would have to pay the creditors. That guarantee gave investors the confidence to extend their own loans to Vienna. Eden and Thugut bolstered that deal with an alliance treaty on May 20. Although Austria did deploy all those troops, they did little fighting and gained no significant ground. This did not stop Thugut from asking Eden for another £3,000,000 loan guarantee in October, prompting Grenville's exasperated refusal. The worst nightmare was that Austria would take the money, abandon the coalition, and default on both the proposed and the earlier loan.[64]

In St. Petersburg, ambassador Charles Whitworth made his latest effort to entice Catherine II into the coalition in early 1795. On behalf of George III, he presented her such gifts designed to flatter her vanity as a ten foot telescope and exotic plants from the Kew conservatory. She was enthralled. The treaty signed on February 18, bound the two realms in an eight year defensive alliance, with Russia and Britain committed to supplying 12,000 troops and twelve warships, respectively, to the other if it were attacked. The trouble was that the current war between Britain and France did not activate the treaty, even through France had started the war with a formal declaration against Britain. Catherine did agree to send a flotilla of twelve ships of the line and six frigates to jointly sail with Britain's Channel fleet. Upon receiving the treaty, Grenville instructed Whitworth to ask Catherine to pack that flotilla with 55,000 troops in return for a £500,000 subsidy or double that if she refused. He also sought a triple alliance among Britain, Russia, and Austria.[65]

Catherine spurned both offers. Russia was still at war with the Ottoman Empire, and the canny tsarina was bolstering her realm's power for a possible knock-out blow. She had secured an Austrian alliance against Turkey with a treaty signed on January 3, 1795. The treaty with Britain also potentially strengthened Russian power if that fleet could sail onward to attack Constantinople via the Mediterranean Sea. Catherine was also secretly conspiring with Francis II for the latest partition of Poland. Entanglement in a war against France would stymie her ambitions against the Turks and Poles.

Once again Poland distracted Austria and Prussia from the war against France. Thaddeus Kosciuszko led an uprising against the Russians at Krakow on March 25 and defeated a Russian army on April 4. That inspired revolts in Warsaw, Vilnius, and elsewhere. Kosciuszko led his army triumphantly into Warsaw on April 20, then, on May, 7, converted that war of independence into a revolution with his Manifesto of Polaniec that promised to abolish serfdom, reduce rent and forced labor, and secure peasants on their land.

The Polish revolution threatened its three neighboring great powers, who allied to destroy it. The Russians and Prussians coordinated offensives that captured most of the rebel cities and joined forces to besiege Warsaw in early July. Not wanting to miss out on the inevitable spoils, the Austrians marched into Galicia. A Russian army routed Kosciusko's army and captured him at Maciejowice on October 10, and the revolt ended with Warsaw's surrender on November 6. The victors wiped Poland off the map by divvying up what was left of it among themselves in treaties between the Russians and Austrians on January 3, 1795, and the Russians and Prussians on October 24, 1795.

Poland's death helped save the French Revolution. To conquer their shares of Poland, the Prussians and Austrians diverted crucial amounts of men, money, munitions, and other material from the western front. Satiated by its share of Poland and financially exhausted from years of war, the Prussians signed, on April 5, a peace treaty with France whereby each country accepted the other's conquests on its side of the Rhine River. A protocol to that treaty on May 17 rendered neutral all German states north of the Main River in Prussia's sphere of influence.

Prussia's withdrawal from the war set off a chain reaction of other peace agreements. Under the Treaty of The Hague, signed on May 16, the Dutch agreed to pay France an indemnity of 100 million guilders, lend vast amounts of money to France at low interest rates, and permit the French to keep 25,000 troops on their soil for the war's duration. Charles IV officially withdrew Spain from alliance with Britain into neutrality when he ratified the Treaty of Basel, signed on July 22, 1795, with France. Peace did come with a price: Spain ceded to France its eastern half of the island of St. Domingue. Yet it was not clear who got the better deal. Slave revolts had plunged both sides of the island into worsening anarchy and violence, and those once rich sources of sugar, known as "white gold," were now ever more costly liabilities to anyone who tried to reimpose the slavocracy. Within a month, the minor states of Tuscany, Venice, and Naples also withdrew from the coalition.

Whitehall persisted in refusing openly to embrace the one group that was eager to be a full coalition partner. The latest awkward diplomatic encounter with the Bourbons came after word seeped to the outside world that France's dauphin had died in prison in Paris on June 8, 1795. This prompted Louis, Comte de Provence, to issue, on July 8, 1795, the Declaration of Verona whereby he claimed to be Louis XVIII, the rightful heir to the French throne that conferred absolute powers on its monarch; he reasserted his vow to destroy the French Revolution. Pitt and his colleagues winced when they read the declaration. Louis's uncompromising stand would only harden most French hearts and minds against him and thus grossly complicate British diplomacy and any chances of peace. Whitehall dispatched George, Earl of Macartney, to Verona to meet with Louis and try to talk him into softening his position, ideally by declaring himself a constitutional rather than an absolute monarch. To encourage the switch, Macartney gave the would-be king £10,000. Louis eagerly grabbed the money but insisted on wielding the same powers as his illustrious predecessors.

Behind the scenes, Whitehall helped organize, equip, and train 1,500 royalists on Jersey Island in the English Channel. On June 27, 1795, a Royal Navy flotilla landed this force at Quiberon Bay, on Brittany's southern coast. The plan was for the Bourbons to join the Chouans and eventually the Vendeans against the French government. But spies sent word of the operation to Paris, and French forces in the region led by General Lazare Hoche swiftly converged and crushed the invaders and Chouans in a series of battles from July 5 to 21. The revolutionary justice was swift and ruthless—of about 3,000 Chouan and 500 invader prisoners, 751 received death sentences and were executed by firing squads. With their small army wiped out, the Bourbons thereafter concentrated on covert and small-scale means of taking power.[66]

Despite the Quiberon debacle, a Bourbon return to the French throne was not as farfetched a notion in the Alien Office as it was with most other people elsewhere. The Alien Office's best-placed foreign agent then was Louis Alexandre de Launay, comte d'Antraigues, who was working assiduously through the Institut Philanthropique for a coup to topple the revolutionary regime. His efforts peaked with the march of several thousand royalists led by National Guard general Auguste Danican against France's government, then known as the Directory, on October 4. Paul Barras, who chaired the council of five directors, empowered General Napoleon Bonaparte to eliminate this threat. Bonaparte gathered what few troops and cannons were available and crushed the rebellion. Barras later expressed his gratitude to Bonaparte for saving the regime by giving him command of the French army of Italy and matching him with Josephine de Beauharnais, who would become his wife. Antraigues was among the insurgents who escaped into exile. He and Bonaparte would have a future fateful meeting in Italy.

The spate of peace treaties in 1795 left the British and Austrians as the sole major powers to fight on against France. Ironically, with 120,000 regular troops, including 35,820 mercenaries, up from a mere 17,000 two years earlier, Britain now had the largest army in its history.[67] But power is not about military muscle per se but what one does with it. As for this, Pitt and his colleagues could not agree.

With the Prussians and Dutch sidelined, the French concentrated their forces for what they hoped would be a knockout blow to Austria. The plan was for Generals Jean-Baptiste Jourdan and Jean-Charles Pichegru to cross the Rhine with their respective armies of 91,000 and 96,000, with Pichegru protecting Jourdan's southern flank and drawing off Austrians as Jourdan captured Mainz. The trouble was that both generals squandered the summer in preparations and complaints that the other did not move first. It was not until September 6 that Jourdan finally crossed the Rhine, while Pichegru dallied until September 20. This long delay let the Austrians mass enough troops to rout first Pichegru then Jourdan back across the Rhine. By mid-December the Austrian army was massed at crossings on the east bank. All the British gold that kept Vienna in the fight merely bought a bloody stalemate.

Important changes affected Britain's position in the Mediterranean in 1795. Admiral William Hotham took command of the fleet when Samuel Hood retired. After Tuscany signed a peace treaty with France, its chief port, Livorno, became a tense neutral rather than safe allied anchorage for British vessels. The French partly rebuilt their fleet at Toulon and were eager to avenge their defeats of 1793 and 1794. As for continuities, the key for Britain was that Nelson remained there in command of the 64-gun *Agamemnon.*

The primary French objective for the Mediterranean in 1795 was to retake Corsica. To this end, an armada of several score vessels packed with 5,000 troops and escorted by fifteen ships of the line commanded by Admiral Pierre Martin sailed from Toulon in early March. British frigates screening Toulon carried word to Hotham, who sailed with thirteen ships of the line, to intercept the armada. The enemy fleets spotted each other on March 10. The British gave chase, with Nelson in the lead. The *Agamemnon* caught up and battered two French ships of the line into surrender, while a British warship ran aground and was lost. But after the French turned back toward their coast, Hotham signaled his captains to end their pursuit. This infuriated Nelson, who insisted that "had I commanded the fleet our fleet . . . the whole French fleet would have graced my triumph."[68] Nelson suffered similar frustrations in July when the enemy fleets clashed near Hyeres Island and Hotham again let the French escape back to Toulon after Nelson's *Agamemnon* destroyed a ship of the line. That want of a killer instinct afflicted another British naval commander that year. Admiral Alexander Hood, Lord Bridport, took over the Channel fleet after Richard, Lord Howe, retired. On June 22, Bridport hoisted the signal for his captains to engage Admiral Villaret-Joyeuse's fleet that had ventured from Brest. But, after three French warships struck their colors, Bridport signaled an end to the battle, thus settling for a limited victory when his captains might have taken many more battered prizes.

The year's potentially most important British victory came at Africa's southern tip. After France conquered the Netherlands, Dutch colonies were fair British game. A squadron commanded by Commodore John Blankett and a score of transports with several thousand troops led by General Keith Elphinstone dropped anchor near the Dutch enclave of Cape Town on June 11. The Dutch fought valiantly and did not surrender until September 16. Britain now possessed a stepping-stone of enormous strategic worth between the Atlantic and Indian Oceans.

Mass death and destruction are not war's sole characteristics, only the most obvious. War can be highly profitable. Neutral flags can literally be worth their weight in gold. and entrepreneurs from countries at peace can make killings by selling essential goods at bloated prices to belligerent countries. After the war erupted in 1792 and ever more countries were sucked into the maelstrom, Americans with verve and luck got ever richer as each side's navies preyed on its enemy's merchant ships, crews, and cargos. Businessmen in the warring countries hired American shipowners to carry their goods. President George Washington underlined America's status when he declared his nation's neutrality on April 22, 1793.

Whitehall, however, issued on June 8, 1793, an Order in Council that was very bad for the neutral carrying trade. Henceforth the Royal Navy would confiscate the cargos of grain and other war contraband on any ship bound for France. Whitehall bolstered this policy on November 6, 1793, by expanding the ban to any vessels carrying any products from France or its colonies anywhere. Within a year, British warships seized several hundred American vessels and their cargos as prizes and pressed into service hundreds of sailors suspected of being British subjects. These were hardly the only blows that the British inflicted on the United States. Whitehall blocked most American goods from British markets at home or in its colonies, still occupied nine forts in America's Northwest region, and armed and provoked

Indians to attack the American frontier. Britain did all that because it was in its interests and power to do so. Without a navy and with just a couple of thousand troops, mostly fighting Indians, the Americans could do nothing but protest.

To end that array of depredations, Washington dispatched John Jay, then the Supreme Court justice, to London to negotiate a treaty that not only protected America's neutral rights under international law but relieved some other festering issues. Under the treaty signed between Jay and Grenville on November 19, 1794, Britain had to evacuate all their forts on American territory by 1796, give the United States most-favored-nation status, and let American merchants ships smaller than seventy tons trade with British colonies. But Jay failed to get the British to stop confiscating American ships and cargos bound for France and its allies and impressing American sailors. Given the overwhelming discrepancies between British and American power, Jay got the best deal possible. This was not, however, how many Americans reacted when they learned the Jay Treaty's details. The Senate ratified the treaty only after a heated debate.

Nonetheless, most American merchants continued to make a killing in the neutral trade. America's balance of trade shifted dramatically during the 1790s. From 1790 to 1801 the tonnage of goods unloaded in American ports from American ships rose from 355,000 to 799,304, and from foreign ships fell from 251,000 to 138,000.[69] This prosperity along the seaboard spread across the nation and continued until the Jefferson White House overreacted to a British atrocity in 1807 with a policy that devastated America's economy.

For Britons, grand farce this year lightened the gloom for some and darkened it for others. Ideally, a royal marriage enhances a nation's power by bolstering ties with another important realm. But, of course, things do not always turn out as hoped. The tragicomic follies emanating from the crown prince's life were compounded when the bride that was chosen for him proved to be his match in licentiousness, searing wit, and madcap antics. Genetics might offer an explanation. The Prince of Wales and Princess Caroline of Brunswick were first cousins. Well aware that Caroline's uncontrollable "passions" inexorably led to "indecent conversations with men . . . and indecent behavior," the royal court's minders ensured that "she was not . . . allowed even to go from one room to another without her Governess."[70] Caroline reveled in the countless tricks she wielded to evade her chaperone. Malmesbury tried to scare her into compliance by warning her "that anybody who presumed to love her was guilty of high treason and [would be] punished with death . . . so also would she." The princess could not suppress her mirth and later sent him a warning of her own, a rotten tooth that she had extracted from her mouth.[71]

George and Caroline were married in the chapel of St. James Palace on April 8, 1795. They shared the royal bed that night for the first and, each insisted, the last time. At fate would have it, the royal coupling defied the odds and produced an heir. Caroline was born nine months later, although her paternity is not absolutely certain given her mother's inclinations.[72] The prince hurried back to his beloved true "wife," Maria Fitzherbert, while the princess bought a mansion in Blackheath where she entertained her paramours in raucous inhibition. Her more famous lovers allegedly included George Canning, William Sidney Smith, and Thomas Lawrence. Caroline's irrepressibly bawdy humor and natural sexuality was perhaps better suited for a brothel's madam than a royal princess. As such, Caroline tended to beguile most men and infuriate most women in her immediate presence. Following this gender divide, the king enjoyed his daughter-in-law while the queen heartily disapproved. The king's will prevailed. He angrily refused his son's plea for an official separation in June 1796. The public, however, mostly adored Caroline and despised George. The estranged royal couple, along with their daughter, would spectacularly embarrass British diplomacy in 1814.

## The 1796 Campaigns

Despite the coalition's dwindling ranks as powerful states dropped out, the British king, prime minister, cabinet, and most members of Parliament were determined to fight on. As such, they defied public opinion. Ever more protests and outright riots erupted across Britain, especially in London. This swelling antiwar sentiment forced diehards to mask their belligerency. Pitt declared before the House of Commons on December 8, 1795, that the government was prepared to enter peace negotiations with France.[73] George III reassured Parliament on December 9, 1795, that his government would "meet any disposition to negotiations on the part of the enemy with an earnest desire to give it the fullest and speediest effect, and to conclude a treaty of general peace."[74]

Actually the time appeared ripe for talks. France certainly seemed to be on the ropes, with an empty treasury, worsening debt, prices, casualties, and unrest, and bitterly divided government. Yet with its withering alliance and relatively small army, Britain lacked the means of delivering a knockout blow. The only alternative to peace was a chronic, low-intensity war at sea and along France's fringes that endlessly devoured more men, money, and material on both sides. Since Pitt and most of his colleagues believed that eventually Britain would win a war of attrition, this was their strategy.

Whitehall justified that stance by pointing to the "peace terms" that a French delegation presented at Berne on March 22, 1796. The French insisted on keeping all their conquests, including the Rhine's west bank, the Austrian Netherlands, and Savoy, while the British had to give back France's West Indian colonies and Corsica. To accept that would grossly violate Britain's security and honor. What no one could have anticipated then was that France's conquests would soon swell thanks to the military genius of a previously little known general.

It was in April 1796 that Britain's second worst nemesis in its history emerged to plague the nation for the next nineteen years and haunt it long thereafter. Napoleon Bonaparte offered Britain and the world then and ever since priceless lessons in the art of power and its related military, diplomatic, economic, cultural, and psychological dimensions. These lessons up through 1808 were mostly on how to wield the art of power, then, starting with his attempt to conquer Spain, were increasingly on how not to do so.

Napoleon Bonaparte may be history's most complex and beguiling "great man."[75] He arrived in Nice to take command of the Army of Italy on March 27, 1796. His field army of around 40,000 troops was split among several towns, overshadowed by the Maritime Alps, on the Ligurian coast. Facing him in the heights and in the valleys beyond were two enemy armies, 15,000 Piedmont-Sardinian troops led by General Michelangelo Alessandro Colli-Marchi and 30,000 Austrians led by General Jean Pierre de Beaulieu. Bonaparte's plan was to split those armies and defeat each separately. In mid-April he ordered his divisions to march north over the mountains and attack the enemy forces before them. Over the next two weeks, in a series of battles, Bonaparte's fast-marching and hard-fighting troops shattered the Piedmont-Sardinians and routed the Austrians. In all, Bonaparte's army "won six victories, captured 21 flags, 55 pieces of artillery, several fortresses, and 15,000 prisoners, and had conquered the richest part of Piedmont."[76]

As a French division marched toward Turin, the kingdom's capital, Victor Amadeus III begged for peace. Under the Armistice of Cherasco, on April 28, Piedmont-Sardinia pledged to sign a peace treaty with Paris, cede three frontier fortresses to France, forbid Austrian troops from its territory, and permit Bonaparte's army to pass through its territory in pursuit of the Austrians. Under the peace treaty of May 15, Piedmont-Sardinia ceded Savoy and Nice to France, paid an indemnity, and permitted French troops free passage through its territory for the war's duration. Bonaparte raced his troops in two pincers after the demoralized Austrian army, clipped its tail at Lodi on May 10, captured Milan on May 15, and bottled Beaulieu and his remaining troops in Mantua. Meanwhile, he crushed revolts that erupted in his rear at Binasco and Pavia.

Bonaparte did not invent the policy of forcing the losers to pay for their defeat; it is as old as history. But few conquerors have ever made war more profitable for the victor than Bonaparte. This summer he squeezed treaties from Tuscany, Naples, Rome, Parma, Genoa, Milan, and Venice that garnered fortunes in cash, provisions, and works of art. By December 1796, he had officially reaped from Italy for the French treasury 45,706,493 francs in cash and 12,132,909 francs in gold, silver, and jewels; unofficially his troops and more venal officers had looted tens of millions of francs' more of wealth.[77]

Bonaparte did more than loot Italy; he began to transform its northern regions into an unified modern state. On October 16 he gathered delegates from Bologna, Ferrara, Modena, and Reggio into a congress that united their realms into the Cispadane Confederation and their troops into the 25,000-man Italian Legion. On December 27 a congress converted the Cispadane Confederation into the Cispadane Republic, with a French-style constitution.

Francis II appointed General Dagobert Sigismond de Castiglione Wurmser to lead 25,000 troops into northern Italy to defeat Bonaparte, rescue Beaulieu at Mantua, and restore Austrian rule. Wurmser pushed past Bonaparte and entered Mantua, but Bonaparte promptly plugged him up there, where he and 30,000 troops would languish amid diminishing supplies and worsening disease for another half year. Francis II then hurried two more armies into northern Italy, but Bonaparte routed them as well.

Pitt and his ministers reacted with stupefaction to report after report of Bonaparte's triumphs. They never considered aiding the Austrians in Italy with British troops and did not even reconsider their existing policy toward the Mediterranean theater. The only change came when John Jervis replaced Hotham to head the fleet, which now numbered twenty-five ships of the line, twenty-four frigates, ten corvettes, and a score of smaller vessels. To more efficiently blockade Toulon, whose harbor was packed with thirteen French ships of the line, Jervis split his fleet into inner and outer squadrons and stationed other warships along the Ligurian coast to keep an eye on French operations there. From April, as Bonaparte's army overran ever more of northern Italy, Jervis had to spread his warships thinner to keep up. The only victory came when Nelson, commanding the *Agamemnon,* captured five ships carrying Bonaparte's siege train on May 30. Britain suffered an economic and strategic blow on June 27, when a column of Bonaparte's troops marched into Livorno to confiscate British vessels and cargos and arrest British merchants and seamen. Deprived of this base, Nelson sailed with his small squadron to the island of Elba and captured Port Ferrario.

The Mediterranean's strategic weight shifted sharply when Spain and France signed an alliance treaty on August 19, 1796. Should the French and Spanish fleets join, they could cut off and destroy Jervis's fleet. Jervis recalled a squadron of six ships of the line and a frigate under Admiral Robert Man that had blockaded Cadiz since October 1795 when a French squadron took refuge there. As Man sailed through the Gibraltar straits, his squadron encountered a Spanish fleet of nineteen ships of the line led by Admiral Don Juan de Langara. Man prudently withdrew his squadron to the nearby shelter of Gibraltar's harbor but, inexplicably, later disobeyed his orders and sailed to Spithead.

This presented Langara with a golden opportunity. He sailed eastward, picked up seven more ships of the line at Cartagena, and headed to Toulon to unite with the thirteen French ships of the line. Outgunned, Jervis was forced not just to break off his Toulon blockade but abandon Corsica, Elba, and other stations and sail westward past Gibraltar, whose port was too small to hold all those combined ships, and then north to safety in Lisbon's harbor. En route Jervis lost three of his three ships of the line in a storm and a fourth to a French squadron. Nelson, now commanding the 74-gun *Captain*, attacked two Spanish warships off Cartagena and briefly captured one of them before having to flee as a half dozen other Spanish warships bore down on him. By January 1797, Jervis had twenty-one ships of the line, twenty-four frigates, fifteen sloops, and a dozen supply ships at Lisbon but the Royal Navy had evacuated the Mediterranean.

On the German front the French commanders got off to another late start, but this time it was not their fault. An armistice did not expire until June 1. Generals Jean-Baptiste Jourdan and Jean Victor Moreau each commanded armies with more than twice the number of troops in Bonaparte's army. Jourdan led his 78,000 men across the Rhine at on May 31, and Moreau his 79,000 men on June 23. Both advanced deep into southern Germany on parallel routes, as Archduke Charles with 92,000 Austrian troops faced Jourdan and General Wurmser with 83,000 faced Moreau. The initial Austrian advantage in numbers dwindled steadily as Vienna diverted tens of thousands and finally Wurmser south over the Alps to battle Bonaparte.

Archduke Charles followed a strategy that Wellington later brilliantly wielded in the Iberian Peninsula. He withdrew before the

French, fighting a series of delaying actions and enticing the enemy further eastward in pursuit. Unable to catch up and inflict a crushing blow, the French faced a worsening problem of strategic consumption: the further they marched, the more troops they had to detach to protect their lengthening supply lines. Charles turned and attacked each enemy army in turn. He defeated Jourdan in a series of battles culminating at Amberg on August 24 and forced him back across the Rhine. He then marched south to defeat Moreau in October and chase him back across the Rhine. Although the defeats of Jourdan and Moreau were as ignominious as Bonaparte's victories were glorious, it did not stop either general from reaping enormous contributions to France's treasury from the German realms that they marched through, officially over 30 million livres by December 1797, and unofficially tens of millions of livres more in loot.[78] The French and Austrians legalized this front's deadlock with an armistice signed on January 9, 1797.

For most Britons, the war was real enough, with its ever-higher taxes, prices, and deaths, but it hardly seemed immediately threatening. This perception changed in 1796. Wolfe Tone and thirty-four other leading Protestant liberals founded the United Irishmen as a reform group in 1791, but harsh British repression radicalized them. The turning point came in May 1794, when Whitehall suspended habeas corpus and began arresting and imprisoning without trial hundreds of those who advocated reforms. This provoked the United Irishmen to commit themselves to revolution and independence. They merged with the secret militant Catholic Defenders, founded in 1784 to protect themselves from attacks by the Protestant Peep O'Day Boys and other terrorist groups in Ulster. Wolfe Tone journeyed to Paris, where he pressured France's revolutionary government to aid Ireland's liberation.[79]

Embracing Tone's idea, the Directory organized a military expedition to invade Ireland and join with Irish patriots in eliminating British rule from their land.[80] On December 16, 1796, General Lazare Hoche and 13,900 troops sailed from Brest packed aboard an armada of forty-three vessels, including seventeen ships of the line, thirteen frigates, six corvettes, and twenty transports commanded by Admiral Morard de Galles. The last of the vessels cleared the harbor as night fell, but this mighty flotilla no sooner reached the open sea when it broke up in violence and bewilderment.

Waiting at the mouth of the long bay leading to Brest was a lone frigate, the HMS *Indefatigable*, commanded by Captain Edward Pellew. This intrepid captain and his crew personified their ship's name. Rather than sail off to a safe distance and shadow the armada to determine its direction, Pellew steered his frigate straight through the enemy vessels and ordered broadside after broadside fired at the dark silhouettes against the night sky. This provoked a chain reaction of broadsides from the French warships, as their captains panicked that they were being attacked by a British fleet. The tragic result was more damage inflicted by the French warships on one another than by Pellew's gunners. One ship of the line sank and two others collided, while the other warships and transports scattered beyond the horizons to evade destruction. The next day Pellew sailed for Falmouth to warn that the French armada would likely strike somewhere in the British Isles.

The French armada's assembly point was Bantry Bay on Ireland's western coast. By Christmas, only Hoche aboard the frigate *Fraternité* and a few transports had dropped anchor there. They did not stay long. A storm that day scattered these vessels as their captains headed for the open sea to avoid being driven against Ireland's rocky shores.

Meanwhile, accompanied by the frigate HMS *Amazon*, Pellew and his HMS *Indefatigable* returned to the coast off Brest. On December 29 much of the French fleet was spotted sailing back to Brest. The two British frigates attacked. During the subsequent chase through stormy seas, with near gale-force winds, several French ships were driven ashore. By the time the last surviving vessels dropped anchor in Brest on January 15, 1797, the French expedition had lost three ships of the line, four frigates, four large transports, and many smaller vessels. The French navy had suffered a devastating defeat while inflicting no damage on Britain.

Meanwhile another invasion force of 1,500 troops known as the Black Legion sailed from France and actually landed in Wales in February 1797. This expedition, however, was as quixotic as Hoche's expedition was a serious threat. Local Welsh militia converged and forced the Black Legion to surrender without a fight.

This was hardly the first nor last time that Britain's fate was determined by brilliant naval captains and nature's wildest forces. Had all gone according to plan and Hoche landed at the head of 13,900 troops, the French could have conquered Ireland. There were only about 12,000 British troops scattered across the entire island, and Hoche could have mopped them up in succession as Irish patriots established a Republic of Ireland. French diplomats then could have wielded Ireland as a trump card in their peace negotiations with Britain.

A formidable threat now rose against Britain in the West Indies. Hope there that the slaves who dreamed of liberating themselves might one day do so came with the stunning news that, on February 4, 1794, France's National Assembly abolished slavery. Then came word that a French expedition had recaptured Guadeloupe in June 1794, then repelled a series of British counterattacks; a French mulatto, commissioner Victor Hugues, was in charge of the island.

Hugues smuggled arms, munitions, and agents into Grenada, St. Vincent, and St. Lucia. In spring 1795 slaves rebelled against their masters on those islands; the free Trelawney Maroons on Jamaica also rose, although the island's slaves remained quiescent. Meanwhile British forces in St. Domingue were besieged in a few key ports by black armies led by generals Pierre Dominique Toussaint Louverture and André Rigaud.

Although Whitehall responded by sending out 13,500 reinforcements, most soon died from the cocktail of tropical diseases. By October 1795, half of all the army's regiments were deployed in the West Indies and were mere skeletons of what had boarded transports in the British Isles. An expedition led by General Ralph Abercromby and Admirals William Cornwallis and Hugh Christian managed to crush the revolts on St. Lucia, Grenada, and St. Vincent in 1796. This same year other British forces quelled the Maroon revolt in Jamaica. Abercromby sailed to take Trinidad from Spain but was repulsed in an attack on San Juan, Puerto Rico. Small expeditions took Dutch Surinam and Curaçao without resistance. General Gordon Forbes and Admiral William Parker, however, were unable to conquer St. Domingue, nor was Forbes's successor, General John Simcoe, any more successful; the final commander, General Thomas Maitland withdrew the remnants of British forces in 1798. Where slaves revolted, the destruction of burned plantations, warehouses, mansions, and refineries was enormous on all the islands, with estimated losses of £4,500,000 on Grenada, £815,532 on St. Vincent, and £580,000 on Jamaica. And all along diseases devoured British soldiers and sailors.[81]

The war's uncertainties for British statesmen worsened when word arrived that Russian tsarina Catherine had died, most likely of a massive stroke, on November 17, 1796. This prompted an insightful quip from Pitt: "It is difficult to say whether one ought to regret that she had not died sooner or lived longer."[82] Her estranged son took the throne as Paul I. He would be a diplomatic loose cannon, complicating the policies of Britain and the other great powers.[83]

## The 1797 Campaigns

The naval war shifted decisively in early 1797. On January 31 a massive Spanish fleet sailed from Cadiz in search of the British fleet that was erroneously reported to have only nine ships of the line. Admiral José de Cordova commanded twenty-seven ships of the line and twelve frigates, with more than 2,300 cannons among them. His flagship was the four-deck, 136-gun *Santissima Trinidad*, the world's largest warship. The British fleet was vastly outgunned, although not as badly as the Spanish believed. John Jervis led fifteen ships of the line, of which only two had 100 cannons compared to seven Spanish warships with 112 or more cannons each.

The fleets collided off Cape St. Vincent on February 14. Despite the daunting odds, Jervis ordered the signal flags hoisted for an attack with words that became immortal: "The die is cast and if there are fifty sail I will go through them. England badly needs a victory."[84] What the British lacked in firepower, they more than made up for with brilliant seamanship, gunnery, and above all, Horatio Nelson with his 74-gun *Captain*. Nelson typically sought and squared off with Cordova's flagship, with fifty more guns than his own, along with three other ships of the line. Fortunately other British warships sailed to his aid. When the cannons finally ceased fire, four Spanish warships had struck their colors and ten were severely battered; Nelson led boarding parties that captured two warships. Cordova escaped with the rest of his fleet back to Cadiz, while Jervis returned with his fleet to Lisbon. Strategically, the Battle of Cape St. Vincent prevented any serious union of the Spanish and French fleets until Trafalgar eight years later.

Nelson emerged from the battle with a commodore's commission and his own squadron. He promptly sailed his warships to bombard Cadiz, then headed south to the Canary Islands to capture Tenerife, its capital. He led 900 marines and armed sailors ashore on July 21, but the Spanish drove them back to their ships. Three days late he headed another assault that was repelled after suffering 146 dead and 105 wounded; grapeshot tore off Nelson's right arm. The losses would have been even heavier had not the Spanish governor agreed to release 300 British trapped in the town if Nelson broke off the siege. Nelson later admitted that emotions trumped reason in determining his tactics: "My pride suffered; and although I felt the second attack a forlorn hope, yet the honor of our country called for the attack, and that I should command it. I never expected to return, and am thankful."[85]

The British scored yet another victory against the Spaniards, this time in the West Indies. On February 17, 1797, Admiral Henry Harvey's squadron of warships encountered a Spanish squadron of four ships of the line and a frigate near Port of Spain, Trinidad. Rather than go down fighting, the Spaniards set fire to their ships, clambered into longboats, and rowed to safety ashore.

Bonaparte continued to be as victorious on land as the Royal Navy was victorious at sea. During a three-day battle that began on January 14 at Rivoli, he decisively defeated the latest Austrian army to march against him. Austrian general Wurmser finally capitulated his 30,000 surviving troops at Mantua on February 2, 1797. On February 19, Pius VI agreed to a treaty whereby he recognized France's takeover of Avignon, the Comtat Venaissin, and the Papal Legations Bologna, Ferrara, and Modena. After rebuilding his army's depleted ranks and supplies, Bonaparte launched his latest campaign on March 16, when he crossed the Tagliamento River and captured Klagenfurt on March

31 and Judenburg on April 7. He was now a mere seventy-five miles from Vienna. Word of his rapid advance inspired his colleagues far to the north to launch their own campaigns, with Lazare Hoche crossing the Rhine with 78,000 troops on April 15 and Jean Victor Moreau, with 57,000 troops, five days later. But the early starts did not compensate for mediocre generalship.

Bonaparte forced the Austrians to sign the Preliminary Treaty of Leoben on April 18, 1797, which ended the war between France and Austria and effectively ended the First Coalition. For the foreseeable future Britain would war alone against France. Under the treaty, Vienna recognized France's takeover of the Austrian Netherlands (Belgium), exchanged Lombardy for Venetia, Istria, and Dalmatia, and retained the Quadrilateral Fortresses of Mantua,

If Britain lacked the power to invade and defeat France, Pitt and his inner cabinet clung to the hope that covert action might be decisive. One of the agents on the Alien Office's payroll succeeded in infiltrating the inner sanction of French power in 1797. General Jean Charles Pichegru won acclaim leading armies against the Austrians and Prussians early in the war. Yet all along he secretly bore a terrible burden—he remained a fervent royalist even as he won battles for the revolution. He decided to capitalize on his fame by running for office, and on May 28, 1797, he was elected to be president of the Council of Five Hundred which, along with the Council of Deputies, formed France's legislative branch. As both a prominent general and politician, Pichegru was perfectly poised to overthrow the Directory and install a royalist government. His key collaborators were Generals Jean Victor Moreau and Louis Charles Desaix, who were still in the field, and directors François Barthlemy and Lazare Carnot. But to the bitter disappointment among the handful of British officials aware of his loyalties, Pichegru got cold feet. His failure to act immediately led to the betrayal and downfall of him and most of his coterie.

French secret agents finally caught up to and arrested one of Britain's best foreign operatives, Louis Alexandre de Launay, Comte d'Antraigues, with incriminating papers in Trieste on May 24, and brought him to Bonaparte's headquarters at Milan. Bonaparte spent hours carefully interrogating Antraigues and finally talked him into confessing. The most vital information Antraigues revealed was Pichegru's conspiracy in Paris. In return, Bonaparte not only spared Antraigues from a hangman's noose but let him "escape" from prison. Bonaparte knew that the royalist exile community would thereafter view Antraigues with suspicion even if he reneged on his promise to be Bonaparte's double agent. Bonaparte hurried General Pierre François Augereau and a detachment of troops to carry word of the conspiracy to Director Paul Barras. On September 1 Barras had Pichegru, Barthlemy, and about forty other conspirators arrested; Carnot escaped; Moreau and Desaix were not implicated. The suspects were convicted of treason and sentenced to the "dry guillotine" of a penal colony at Guyana. In 1798 Pichegru and seven others escaped and late the following year reached London, where the Alien Office enlisted them for a plot to assassinate Napoleon Bonaparte, who by then had taken over France's government.

Meanwhile, Britain teetered at bankruptcy's brink in early 1797. The war's costs had tripled over the three previous years, from £8,123,000 in 1793 to £16,837,000 in 1794 to £26,273,000 in 1795. The national debt soared from £241,600,000 in 1793 to £310,400,000 in 1796. Revenues dropped further behind the war's skyrocketing costs, and loans filled the steadily widening gap, soaring from £6,700,000 in 1793 to £32,500,000 in 1796. Interest rates rose as ready money grew more scarce. On top of that, the nation suffered worsening international balance of payments. Gold and silver coins flowed from the British Isles to fill the pockets of soldiers, sailors, allies, spies, and counterrevolutionary groups. The Royal Mint was starved for precious metals. The value of new coins dropped from £2,558,000 in 1794 to £493,000 in 1796, while gold reserves to £5,632,000 worth in 1795 to £2,331,000 in 1796.[86]

Before the king and Privy Council on February 25, 1797, Pitt explained the decisive measures that could pull Britain back from bankruptcy's brink. Seeing no alternative, the king and his council approved. The next day, Whitehall suspended cash payments to its suppliers and creditors and began issuing paper money. Critics blasted

Whitehall's policy of paying British creditors and supplies with paper promises while ladling gold to its allies, especially Austria. This provoked a panic among private financiers that Pitt only quelled when he promised that the government would uphold the printed value of its obligations. He got the House of Commons to back his policies with a 244 to 86 vote on February 28.

Pitt followed up that short-term emergency measure with efforts to make revenue collection and distribution more efficient by having all taxes forwarded to a consolidation fund. He raised taxes on excises, customs, posts, stamps, imposts, and land and imposed new taxes on a bewildering array of items, including glass, bricks, carriages, documents, hair powder, marine insurance, wine, tobacco, hats, dogs, and horses. Most importantly, he insisted that the lion's share of taxes was paid by those most capable of paying. The rich grumbled but did not revolt. They understood that their future wealth might vary starkly, depending on whether Britain won or lost its death struggle with France.

As if Britain's financial burdens were not onerous enough, the Austrians would grossly worsen it. In April 1796 Pitt yielded to Vienna's pleading for more money by authorizing Colonel Charles Craufurd, Britain's liaison with the Austrian army in Germany, to secretly hand over £100,000 of treasury bills immediately and £150,000 more each month thereafter.[87] The first transfers took place when Parliament was still in session but without its permission. Pitt did not inform his colleagues until December 1796, after they returned from nearly a half year's recess and the Austrians had pocketed £1.2 million worth of treasury notes. Charles James Fox led the outcry against Pitt's deceit. His censure motion, however, fell short of passage. Pitt then motioned that parliament approve the transfers; an overwhelming majority of 285 to 81 did so. The House of Commons followed this up on April 4, 1797, when it appropriated by a 266 to 87 vote £1.62 million in subsidies to Austria for that year.[88] Pitt dispatched diplomat George Hammond to Vienna with this money and a plea that Austria stay in the fight.

The Austrians replied with one of history's most outrageous acts of ingratitude. Not only did they palm the money after signing with France the peace treaty at Leoben on April 18, they defaulted on their

£3 million loan of 1795. Foreign Secretary Grenville tried to talk them out of this act of perfidy, arguing that over the long term Austria would suffer far more than Britain: "We will lose some money for having believed in the good faith and probity of the Austrian government. The Court of Vienna will forever lose its credit, its honor, and the chance of finding here any financial aid which it might require in the future. All things considered, I really believe that if we are the dupes, it is the Duper who will be the loser." When that moral reasoning failed to move them, he toughened his rhetoric, declaring that with their deceitful grand act of larceny, the Austrian denied themselves "forever the possibility not only of any future assistance of a pecuniary nature from Great Britain to Austria, but of any intercourse of Councils or confidential Concert being established between them at a moment when depends . . . the common safety of the two Monarchies and the fate of the rest of Europe."[89]

On top of this financial crisis came a naval crisis. On April 16 the sailors in the fleet at Spithead, near Portsmouth, refused an order to put to sea. They did so in protest that the government had not acknowledged let alone acted progressively on a series of petitions, dating back to December 1796, for a long redress of grievances. One petition warned that the "ill treatment which we receive . . . is more than the spirits and hearts of true Englishmen . . .can . . . bear, for we are born free but now we are slaves."[90] This was only a slight exaggeration. The last time that sailors had got a pay raise was during the reign of Charles II, more than 120 years earlier! The food and care for the sick were wretched, and the lashings for the slightest offenses were severe. On top of this the Admiralty had recently replaced as their commander "sailor's sailor" Richard Howe with Alexander Hood, Lord Bridport, renowned for his harsh discipline. The strike became a mutiny when one crew after another arrested their officers for insisting that the sailors obey their commands.

This certainly got the Admiralty's attention. First Lord George Spencer met with Pitt, who asked him to dash to Portsmouth and speak with the mutiny leaders. The crews of each of the fleet's sixteen ships selected two delegates to meet with Spencer and present a list of demands that included better pay, food, medical care, and pensions; less cruel punishments; a more equitable distribution of prize money; and pardons for all the protesters. Spencer found that reasonable enough and raced a courier off to Pitt, asking him to accept the demands.

Pitt convened the cabinet early on April 22, and they swiftly approved. He then hurried to Windsor Castle to consult George III. The king at first angrily opposed any concession but finally gave in and issued a royal pardon that evening. Pitt had a hundred copies printed and sent to the mutinous fleet, along with a request for patience. To fulfill the promises, he not only had to rewrite that year's budget but borrow more money.

Meanwhile, the pressure on Whitehall mounted. Radicals among the sailors threatened to defect to the French if Parliament and the Admiralty did not soon act. This caused Spencer to despair that "the Channel fleet is now absolutely lost to the country as if it was at the bottom of the sea."[91] The crisis worsened on May 9, when the mutineers sent their officers ashore and sailed to St. Helens, a bay on the Isle of Wight.

It was not until May 5 that Pitt was able to submit to the House of Commons a bill that increased navy pay and allowances. After Parliament passed it on May 8, Pitt sent Admiral Howe to Portsmouth to share that good news with the sailors. The sailors were jubilant, and a group of them hoisted the admiral on their shoulders and paraded him through the town. Howe then invited the strike leaders to dine with him and his wife at their nearby home. The fleet put to sea on May 17.

Unfortunately, this unprecedented display of generosity and familiarity only ended Portsmouth's troubles. Strikes erupted in Torbay, Plymouth, Weymouth, Yarmouth, and Nore. Britain would suffer a devastating humiliation and defeat if any, let alone all, of the mutinous fleets sailed to France and there defected. Compromises defused this danger in every port except Nore, which ended with violence and repression. This strike was led by Richard Parker, a former midshipman who was severely punished for a minor offense and busted to the ranks. He refused to negotiate with anyone other than the first lord of the admiralty. Spencer journeyed to Nore and offered a royal pardon to the mutineers if they promptly resumed their duties. Most did, but the Admiralty eventually had 412 tried on treason charges and found 59 guilty, of which 29 including Parker were hanged, 29 were imprisoned, and 9 were flogged.[92]

Britain's war against France sputtered on as the nation's debts and deaths soared, with no end in sight. Parliament and the public split over whether to stay the course or cut their losses and end the fighting. King George III was deeply pessimistic about either course: "I do not see the hope that either war can be continued with effect or peace obtained but of the most disgraceful and unsolid tenure."[93]

Pitt was now so strongly committed to peace that "he would stifle every feeling of pride to the utmost to produce the desired result."[94] On June 1 he got the cabinet to accept a French offer for talks and sent Malmesbury to Lille to negotiate with a French delegation. Talks began shortly after Malmesbury arrived on July 4, 1797. Pitt had armed him with some very generous terms, including British recognition of France's conquest of the Austrian Netherlands, Nice, and Savoy, while Britain would return all its conquests to their previous owners except Trinidad, the Cape of Good Hope, and Ceylon. Yet week after week passed with the talks deadlocked.

The stalemate came from the inability of the French government's five directors to agree on just what to win from the war. Barras and two others believed that Britain's willingness to concede so much revealed its imminent defeat, so France could win more if it fought on. The best evidence for this were the Royal Navy's mutinies on top of years of worsening riots in the cities for bread and peace. Then a seeming diplomatic victory bolstered that position when on August 10 French and Portuguese ministers signed a treaty in Paris whereby Lisbon would sever its trade with Britain. Portugal's government, however, refused to ratify the treaty after receiving it.

Meanwhile, on September 4, Barras purged the government of moderates and replaced them with Jacobins. He then sent word to the negotiating delegation to give Malmesbury an ultimatum, either to agree to all of France's demands within twenty-four hours or leave. Malmesbury promptly packed up and headed back to

London. Whitehall formally informed the French on October 5 that the talks were terminated. Barras, however, was driven primarily by greed for money and power rather than ideology. He sent a trusted underling to London with the offer to accept Britain's offer in return for a secret payment of £2 million. Pitt countered with an offer of £450,000. This last chance for a deal died when neither side budged from its position.

The latest naval victory briefly lifted some of the prevailing gloom. Admiral Johan de Winter sailed with his Dutch fleet of sixteen ships of the line, four frigates, and six sloops from Texel on October 8, 1797. A British frigate immediately raced to Yarmouth and informed Admiral Adam Duncan, who commanded sixteen ships of the line. Duncan ordered his captains to put to sea. Duncan's fleet caught up to and attacked Winter's fleet five miles offshore from the village of Camperdown on October 11. The British battered seven Dutch ships of the line, two 50-gun warships, and two frigates into striking their colors. George III awarded Duncan by naming him a viscount. Camperdown restored a portion of national confidence.

Britons would need all the confidence they could muster after learning that Austria had abandoned the Coalition. By signing the Treaty of Campo Formio on October 18, 1797, Vienna recognized France's acquisition of the Austrian Netherlands, Savoy, and Nice, its eastern frontier on the Rhine River, the Ionian Islands, the enclave of Nicopoli in Albania, and Bonaparte's creation, the Cisalpine Republic, whichembraced Piedmont, Lombardy, Mantua, and the Papal Legations. In return, France accepted Austria's takeover of the Republic of Venice, Dalmatia, and Istria. Those rulers who lost their Italian realms would be compensated with German lands at a congress at Rastadt within a few months.

Britain was now fighting alone against France, with no power to inflict a decisive blow against its enemy, let alone win the war. And yet it fought on.

CHAPTER 5

# The Second Coalition, 1798–1802

"The all-searching eye of the French revolution looks to every part of Europe, and every quarter of the world in which can be found an object either of acquisition or plunder. Nothing is too great for the temerity of its ambition, nothing too small or insignificant for the grasp of its rapacity."

William Pitt

"I, who ought not to love you . . . have become your antagonist and have compelled you in the midst of the sands of Syria, to raise the siege of a miserable, almost defenseless town? . . . Believe me, general, adopt sentiments more moderate . . . Asia is not a theatre made for your glory. This letter is a little revenge that I give myself."

William Sidney Smith to Napoleon Bonaparte

As 1798 dawned, Britain again teetered at bankruptcy's brink. Whitehall desperately needed money to pay its soaring expenses and service its soaring debt. This forced Pitt to raise taxes in January, but carefully, so that the heaviest burden lay on those most capable of bearing it. He lowered the minimal two-pence-a-pound tax for annual incomes from £65 to £60 and raised rates in steps to a maximum of two shillings a pound for incomes over £200. The very rich also gave more to the nation's security when Pitt tripled existing taxes on houses, windows, male servants, horses, and carriages. He followed this up in December 1798 by getting a bill passed that established income and land taxes.

Pitt may have spared the legions of poor from taxes but he could do nothing to help extract them from their dismal and worsening conditions. Prices, homelessness, crime, malnutrition, and despair climbed as jobs, income, lodgings, and food dwindled. What the prime minister could do was amass enough legal power to deter radicals from mobilizing and unleashing those revolutionary forces against the government, then crush them if they did. To that end this year, he pushed two laws through Parliament for the King's approval, the Combination Act, which outlawed seditious groups and labor unions, and the Defense of the Realm Act, which required the forty counties to provide lists of all able-bodied men in each parish that would be mustered to repress any revolts.

Pitt struggled to create a new coalition from the previous one's ruins. Vienna expressed its willingness to war again against France, but only if the price was right. In doing so, the Austrians shamelessly ignored two treaties they had signed the previous year, one to repay their debt to Britain and the other to keep their peace with France. Pitt and his colleagues saw this as a chance to get the Austrians to recall their default and to pay what they owed. When Foreign Minister Grenville informed Ambassador Louis Starhemberg of this precondition for a £1 million subsidy, the Austrian promised that his country would do so as soon as possible. Whitehall would be a long time waiting.[1]

Meanwhile, Grenville had Ambassador Charles Whitworth entice Tsar Paul into an alliance by promising subsidies of up to £300,000 up front and £100,000 each month thereafter for 60,000 troops. Paul stalled an answer to Whitworth while his foreign ministry put the finishing touches on an alliance treaty with Austria that included a tenet making it contingent on British subsidies. With this deal in hand, Paul summoned Whitworth and talked him into signing a bilateral treaty with Austrian ambassador Ludwig Cobenzl whereby Britain guaranteed a £3.6 million loan to Vienna. The tsar then got Whitworth to sign a treaty committing Britain to pay Russia £225,000 up front, £75,000 thereafter until a peace treaty was signed, and £35,000 as a going away gift for 45,000 Russian troops. Although Grenville was pleased that Whitworth cut a deal with Russia well below his ceiling, he was enraged that the ambassador had signed an unauthorized loan guarantee treaty with Austria. When Paul heard that Whitehall had rejected the treaty with Austria, he repudiated his treaty with Britain. And there the Second Coalition stalled for now.[2]

A treaty ended the impasse on February 17, 1799; Paul pledged to send a 45,000-man army to fight alongside the Austrians in return for an annual subsidy of £900,000, plus £225,000 up front to mobilize the troops, £75,000 when they joined the campaign, and thereafter £37,500 a month until a formal peace treaty was signed by all belligerents. Grenville wanted an additional 45,000 Russian troops to join British forces for a campaign in the Low Countries, but the best deal Whitworth could strike was a treaty signed on June 22, 1799, whereby Britain would pay Russia £88,000 to mobilize a 17,500-man army, £44,000 a month thereafter for the war's duration, and £19,000 a month for the transport fleet that carried and supplied the troops for a British-led campaign in the Low Countries.[3]

As usual, Britain's taxpayers did not get their money's worth. After Whitehall learned that the Russian army marching to Austria numbered only 27,000 of the 45,000 troops pledged and paid for, Grenville fired off instructions to Whitworth to pressure the tsar to fulfill the treaty or else suffer the cutback of future payments. Paul admitted the complaint's justice but pleaded that he had no more troops to spare. Then, faced with the imminent paring of his subsidy, he found 10,000 troops that he promised to send to the Switzerland front. Grenville, realizing that was the most that Britain would get, accepted it. When those troops failed to arrive, Whitehall would adjust its payments accordingly. If the shortfall in Russian troops disappointed Pitt and his colleagues, what the Austrians did would enrage them.[4]

Meanwhile, the British enjoyed an indirect ally when the United States got into what became known as the "Quasi-War" with France. While British depredations against American shipping dropped after the 1795 Jay Treaty was ratified, French seizures persisted. President John Adams hoped to strike a similar deal with France by sending a three-man diplomatic team to Paris in 1797. What the envoys experienced was not diplomacy but blatant and persistent attempts by Foreign Minister Charles Maurice Talleyrand and his underlings to squeeze bribes from them. Revelation of those attempted shakedowns, known as the XYZ Affair for the letters that masked the names of the officials, shocked and enraged America's government and people. In the spring and summer of 1798, Adams got Congress to approve a series of bills that prepared and unleashed a naval war against France. Although America went to war with only three 44-gun frigates and half a dozen smaller warships, the intrepid captains and crews won each of the dozen or so battles that they fought against French warships. Napoleon Bonaparte finally resolved the war with the Treaty of Mortefontaine on September 30, 1800. These victories gave the Americans a confidence that helped carry them to war against the British empire a dozen years later.

At times political tensions in and beyond Parliament could literally explode in one's face. On May 25, 1798, Pitt introduced a naval appropriations bill and urged a vote on it later that day. George Tierney, who was opposition leader Charles Fox's right-hand man, rose to insist that such an important bill demanded more time to consider. Without a counter to that reasonable request, Pitt resorted to the foul tactic of questioning Tierney's patriotism and accusing him of trying "to obstruct the defense of the country." Tierney angrily called on Henry Addington, the House Speaker, to rebuke Pitt for making such an defamatory statement. The speaker refused to do so but did ask Pitt to explain himself. Pitt could have defused the insult with some vague expression of regret that he had been misunderstood. Instead, he haughtily replied: "I will neither retract from nor further explain my former expression." That evening Tierney sent Pitt a challenge to a duel.[5]

They met with their seconds in a meadow near Kingston Vale shortly after dawn on May 27. At twelve paces, each lowered his pistol and fired. The shots missed. Tierney insisted that his honor remained unsatisfied. Their seconds reloaded the pistols and handed them back. This time Pitt fired in the air while Tierney again shot wide. After their seconds insisted that the duelists had amply defended their honor, Pitt and Tierney shook hands and went their separate ways.

The next day Pitt reassured his mother that the "business terminated without anything unpleasant to either party, and in a way which left me perfectly satisfied with myself and my antagonist, who behaved with great propriety."[6] Pitt's outward sangfroid over the duel masked enormous stress. He took to bed for several days, explaining that he had been "making Exertions beyond my real strength."[7]

Duels represented a conflict between law and culture that would take several generations to resolve. It was at once illegal and acceptable to duel, at least for men of "honor" among the political and economic elite. The custom, however, undermined national power by imposing a hair-triggered sensitivity on its leaders for any slight that questioned their honor. King George III was among those who understood this toll. In a private letter he firmly but gently rebuked Pitt: "I trust what has happened will never be repeated. . . . Public characters have no right to weigh alone what they owe to themselves; they must consider also what is due to their country."[8]

The worst crisis that Britain faced in 1798 erupted in Ireland. This happened despite or perhaps because Whitehall reacted to the invasion scare of 1796 and a series of subsequent uprisings by boosting the number of British regulars and militia to 130,000, the largest force Britain massed during the entire era in one region, by June 1798. Yet even this was not enough. Although the British brutally repressed each revolt, they could not kill or capture all the insurgents or be everywhere at once.

This in turn encouraged France to mount another invasion, but one far more elaborate than the first.[9] Of the seven expeditions that the Directory organized, five actually set sail, three reached the Irish coast, and one put troops ashore. General Joseph Humbert and 1,099 French troops landed at Killala Bay on the remote northwestern coast of Mayo on August 22. These troops were too few and too late to aid the rebellion. Nonetheless, Humbert left a couple of hundred men to guard his landing and marched with the rest into the interior. Learning of the invasion, General Gerard Lake ordered forces to converge. Humbert surrendered 844 French troops and 1,500 Irish rebels on September 8. The British executed the Irish leaders and imprisoned the rest of the rebels along with the French. Commodore Jean Baptiste Bompard led a squadron of one ship of the line and eight frigates packed with 3,000 troops from Brest on September 16. British frigates carried word to Commodore John Warren, who pursued Bompard with his squadron. On October 11, Warren caught up, attacked, and forced the French ship of the line and six of the frigates to surrender. Wolfe Tone was among the prisoners. He was charged with treason, found guilty, and sentenced to be executed, but he cheated the hangman by slitting his throat on November 19.

The Irish revolt spread despite the limited French aid. Pitt ordered ruthless measures to crush the insurgents. He condemned the "traitors and rebels . . . who are industriously propagating the most dangerous principles, engrafting upon the minds of the people the most destructive doctrines, wantonly seducing and deluding the ignorant multitude, encouraging the most criminal correspondence with the enemy . . . and for converting Ireland into a jacobinical republic under the wing and protection of republican France."[10]

The British retained their colony of Ireland by slaughtering perhaps as many as 50,000 people, mostly Catholics. Indeed, of all the massacres during that blood-soaked age, none exceeded Britain's genocide in Ireland, including the French Revolution's murder of perhaps 30,000 French from 1792 to 1799 and Russia's slaughter of perhaps 20,000 Poles in 1795. This brutal assertion of overwhelming hard power reflected the abject failure of British soft power to enact reforms that likely would have prevented the rebellion.[11]

Britain's second worst security crisis this year came in Egypt. Napoleon Bonaparte's lifetime dream of emulating Alexander the Great began to come true on May 19, 1798, when his expedition sailed to conquer Egypt as a stepping-stone to India. His armada included 13 ships of the line, 7 frigates, 18 sloops, and 300 transports packed with 36,000 men, including 276 officers, 28,000 infantry, 2,800 cavalry, 2,000 gunners, 1,157 military engineers, and 900 nonmilitary personnel—among them doctors, scientists, anthropologists, artists, and writers—along with 60 field guns, 40 siege guns, and hundreds of tons of munitions and provisions.[12] Bonaparte and most of these vessels sailed from Toulon, while others departed from Genoa, Livorno, and Cittavecchia to rendezvous at Malta.

The armada dropped anchor at the entrance to the port of Valletta, Malta's capital, on June 9. When Malta's ruler, Ferdinand von Hompsech, refused to let all those vessels into the harbor to replenish their water supplies, Bonaparte ordered his troops to land on a nearby beach and arc around to seal off the city. On June 12 Hompsech capitulated after a brief and bloodless artillery duel designed to preserve both his honor and that of his 332 Knights of St. John's, as well as his 2,000 militia. Bonaparte then made Malta a dress rehearsal for what he hoped to do in Egypt: he abolished slavery and feudalism; organized modern administrative, legal, tax, and school systems; and left behind a 3,400-man garrison before sailing on to Egypt.

Bonaparte landed with 4,000 troops on a beach four miles west of Alexandria on July 1 and fought his way into the city. It took several days to disembark the rest of the soldiers, horses, munitions, and provisions, but then, on July 9, after garrisoning Alexandria, he headed east toward the Nile River. Before leaving, he told Admiral François Paul Brueys d'Aigalliers, his naval commander, either to crowd his fleet into Alexandria's harbor or sail to a safe port in Corfu, one of the seven Ionian Islands ceded to France by the Treaty of Campo Formio. Brueys would disobey this order, with catastrophic results.

After reaching the Nile, Bonaparte led his army alongside its west bank toward Cairo. On July 21 the French were within a day's march of Cairo and could see the pyramids on the horizon. Blocking their way were 15,000 Egyptian infantry, 3,000 light cavalry, and 6,000 Mameluk cavalry. Bonaparte ordered his regiments to form squares as the horsemen charged, and his infantry and gunners decimated and routed the enemy. He then began what became four days of negotiations for Cairo's surrender, after which, on July 26, he led his army into the city. After sending columns after the remnants of the Mameluk forces, Bonaparte launched a campaign to transform Cairo from a medieval into a modern city. Then, on August 14, amid his flurry of reforms, he got horrifying news.

Spy reports of a naval and troop buildup at Toulon had reached Whitehall as early as mid-April. The French were clearly preparing an expedition, but to where? The first fear was for Ireland, followed by the West Indies. The crucial question was how best to stop it, regardless of its destination. Should all available warships mass at Gibraltar to cork the Mediterranean or should a fleet sail into that sea and destroy the enemy armada as it left its lair? Pitt and his cabinet chose the latter strategy. On April 29, 1798, a fast frigate carried orders from the Admiralty to Admiral John Jervis, now Earl of St. Vincent after his decisive victory in the Battle of Cape St. Vincent in 1797, who commanded the fleet blockading Cadiz, to dispatch Captain Horatio Nelson with fourteen ships of the line and several frigates to Toulon. [13]

But St. Vincent was way ahead of those orders. On May 2, acting independently on the same intelligence, he ordered Nelson with his 74-gun Vanguard and two other ships of the line to ferret out just what the French were up to at Toulon, sending ten additional ships of the line to reinforce Nelson after he read the Admiralty's dispatch on May 19.. By the time Nelson and his fleet reached Toulon, however, Bonaparte's armada was long gone. Guessing that Bonaparte was bound for Egypt, Nelson had his captains spread sail and race there as fast as possible. His hunch was correct. but he got to Alexandria too early, on June 28, two days before the French armada arrived. He then sailed for Constantinople, hoping that was Bonaparte's objective, but after a few days decided to steer west to the British rendezvous port of Syracuse, Sicily. There he learned that Bonaparte had indeed gone to Egypt after capturing Malta, so Nelson ordered his captains to turn eastward once more.

As Nelson's fleet approached Alexandria in late afternoon on August 1, lookouts spied not a single French warship in the city's harbor. Admiral Brueys had rejected Bonaparte's order either to shelter his fleet there or at distant Corfu. His reason for avoiding Alexandria's port was sound enough. He could only crowd his warships in that shallow basin if they were neutered of their guns. Then, if a British fleet appeared just beyond cannon shot, he would suffer the humiliation of being corked there impotently and indefinitely. But he did not sail on to safe harbor at Corfu. Instead, like so many sitting ducks, his thirteen ships of the line were anchored prow to stern a hundred and sixty yards apart across a mile and a half of Aboukir Bay's placid waters a dozen miles east of Alexandria. The fleet was unprepared for combat. None of the warships had springs and ropes attached to their cables to let them be turned quickly, and skeleton crews manned each vessel, as most sailors were either ashore or sickened from dysentery. Inexplicably, Brueys had failed to post frigates as sentinels a score or so miles off shore to give him and his men time to react should an enemy fleet appear.

Spotting Bruey's fleet in the distance, Nelson immediately had signals hoisted for his warships to attack in two lines and blast the French vessels between them as they sailed across the bay. The battle raged into the night, climaxing with the explosion of Admiral Bruey's flagship, the *Orient.* The British victory was decisive. The French fleet was virtually destroyed, with two ships of the line sunk, nine captured, and just two escaped. Over 5,235 French were killed or missing and 3,305 captured to 218 British killed and 678 wounded.[14] Bonaparte and his army were now marooned in Egypt.

Nelson left behind a small blockading squadron and sailed with most of his fleet to Naples to reequip and repair his vessels. He soon mixed sensual delights with his business. After moving into Ambassador William Hamilton's mansion, Nelson took his host's voluptuous wife Emma as his lover. He soon found himself besotted not just with her but with the royal couple Ferdinand IV and Marie Caroline, who he saw as enlightened rulers rather than the doltish king and shrill queen that they were. These feelings were partly stirred when Ferdinand named Nelson Duke of Bronte, with an annual £3,000 stipend, and relied on him as his unofficial viceroy. In the months ahead, Nelson asserted his powers in ways that undercut British diplomacy, eventually lost his royal hosts half their realm, and blackened his name.

A fast vessel brought word of Nelson's victory to Constantinople on August 12. It then took nearly a month before Selim III and his advisers resolved their debate over whether to accept or resist France's invasion of Egypt, an Ottoman Empire protectorate. On September 9, Selim III declared war against France. Then an extraordinary event happened. The Turks and the Russians set aside a century or so of wars and hatreds and signed a treaty of alliance against France. Admiral Feodor Ushakov and Admiral Kadir Bey combined their fleets and sailed through the Dardanelles Strait on October 1, bound first to retake the Ionian Islands extending southward from the mouth of the Adriatic Sea along Greece's western coast. The Russo-Turkish fleet captured Cerigo on October 15,

Zante on October 25, Cephalonia on October 29, Nilopolis on the Albanian coast on November 1, and Santa Maura on November 13. The only French holdout was Corfu, which defied an allied siege that opened on November 5 until the garrison finally surrendered, on March 1, 1799. The Russians and Turks then turned their guns on Bonaparte in Egypt, and in doing so they were joined by the British. Britain's greatest naval commander, however, did not join this campaign.

After the battle of the Nile, Nelson, while enjoying Emma's ample charms, spent months in Naples trying to entice Ferdinand IV to war against France. Lacking confidence in his own officers and troops, Ferdinand asked Francis II to lend him a prominent Austrian general to lead his army against France. Francis dispatched General Karl Mack along with the sensible advice to let the French attack first. Instead, egged on by Nelson, Ferdinand ordered Mack to invade the Papal States on November 23, 1798. The Neapolitans scattered the handful of French in their way and entered Rome six days later, but General Jean Antoine Championnet rallied his forces north of Rome, counterattacked, and routed Mack's army on December 12. The Neapolitan remnants stumbled into Naples a week later, with the French hot on their heels. Nelson, meanwhile, had sailed with his squadron to Livorno to aid the Neapolitan army as it swept the French from Italy. Upon learning that Mack's campaign had ended in disaster, he hurried back to Naples. He had only a few days to pack the royal family, the Hamiltons, and 3,000 other refugees aboard his squadron, and it sailed for Palermo on December 22.

Championnet led his victorious troops into Naples on January 23. After consolidating his power, he sent columns of troops to occupy strategic southern Italy ports like Reggio, Taranto, Otranto, and Bari. He also assisted a group of Neapolitan liberals in establishing the Parthenopean Republic on January 22, 1799. Except for Venetia in the northeast, French troops now occupied the key positions throughout the Italian peninsula.

Nelson's foray into diplomacy and grand strategy was disastrous for Britain and the coalition. Yet by the end of 1799 the allies would clear Italy of virtually all French troops and Nelson would play a significant but controversial role in this astonishing victory.

Meanwhile, France's Directory planned to overrun Germany in spring 1799, much as they had Italy the previous autumn. By launching the campaign on the late winter date of March 1, 1799, the strategists hoped to catch the Austrians while they were short of troops, forage, and provisions. General Jean-Baptiste Jourdan would lead the central thrust with his 39,000 troops across the Rhine at Strasbourg, march through the Black Forest to the upper Danube River, then follow it to Vienna. With 28,000 troops, General Jean-Baptiste Bernadotte would cross the Rhine near Mannheim, then angle southeast to join Jourdan on the Danube. General André Masséna would march his 26,000 troops across northern Switzerland to Bavaria to link up with Jourdan and Bernadotte.

As he had in previous years, Archduke Charles upset that elegant French plan. He beat Jourdan at Ostrach on March 20 and again at Stockach on March 25, forcing him to withdraw to Strasbourg. He then headed north against Bernadotte, who, fearing he would be cut off, abandoned his siege of Philipsburg and withdrew west of the Rhine. Charles could now concentrate on Massena, who had withdrawn to Zurich after Jourdan's defeat and retreat. Although the French repulsed a series of Austrian attacks starting in late May and culminating on June 4, Massena led his army westward to avoid encirclement. A lull settled on that front as both commanders awaited reinforcements.

Meanwhile, the French fared even more disastrously in Italy. By the spring of 1799, 92,000 French troops were occupying Italy's key cities and regions, with 33,000 led by General Barthelemy Scherer west of the Mincio River, 34,000 led by General Etienne Macdonald in the Papal States and Kingdom of Naples, and 25,000 guarding supply lines heading back to France. The Directory ordered Scherer to cross the Mincio and attack General Paul Kray's 58,000-man Austrian army. Not surprisingly, the Austrians routed the outnumbered French at Magnano on April 5. In pursuing Scherer beyond the Mincio, Kray was joined by Russian General Alexander Suvorov, perhaps the era's least-known brilliant general. On April 19 Suvorov deployed his army of 11,000 Russian and 29,000 Austrian troops around Brescia, defended by 11,200 French troops; the French capitulated two days later. General Jean Victor Moreau replaced Scherer but was no more capable of repelling the enemy onslaught. Suvorov led his army across the Adda River on April 27, routed Moreau at Cassano, then marched unopposed into Milan the next day.

Macdonald received orders to abandon all of southern Italy, except for Naples, and join Moreau. With 29,000 troops, he began his long march up the peninsula on May 7. After learning that Macdonald had taken Modena on June 12, Suvorov turned east and blocked him at the Tidone River on June 17. After three days of fighting, Macdonald withdrew his army toward Genoa. Meanwhile, Moreau sat on his heels rather than hurried to join Macdonald. General Barthelemy Joubert replaced Moreau, rallied the army, and advanced against Suvorov at Novi on August 12. There, when he hesitated to attack the masses of Russian and Austrian troops on the plain before him, Suvorov attacked instead and routed the French; Joubert was among those killed. Moreau took command again but withdrew his army into northwestern Italy.

Rather than pursue Moreau, Suvorov left enough Austrian troops to block him and headed north with his Russian troops into Switzerland to join the allies against Masséna. He did not get there in time. Masséna launched his army in a series of attacks that routed General Alexander Korsakov's Russian army at Zurich on September 25 and 26. Masséna then turned against Suvorov, who escaped eastward over snowbound alpine passes to safety in Austria after losing most of his troops to starvation and capture.

Meanwhile, the Parthenopean Republic in Naples survived only a few months. The leaders squabbled among themselves, failed to organize an administration and army, and instead depended on French troops for protection. Their liberal constitution puzzled rather than inspired most Neapolitans, while their policy of confiscating Catholic Church property alienated the devout. Backed with British supplies and adviser Captain Edward Foote, Cardinal Fabrizio Ruffo organized a crusade against the godless Neapolitan liberals and the French that began in the toe of Italy and eventually spread up the peninsula to Naples itself. The rebels forced Championnet to withdraw his scattered detachments back to Naples, and on April 22 he and his army, except for a 500-man garrison in Fort St. Elmo, headed toward northern Italy. Ruffo and Edward signed a treaty with the Parthenopean Republic leaders that either pardoned them if they pledged allegiance to the king or sailed them to Toulon if they did not.

Nelson's fleet sailed from Palermo on June 21 and three days later dropped anchor in Naples Bay. Armed with martial law powers by King Ferdinand, Nelson repudiated the treaty and had 8,000 Parthenopean Republic leaders and followers imprisoned. He later had liberal leader Francesco Caracciolo and 99 others summarily hanged without trial. In doing so, Nelson forever blackened the fringe of what otherwise was a brilliant naval career.[15]

Nelson split his command into three. He remained at Naples with several warships; Captain John Duckworth sailed with four ships of the line to take Port Mahon, Minorca; and Captain Thomas Troubridge and three ships of the line slowly made their way up the Italian coast, parallel with the march of Neapolitan and British troops, to drive the French from the Kingdom of Naples and the Papal States. Capua fell on July 29, Gaeta on July 31, and Civitavecchia on September 29. News of a revolt on Malta prompted Nelson to dispatch a flotilla to aid those rebels against the French. Although the French there rejected the British demand for surrender on September 25, the subsequent blockade effectively eliminated Malta as a French asset. After Duckworth's flotilla dropped anchor off Port Mahon on November 7, General Charles Stuart led 3,000 troops ashore to besiege the town, and the Spanish garrison surrendered on November 15. Britain now had an excellent base of operations in the western Mediterranean.

Meanwhile, a British and Russian army scored an initial victory, then bogged down and suffered a humiliating defeat in the Low Countries. General Ralph Abercromby led 12,000 British infantry, 600 gunners, and 218 horsemen ashore near Helder, in the Netherlands, on August 27. The next day those troops captured the nearby naval port of Nieue Werk, and twelve Dutch frigates anchored there. Had Abercromby evacuated his troops along with the captured warships and naval supplies, that victory would been bought extremely cheaply. Unfortunately, however, the expedition stayed and the losses steadily mounted. Within a week, 6,000 Russian troops arrived, the first contingent of 17,500 promised. Edward, Duke of York and the British army's commander-in-chief, arrived to take over from Abercromby on September 13. The allied army peaked in strength with 32,000 troops in mid-September.

York ordered his army to attack General Guillaume Brune's 19,000 French and Dutch troops at Bergen on September 19, and at Castricum on October 6. Brune's men repulsed both assaults, inflicting 8,000 casualties on the British and Russians. Now York faced a terrible dilemma. He and his army were trapped. If he ordered yet another attack on the French lines, his troops would be repelled with heavy losses. If the army stood its ground, disease would devour its ranks. If he tried to evacuate his army to the flotilla, the French could attack and overrun most of his forces before they embarked. Only one choice avoided destruction. York signed an armistice with Brune on October 18, whereby the British freed and sent back 8,000 French and Dutch prisoners of war in England in return for York's withdrawing his army, unmolested, to Britain by November 30.

The Dutch campaign debacle frosted relations between Foreign Secretary Grenville and Secretary at War Dundas. Grenville asserted that the evacuation agreement was void because York had exceeded his authority by pledging to release French prisoners in Britain. Dundas insisted that the deal must be upheld for the sake of national honor. George III ended the deadlock predictably by siding with his son.

Nelson's annihilation of the French fleet at Aboukir Bay may have severed Napoleon Bonaparte's link to France but not to his dreams. This would-be modern Alexander the Great led 13,000 troops from Cairo on February 6 and quick-marched them across the Sinai desert in just two weeks. Facing the invaders were 4,000 Turkish and Palestinian troops at Jaffa, 5,000 at Acre in Palestine, and 25,000 more scattered across Syria's key cities and fortresses. The French captured El Arish on Palestine's western frontier on February 20, Gaza on February 24, Jaffa on March 3, and Haifa on March 17. Just a few miles away across the bay from Haifa was the fortress town of Acre, commanded by Ackmed Djezzar Pasha, with his well-deserve nickname, "The Cut-Throat."

Bonaparte most likely would have vanquished Djezzar had not yet another intrepid British sea warrior thwarted his plans. Captain William Sidney Smith's fleet blockaded Alexandria. Upon learning of Bonaparte's campaign to conquer the Holy Land, Smith split his squadron, and leaving half his warships at Alexandria, with the rest, including his 80-gun flagship, *The Tigre*, he shadowed the invaders along the coast. Smith's flotilla reached Acre on March 15, just two days before the French appeared, and bolstered that fortress with British guns, gunners, and munitions. Three days later, Smith's warships captured a half dozen vessels packed with Bonaparte's siege guns.

Upon learning of this loss, Bonaparte could only fume and send couriers galloping back to Egypt with orders to send another shipment of heavy cannons. Meanwhile, the French field guns chipped away at the fortress, but it took nearly ten days for his gunners to pound a small breach in the walls. On March 28 Bonaparte ordered an assault, but the Turks and British repelled it, with heavy losses. Word reached Bonaparte that a Turkish army was advancing from Damascus and threatened to engulf him, trapping him against the sea. He detached part of his army to rout the Turks at the Battle of Mt. Tabor. Although the French army's rear was secure for now, Acres's defenders repulsed every attack. Smith triumphantly sent Bonaparte this message: "I, who ought not to love you . . . have become your antagonist and have compelled you in the midst of the sands of Syria, to raise the siege of a miserable, almost defenseless town? . . . Believe me, general, adopt sentiments more moderate. . . . Asia is not a theatre made for your glory. This letter is a little revenge that I give myself."[16] With these words probably searing his mind, Bonaparte finally gave up and ordered his army on the long, grueling march back to Egypt on May 16. All along the way, Smith's flotilla shadowed Bonaparte's journey.

Within a month, Bonaparte and his army's remnants had rejoined their comrades in Egypt. Shortly thereafter, news arrived that an armada of 113 mostly Turkish and Russian vessels had dropped anchor off Aboukir Bay on July 11, and over the next few days had disgorged 18,000 Turkish troops on the beach. Bonaparte gathered 10,000 troops and raced from Cairo. Upon reaching Aboukir on July 25, he launched an attack that annihilated the Turkish army. Among the spoils were several newspapers, which gave Bonaparte his first news of continental affairs in eight months, and what he learned infuriated him. To his aide Louis Antoine Bourrienne, he exclaimed: "Italy is lost! . . . All the fruits of our victories have disappeared! It is essential that I leave."[17] He soon got his chance.

Although the Royal Navy emerged from the Battle of the Nile as the Mediterranean's premier sea power, this position was vulnerable. On April 25, 1799, Admiral Eustache Bruix sailed from Brest with twenty-five ships of the line and five frigates after a storm blew off the blockading British fleet of sixteen ships of the line led by Alexander Hood, Lord Bridport. Bruix's mission was wildly ambitious—he was to join forces with the Spanish fleet, sail on to drive the British from Minorca and Malta, land supplies at Alexandria for Bonaparte's army in Egypt, and, finally, destroy the British fleet. In the end, he fulfilled only one of these objectives.

After Bridport learned of Bruix's escape, he sailed to screen Ireland while spreading word to the Admiralty, Admiral John Jervis, Earl of St. Vincent, with seven ships of the line at Gibraltar, and Admiral George Keith, whose squadron of fifteen ships of the line blockaded Cadiz. The Admiralty promptly dispatched Admiral Charles Cotton with twelve ships of the line to reinforce Keith. St. Vincent, stunned to watch Bruix's fleet sail through the Strait of Gibraltar on May 5 sent orders to Keith to join him. After Keith arrived on May 10, he and St. Vincent sailed eastward to join forces with as many of the fifteen ships of the line scattered across the Mediterranean as possible, including Admiral George Duckworth's four at Port Mahon, Captain Thomas Troubridge's three at Naples, Captain Alexander Ball's three at Malta, Captain Smith's two at Alexandria, and Admiral Nelson's 80-gun *Foudroyant,* his pick of the prizes at Aboukir Bay, at Palermo. The trouble was that it might take months to unite these squadrons, if Bruix did not wipe them out one by one.

With the horizon empty of British warships, Spain's fleet at Cadiz sailed on May 17 and reached Cartagena three days later. Bruix, meanwhile, reached Toulon, where he received new orders to convoy supplies to Genoa, then head to Cartagena. After reaching Cartagena on June 22, the Franco-Spanish fleet numbered thirty-four ships of the line. Rather than seek out and attack the British fleet, the combined fleet sailed on June 29 for the safe harbor of Cadiz. When Bruix departed on July 21, the Spanish fleet stayed behind. Bruix's fleet reached Brest on August 13, nearly four months after it had departed from Brest. During that time, although the expedition never fought a battle, the wild goose chase that it provoked helped change the course of history.

Bonaparte capitalized on all the confusion. Smith's warships blockading Alexandria had departed on different missions, leaving behind a half dozen Turkish vessels. Bonaparte turned over his army's command to General Jean-Baptiste Kléber, and on August 23 he and an entourage escaped aboard two frigates and two smaller vessels bound for France. They stepped ashore at Frejus, on October 9, and hurried north to Paris.

A month later, on November 9, Bonaparte deposed France's Directory in a bloodless military coup. He did not immediately become a dictator. Instead, he supervised the writing of a constitution that created a government known as the Consulate, with three consuls as executives, three legislatures with various powers, an electoral system, and guaranteed civil rights for citizens. He assumed the post of the first consul, or chief executive, and wielded his powers to reform France's law, administration, and taxes; bolster and diversity France's economic infrastructure and industries; crush a revolt by the Chouans and Vendeans in western France; and forge peace with its enemies. The heart of his diplomacy were direct appeals to the monarchs of Britain and Austria to end the war that he sent, pointedly, on Christmas Day 1799.[18]

Bonaparte's plea to King George III, accompanied by Foreign Minister Talleyrand's cover letter, reached Foreign Minister Grenville on New Year's Eve. Grenville promptly forwarded it to the king and got together with Pitt and the rest of the inner cabinet to discuss how to respond.[19] Playing to type, the first reaction of those very English ministers was on the message's form rather than its substance. They sneered that Bonaparte had violated protocol by directly addressing His Royal Highness. Properly, the letter should have gone from the First Consul to the First Minister. Yet they admitted that, if nothing else, Bonaparte's missive, which he had published in French newspapers, was a very clever propaganda ploy that boxed in the British government. Pitt could "not see on what Grounds We could justify to ourselves a refusal to Treat, and much less how We could expect to be supported by Public Opinion."[20] On the other hand, if they did negotiate and a deal was struck, what if Bonaparte took advantage of the peace to prepare for the next war? The decisive argument was that Britain could not make peace until after it had decisively defeated France. Anything else would lock Britain into an inferior position that the French would exploit mercilessly until the next war erupted. Pitt reasoned that "we can have nothing to do but to decline all negotiation at the present moment on the ground that the actual situation of France does not as yet hold out any solid security to be derived from negotiation. . . . This may, I think, be so expressed as to convey to the people of France that the shortest road to peace is by effecting the restoration of Royalty."[21]

With this argument, Pitt forged a consensus to spurn Bonaparte's olive branch on January 2, 1800, a mere two days after it arrived. When Pitt informed the king of this decision, George III was happy to comply, later explaining: "Peace can be nothing but an armed neutrality, which is a most hazardous situation. . . . While French principles are victorious no peace can be safe."[22] The king and his ministers rejected even the notion of dignifying Bonaparte with a direct reply but had Grenville send the rejection notice to his counterpart Talleyrand.[23]

Of all the decisions Pitt made during his eighteen years in power, this was his most controversial. Historian J. Holland Rose condemned it as "among the greatest mistakes of the time."[24] Pitt justified his decision by arguing that peace was impossible because Bonaparte could never be trusted to live up to it. A judicious look at the evidence, however, contradicts this assertion and upholds Rose's rebuke.

The treaties that Bonaparte negotiated at Leoben in April 1797 and Campo Formio in October 1797, after soundly thrashing the Austrians earlier that year, were actually quite restrained. This evidence was immediately at hand for Pitt and his cabinet, who would soon observe Bonaparte repeat his generosity. Although Vienna had broken these treaties and attacked France in 1798, he was just as lenient with the Treaty of Luneville of February 1801, after trouncing the Viennese again the previous year. He could have been more ruthless, but he then believed that a gentle peace would endure longer than a harsh peace. It was not until after he defeated Austria a third time, in 1805, that he reasoned a Draconian settlement was the best way to deter Vienna from future aggression. Bonaparte was indeed eager for peace after taking power in November 1799. War would stymie his ambitious plans to modernize France's economic, educational, and legal systems and promote art, science, and innovation. He tried to rally France's political and business elite behind his plans through a series of speeches and newspaper articles.

In a classic case of cognitive dissonance, Pitt and his colleagues ignored all this and clung to the scary caricature that Bonaparte was nothing more than an insatiable warmonger. In doing so, they failed to uphold the most vital element in wielding the art of power—to know one's enemy.

Regardless of how Pitt justified his decision, it was quite a policy flip-flop. The prime minister who urged peace at nearly any price two years earlier was now dead set on fighting to the bitter end. In 1797 he sought to extract Britain's people and economy from the burden of soaring debt and death, but the terrible toll had steadily mounted since then. And this, paradoxically, may explain his reversal. Like a high-stakes gambler, Pitt had suffered such severe losses that emotionally he could only justify them by continuing to double down, which, of course, only compounded the losses. He and his colleagues were increasingly determined that the dead should not have died in vain, so they continued to send a steady stream of other men to their deaths. This mentality was not a historic anomaly; it has afflicted countless wartime leaders. But it sharply violates the art of power, in which knowing when to cut one's losses is a crucial element.

If rejecting peace was easy enough for the king and cabinet, justifying to Parliament and the public an ever-costlier war for the indefinite future for an elusive end was a challenge. Pitt made his case before the House of Commons on February 3, 1800. His key rationale was that the French could not be trusted to keep the peace:

> But supposing the confederacy of Europe prematurely dissolved, supposing our armies disbanded, our fleets laid up in our harbours, our exertions relaxed, and our means of precaution and defense relinquished, do we believe that the revolutionary power, with this rest and breathing-time given it to recover from the pressure under which it is now sinking . . . will not against prove formidable to Europe? . . . As a sincere lover of peace, I will not sacrifice it by grasping at the shadow when the reality is not within my reach.

As for Bonaparte, Pitt condemned him as "this last adventurer in the lottery of revolution." He condemned the French Revolution as "the severest trial which the visitation of Providence has inflicted upon the nations of the earth. . . . The all-searching eye of the French Revolution looks to every part of Europe, and every quarter of the world in which can be found an object either of acquisition or plunder. Nothing is too great for the temerity of its ambition, nothing too small or insignificant for the grasp of its rapacity."[25]

This speech convinced a resounding majority in the House of Commons, which approved the policy by 265 to 64 votes. Uninhibited by its sharply diminished ranks, the opposition expressed its astonishment that the government would spurn what appeared to be a sincere plea for peace. Charles Fox led the opposition's criticism of Pitt's war without end.

Pitt's brilliant rhetoric masked a dilemma. If revolutionary France under Bonaparte's rule could never be trusted, then logically Britain would have to wage war until that regime was destroyed and replaced by a friendly monarchy. And this indeed is what happened fifteen blood-soaked years later. Meanwhile, within five years the French actually did restore royalty to France, but as an imperial throne for Napoleon rather than a king's throne for Louis XVIII.

Having rhetorically chiseled in stone a fight to the death struggle against the French Revolution and Bonaparte, Whitehall now had to realize it. The perennial trouble was that, militarily, Britain's sea power was as mighty as its land power was puny. For months Pitt and his ministers mulled various options, of which only one directly attacked France's mainland. Proposals were raised and discarded for launching expeditions against New Orleans, Louisiana; Buenos Aires, Argentina; Tenerife, Canary Islands; Walcheren Island, Holland; Minorca, Spain; Brest, France; and Belle Isle off Brittany's south coast.[26]

Pitt finally reached a decision after meeting with Charles, comte d'Artois, the would-be Louis XVIII's younger brother. A British army would land on the Ruis Peninsula near Quiberon Bay in southeastern Brittany, then march north to capture Rennes and sever the main road linking Brest and Paris. Artois assured Pitt that at least 25,000 rebels awaited a British invasion, and tens of thousands more would rally to the Bourbon colors thereafter. The army would then march west on Brest. Capturing France's largest and most threatening naval base would be a decisive military victory and a huge bargaining chip to win a decisive diplomatic victory.

Dundas was skeptical when Pitt shared the plan with him. He asked General Charles Grey to crunch the numbers and evaluate the plan's plausibility. The report that Grey issued on January 16, 1800, was unequivocal: "I earnestly hope you will not embarrass yourself with this enterprise."[27] The reason was simple. The plan's ambitions exceeded its abilities, a rather grievous shortcoming in the art of power. The original hope was to muster 80,000 troops for the invasion, but that proved to be impossible with the "thin red line" already stretched to the snapping point. So Whitehall dropped the army's ranks to 50,000 troops, but even this exceeded British power. A crucial related problem was how to sustain all those troops along with the rebels. Somehow the Admiralty had to gather enough transports to carry 200,000 tons of provisions, munitions, wagons, draft animals, and cavalry mounts in their holds along with all the soldiers. For the rebels alone, Whitehall earmarked 22,000 muskets, 32 cannons, and 18,000 pairs of shoes aboard the flotilla. But the demands on Britain's transport fleet, like its army, exceeded its power.[28]

These insurmountable obstacles were enough to spike the plan. Then came word that First Consul Bonaparte had sent General Guillaume Brune, who had defeated York in the Netherlands, against the rebels in northwestern France. Brune waged an utterly ruthless and ultimately successful campaign.

With Grey's damning report, Pitt sharply pared back the operation and shifted the objective to Belle Isle. In early June a flotilla sailed, packed with 4,200 troops led by Major General Thomas Maitland, and guarded by a half dozen ships of the line led by Captain Edward Pellew. Nature rather than the French defeated them: a storm scattered the fleet. When Pellew managed to reassemble his vessels, he received bad news. A spy sent word that Belle Isle's garrison was far stronger than was initially reported. Pellew and Maitland reluctantly decided to cancel their campaign. Whitehall responded by ordering the flotilla to sail to Gibraltar and there await further orders. Over the summer the flotilla received reinforcements and instructions to sail in different directions but never a target to attack. General Charles Cornwallis expressed the prevailing frustration at Whitehall's dithering: "Twenty-two thousand men . . . floating round the great part of Europe, the scorn and laughing stock of friends and foes."[29]

Meanwhile, the cabinet engaged in the latest debate over how much money to hand out to the allies and what to ask in return. Unable to decide either question, Pitt had Grenville instruct Britain's ministers in St. Petersburg and Vienna to open talks and find out how much money they wanted and what they intended to do with it. With this information, the British could make counter offers and proposals. But this diplomatic offensive soon ground to a halt.[30]

Tsar Paul shared his officers' rage that during the 1799 campaign the Austrians had treated Russia's generals like oafs and Russia's troops like cannon fodder, capped by abandoning General Korsakov and his army at Zurich, where Massena routed them. He demanded that Francis II fire Foreign Minister Johann Thugut and divide between Russia and Austria the conquered Italian lands. When Francis demurred, Paul severed Russia's alliance with Austria and ordered his troops to head for home.[31]

After doing so, the mercurial tsar assured Ambassador Whitworth that he still upheld his alliance with Britain. The 15,000 Russian troops then quartered on the Guernsey and Jersey Channel Islands remained at Whitehall's disposal. The trouble was that these troops were in a deplorable condition, with ragged uniforms, half rations, and rock-bottom morale, an armed, half-starved mob rather than an army. During a War Department inspection, William Huskisson was appalled by "the sulkiness, filth, torpor, and wretchedness that prevail among them. Their officers appear to care much less about them than we do for our sheep."[32] But a far worse strategic problem came soon after the tsar once again changed his mind.

British diplomacy with the Austrians was just as rancorous. The year 1800 opened with Whitehall and Vienna haggling over how much and under what conditions Britain would subsidize Austria's war efforts. It took half a year before three separate deals, two public and one secret, were signed, on June 23, 1800. Under the two public documents, the Austrians finally promised to pay back the 1797 loan that it had defaulted; Britain would give Austria three separate installments of £666,666 this year in return for keeping 200,000 troops in the field; neither country would take any territory from France that it held in 1789; and there would be no separate negotiations, let alone peace. Secretly, Britain recognized whatever Italian territory that Austria was able to conquer. The Austrians signed this deal the day after they learned of an utter disaster to one of their armies. They did not share this stunning news with British Ambassador Charles Elliot, Lord Minto. On top of this deception, the Austrians would typically break their promise, in this case over no separate negotiations or peace.[33]

The decisive defeat came on June 14, near Marengo, in northwestern Italy. Marengo was the culmination of a two pronged offensive that Bonaparte unleashed against Austria in May 1800. General Jean Moreau marched his army over the Rhine and down the Danube River valley, while Bonaparte himself led an army over the Alps into northwestern Italy. Typically Bonaparte's movements were as swift as Moreau's were plodding. In a seesaw battle, Bonaparte's army finally routed General Michael Melas's Austrians at Marengo. Bonaparte hoped that generosity might induce Vienna to peace. Rather than force Melas to surrender, he let the Austrians withdraw with honor behind the Adige River in return for talks over an armistice and then a peace that simply restored the terms of the 1797 Treaty of Campo Formio. Meanwhile, Moreau's troops crossed the Rhine and besieged Austrian garrisons in Ulm, Ingolstadt, and Phillipsburg.

Bonaparte's hope for peace soared when French and Austrian envoys signed an armistice on July 28, 1800. Then a setback came on August 10, 1800, when Vienna invited Whitehall to join the peace negotiations and the British refused. Bonaparte made his latest peace offering to London on August 24, forwarded via diplomat Guillaume Otto, whereby France and Britain would forge peace in two stages, with an armistice and prisoner exchange leading to a comprehensive settlement.

This time Whitehall split over whether to give peace a chance. Prime Minister Pitt and Foreign Minister Grenville favored grasping Bonaparte's outstretched hand, while King George III, Secretary at War Dundas, and Secretary for War Windham adamantly spurned it. Eventually the reasoning prevailed that a truce would lead not to a genuine peace but to a stronger France that warred more voraciously against Britain. To justify his government's policy of continuing the war, Pitt repeated the rationale that peace with a revolutionary regime led by Bonaparte would never last, and that only a decisive victory would bring a decisive peace.[34]

Yet, defying that logic, Whitehall did agree to discuss a prisoner swap that would potentially benefit France far more than Britain. Any returned French soldiers could swiftly rejoin their regiments facing the Austrians. But where would returned British soldiers be deployed? It was a far longer journey to the Caribbean or Mediterranean seas, where dozens of British regiments were conducting operations. The foreign secretary tapped his brother, Thomas Grenville, to head the talks, but in the end nothing came of them.

The British nearly scored a bloodless victory in early 1800, but cabinet hardliners scuttled it. Captain Sidney Smith assisted negotiations between the French and Turks that led to the Convention of El Arish on January 24, 1800, whereby the French army gave up Egypt in return for being transported back to France. Whitehall, however, refused to ratify the treaty, reasoning that the French army was so weak that it could be captured and imprisoned for the war's duration rather than repatriated to fight again. Kléber's army was already packed up and ready to go when Smith got orders in February to repudiate the deal and demand Kléber's surrender. Kléber refused. The Turks landed an army near Alexandria on March 10. Kléber launched a attack that routed and forced it to reembark on the allied flotilla. The French would cling to Egypt for another year and a half. After an Egyptian assassinated Kléber on June 14, 1800, General Jacques Menou assumed command. The British themselves would lead the next attempt to defeat the French in Egypt, and it would cost an enormous amount in treasure and blood.

Eventually a few rays of good news reached London and briefly lightened the prevailing gloom. During the blockade of Valletta, Malta's capital, the Royal Navy captured the two French ships of the line that had escaped from Aboukir Bay. Nelson commanding the Foudroyant accompanied by the Northumberland battered one into striking its colors, as it escorted a supply flotilla sailing to Valletta; after his latest coup Nelson sailed to join his mistress, Emma Hamilton, in Naples, then, still besotted with love, resigned his command and journeyed with her and her husband back to London. The blockading squadron captured the final survivor when it attempted to slip out of Valletta harbor to the open sea. With swindling supplies and no chance of rescue, the French garrison on Malta surrendered on September 4, 1800.

Austria's hardliners welcomed Britain's rejection of peace and pressure to resume the war against France in return for all the British gold that Vienna had received. The armistice ended on November 15. Moreau resumed his campaign down the Danube valley and routed the Austrians at the Battle of Hohenlinden on December 3, 1800. The Austrians hastily agreed to the latest cease-fire and negotiations. Two months later peace between France and Austria came with the Treaty of Luneville, signed on February 9, 1801. Austria recognized France's "sister" Batavian (Dutch), Helvetian (Swiss), Ligurian (Genoa), and Cisalpine (northern Italian) republics and the annexation of the Austrian Netherlands (Belgium) to France. In return, the French had to withdraw their troops from those countries.

Whitehall tolerated Austria's separate peace with France even though it violated the alliance treaty's terms. Foreign Minister Grenville accepted "the necessity under which the [Austrian] Emperor has acted, being unquestionably such as fairly to come within the descriptions of those circumstances which release a Power from any engagements of this Nature."[35]

Britain was now once again fighting alone against France. The demands for peace rose steadily among the public, in Parliament, and in the cabinet itself. Pitt and his government insisted that peace could come only after Britain and any future grand alliance crushed both Bonaparte and revolutionary France, which were now viewed as inseparable. If so, then any means to that end were justified. Indeed, if Bonaparte and the French revolution had morphed, then destroying one logically would destroy the other.

The Alien Office tried to realize this by working with the Institut Philanthropique's English Committee, led by Paul Hyde de Neuville in Paris. Neuville nurtured links with police minister Joseph Fouche and foreign minister Talleyrand, who both at once admired, loathed, feared, and undermined Bonaparte. With his extensive spy system and periodic arrests of dozens of suspects, Fouche was well aware of what lurked beneath the Institut Philanthropique's cover, but he deliberately nibbled around its edges rather than devoured it. Like Talleyrand, Fouche was hedging his bets in case a royalist coup overthrew Bonaparte and brought back the Bourbons. In doing so, of course, he made that highly unlikely event less so.

The plan was to murder Bonaparte with a cart bomb. Joseph Picot de Limoelan, a major general in the Chouan army, arrived in Paris on November 16, 1800, fresh from a training course in terrorism and bomb making, courtesy of Whitehall's Alien Office. Assembling the bomb was easy enough. The hard part was finding a chance to detonate it. This came when the conspirators learned that Napoleon and Josephine Bonaparte intended to hear Josef Haydn's *La Création* at the Opera House on Christmas Eve. Another Alien Office agent, Robinault de St-Régent, who reached Paris on November 26, led the horse-drawn cart packed with gunpowder to the Rue St. Niçaise on the route from the Tuileries to the Opera House, hired a young girl to hold the reins, and nervously awaited a hand signal from a lookout of the approach of the first consul's carriage. Seeing the signal, he sparked the fuse and hurried away.

The timing was nearly perfect. The Bonapartes were in separate coaches, with Napoleon in the lead and Josephine a few minutes behind. Bonaparte's coachman saw the cart partly obstructing the street and, suspecting the worst, whipped the horses into a canter. The bomb exploded seconds after Bonaparte's carriage passed, murdered the girl and a dozen or so others, and grievously wounded a score more. Upon learning that Josephine was safe, Bonaparte continued to the Opera House, where the assassination attempt was announced and he received a standing ovation. Bonaparte ordered Fouche to arrest everyone involved in the plot. Fouche's police rounded up 130 "suspects," but initially Jacobins rather than royalists. Only later, after the most prominent got away, did Fouche order the arrest of a dozen royalists, including Limoelan, who had foolishly lingered in Paris.

The viciousness of the mass murder resulting from that assassination plot horrified morally sensitive people, including those who otherwise counted themselves among the enemies of France and Bonaparte. The "collateral damage" would have been morally acceptable to those involved in the conspiracy had Bonaparte been killed. The belief at the Alien Office and across the counterrevolutionary network was that they could wash the innocent blood from their hands only by killing the tyrant, so they redoubled their efforts to this end.

As if the chronic war with France was not daunting enough, Whitehall nearly mired Britain in war with Russia. Napoleon Bonaparte was hardly the only British target for assassination. In St. Petersburg, ambassador Charles Whitworth conspired with a coterie of Russian ministers and generals seeking to depose Paul and place his son Alexander on the throne. Getting wind of Whitworth's machinations, on March 31, 1800, Paul declared him persona non grata. When the tsar learned that General Ralph Abercromby had barred Russian troops from joining Britain's occupation of Malta, he angrily expelled the rest of Britain's diplomatic delegation and closed Russian ports to British ships. The alliance between Britain and Russia was now effectively dead.

Paul did not stop there. His rage at a series of real and imagined affronts by London and Vienna drove him to outright war against them. He revived the League of Armed Neutrality that his mother,

Catherine, had established during America's War of Independence. During the 1780 alliance, Russia, Prussia, Sweden, Denmark, and the Netherlands had allied to deter British searches and seizures of neutral merchant ships accused of carrying "war contraband" goods to France, and to bar British naval and merchant vessels from the Baltic Sea. The League of Armed Neutrality of Russia, Sweden, Denmark, and Prussia officially announced its formation on December 16, 1800.

Word of the league reached London on January 13, 1801. Prime Minister Pitt condemned the league for endangering "not only our character but our very existence as a maritime power."[36] Thomas Grenville, the secretary of state's younger brother, explicitly warned of the consequences if the league did not swiftly dissolve itself: "Sir Hyde Parker and Lord Nelson will be our best penitentiaries as soon as the Baltic will thaw enough to receive them."[37] Whitehall declared an embargo on all league members, effective January 14, 1801.

Although Whitehall had squared off with four countries, no one lost sight of just who was the number one enemy. George III asserted that "with such a strange character as that of the Russian Emperor, nothing can be gained but by shewing him he is not feared."[38] Foreign Secretary Grenville expressed the prevailing astonishment at Paul's behavior: "I cannot conceive how so manifest a madman can be permitted to go on even so long as he has."[39] The wish that somehow he would be deposed soon came true.

The trouble was that Russia was the league's least vulnerable member. To get to St. Petersburg a British expedition would have to run the gauntlet past the forts and fleets of Denmark, Sweden, and Prussia. Whitehall decided systematically to pick apart the league, with Denmark the first target. Grenville dispatched Charles Whitworth to Copenhagen with a diplomatic stick and carrot. He was to warn the Danes to withdraw from the league or else suffer retaliation. If the Danes stood down, he was to cut a deal that restored bilateral trade while restricting Danish trade with France. The stick was the British fleet of eighteen ships of the line and thirty-five lesser warships commanded by Admiral Hyde Parker that had conveyed Whitworth on his mission. But when at Copenhagen Whitworth made no progress during ten days of talks, he issued an ultimatum and withdrew to the fleet.

Parker was authorized to attack if talks failed, but he hesitated to assault a capital that was not only technically neutral but appeared impregnable. He summoned his captains and promised to heed their advice. Horatio Nelson sought to shame Parker into belligerence: "Here you are, with almost the safety, certainly with the honour, of England more intrusted to you than ever yet fell to the lot of any British officer. On your decision depends whether our country shall be degraded in the eyes of Europe or whether she shall rear her head higher than ever." He summed up his view with this advice: "Beat the enemy first, and negotiate afterward."[40] Parker gave in but still hoped to evade responsibility for what happened. He asked Nelson to lead the assault with ten ships of the line, two 50-guns, seven frigates, and nine bomb ketches, while he remained anchored safely in reserve north of the city with the rest of the fleet.

This appeared to be all but a suicidal mission. Copenhagen lay on the western side of the strait between Denmark and Sweden. A huge shoal split that strait into two relatively narrow, shallow channels. The Danish warships were anchored prow to stern offshore, backed by fortresses and batteries. The British could only attack the Danes from two directions, directly south down the western channel or down the eastern channel and then north around the shoal. The prevailing winds would determine the attack's direction.

Nelson took the latter route when he sailed with ten ships of the line and twenty-four smaller warships on April 2. As his flotilla approached from the south, three of his warships ran aground. Nelson aboard the 74-gun *Elephant* and the other warships sailed forward under a rain of fire from the shore batteries, fortresses, and warships. Then Nelson's *Elephant* ground to a halt on a shoal as one cannonball after another smashed into it.

A half dozen miles to the north, Parker was with the reserve squadron of eight ships of the line. His alarm worsened as Danish guns pounded Nelson's warships until finally he had a signal raised calling for a withdrawal. When an officer pointed out Parker's signal, Nelson reputedly replied: "Then damn the signal; take no notice of it, and hoist mine for closer battle." He turned to Captain Thomas Foley, his second in command, placed his spyglass to his blind eye, and quipped:

"I have only one eye—I have a right to be blind sometimes and damn me if I'll see that signal."[41] Did Nelson actually utter those celebrated remarks? Possibly. The *Elephant*'s surgeon who recorded them was below with the wounded when Nelson allegedly said them, but he may well have heard them later from someone who was actually on the quarterdeck at the time.[42]

Parker's order confused Nelson's captains. Some sailed off and others fought on. This allowed the Danes to concentrate their fire on the remaining warships. Nelson finally had his own withdrawal order hoisted. Three warships remained stranded and had to await high tide to float free. Nelson had a request for a truce and talks rowed ashore, and when the Danes agreed, the battle ended in a bloody draw. The British suffered 250 dead and 700 wounded, and the Danes possibly as many casualties.

Parker authorized Nelson to lead the diplomacy. Nelson demanded that the Danes withdraw from the league or else suffer Copenhagen's destruction. The Danes feared Russian retaliation if they did so and asked for British protection, but Nelson was not authorized to promise that. When the talks stalled, Parker had General William Stewart, who commanded the army contingent, join Nelson, and on April 9 the Danes finally agreed to a fourteen-week armistice. Nelson boasted that his threat to destroy Copenhagen had done the trick: "We wish to make them feel that we are their real friends, therefore we have spared their town, which we can always set on fire, and I do not think if we burnt Copenhagen it would have the effect of attaching them to us, on the contrary they would hate us."[43]

The next objective was Russia's Baltic fleet at Reval, and on April 12 Parker ordered his fleet to sail for that naval base. The following day electrifying news reached the fleet. On March 23 a cabal had murdered Tsar Paul and elevated his son Alexander to the throne. Meanwhile, learning of the approaching British fleet, the Russians withdrew to Kronstadt, near St. Petersburg. More good news followed. The new tsar dissolved the Leagueof Armed Neutrality on May 19. The war was over before it started for the Russians, Prussians, and Swedes; only the Danes were not spared its horrors.

Amid the Copenhagen expedition, William Pitt resigned as prime minister over a dispute with the king over what to do about Ireland.[44] He had hoped to follow the crushing of the 1798 Irish revolt with genuine reforms that might prevent future uprisings. Before the House of Commons, he expressed his vision for Ireland in the British empire: "If the Kingdoms are really and solidly united, they feel that to increase the commercial wealth of one country is . . . to increase the strength and power of both . . . if . . . Ireland is to continue [to be] for ever an essential part of the . . . British empire; if her strength is to be permanently ours, and our strength to be hers."[45] To this end, he planned a two-bill process, with the first uniting Britain and Ireland and the second freeing Catholics for worship, business, and politics.

His union plan was to dissolve Ireland's parliament and expand Britain's with Irish representatives. In all twenty-eight Irish peers and four protestant bishops would join the House of Lords; as for representation in the House of Commons, most of Ireland's rotten boroughs would be eliminated by buying them off with £1.260 million. The remaining members of Ireland's lower house would join the House of Commons by adding a hundred seats to the latter, bringing the total to 658. Britain and Ireland would also economically unify, as all restrictions on the later would be eliminated and a common market with common tariffs prevail thereafter.

Ireland's House of Commons passed the bill by 106 to 105, with a single member determining the difference between victory and defeat on January 22, 1798. The votes of those in favor may not have reflected the true feelings of those who cast them; many of those votes were blatantly bought with £30,000 in secret service funds. The bill passed more enthusiastically in Britain's House of Commons, with 158 for and 115 opposed on February 6, 1800. The Act of Union with Ireland passed both houses of Parliament in May 1800, was approved by Ireland's parliament in June, and took effect on January 1, 1801.[46]

With that done, Pitt now promoted a bill to emancipate Catholics. He insisted that for the Union to be genuine, Catholics should enjoy the same political rights as protestants. To this end, the Test Acts had to be repealed so that officeholders no longer swore allegiance to or tithed the Church of England regardless of their faith. National security was as important as natural rights in justifying that reform. He wholeheartedly agreed with General Charles Cornwallis's assessment: "Until the Catholics are admitted into a general participation of rights (which when incorporated with the British government they cannot abuse) there will be no peace or safety in Ireland."[47]

Although many people in and beyond Parliament opposed Catholic emancipation, only one had the power to crush it. George III could not have made his royal will clearer to Pitt during two previous times when the issue arose. In a 1795 letter, he condemned the idea for resulting in "a total change in the principles of government" and "overturning the fabric of the Glorious Revolution," and he insisted that "the subject is beyond the decision of any Cabinet of Ministers."[48] In 1798 he restated his indomitable position: "No further indulgences must be granted to the Roman Catholics, as no country can be governed where there is more than one established religion; the others may be tolerated, but that cannot extend further [than] to leave to perform their religious duties according to the tenets of their Church, for which indulgence they cannot have any share in the government of the State."[49]

The king was naturally enraged that Pitt and other reformers in Parliament had resurrected what he fervently believed should have been a dead issue. At his levee on January 28, 1801, he demanded of his mostly embarrassed audience: "What is the question which you are all about to force upon me? What is this Catholic Emancipation . . . that you are going to throw at my head? . . . I will tell you that I shall look on every Man as my personal Enemy who proposes that question to me."[50]

Undaunted by the king's will, Pitt forged ahead. In doing so, he miscalculated and thus mishandled the politics behind Catholic emancipation. He believed that he had enough support in the House of Commons to pass the measure, but before scheduling a vote he sought to rally every cabinet member behind it. That proved to be impossible, as Portland, Liverpool, Westmoreland, and even his own brother Chatham were adamantly opposed. Without a united front, the king would never agree to the bill.

Pitt made a final attempt to change the king's mind with a long letter he penned on January 31, 1801. In a polite reply the next day,

George III explained that his "sense of religious as well as political duty" prevented him "from discussing any proposition tending to destroy this groundwork of our happy Constitution." He then asked Pitt to postpone indefinitely the Catholic emancipation question. Finally, he implored Pitt not to resign over the matter.[51]

The king's zealous opposition to Catholic emancipation was hardened by the peculiar state of his character and health. Irascible in the best of times, stress was dragging him steadily back into madness. He bristled at what he saw as the disdain for his royal power by Pitt, Grenville, and Dundas. He increasingly longed to send them all packing. The only trouble was finding loyal, deferential, and like-minded subjects to take their places. For his next prime minister, George III did have someone in mind.

Henry Addington was bright, articulate, conscientious, and knowledgeable, and he proved to be an able Speaker of the House of Commons after succeeding William Grenville at that post in 1789[52] Like the king, he was devoted to his family and church. His most notable political flaw was that his need to be liked often prompted him to dilute or avoid tough decisions. This was fine with George III, who would supply the backbone that Addington lacked. But the final quality that attracted the king was that Addington also adamantly opposed Irish emancipation. Indeed, George III had pressured him to "open Mr. Pitt's eyes on the danger of his ever speaking to me on a subject on which I can scarcely keep my temper."[53]

Although they differed over emancipation, Pitt had been nurturing Addington as a possible successor to himself for some time. Addington later recalled that "Pitt told me as early as 1797, that I must make up my mind to take the government."[54] The prime minister sought Addington as his heir because he was at once devoted to Pitt and weak willed, and Pitt hoped to exploit these traits to rule through him.

Pitt formally resigned on February 5. The king promptly summoned Addington and asked him to form a government. Addington was reluctant and asked the king to consider much more qualified men. In a touching scene, George III implored him to "lay your hand upon your heart and ask yourself where I am to turn for support if you do not stand by me."[55] Addington finally yielded to the king's will later that day.

Pitt resigned as much from his hurt feelings as his principled stand on Catholic emancipation. He confided to George Canning, then a rising star among his followers, that he "went out, not on the Catholic Question simply as a measure in which he was opposed, but from [the] manner in which he had been opposed, and to which, if [the king] had assented, [Pitt] would as a Minister have been on a footing totally different from what he had ever before been in the Cabinet."[56]

Pitt's resignation did not take place immediately. He would retain power until Addington formed his own government. Then, on February 19, madness again gripped George III. This put a hold on everything. The crisis deepened when the king descended into a coma on March 2. The court went into its latest death watch and the cabinet into its latest debate over how to structure a regency. Yet once again the king confounded the fears of many and hopes of some when he struggled free. By March 14, he was lucid enough to take back the seals from Pitt and pass them to Addington.

One can only imagine Pitt's feelings on March 16, as he entered the House of Commons and passed the treasurer's seat to squeeze among his colleagues in the benches. He had led the government for seventeen years and eighty-five days. He was forty-one years old when he gave up power. He must have felt just as displaced that night when he went to bed in a flat off Park Place rather than Number 10 Downing Street.

Pitt may have ruefully wished that he could have shed his £46,000 worth of debts as easily as he had his power. The king sought to assuage any ill feeling between him and Pitt by offering magnanimously to pay off his debts. But Pitt respectfully declined the offer, privately fearing that to accept would render himself the royal poodle. This same fear of becoming a political prostitute caused Pitt to reject a £100,000 offer by London's rich bankers and merchants, yet desperation led him to accept a private subscription among his friends that eventually raised £11,700. This at least let him stiff-arm the most pressing of his creditors for now.[57]

Addington found Pitt a nearly impossible act to follow and never quite escaped his predecessor's daunting shadow.[58] For years he had been Pitt's devoted disciple, hanging on his every word and stance. He was well aware that his political and oratorical skills were a fraction of the master's. Addington was hardly alone in questioning his ability to be prime minister. Elizabeth Pretyman, the wife of George Pretyman, Pitt's secretary, spoke for countless politicians and well-informed Britons when she exclaimed at the news: "Addington! . . . Are you all mad?"[59]

Just forming a government was tough enough. About half the cabinet that had backed Pitt on Catholic emancipation resigned with him, and the House of Commons was split among a half dozen factions, including followers of Pitt, Addington, Canning, Grenville, Fox, and even the Prince of Wales. Somehow Addington had to forge a coalition from these rival egos and interests. Further complicating matters was the king's refusal to let Fox into any government. The breakthrough came when Grenville finally talked Robert Jenkinson, Lord Hawkesbury (later the Earl of Liverpool), into being the foreign secretary.

Addington gradually asserted himself, and the more he did, the more conflicts emerged and festered with his mentor. This turned Pitt from supporting to denigrating his former disciple. In July he condemned Addington as a man "of consuming vanity and of very slender abilities."[60] Apparently Pitt was blind to those faults when he was prime minister but awakened to them as Addington struggled to be his own man.

In 1801 Whitehall targeted Egypt for conquest from France in.[61] The expedition included 16,000 troops led by General Ralph Abercromby packed aboard eighty transports protected by twenty-two ships of the line and thirty-seven frigates led by Admiral George Keith. The armada dropped anchor in sight of Alexandria on March 2, 1801. Six days later, Abercromby led his army ashore to besiege that city. General Jacques Menou was in Cairo at the time. Learning of the invasion, he rushed most of his troops northward and launched them against the British near Alexandria on March 21. Although the redcoats repelled the French, Abercromby was among the dead. Menou withdrew with his 7,000 troops into Alexandria.

Bonaparte reacted to the British invasion by ordering Admiral Honoré Joseph Ganteaume to sail with four ships of the line and a frigate packed with 5,000 troops to reinforce Menou. The flotilla left Toulon on April 27, reached the Egyptian coast in mid-June, then turned back to Toulon in the face of Keith's superior fleet. Bonaparte reasoned that if France's fleet was too weak to drive the Royal Navy from Egypt, it might divert it. He ordered Admiral Charles Alexandre Linois to threaten Gibraltar with three ships of the line and a frigate. The result was a rare French naval victory, the capture of the British brig HMS *Speedy*, commanded by Captain Thomas Cochrane; Cochrane was later exchanged for and would avenge himself with relentless attacks against the French navy. Linois led his flotilla on to Gibraltar, which they reached on July 4. Gibraltar then had only a single British sloop in the harbor, albeit backed by the fortress's massed guns. Rather than order an attack, Linois sailed his warships to the Spanish port of Algeciras, four miles across the bay from Gibraltar.

British admiral James Saumarez and his fleet were blockading Cadiz. When word of the French flotilla reached him, he split his command, leaving three warships off Cadiz and sailing with six ships of the line against Linois. His warships closed for action on July 6. Although outgunned, the French flotilla not only repelled the British attack but captured one of Saumarez's ships of the line, causing Saumarez to withdraw his battered flotilla to Gibraltar. Linois tried to follow up his victory by sending a message to the Spanish fleet captain at Cadiz, Don Josef de Mazarredo, announcing his victory and urging him to drive off the three blockading British warships then join forces at Algeciras to attack Saumarez at Gibraltar. Mazarredo dispatched six ships of the line commanded by Admiral Don Juan de Moreno. The combined allied fleet of nine ships of the line outgunned Saumarez's five ships of the line on the night of July 12 and might have won had not tragedy struck. Captain Richard Keats aboard the 64-gun *Superb* sailed between two 112-gun Spanish warships, which belatedly opened fire after he passed and fired devastating broadsides against each other until each blew up. Meanwhile, British gunners battered and drove off the remaining allied fleet to Cadiz.

Word of that British victory crushed Menou's last hope for relief for his army stranded in Egypt. He agreed on September 2, 1801, to surrender with honors of war and passage of his army back to France. Only 13,000 French soldiers remained of the 35,000 that had landed in Egypt with Bonaparte three years earlier.

This year Britain officially lost a longstanding tug-of-war with France over Portugal. In 1793 the Portuguese had allied with Britain and Spain against France. This alliance, however, was far more symbolic than substantive. Portugal's soldiers remained in their barracks while its warships tended to flee rather than fight the French at sea. The reason was simple. Portugal faced no direct threat from France but had, for centuries, faced an existential threat from Spain. The essence of Portugal's foreign policy was to placate imperial Spain and nurture relations with Britain as a counterweight. Upon learning in July 1796 that part of the deal cut between France and Spain was to conquer and divide Portugal between them, Lisbon sent an urgent appeal to London for help. The specific requests were easy credit to borrow, enough arms for 16,000 troops, and 12,000 British redcoats to deter a Spanish invasion. Whitehall promptly responded by sending to Lisbon, by the year's end, General Charles Stuart and 6,000 troops, along with 12,000 muskets, 3,300 carbines, 1,300 pistols, 3,300 swords, and 200 tons of saltpeter. From 1798 to 1800, Britain supplied Portugal with 19,000 muskets, 1,000 carbines, 5,000 swords, and 250 tons of saltpeter. Finally, atop all that, from 1797 to 1801 Britain loaned Portugal £210,688.[62]

As this aid poured in, France upped its pressure on Lisbon to end its alliance with Britain, or else. In August 1797 the Portuguese succumbed and signed a treaty with France that required them to close their ports to British war and merchant vessels. Now it was Whitehall's turn to get tough. Prince John, the heir to the Portuguese throne and regent for his mad mother, finally agreed not to ratify the treaty but requested more money, equipment, and redcoats in return. Whitehall gave more money but had to withdraw Stuart and his small army for operations against the French in Egypt. With the British tripwire removed, the Spanish threatened invasion and the Portuguese finally succumbed. Under the Treaty of Badajoz, signed on June 6, 1801, Regent John diplomatically seesawed once again by promising to shut Portuguese ports to the British.

Nelson returned to London in May 1801 to bask in adulation for his victory at Copenhagen. The acclaim was not universal. Moralists and lampoonists attacked him for abandoning his wife and shacking up with Emma Hamilton. This and his naturally kinetic restlessness soon drove him back to war in a relentless search for more glory, which he hoped to find literally at Britain's threshold. Just across the Channel at Boulogne, a French army was massing with the mission of invading and conquering England. Nelson devised a scheme for a surprise attack on Boulogne's harbor to destroy the vessels that would convey that enemy army across the Channel. His plan got the reluctant approval of First Lord of the Admiralty John Jervis, Earl of St. Vincent, who worried that "reckless" and even "suicidal" might better than "bold" characterize the operation.

Nelson's squadron first attacked Boulogne on the night of August 3 and 4, 1801, and managed to sink a brig and three transports before withdrawing under heavy fire. He tried again on the night of August 15 and 16, this time with marines and sailors packed aboard fifty-five longboats commanded by Captain Edward Parker. The French were ready and opened a withering fire of cannon and musket shots as the raiders skimmed into the harbor, killing 44 and wounding 128, including Parker with a shattered thigh, and sinking a dozen longboats. The British rowed frenziedly to safety without having destroyed a single one of the invasion boats chained together around the harbor and on the quays.

Nelson at once accepted responsibility and bristled at the public condemnation for his bloody defeat. His mind churned with notions for burying that debacle beneath a dazzling naval victory, with his favorite an attack on Flushing, when an event rendered this all but impossible for the foreseeable future.

After Austria dropped out, the Pitt government's war-at-any-price policy seemed absurd and self defeating to Addington and his colleagues.

Britain was expending ever more blood and treasure to what end? Warring against an enemy without the means of vanquishing it was a kind of madness, especially when its leader repeatedly called for ending the fighting. The cabinet agreed to signal Bonaparte its willingness to talk. The first consul eagerly accepted.

An armistice was signed on October 1, 1801. Negotiations began in December and culminated with the Treaty of Amiens on March 23, 1802. Britain agreed to recognize France's territorial expansion to the Rhine, along with its "sister" Dutch, Swiss, Ligurian, and Cisalpine republics. Of its conquests, Britain kept Ceylon and Trinidad and returned Martinique, St. Lucia, and Tobago to France; the Cape of Good Hope and Guinea to the Netherlands; Minorca to Spain; Egypt to Turkey; Elba to Tuscany; and Malta to the Knights of St. John. France had to withdraw troops from the Kingdom of Naples and its four sister republics. Both sides had to withdraw all their forces within three months of the treaty's ratification.

The spoils of war naturally reflected the asymmetrical power between France's army and Britain's navy. The French had prevailed on land, especially when Bonaparte commanded. The British had even more decisively won the war at sea, having sunk or captured fifty French ships of the line while losing only five of their own. As with France, one man largely scored the lion's share of British victories. Admiral George Keith explained to Nelson "how very important it is that the enemy should know that you are constantly opposed to him."[63] After a brief retirement, Nelson would once again be called upon to fulfill that duty to his nation.

King George III (1738–1820), 1761–1762 (oil on canvas), by Allan Ramsay (1713–1784). 

William Pitt the Younger (1759–1806), 1805 (oil on canvas), by John Hoppner (1758–1810). Private Collection, Bridgeman Images.

Edmund Burke (1729–1797), c. 1769 (oil on canvas), by Joshua Reynolds (1723–1792). © National Portrait Gallery, London.

Henry Dundas (1742–1811), 1st Viscount Melville, c. 1810 (oil on canvas), by Thomas Lawrence (1769–1830). © National Portrait Gallery, London.

William Wyndham Grenville (1759–1834), 1st Baron Grenville, c. 1800 (oil on canvas), by John Hoppner (1758–1810). © National Portrait Gallery, London.

Horatio Nelson (1758–1805), 1797 (oil on canvas), by Lemuel Francis Abbott (1760/61-1802). © National Portrait Gallery, London.

*Battle of the Nile*, 1899 (oil on canvas), by William Lionel Wyllie (1851–1931). © Tate, London 2015.

*The Battle of Alexandria, 21 March 1801*, 1802 (oil on canvas), by Philip James de Loutherbourg (1740–1812). National Galleries of Scotland, Edinburgh.

*Battle of Trafalgar, and the Victory of Lord Nelson over the Combined French and Spanish Fleets, October 21, 1805*, 1836 (sketch), by Clarkson Frederick Stanfield (1793–1867). © Tate, London 2015.

Robert Stewart (1769–1822), 2nd Marquess of Londonderry (Viscount Castlereagh), c. 1809 (oil on canvas), by Thomas Lawrence (1769–1830). © National Portrait Gallery, London.

George Canning (1770–1827), 1825 (oil on canvas), by Thomas Lawrence (1769–1830). © National Portrait Gallery, London.

Arthur Wellesley (1769–1852), 1st Duke of Wellington, 1804 (oil on canvas), by Robert Home (1752–1834). © National Portrait Gellery, London.

*Scotland For Ever!* 1881 (oil on canvas), by Lady Butler (Elizabeth Southerden Thompson) (1846–1933). Leeds Museums and Galleries (Leeds Art Gallery) UK, Bridgeman Images.

CHAPTER 6

# The Third Coalition, 1803–1805

England expects that every man will do his duty!

Horatio Nelson

They feel they are a distinct and superior class to the rest of the world that surrounds them, and their actions correspond to their high notions of their own superiority . . . and they show in what manner nations consisting of many millions are governed by 30,000 strangers.

Arthur Wellesley

I do not say the French cannot come. I only say they cannot come by water.

John Jervis, Earl of St. Vincent

England has saved herself by her exertions, and will, as I trust, save Europe by her example.

William Pitt

The "peace" of Amiens was little more than a fourteen-month breather before the next round of war.[1] Although neither the British nor the

French wanted to resume fighting, each committed acts that made that increasingly likely. A security dilemma prevailed in which each interpreted the other's behavior as aggressive, while insisting that its own "counter" measures were purely defensive. The result was a self-fulfilling prophecy. The inability to understand let alone extract themselves from this psychological trap reflected a severe lapse in the art of power wielded in the Tuileries and Whitehall.

Napoleon Bonaparte certainly appeared oblivious to the impact of his policies across the English Channel. With his vision of Asian conquests thwarted for now, he dedicated himself to rebuilding France's New World empire. He had taken the first step secretly before the treaty of Amiens with Britain. Under the Treaty of St. Ildefonso, signed on October 1, 1800, France ceded Tuscany and Parma to Spain for the Louisiana Territory. The next step was to crush the rebellion in St. Domingue, France's most lucrative sugar-producing island, which he could freely do only after Amiens. To that end, the first consul dispatched an armada of thirty-three ships of the line, a half dozen frigates, and a hundred or so transports packed with 20,000 troops led by General Victor Emmanuel Leclerc, his brother-in-law. The result was a disaster, as yellow fever, malaria, typhoid, and rebels wiped out virtually all of these troops, including its commander. Bonaparte's New World dream had become a nightmare from which the first consul was increasingly eager to escape.

Meanwhile, the rumor that Spain had ceded the Louisiana Territory to France worried President Thomas Jefferson and his administration. A weak neighbor like Spain was not just acceptable but desirable, because the United States would eventually force Madrid to cede the Louisiana Territory and the Floridas as they filled with American settlers. But as Jefferson put it, the moment France took New Orleans, "we must marry ourselves to the British fleet and nation."[2] He dispatched James Monroe to Paris with instructions to purchase New Orleans from France. When Napoleon offered the entire Louisiana Territory, Monroe eagerly snapped it up, for $15 million, in a treaty signed on April 30, 1803.

The Louisiana Purchase crucially shifted the international distribution of power. The United States at once doubled its territory and no longer had any good reason to war against France. American foreign policy now could focus on pressuring Whitehall to revoke its Orders in Council that caused the capture of neutral ships carrying contraband war goods to Britain's enemies and the impressing of foreign sailors into the Royal Navy> The failure of first the Jefferson then Madison administrations to win these concessions would result in an American declaration of war against Britain nine years later.

Bonaparte's New World setbacks prompted him to strengthen his grip in the Old World. Rather than withdraw from the "sister republics" as required under the Amiens Treaty, he expanded his power over them. The means that he wielded were mostly behind-the-scenes political intrigues that played off factions against each other, but in Switzerland he ordered an invasion by 30,000 troops to crush a swelling anti-French political movement. He then annexed to France Piedmont and Elba in September 1802 and the Netherlands in February 1803. Meanwhile, he launched a major naval buildup with thirty-two ships of the line in construction at French ports. As disturbing in British eyes were Bonaparte's growing dictatorial powers. The legislature named him first consul for life in August 1802.

Bonaparte's swelling power warped his mind. While he violated the Amiens Treaty with impunity, he castigated the British for their own violations. On February 21, 1803, he summoned ambassador Charles Whitworth for a two-hour harangue against British perfidy and demands that Britain evacuate Malta as required by Amiens or else be responsible for renewing the war. The first consul impatiently awaited a reply, then, when he did not receive one, vented his rage at Whitworth during a reception for the diplomatic community on March 18.[3]

Whitworth's silence was not his fault. He had dutifully reported Bonaparte's demand to Whitehall, but Addington and colleagues debated for nearly two months before reaching a decision. On April 23 Foreign Minister Jenkinson instructed Whitworth to demand that Bonaparte withdraw his army from the Netherlands and Switzerland, and to inform him that Britain would retain Malta for another decade.

Bonaparte reacted to that ultimatum by having Foreign Minister Talleyrand present Whitworth diplomatic notes expressing the first consul's dismay over how the British could go to war knowing the horrendous results and calling on Whitehall to cede Malta to a joint guarantee of its independence by Russia, Prussia, and Austria. When Whitworth upheld the ultimatum, Bonaparte once again compromised—he would accept Britain's occupation of Malta for ten years in return for France's occupation of Otranto and Taranto in southern Italy for the same time. Whitworth's rejection of this offer provoked Bonaparte's latest public tirade against him. Whitworth left Paris on May 11.[4]

Although Bonaparte did not want war, at least not then, he had heedlessly played the potentially disastrous game of brinksmanship to frighten the British into ceding more to him than he ceded to them. That strategy failed, as the more threats he made, the more he bolstered the hawks against the doves in Addington's government. He was stunned to learn that George III had formally declared war against France on May 18, 1803.[5] Given the asymmetrical power between them, with Britain dominate at sea and France on land, neither could immediately inflict much harm against the other.

Bonaparte reacted to Britain's war declaration by ordering all British subjects in France arrested and all British ships and their cargoes in French ports confiscated. He banned all imports of British goods aboard neutral ships. Finally, he ordered French troops to occupy Naples, Brindisi, and Taranto in southern Italy and take over Hanover, missions that were accomplished within a few weeks. But this was all he could do to hurt Britain for now.

Whitehall swiftly reasserted its time-tested strategy of blockading enemy ports, picking off enemy colonies, cobbling together and subsidizing a coalition, and somehow raising enough money to pay for it all. This time the pieces fell into place quicker and easier than in the past. The only trouble was that France had twice defeated this now familiar formula. But what else could be done? Had Britain's leaders overlooked some potentially winning strategy?

The Royal Navy went to war with 72 ships of the line and 120 frigates compared to France's 25 ships of the line and 25 frigates, and this gap widened steadily over the next dozen years.[6] The blockading squadrons included Admirals William Cornwallis's at Brest, Cuthbert Collingwood's at Rochefort, Edward Pellew's at Ferrol, Horatio

Nelson's at Toulon, and, most importantly, the separate squadrons of James Montagu and William Sidney Smith along the stretch of coast from Boulogne to Flushing.

The army, now 94,000 men strong, took a back seat in this strategy.[7] Its only offensive role was to supply contingents for naval expeditions that sailed off to seize enemy colonies. But for the foreseeable future, the redcoats' chief task was to guard the British Isles against the remote chance of an invasion from the army that Bonaparte was massing at Boulogne and nearby ports. A successful invasion depended on the French winning control of the English Channel long enough for the army to cross over. For Bonaparte this was a dream that could never come true.

While the British played defense in Europe, they launched an offensive designed to sweep the enemy from the Caribbean. Flotillas captured the French islands of St. Lucia and Tobago in June; the Dutch colonies of Demefara, Essequibo, and Berbice in September; and Cape François and St. Nicolas Mole, the last French toeholds on St. Domingue by December. The largest British imperial gains, however, were on the far side of the world.

It was during the nineteenth century's first decade that the British expanded their three separate colonies of Bengal, Bombay, and Madras to join each other and engulf much of the Indian subcontinent.[8] The general who played the most decisive role in this triumph of British imperialism returned to Europe to command a series of campaigns that drained French power and culminated in Napoleon's final devastating defeat.

The man to be renowned as Arthur Wellesley, Duke of Wellington, was born at an unrecorded site in County Meath, Ireland, on an unrecorded date in spring 1769, and with a last name that the family later changed from Wesley to Wellesley.[9] He was the third son of a rich Anglican landowner whose ancestors had migrated to Ireland generations earlier. He was a late bloomer, overshadowed for decades by his older brothers Richard and William who excelled in politics, government, and diplomacy. He was formally educated at Eton, then at France's Royal Academy of Equitation at Angers, where he learned the rudiments of military art and science. His army career began in 1786, when his father bought him an ensign's commission, and thereafter he rose steadily through one purchased rank after another. In 1790 he was elected at age nineteen to the family seat of Trim in Ireland's parliament, and for the next three years he took a series of leaves to serve there. The year 1793 was a crucial turning point for Wellesley. Until then he had dabbled at soldiering and politics, while his most notable skill was music. But he literally burned his violin and the romanticism it symbolized when his lack of wealth forced him to break off his courtship of a rich girl he loved named Kitty Pakenham. He soon resigned his parliamentary seat and devoted himself to being the best possible soldier and officer.

As for character, Wellesley exemplified the snobbish, arrogant, aloof English aristocrat and officer. He got this from his mother, who lost no chance to denigrate him for being, in her mind, ugly, lazy, and dull, "food for powder and nothing more."[10] With such a maternal harpy it is no wonder that he was so rigid in many ways. But he would never have won greatness were he only this. He strove constantly to control not just others under his command but himself above all. He was Spartan in his habits and tastes, pushed himself to be as tough as any of his soldiers, and was a model of probity in an especially corrupt age. William Pitt was among his admirers, noting: "I have never met a military officer with whom it is so satisfactory to converse. He never . . . hides in ignorance in vague generalities. If I put a question to him he answered it distinctly; if I wanted an explanation he gave it clearly; if I desired an opinion I got from him one supported by reasons which were always sound. He states every difficulty before he undertakes any service, but never after he had undertaken it."[11] Wellesley's concept of honor compelled him to wed Kitty Pakenham in 1805, fulfilling a promise that he had made during his failed courtship of her a dozen years earlier that he would return when he could afford to provide her a life at least equal to her luxurious upbringing. It was definitely a marriage of duty rather than passion, for in the interim Kitty had, in his blunt words, "turned ugly, by Jove!"[12]

Wellesley first experienced war in June 1794 as the Thirty-third Regiment's lieutenant colonel in York's Flanders campaign. During the next half year he took priceless lessons in how not to lead and fight: "I learnt more by seeing our own faults and the defects of our system in the campaign of Holland, than anywhere else."[13] From this foundation he developed his art and science of war to ever higher levels first in India then, after a fleeting interlude in Denmark, for five continuous years in the Peninsula, and, finally, in the Waterloo campaign.[14]

The age's greatest British general attributed his military prowess to being a hands on master of detail: "The real reason why I succeeded in my own campaign is because I was always on the spot—I saw everything and did everything for myself." The man who once called his troops "the scum of the earth," toiled ceaselessly to ensure that they had the best possible nutrition, hygiene, and shelter. As for battle, "I owe most of my success to the attention I always paid to the inferior part of tactics as a regimental officer. There were few men in the Army who knew these details better than I did; it is the foundation of all military knowledge."[15] But he also knew how to delegate authority and to this end carefully selected and groomed his staff: "I assembled my officers and laid down my plan and it was carried into effect without any more words."[16]

Before sailing to retake Portugal from the French in 1808, Wellesley penned lines that captured the essence of his conception and exercise of the soft and hard dimensions of military power:

> I am thinking of the French that I am going to fight. I have not seen them since the campaign in Flanders when they were capital soldiers, and a dozen years of victory under Bonaparte must have made them better still. They have besides . . . a new system of strategy which has outmaneuvered and overwhelmed all the armies of Europe. It is enough to make one thoughtful; but no matter, my die is cast; they may overwhelm me, but I don't think they will outmanoeuvre me. First, because I am not afraid of them, as everybody else seems to be; secondly, because, if what I hear of their system of manoeuvres be true, I think it a false one as against steady troops. I suspect that all the continental armies were more than half beaten before the battle was begun. I, at least, will not be beaten beforehand.[17]

Wellesley understood how vital the soft power of psychology was in bolstering the hard power of armed men in ruling peoples and defeating enemies. In a war of imperialism, victory depended on following up the defeat of enemy armies by winning the population's hearts and minds, an impossibility if one wielded only brute force. On July 31, 1808, the eve of the army's landing in Portugal, he issued this command: "The troops are to understand that Portugal is a country friendly to his Majesty."[18]

Wellesley was ordered in April 1796 to lead his regiment to India. Illness delayed his departure, and he did not step ashore at Calcutta until February 1797. He was lucky that his older brother Richard Wellesley, then Earl of Mornington, arrived in May 1798 to be India's governor-general, accompanied by their younger brother Henry as his secretary. The three brothers would work closely together to expand the empire and enrich themselves.

Like nearly all Britons in India, Arthur Wellesley soon harbored a jaundiced view of the natives: "I have not yet met with a Hindoo who had one good quality, and the Mussulmans are worse. Their meekness and mildness do not exist. It is true that the feats which have been performed by Europeans have made them objects of fear, but wherever the disproportion of numbers is great than usual, they uniformly destroy them if they can, and in their dealings and conduct among themselves they are the most atrociously cruel people I ever heard of."[19] It was despite or more likely because of such attitudes that Wellesley was able to forge Hindus and Muslim recruits into loyal, disciplined, courageous sepoys, or native soldiers.

The worst threat to British India was Tipoo Sultan, "the Tiger of Mysore," with his capital at Seringapatam. Tipoo was determined to drive the British from the subcontinent. To this end, he signed treaties with France to receive scores of military advisers and shiploads of muskets, cannons, and munitions. General George Harris commanded the 50,000 British and native troops in India. He devised a two pronged offensive against Tipoo: Harris marched with 16,000 troops, including Wellesley and his Thirty-third Regiment from Madras, while General James Stuart led 6,000 troops from Canamore in February 1799. Tipoo hurled his men against those converging armies, but he was driven further back until he and his army's remnants holed up in Seringapatam for a last stand. The two British armies met there in early April 1799 and immediately began zigzagging trenches and batteries closer to the city's walls. After the walls were breached on May 4, Harris ordered a massed assault that slaughtered Tipoo and thousands of his troops and civilians.

Mornington rewarded his brother's role in the campaign by naming him Seringapatam's governor and commander of British forces in central India. In 1800, Wellesley marched against Dhoondiah Waugh, a Mahratta ruler, who threatened Britain's grip over Carnatic and Mysore. In the first battle under his exclusive control, he led a cavalry charge that routed the enemy at Conahgull on September 10, 1800. A peace treaty was soon negotiated between the British and the Mahrattas.

That peace lasted until 1803, when Scindiah and Bhoonslah, two Mahratta leaders, revolted against British rule. The first stage of Wellesley's campaign climaxed with the capture of the fortress of Ahmednuggur on August 12. He then marched his 9,500 troops to rout the enemy at Assaye on September 24. Wellesley later reckoned Assaye his best fought battle as he directed a series of brilliant maneuvers and attacks that devastated an army of 40,000 men, more than four times larger than his own army.[20] From there he led his men on to win the battle of Argaum on November 26 and capture the fortress of Gawilghur on December 15, victories that forced the Mahrattas to surrender.

Wellesley revealed his expanding expertise in the art of power by recognizing that a lasting peace was more likely if it were generous rather than harsh: "I am decidedly of the opinion that all animosity should be forgotten. The war will be eternal if nobody is ever to be forgiven. When the empire of the Company is so great, little dirty passions must not be suffered to guide its measures." In this he opposed the policies of his brother, who, pressured by the East India Company's board of directors, wrung as many land and trade concessions as possible from every victory over native rulers. Wellesley later complained that "the demons of ambition appear now to have pervaded all."[21]

Prime Minister Henry Addington was fumble fingered in wielding the art of power. Leading a government is like managing a team of spirited horses: it demands deftness, firmness, confidence, and a clear direction. Addington was deficient in all those skills. Atop that, his followers cringed and his opponents jeered when he debated; he was void of Fox's embracing emotionalism and Pitt's killer logic. Not surprisingly, his honeymoon in office was short. Criticisms from all directions grew more acidic, and his faction in the House of Commons steadily dwindled.

Some of the sharpest attacks came from within the cabinet as one minister after another sadly concluded that Addington was just not the man for the job. By January 1803, Grenville had written in despair to Pitt "that the government which now exists is manifestly incapable of carrying on the public business." He urged Pitt to climb back into the political center ring and put together "an administration comprehending as large a proportion as possible of the weight, talents, and character to be found in public men."[22] What Grenville had in mind was reaching across the aisle to the opposition, with the hand of Charles Fox the first to grasp.

The notion of joining forces with his most implacable foe enraged Pitt. Yet, in harshly condemning Grenville's plea, he seemed to question the character of his cousin, friend, and ally—which pushed Grenville into Fox's arms. The shock of the defection sobered Pitt. He tried to make amends with a grand concession: on second thought, perhaps bringing Fox and other opposition leaders into a grand coalition government might best serve the nation's interests after all. Although this stunning reversal relieved Grenville, relations between them had forever cooled.

Further fouling the situation was the king's relapse into madness in February 1804. Once again Britain's political elite debated whether to establish a regency and, if so, what powers to give it. And once again George III emerged from the maelstrom of his madness as suddenly as he had descended into it. By March he was lucid enough to speak with Addington and his Privy Council.

This latest crisis was Addington's breaking point. On April 29, 1804, he informed the cabinet that he would resign as soon as Parliament approved the national budget. Upon hearing that news, Pitt fired off to George III a letter in which he offered to form a government. The king was cool to the idea. He found the affable Addington far more pleasant to work with than the remote, haughty, and laser-witted Pitt. But what appalled him was Pitt's suggestion that Fox be among his ministers. Yet what else could he do? He summoned Pitt on May 6.

George III was gracious when they met. When Pitt complimented his healthy appearance, the king credited that to his relief that although he was "parting with an old friend," he was "about to regain one."[23] As for Pitt's cabinet, George was open to anyone except Fox, although he would be happy to dispatch his nemesis as the chief diplomat to some distant land.

With this go-ahead, Pitt busied himself cobbling together a cabinet. This time he would have to make do politically with far less: of all the ministers, his only firm allies were Henry Dundas, now Viscount Melville, as first lord of the admiralty, and his brother John, Earl of Chatham, as ordnance general. The rest had either distanced themselves politically or were outright rivals such as Charles, Lord Camden as secretary of state for war; Robert Stewart, Viscount Castlereagh as president of the Board of Control; Charles Jenkinson, Lord Hawkesbury as home secretary; Dudley Ryder, Earl of Harrowby, as foreign secretary; William Bentinck, Duke of Portland, as lord president; John Scott, Earl of Eldon, as lord chancellor; and John Fane, Earl of Westmoreland as lord privy seal. Mediocrity compounded the political divisions—aside from Melville, Hawkesbury, and Castlereagh, the men in these vital posts were second-stringers as thinkers and leaders. Notably missing were first-rate leaders like William Grenville; George Fox; George, Earl of Spencer; William, Earl of Fitzwilliam; and George, Earl of Gower.

That weak and split cabinet reflected the realty that Pitt himself was well beyond his zenith of political and cognitive powers; decades of eating and drinking to excess were ever more embarrassingly evident. The king gave him and his colleagues the seals of office on May 18, 1804. Pitt was just ten days shy of his forty-fifth year—and he had less than two years to live.

The symbolic timing of Pitt's comeback was appropriate. The same day that George III proclaimed Pitt his prime minister, the French Senate proclaimed Napoleon Bonaparte the emperor of France. A crucial element of the art of power is knowing one's enemy, and Pitt had no delusions about the newly minted emperor: "I see various and opposite qualities—all the great and all the little passions unfavorable to public tranquility—united in the breast of one man . . . whose caprice can scarce fluctuate for an hour without affecting the destiny of Europe."[24]

Once again, powerless to defeat France militarily, Whitehall attempted covert means of destroying Bonaparte and his regime. In early 1804 the Alien Office concocted a plan with General Georges Cadoudal and General Jean-Charles Pichegru to slip across the Channel and make their way to Paris, where they would mobilize the royalist underground led by the Institut Philanthropique's English Committee and overthrow Bonaparte in a coup. Of the officers that they hoped to enlist in that plot, General Jean Victor Moreau was the key.

Among the many ingredients for pulling off such a venture, none was more vital than secrecy and trust. These proved to be a fatal Achilles' heel for this latest Alien Office operation. Jean-Claude-Hippolyte Méhée de la Touche was among the hundreds of French refugees and would-be counterrevolutionaries who knocked on the Alien Office's door. What made Touche special was that he had defected from Joseph Fouche's police ministry and brought along a trove of secret documents. After debriefing and training him, the Alien Office sent him to join spymaster Francis Drake in Munich. Touche was actually a double agent loyal to Bonaparte's France. Although Drake never revealed to him the latest royalist conspiracy in Paris, Touche suspected something was up and sent word back to Fouche to be on guard. Fouche was actually well aware of the latest unfolding conspiracy, since he was part of it.[25]

Fortunately for Bonaparte, he did not have to rely solely on Fouche for the security of himself and France. Shortly after taking power, he had set up an alternative internal security system led by Paris police chief Louis Nicolas Dubois. Starting in February 1803, Dubois's men arrested a series of royalists linked with the 1800 Christmas Eve bomb-cart assassination attempt against Bonaparte, with the interrogation of each suspect leading to more arrests, culminating with that of Jean Talon, who headed the Institut Philanthropique's English Committee on September 25, 1803.

Upon learning of these arrests, the Alien Office should have instantly canceled the coup plan, but it failed to do so. In January 1804 Cadoudal, Pichegru, and a half dozen underlings reached Paris and disappeared into the underground. They did not stay hidden for long: the police systematically arrested and interrogated more links in the network until prisons swelled with 356 suspects, including Pichegru, Cadoudal, and Moreau. Pichegru committed suicide; Cadoudal was among the dozen plotters sentenced to death; Moreau got off with a two-year sentence but was later released into permanent exile; several score lesser figures received long prison terms.

Bonaparte naturally was furious to learn that Britain had bankrolled, organized, and launched this latest attempt to murder him. Among the bits of information gleaned from interrogations of the conspirators was that an unnamed nobleman lurked in a neighboring country to take power after Bonaparte was deposed. In running down a list of suspects, one stood out. Louis Antoine, duc d'Enghien was an unabashed royalist who had served with the prince de Condé's army of exiles before settling into a palace in Ettenheim, Baden, just across the Rhine River. What was unknown in Paris was that he had turned down efforts, most notably by William Wickham, to talk him into seconding Charles, comte d'Artois, as a counterrevolutionary leader.

After consulting with his key advisers, Bonaparte ordered a rendition operation that nabbed Enghien on March 15 and brought him back to Vincennes castle on the edge of Paris. Then Bonaparte made a fateful decision. He agreed with a majority of his advisers that a military commission should try Enghien on charges of treason and, if he was found guilty, order his execution. A firing squad killed Enghien before dawn on March 20.

Word of the execution lost Bonaparte what little sympathy he might have garnered for the aborted coup attempt. Most people were appalled at what they saw as the rigged trial and cold-blooded murder of an innocent man. Yet, although St. Petersburg, Vienna, and Berlin were among the governments that protested Enghien's fate, they stayed on the sidelines in the war between Britain and France.

Far more disturbing to most of Europe's royal heads was the Senate's unanimous vote on May 18, 1804, that declared Napoleon Bonaparte to be France's emperor. This provoked Alexander to edge closer to war. He talked Frederick William, then Francis, into signing treaties in May and November 1804, that respectively bound Prussia and Austria in defensive alliances with Russia. Yet the tsar's antipathy toward Britain, especially its blockade against France that inevitably damaged Russian trade, kept him from seeking a similar defensive alliance with London.

Whitehall was determined to assert the full span of its naval power regardless of the diplomatic consequences. As 1804 dawned, the Royal Navy numbered 88 ships of the line, 128 frigates, and 189 smaller warships, several times more than the French vessels in each category. The largest fleets were Admiral William Cornwallis's 33 ships of the line blocking Brest, Admiral George Keith's 21 ships of the line blockading the stretch of English Channel from Boulogne to Flushing, and Admiral Horatio Nelson's 13 ships of the line off Toulon.[26] Elsewhere, British expeditions captured Goree on the Senegal River on March 7 and Surinam on May 5.

Nelson typically conducted a distant blockade by screening Toulon with frigates and stationing his five ships of the line in an arc far out to sea. By doing so, he hoped to lure out Toulon's fleet commander, Admiral Louis-René Latouche-Tréville. The French commander took the bait of an open sea and sailed forth with eight ships of the line on June 15, 1804. Nelson soon learned of the sortie and launched his squadron in pursuit. Upon sighting Nelson's flotilla, Larouche-Tréville ordered his captains to reverse course back to Toulon, despite outnumbering Nelson.

Ironically, Britain struck the war's first decisive blow against a neutral country rather than France. Word reached Whitehall that four Spanish vessels packed with silver and gold from the New World were sailing across the Atlantic. Pitt and his cabinet debated whether to seize this treasure from a country with whom their nation was at peace. In this case, the need for cash trumped the need to uphold national honor, so on September 18, 1804, four frigates commanded by Captain Graham Moore received an order to capture or destroy the Spanish flotilla. Miraculously, somehow in that vast ocean, the British intercepted and attacked the Spanish on October 5. During the battle, one treasure ship blew up and sank into the ocean's depths. This prompted the other three vessels to strike their colors and yield over £1 million in prize money.

Charles IV reacted with a diplomatic protest and demand for compensation. When Whitehall ignored this demand, the king finally and reluctantly declared war on Britain on December 12, 1804. After waiting weeks, hoping vainly that the British might offer some concession so Spain could sidestep war, Charles reluctantly agreed to a treaty of alliance with France, signed on January 4, 1805. He and his government reasoned it would be less costly to fulfill its alliance duties to France with money than men and so promised annually to pay France 72 million francs. The treaty's most important clause gave France control over Spain's navy. This could lead to a mortal threat to Britain if France's then forty-three ships of the line combined with Spain's twenty-nine and somehow massed them in the English Channel. The Royal Navy then numbered about eighty operational ships of the line. In all, Napoleon could not have been happier with the terms of his alliance with Spain.[27]

The unprovoked British attack and seizure of Spain's treasure flotilla infuriated Tsar Alexander. Yet, after months of debating with his advisers over what to do, he finally reasoned that Britain's threat to Russian interests was not as menacing as that of France's. The most recent event that the tsar used to justify this belief happened on October 24, when French troops marched into Hamburg to seize George Rumbold, Britain's envoy there, and all his papers. Napoleon ordered the operation after learning that Rumbold was part of the espionage network operated by Francis Drake in Munich. The French released Rumbold a few days later without his papers, Napoleon reasoning that surely violating Hamburg's neutrality and Rumbold's diplomatic immunity was petty compared to Britain's attack on neutral Spain's treasure fleet that led to a sunk Spanish frigate, hundreds of Spanish deaths, and the capture of three Spanish frigates and £1 million's worth of prize money. This was certainly how Frederick William III, the king of neighboring Prussia, responded, agreeing with Foreign Minister Charles Augustus, Prince von Hardenberg that one does not go to war for "a box of papers."[28] Maybe so, but this was not how the tsar reacted.

Alexander was looking for an excuse to launch a diplomatic initiative with Britain, and the Rumbold incident served this end. He sent Nicholas Novosiltsev to join ambassador Simon Vorontsov in London in December 1804, to discuss a possible alliance and subsidies with Pitt and his ministers. The envoys explained that the tsar would openly join Britain against France only if Whitehall forged and subsidized an alliance among the four great powers—Britain, Russia, Austria, and Prussia—whose combined military power would be great enough to crush even Napoleon. Pitt agreed that such a coalition would be ideal but would take time to construct. Russia could accelerate that process if it declared war and joined Britain, and these acts in turn might well boost the confidence in Vienna and Berlin high enough that they joined the coalition. But the tsar refused to commit Russia without a treaty binding all four great powers in a coalition underwritten by Britain. So for now the diplomacy stalemated.

The New Year of 1805 opened with an artfully designed peace message from Emperor Napoleon I to King George III that echoed many of the sentiments and themes of his previous effort in December 1799. He appealed mostly to the king's heart, lamenting the wars between France and Britain over the centuries that had "shed blood so futilely" and "destroyed our finances." He called on the king to listen to the appeal of humanity and reason for peace.[29]

Once again, Pitt and his colleagues chose to snub both the protocol and substance of Napoleon's plea for peace. The emperor waited impatiently in vain for a response from his fellow monarch. Instead, on January 14, Foreign Secretary Mulgrave sent a letter to Foreign Minister Talleyrand, icily rejecting any notion of negotiations.[30]

Pitt recommitted Britain to a total war that destroyed Napoleon and revolutionary France. He revealed his grand strategy to this end later that month in a report, partly titled "The Restoration of Peace," that he wrote and submitted to the cabinet in January 1805.[31] After crushing France and reducing it to its pre-1789 frontier, Europe's great powers would thereafter work closely together to keep the peace by resolving conflicts through diplomacy. A decade later the Concert of Europe would be founded on this idea.

Pitt introduced the Force Bill, which empowered him to reorganize and aggrandize the army. Though the bill passed by 265 to 223 votes on June 18, 1804, the size of the opposition against such a vital measure in wartime revealed the fragility of Pitt's coalition. It was payback time for Addington against Pitt, who had blistered him with criticism before finally pushing him from power. Addington had his faction pointedly vote against the man who he had once adored and now loathed.

Pitt eventually enticed Addington back into his camp, but it took some doing. In December 1804, wielding Hawkesbury as a go-between, he met with Addington and reknit a relationship. Horse trading rather than sentiment, however, were now the most crucial bonds, and Pitt went to the king with a special request. On January 14, 1805, George III named Addington Viscount Sidmouth and appointed him lord president of the council.

This addition to his cabinet only slightly lightened Pitt's burden of governing. During his previous time in power, assembling a majority behind a bill had rarely been easy, but now every vote was preceded by a prolonged, often acrimonious struggle to entice supporters, and politics were steadily fragmenting.[32] Now five factions, led by Pitt, Fox, Grenville, Addington, and the crown prince, vied for power, with none commanding numbers remotely close to a majority. One anonymous politician captured the political flux. When asked in 1801 whether he was a Pittite or a Foxite, he explained that the choice was not so clear cut: "We knew what we were about but now the main armies are broke down into independent corps, and each has its own discipline, we know not how to handle our votes, shoulder our consciences, or where to look for the word of command."[33]

Atop this, Pitt had lost the political finesse of his younger years as prime minister. Like Napoleon and countless others, power went to his head. For instance, he confronted the king over an issue that should have been of peripheral attention, let alone importance, to Britain's war leader. John Moore, the archbishop of Canterbury and head of the Anglican Church, died on January 18, 1805. The king wanted to replace him with Manners Sutton, the bishop of Norwich. Pitt, however, insisted that his friend George Pretyman Tomline, the bishop of

St. Paul's Cathedral, was more qualified. George III rejected Pitt's proposal. An enraged Pitt insinuated that he would resign if he did not get his way, but the king held firm. A shouting match flared then subsided as Pitt backed off with apologies. But the damage in the relationship between them was irreparable.[34]

Then Pitt's cabinet suffered a blow with accusations that Henry Dundas, Viscount Melville, and several underlings had misappropriated funds. The House of Commons formed an investigative committee. The evidence appeared damning, and Pitt accepted his old friend's resignation on May 6, 1805. Melville eventually won acquittal, but only after a long trial that began in April 1806 and ended in June 1807. Before that final vindication, his fortune and reputation were ruined.

Then, in May 1805, Pitt himself came under scrutiny for alleged fiscal impropriety, and he appointed a committee to investigate. The committee found some questionable entries in the Treasury books but not enough for criminal charges. Honest mistakes in mathematics rather than venality most likely explained the discrepancy. Indeed, Pitt was noticeably declining in his powers of patience, attention to detail, and memory. On July 7 a majority in the House of Commons voted to mildly censure him.[35]

Those scandals could not have come at a worse time. Once again the most crucial immediate need was raising enough money to pay for the latest war. Addington's government had revoked the income tax in 1802, and Pitt had to reimpose that and an array of other taxes as the budget soared from £12,350,600 in 1804 to £18,864,000 in 1805.[36]

This money was crucial as Whitehall sought to shore up and expand the coalition. St. Petersburg was now seen as the linchpin of an alliance with Vienna and Berlin. It was assumed that the Austrians and Prussians would join the coalition if presented with enough British gold and Russian troops. To this end, Foreign Secretary Henry Phipps, Earl of Mulgrave met repeatedly with Russian minister Simon Vorontsov in London and sent a draft treaty of alliance and proposals for crushing the French empire and reconstructing Europe to British minister George Leveson, Earl of Gower in St. Petersburg.

Typically the Russians were tough and canny bargainers. They had good reason to be so. Britain's expansion of power worried them as much as Russia's expansion of power worried the British. They insisted that any peace treaty must include Britain restoring all its conquests, ceding Malta to Russia, and lifting its restrictions on Russian vessels carrying goods to British ports. Gower conceded these points. In addition, Britain would subsidize Austria and Russia with £3.5 million split between them in proportion to the 250,000 and 112,000 troops each respectively fielded. He and Foreign Minister Nicolas Novosiltsev drew up and signed a provisional treaty on April 11, 1805.[37] News that Napoleon had been crowned king of Italy on May 26 and had annexed the Ligurian Republic to France on June 6, cinched the deal. Alexander eagerly exchanged ratifications with Gower on July 28, 1805.

Count Phillip Johann von Stadion, Austria's ambassador at St. Petersburg, protested when he learned the details of this deal supposedly cut on Austria's behalf. He demanded £4 million for Austria, of which £3 million must be paid immediately. Gower rejected this amount as impossible, then offered £1,666,665 to help jump-start Austria's campaign. Stadion dismissed this as far too little and insisted on his original demand. The stalemate persisted another four months until Stadion finally accepted Gower's offer and signed an agreement on August 9, 1805.[38]

Ferdinand IV had joined Britain's payroll in 1803, when he gratefully received £170,000. To get the king's attention, Whitehall slightly dropped the subsidy to £150,000 in 1804, then, in June, offered to double that year's amount if the Kingdom of the Two Sicilies openly joined the coalition. Ferdinand explained that for him to do so would be suicidal, with 20,000 French troops occupying strategic ports in his realm, including Taranto, Otranto, Brindisi, and even his capital of Naples. For now he could only secretly palm British gold and dream of one day routing the French from his land.

Whitehall also sought to bring Sweden into the coalition, a mission that demanded delicate diplomacy. Gustavus IV was a very addled king, bloated with a volatile brew of paranoia, power, and pride. Yet he had his calm and lucid moments when he recognized that Sweden was far better off fighting with rather than against Britain. Nelson's crushing of the Danish fleet in 1801 had been a sobering spectacle from neighboring Sweden. The Swedes naturally feared that a British fleet could sail to Stockholm to sink their fleet and reduce the city to rubble, and they were only slightly less fearful of Russian and Prussian aggression from just across the Baltic Sea basin. The Swedish provinces of Pomerania in northern Germany and the island of Rutland would be easy pickings.

So Gustavus agreed to open talks with British ambassador Henry Pierrepont in August 1804. It took five months to cut a deal. Pierrepont offered Gustavus £60,000 a month if he let the British military use Pomerania as a base and opened Stralsund to British merchants. The king was willing to do so, but for £2 million a year, he would also lend Britain 25,000 troops. Pierrepont explained that for now Britain only needed the base and market. The king finally succumbed and on December 3, 1804, ratified a treaty based on Pierrepont's original proposal, but as 1805 unfolded, the king's troop offer appeared more appealing to Whitehall. On August 31, 1805, Pierrepont got Gustavus to accept a treaty whereby Sweden supplied Britain with 12,000 troops for £150,000 a year. The king soon believed that he had struck a bad deal, and demanding more subsidies, on October 3, 1805, he agreed to Pierrepont's offer of £62,500 to initiate the troop transfer and £50,000 to upgrade Stralsund's fortress.[39]

If Prussia joined Britain, Russia, and Austria in the alliance, France's defeat was likely if not certain. Whitehall authorized Francis Jackson, Britain's minister at Berlin, to offer Frederick William III £1.25 million if he joined 100,000 Prussia troops to the coalition. The king's council split between Kurt von Haugwitz, who insisted that Prussia must strictly uphold its neutrality, and Charles Augustus, Prince von Hardenberg, who just as adamantly implored the king to join the coalition. This posed a painful dilemma for the king, notorious for being weak willed and vacillating. After pondering the choice for days, he typically decided that inaction was the lesser evil. After getting this disappointing news, Pitt sent Dudley Ryder, Earl of Harrowby, to Berlin with an offer of £2.5 million for 100,000 troops to join the coalition or £1.25 million to offer Napoleon mediation that, if spurned, would trigger Prussia to declare war against France.[40]

Napoleon meanwhile lined up his own allies. Although Frederick William played just as hard to get with him as he did with the coalition partners, the emperor was able to entice other German leaders that feared Austria far more than France. He ratified treaties of alliance signed with Bavaria on August 24, Baden on September 5, and Wurttemberg on October 5, along with a treaty of neutrality with the Kingdom of the Two Sicilies on September 21, 1805.

The coalition partners devised a strategy to assault Napoleon's empire initially on three fronts. The main effort would be in southern Germany, where a combined Austrian and Russian army would either invade eastern France or defeat an attack by Napoleon if he marched with his army from Boulogne. Austrian general Karl Mack would secure that region by overrunning Bavaria with 40,000 troops, then await 150,000 Austrian and 100,000 Russian reinforcements. Meanwhile, Archduke Charles with 50,000 troops would invade the Kingdom of Italy. Finally, 16,000 Russian and several thousand British troops would land at Stralsund, Pomerania to march with Sweden's 25,000 troops against the French.

The plan suffered several flaws. Each ally failed to muster its promised quota of troops and to get what troops it did muster to the front on time; indeed the Stralsund expedition did not land until after the French had decisively defeated the allies on the other fronts. Also, these armies were so spread out that coordinating them was impossible. Finally, these coalition troops were a very long way from France, so any victories would probably not be decisive in defeating Napoleon's empire.

Napoleon, meanwhile, was unaware of these plans and remained bound by the logic that the only way for France to defeat Britain was to conquer it. To this end, he massed ever more forces in camps along a stretch of the English Channel centered around Boulogne until, by August 1805, there were 165,000 soldiers, 40,000 horses, and 400 cannons. To convey this army across the English Channel, he ordered built several thousand boats in four classes with each carrying a different load of sailors, troops, supplies, and cannons; other craft were designed to carry horses. His army could only reach English soil if the French navy controlled the Channel during its crossing. This meant that the French squadrons in Brest, Rochefort, Toulon, and lesser ports somehow had to break through the British blockades, unite in the Channel, and hold that narrow passage long enough for the army's passage.[41]

Two flaws rendered this mission all but impossible. The second-, third-, and fourth-class vessels that were supposed to carry most of the army to the conquest of England were not seaworthy, since they lacked keels and were shallow draft. That invasion army would need an extremely rare calm Channel day for the crossing. The second unlikely event was that enough French and Spanish ships of the line had to break out of their blockaded ports, mass in the Channel, and keep the British navy at bay until Bonaparte and his army were safely ashore. Britain's naval commanders were well aware of these debilitating French weaknesses. While some were worried about a French invasion, John Jervis, Earl of St. Vincent, the first lord of the admiralty, was unflappable: "I do not say the French cannot come. I only say they cannot come by water."[42]

The alliance with Spain bolstered the odds of that plan succeeding, however. Under the treaty signed on January 4, 1805, Spain made the extraordinary concession of ceding control of its navy to France. Napoleon launched the campaign to dominate the English Channel during the month of negotiations leading to the alliance. His plan was ingenuous, ambitious, and, typically, changed with circumstances until eventually there were five versions. The essence, however, remained constant. The first stage was to confound and disperse the British fleets in wild goose chases. One fleet of five ships of the line led by Admiral Edouard-Thomas de Missiessy at Rochefort was to sail directly to the Caribbean, while two others, those of Admirals Honoré Joseph Ganteaume with twenty-one ships of the line at Brest, and Pierre Charles Villeneuve with eleven ships of the line at Toulon, were to break through the British blockades of Ferrol and Cadiz, respectively, unite with the Spanish fleets there, then sail westward. The three fleets were to rendezvous at Martinique. Then, after much of Britain's naval power was massed in the West Indies, the allied fleet of over fifty ships of the line was to recross the Atlantic to wedge itself in the English Channel and guard the passage of the French army to Dover.[43]

Nature, incompetence, and cowardice fouled Napoleon's grand strategy. Villeneuve's cruise was short lived; a punishing gale forced him back to Toulon to repair his vessels. Ganteaume's fleet sailed only a few days before encountering Admiral Alan Gardner's twenty-four ships of the line; the admiral ordered his captains to hurry back to the safety of Brest. Missiessy, however, reached the West Indies, where a storm damaged many of his vessels. Fearful that he would be trapped by a superior British fleet, he had his men make hasty repairs then sail back to Rochefort. Villeneuve did not put to sea again until March 30, but this time he fulfilled his mission of scattering the blockade of Cadiz and sailing with the Spanish fleet commanded by Admiral Frederico Gravina to Martinique. Upon arriving there, he found not Missiessy but new orders from Napoleon. His first duty was to capture the British garrison atop Diamond Rock, which he accomplished. He then was to sail to Ferrol, liberate the Spanish fleet there, head to Brest to join forces with Ganteaume, and, finally, his massive fleet was to plug the English Channel as Napoleon's army crossed to conquer Britain.[44]

Villeneuve's twenty ships of the line were a hundred miles west of Finisterre when Admiral Robert Calder and his fifteen ships of the line intercepted them on July 22. Although his fleet outgunned Calder's, Villeneuve ordered his captains to evade rather than engage. As the British battered two Spanish warships into striking their colors, the rest of the allied warships sailed safely to Vigo, then Ferrol. Upon learning of these events, Napoleon dashed off orders for Villeneuve to drive off the blockading fleet, join forces with Ganteaume at Brest, then seize the Channel.[45] Fearing that if he did so, he would sail to his destruction by a superior British fleet, Villeneuve instead headed south to Cadiz, where he arrived on August 22.

Meanwhile, where were Nelson and his eleven ships of the line? Villeneuve had exposed not once but twice the downside of the distant blockade so favored by Nelson. The strategy of keeping just a few frigates to watch a port and most of the fleet far beyond the horizon can certainly tempt an enemy fleet to sail forth. Ideally, the frigates then would shadow the enemy while sending smaller vessels with word of its movements to the main fleet, which would pursue and close for a battle of annihilation. But Villeneuve twice managed to evade the frigates and leave Nelson perplexed. Valuable weeks were lost until Nelson finally learned that Villeneuve had sailed for the West Indies, and he sailed in pursuit. He reached the West Indies in late June just as Villeneuve was heading east. Once again Nelson lost crucial time as he searched in vain for Villeneuve. He recrossed the Atlantic and reached Gibraltar on July 19. There he stepped ashore for the first time in twenty-two months. And there he remained until he received word that Villeneuve was holed up in Ferrol. With the French and Spanish fleets all corked in ports, Nelson reckoned he could finally take a well-deserved leave with his beloved Emma in England.

It was on September 13, 1805, that Britain's two greatest military leaders of that era met briefly for the first and last time. Wellington left an insightful account into both their characters:

> Lord Nelson was in different circumstances, two quite different men as I myself can vouch, although I only saw him once in my life . . . for perhaps an hour . . . [at] the Colonial Office. . . . He could not know who I was, but entered at once into conversation with me, if I can call it conversation, for it was about himself . . . in a style so vain and silly as to surprise and almost disgust me. I suppose something that I happened to say may have made him guess that I was somebody, and he went out of the room for a moment . . . no doubt to ask . . . who I was, for when he came back he was altogether a different man. . . . All that I had though a charlatan style had vanished, and he talked of this country and . . . of affairs on the Continent with a good sense and a knowledge of subjects both at home and abroad . . . he talked like an officer and a statement . . . I don't know that I ever had a conversation that interested me now . . . luckily I saw enough to be satisfied that he was really a very superior man.[46]

As Napoleon prepared to invade England, he kept glancing eastward over his shoulder at Prussia and Austria, and far beyond them at Russia. The ultimate nightmare scenario would be for these three to ally with Britain against him. In August the emperor began stockpiling supplies on routes leading to the heart of Germany just in case. This nightmare was partly realized when Napoleon learned that General Karl Mack and 42,000 Austrian troops had invaded Bavaria on September 8.

Napoleon devised and launched a plan to quick-march seven infantry corps and one cavalry corps from the English Channel to the Danube River valley to cut off and destroy Mack's army before reinforcements arrived. The plan worked nearly perfectly. The surrender of Mack with 25,000 men at Ulm, on October 17, brought to 40,000 the total number of Austrian troops so far captured or killed by the French. After detaching a corps southward to attack Archduke John's army in the Tyrol, Napoleon then raced the rest of his army east down the Danube valley. As the Austrian and Russian armies retreated hastily before the onslaught, they lost thousands of men to battle and exhaustion along the way before finally halting at Olmutz, in Moravia, where the forces concentrated. Meanwhile, on November 12, French troops marched into an undefended Vienna.

None of these dazzling victories would have been possible had Prussian king Frederick William III not sat uneasily on the sidelines and resisted the urging of Francis and Alexander to join them. Meanwhile, in northern Italy, Marshal André Masséna defeated Archduke Charles's army and marched toward Vienna. However, any lingering elation from his brilliant string of victories dissipated on November 18, when Napoleon learned that the Royal Navy had inflicted a crippling defeat on the Franco-Spanish fleet near a cape at Spain's southwestern-most coast named Trafalgar.

Nelson enjoyed only twenty-five days of leave in England before he sailed with the *Victory* toward his final command, victory, and immortality. With the *Victory*'s arrival on September 26 at the fleet hovering off Cadiz, the ships of the line numbered twenty-three. Four more ships of the line would soon arrive.

Napoleon naturally was furious when he learned that Villeneuve had disobeyed his orders and sailed south to Cadiz rather than north to Brest. In September, he sent new orders to Villeneuve to sail into the Mediterranean to Italy's western coast and cooperate with the army in conquering the Kingdom of Naples. The following day he issued an order replacing Villeneuve with François Etienne de Rosily-Mesros as the fleet's commander. Villeneuve, who opened the first order on September 27 and heard rumor of the second and Rosily's presence at Madrid on October 11, made haste to be at sea before he got the official order to relinquish his command. His fleet cleared Cadiz's harbor on October 20.[47]

Nelson's fleet of twenty-seven ships of the line with 17,000 sailors and 2,148 cannons intercepted Villeneuve's thirty-three ships of the line, eighteen French and fifteen Spanish, with 30,000 sailors and 2,568 cannons off Cape Trafalgar, thirty miles southwest of Cadiz on October 21. Nelson was undaunted by these numerical odds. He knew that his captains and men would exceed the enemy in seamanship, gunnery, and courage. Nelson split his warships into two nearly equal columns and led one toward the enemy's center, while Admiral Cuthbert Collingwood closed with the other against the enemy's rear. As his fleet sailed to battle, this message in signal flags was hoisted: "England expects that every man will do his duty!"[48]

Nelson's fleet devastated the enemy, capturing or destroying eighteen warships, inflicting 6,953 casualties, and capturing 20,000 sailors. In the pursuit over the next several days, the British captured another seven ships of the line, bringing the total to twenty-five of the thirty-three present at the start of the battle. The victory cost the British 1,690 killed and wounded but no warships, although eight were battered so badly they had to be towed to a safe port. Britain's worst loss was Nelson, who received a mortal wound from a sharpshooter. He muttered these immortal last words: "Thank God I have done my duty."[49]

Word of this stunning victory reached London on November 7. An exuberant crowd unhitched the horses from Pitt's carriage and pulled it through the streets to Parliament. There, in a speech before the Commons, Pitt at once celebrated that victory and placed it a broader context of Britain's nearly nonstop sacrifices over a dozen years against France: "England has saved herself by her exertions, and will, as I trust, save Europe by her example."[50]

The next phase of Napoleon's campaign was as decisive as it was short. After Francis spurned his offer to negotiate a peace treaty,

Napoleon advanced his army into Moravia, encamped much of it around the village of Austerlitz, and made it appear to visiting allied envoys that he was going into winter quarters. Francis and Alexander launched their combined army of 85,400 troops against Napoleon's 66,800 troops on December 2. After his troops blunted that assault, Napoleon launched a counterattack that smashed through the center of the allied line and routed the enemy. During the Battle of Austerlitz and the pursuit, the French killed or captured nearly 27,000 allied troops while suffering 9,000 casualties.

Napoleon was savoring his victory when he was furious to learn that a new allied front had opened against him. Ferdinand IV and Marie Caroline played a double game that they ultimately lost. The queen was the royal couple's backbone, constantly prodding her husband to drive the French from their realm. More than nationalism motivated Marie Caroline: she hated the French revolutionaries for guillotining her younger sister, Queen Marie Antoinette. On September 10 Ferdinand secretly agreed to permit a Russian expedition to land 25,000 at Naples to join forces with his Neapolitan troops against the French. The trouble was that 20,000 French troops already occupied key ports in his realm, including Naples, but Ferdinand got rid of them with a few strokes of his pen on October 8, when he ratified a treaty with France pledging to remain neutral if Napoleon withdrew his troops to join his armies far to the north.

As the last French troops left his kingdom, Ferdinand passed word to the allies that the coast was clear. An army that included 7,350 Russians and a few hundred Greeks led by General Peter von Lacy, and 6,000 British led by General James Craig, disembarked at Naples on November 20. The Russian contingent was far short of the 25,000 troops that Alexander had promised. Sickness soon dwindled the allied ranks to about 8,000 healthy troops, and they did not linger long. Lacy and Craig got ever colder feet with reports of the string of crushing French victories culminating with Austerlitz. It was only a matter of time before Napoleon launched a campaign to overrun the Kingdom of the Two Sicilies and vent his wrath at the king and queen who had betrayed him. In mid-January 1806, Lacy withdrew with his troops to Corfu and Craig with his to Malta, leaving behind Ferdinand

and Marie Caroline to be defended by their 22,000 second-rate troops. Word that a 41,000-man French army led by Marshal André Masséna had invaded the kingdom on February prompted the king, queen, and their entourage to cram aboard ships and flee to their palace in Palermo, Sicily. The Neapolitan army swiftly capitulated and after French troops secured Naples, Joseph Bonaparte, Napoleon's older brother, arrived and had himself declared king. French divisions fanned out to occupy southern Italy, and to complete the conquest, all that remained was for the French to invade and overrun Sicily.[51]

The other British expedition also failed miserably. The plan was for an Anglo-Russian army to land at Stralsund, Pomerania, and there join a Swedish army promised by Gustavus IV. Whitehall changed the mission to Hanover both because it was the king's ancestral home and the port of Bremen was much closer to Britain. The first contingent of British troops sailed on November 5, with others following over the next three weeks. When a gale sank several transports and drowned 2,000 troops, the remnants returned to port. The expedition sailed again on December 22, and this time it disembarked in Hanover only to learn of Austerlitz and the subsequent peace treaties. The troops packed up and sailed for home.

After Austerlitz, Alexander withdrew his army on the long road back to Russia and Francis asked Napoleon for a truce. An armistice was signed on December 6, and peace talks opened. The terms that Napoleon imposed on Austria with the Treaty of Pressburg on December 26 were as harsh as the terms of his previous treaties of Campo Formio in 1797 and Luneville in 1801 were lenient. The emperor reasoned that a lasting peace could only come if Austria were weakened to the point where it was incapable of launching another aggressive war against France, as it had in 1792, 1799, and 1805. He rewarded his allies by aggrandizing Bavaria and Wurttemberg with territory at Austria's expense and converting their grand dukes into kings. He did the same with Baden, promoting its duke to a grand duke. He pressured Prussia to ally with France in a treaty signed on December 15. Russian envoys did not attend the negotiations let alone sign a treaty, but although France and Russia remained technically at war, they had no means of striking each other. In all, Napoleon decisively shifted

Central Europe's balance of power in France's favor with treaties that diminished Austria's territory and army; expanded the territories of Bavaria, Wurttemberg, and Baden as French allies; and enlisted Prussia as a French ally.

Upon learning of Napoleon's triumphs, Pitt allegedly pointed to a map of Europe and said, "Roll up that map. It will not be wanted these ten years." While historians dispute that story's veracity, the heartbreak of that crushing news undoubtedly hastened Pitt's demise.[52] Decades of heavy drinking and eating, and the stress of leading Britain at war finally caught up to him. Pitt died at age forty-six on January 23, 1806, done in by some toxic mix of peptic ulceration of his stomach, cirrhosis of the liver, kidney failure, and uremia, a pernicious version of gout. His last words were: "Oh, my country! How I leave my Country!"[53]

CHAPTER 7

# The Fourth Coalition, 1806–1807

We have now what we have had once before and once only, a maritime war in our power—unfettered by any consideration of whom we may annoy—or whom we may offend—And we have . . . determination to carry it through.

George Canning

Our interest is that till there can be a final settlement that shall last, everything should remain as unsettled as possible: That no usurper should feel sure of acknowledgement; no people confident of their new miseries; no kingdom sure of its existence; no spoliator secure of his spoil; and even the plundered not acquiescent in their losses.

George Canning

We are hated throughout Europe and that hate must be cured by fear.

George Canning

Pitt's death led to a coalition government known as the Ministry of All Talents, whose inner cabinet included William Grenville as first lord of the treasury and prime minister, Charles Fox as foreign secretary, Henry Petty as chancellor of the exchequer, and William

Windham as secretary for war. Grenville was a fine choice to head the government.[1] He had an outstanding resume, having served as Ireland's chief secretary in 1782 and 1783, home secretary from 1789 to 1791, and the foreign secretary and leader of the House of Lords from 1791 to 1801. Like his cousin William Pitt, he was an Oxford graduate who entered Parliament in 1782. He also shared his cousin's penchant for being haughty and aloof, although he lacked Pitt's rapier-edged wit and, fortunately, his gluttony and alcoholism. He was a devoted husband and father, who hurried home as soon as his long day's work was done. Finally, he had a fine mind for numbers, which he would put to good use at the treasury.

Yet all the sharp minds and stiff backbones of Grenville and his colleagues faced an impossible duty for the foreseeable future. Shorn of viable allies, how could Britain stop, let alone destroy, Napoleon and his swelling empire? After prolonged debate, Whitehall resumed the shopworn strategy of nibbling around the edges of French power. George Canning bluntly explained British power and strategy: "We have now what we have had once before and once only, a maritime war in our power—unfettered by any consideration of whom we may annoy—or whom we may offend—And we have . . . determination to carry it through."[2]

Complicating this already challenging strategy was Prussia's conversion from a fence-sitter to an outright enemy. Frederick William III's Hamlet-like indecision during autumn 1805 over whether to join the allies undercut the military campaign of Austria and Russia and ultimately led him to sign the Treaty of Schönbrunn that allied Prussia with France. The ink on this treaty was no sooner dry than Napoleon began pressuring Frederick William to prove his loyalty. On February 26, 1806, the Prussian king submitted two orders, one for his customs officials to bar British merchants from Prussian ports and the other for his troops to march into Hanover.

This posed a dilemma for Grenville and his cabinet. They wanted neither to war against Prussia nor appease its aggression. Weeks of debate led to a compromise: Whitehall issued an Order in Council to sweep the seas of Prussian vessels and bring them back to British prize courts. Of course, any land campaign against Prussia was inconceivable.

The total number of British troops was far below that of Prussia, and the redcoats were already widely dispersed across Britain and in dozens of strategic spots around the world.

Beyond Europe the year started out well for British arms. The previous year, Pitt had dispatched an armada of 6,000 troops led by General David Baird packed aboard three ships of the line, two frigates, a sloop, a brig, and sixty-one transports led by Commodore Home Popham. These troops landed near Capetown at Africa's southern end on January 6, 1806. Facing overwhelming odds, the Dutch capitulated on January 18, 1805.

Popham was not content with this easy victory. A restlessness seized him to sail to distant horizons in search of action, glory, and prize money. He pressured Baird to leave a skeleton force at Capetown and head for South America. Baird initially dismissed the idea. His orders were to station half his troops at Capetown and forward the rest to India, while nothing authorized a South American campaign. This prompted Popham to ask whether anything in his instructions prevented him from doing so. Baird reluctantly lent 2,500 troops and General William Beresford to Popham's expedition. He would eventually regret this decision.

As first all went well. Popham, Beresford, and their men sailed on April 20 and forced the authorities to surrender Buenos Aires and its 70,000 inhabitants on June 27. Leaving Beresford and his troops, Popham and his flotilla carried home the equivalent of £1.1 million in prize money. The shock and awe of this unexpected British invasion soon wore off. Spanish soldiers and Argentinean militia converged on Buenos Aires until vast numbers surrounded the British garrison. Beresford surrendered on July 7.

Oblivious to this event, Whitehall sent as reinforcements General Samuel Auchmuty with 2,000 troops aboard a flotilla commanded by Admiral Charles Sterling. The expedition learned of Beresford's surrender only after dropping anchor off Buenos Aires in December. Auchmuty and Sterling decided to sail across the Plate River to nearby Montevideo, Uruguay, and seize that port. The defenders mounted a stout resistance and did not surrender until February 3, 1807. When the news of the Buenos Aires disaster reached London, on January 25,

1807, Whitehall hastily organized an expedition of 11,180 troops led by General John Whitelocke to retake Buenos Aires. Whitelocke did so at the cost of 3,000 casualties but was unable to control the city. Whitehall eventually sent orders for Whitelocke and Auchmuty to withdraw from Buenos Aires and Montevideo.

Meanwhile, the navy racked up more victories in 1806. After the shock of Trafalgar wore off, Napoleon ordered two squadrons at Brest to put to sea, Admirals Corotin de Leissegues with five ships of the line, two frigates, and a corvette, and Jean-Baptiste Willaumez with six ships of the line and two frigates, and two corvettes. Their mission was to devastate enemy shipping in the West Indies and show the British that they might have won a victory at Trafalgar but the war persisted.

Admiral John Duckworth was blockading Cadiz with six ships of the line when he learned about those expeditions and immediately headed west in pursuit. He caught up to Leissegues off St. Domingue and captured three and destroyed two of the enemy ships of the line; the frigates and corvette escaped. Willaumez evaded Duckworth and other British squadrons and captured and destroyed a number of merchant vessels in the West Indies before sailing back to Brest via America's coast. In Chesapeake Bay a hurricane crippled two of his ships, which he burned to prevent the British from capturing them.

The British army scored a field victory in 1806 that redeemed some of its tarnished reputation and tested tactics that Wellington and other field commanders would successfully wield against the French in future battles. Although Admiral Sidney Smith's fleet deterred a French invasion of Sicily, General John Stuart, who commanded British forces on the island, was determined to carry the war to the enemy. He sailed with 5,200 troops aboard transports from Messina on June 30 and landed at St. Eufemia the following day. The closest French troops were General Jean Louis Reynier's division deployed in Reggio, Scylla, and other important towns in the peninsula's toe. Leaving small garrisons behind, Reynier gathered 6,440 troops and marched against Stuart. On July 3 he launched his small army in columns against the redcoats drawn up in a line across a ridge top near Maida. The British fired volley after volley into the French until they broke and ran. In all, Reynier lost 3,000 men killed, wounded, or captured, or nearly half his command, while Stuart suffered only 350 casualties.[3] Wellington would repeatedly defeat the French by deploying his men in lines against their advancing columns during five years of war in the peninsula.

As if fighting a world war were not challenging enough, British humanitarians returned to an issue that had long weighed heavily on their consciences. Grenville and Fox shared similar views on most issues and worked closely together to address them, none more so than the slave trade, which a royal proclamation in 1803 had condemned but not outlawed. Uncertain whether they could round up enough votes for complete abolition, they devised a bill that aimed to reduce Britain's share of the trade by about two-thirds. In spring 1806 the bill passed the House of Commons by an overwhelming majority and Lords by 43 to 18 votes. This relatively swift passage inspired them to press for a resolution that committed Parliament to full abolition in the future. Both houses approved that resolution in June.[4]

The most important issue that Grenville and Fox collaborated on was peace. Looking at the world as it was and was likely to be, they conceived no way to destroy Napoleon and the French empire. Instead, they foresaw only endless warfare with soaring debts and death that drained Britain's economic vitality and provoked worsening poverty, despair, unrest, and violence. National security was best promoted by peace and prosperity. The question was how to initiate talks without appearing weak. A possible ice breaker arose after Fox received intelligence in February 1806 of a royalist plot to assassinate Napoleon. Rather than let it go forward and hope for the best, he decided that a good will gesture might actually reap a greater benefit.

Fox had Foreign Minister Talleyrand secretly informed of the plot. Napoleon expressed his gratitude and released France's highest-ranking prisoner, General Francis Charles Seymour, Earl of Yarmouth, back to London with word that the emperor was interested in negotiations. This provoked a heated debate between the cabinet's hawks and doves over whether to talk and what terms to win. Grenville and his colleagues finally agreed to negotiate a grand deal with Napoleon based on uti possidetis, or each keeping what it had. This position, however, would be complicated by the British insistence that no peace was possible unless the treaty protected the interests of its allies: Russia, Portugal, the Two Sicilies, and Sweden.

Fox had dreamed of winning a lasting peace for Britain, but ill health forced him to take leave in June. For now Grenville added the duties of foreign secretary to his already heavy burden as treasury secretary and secretary of state. He sent Yarmouth back to Paris to negotiate with Talleyrand but soon had to recall him when a scandal erupted over the envoy's misuse of public funds. James Maitland, Earl of Lauderdale, took Yarmouth's place but made little progress. One obstacle was the fate of the Kingdom of the Two Sicilies, now split between Napoleon's brother Joseph ruling southern Italy from Naples and Ferdinand ruling Sicily from Palermo. Napoleon demanded that Joseph should take Sicily as well while compensating Ferdinand with a realm elsewhere, like the Balearic Islands. Another obstacle was Malta, which the British insisted on keeping and Napoleon demanded that they evacuate.[5] The last hope for peace died with Fox on September 13, 1806, as the cabinet's hawks now outnumbered the doves. Grenville tapped his brother Thomas to replace Fox as foreign secretary and also fill a vacancy as the exchequer.

Peace talks with France failed partly because peace talks with Prussia succeeded. For this, Napoleon was largely responsible. He tried to sweeten a deal with Whitehall by promising to force Prussia to return Hanover to Britain, a betrayal the British promptly shared with the Prussians. This was the snapping point for Frederick William and his advisers, who repudiated Prussia's alliance with Napoleon and opened talks with the British for an alliance. The result was a secret treaty signed on June 27, whereby Britain paid Prussia £100,000 immediately and £1 million in three equal slices over the rest of the year in return for devoting itself to defeating Napoleon. Atop this Whitehall sent Berlin 40 artillery pieces, 10,000 muskets, 100,000 flints, and 3 million cartridges.[6] Once again Whitehall placed a huge bet on what would be a lost cause.

As in 1805, Napoleon did not want war in 1806. He sent his first plea for peace to Frederick William after he began mobilizing his army and two more after the king issued, on October 1, an ultimatum that French troops withdraw west of the Rhine River.[7] The campaign that

Napoleon launched on October 8 was among his most decisive. His army routed the Prussians at the twin battles of Jena and Auerstadt on October 14, marched unopposed into Berlin on October 24, and by early November had overrun nearly all of Prussia except the far eastern city of Konigsberg, where Frederick William, his family, his court, and his army's remnants holed up. In just a month the French had killed or wounded 25,000 Prussians and captured 140,000 troops and 2,000 cannons. The second phase of Napoleon's campaign led him into Poland, where he captured Thorn and Glogau in November, and marched unopposed into Warsaw in December as the Prussian and Russian forces withdrew beyond his grasp.[8]

Napoleon's brilliant whirlwind campaigns left him at once elated and infuriated. He viewed the war as a completely unnecessary tragedy. The Prussians would never have mustered the troops and will to fight had British gold not filled their royal coffer and gilded many of their leaders' palms. He would make Prussia pay heavily for the folly of its king and ministers as soon as he destroyed its remaining troops, now backed by a Russian army.

Meanwhile, Napoleon would do what he could to bring the paymaster for Europe's wars to its knees. Without command of the sea, the emperor could not invade and conquer Britain. If he could not strangle Britain with arms, he would do so with trade by depriving it of European markets and goods. The hope was that as Britain's economy faltered, ever more bankers, merchants, and households would reason that only peace could revive trade with the continent and thus prosperity. To this end, Napoleon's Berlin Decree of November 21 and Milan Decree of December 17, 1807, asserted that henceforth the French empire would blockade all British trade; any vessel from any country that violated that blockade would be confiscated, along with its cargo. He pressured other states to join what he called his Continental System.[9]

The blockade did sharply reduce British exports from northern European markets, with the value halved from £10.32 million in1805 to £5.09 million in 1807. Britain's total exports also fell, although eventually they found markets elsewhere, especially in Latin America, with the value ranging from £50.1 million in 1806, £45.5 million in 1807,

£43.8 million in 1808, £61.7 million in 1809, £60.9 million in 1810, £39.6 million in 1811, £51.1 million in 1812, £70.3 million in 1814, and £68.4 million in 1815 (the statistics are apparently lost for 1813).[10]

This roller coaster ride for Britain's exports and economy lay ahead. Meanwhile the gloom worsened for Grenville and his colleagues as they read increasingly dire reports of Napoleon's systematic destruction of the Prussian army and takeover of the realm. Hoping for a rally-round-the flag effect, the prime minister asked the king to dissolve Parliament and call for an election in November 1806. The gamble paid off, as the results bolstered the coalition's hold on power with the combined strength of its factions numbering about 350 members compared to about 100 opponents and 230 independents.

An emboldened Grenville acted on two long-standing progressive priorities in February 1807, winning the first and losing the second. A bill abolishing the slave trade passed the House of Commons by 283 to 16, and Lords by 100 to 36. As party leaders began rounding up votes for a Catholic emancipation bill, George III demanded that Grenville and his other ministers sign a pledge not to renew this issue. Grenville replied with two practical arguments: giving Catholics political rights would undercut support for another Irish rebellion and help replenish the army's ranks by letting Catholics serve without taking the oath to the Church of England. This was immaterial to the king; what was essential was his coronation oath to uphold the Anglican Church as Britain's only legitimate religion and to suppress all heresies. The king's angry and unwavering stand left Grenville and his colleagues with only one honorable act: they resigned and turned in their seals on March 24, 1807.[11]

William Bentinck, Duke of Portland, was sixty-nine years old when the king appointed him prime minister for the second time, and his age showed.[12] He was even more a figurehead this time as he happily left the political heavy lifting to his colleagues. The cabinet's two most powerful ministers running the war effort were Robert Stewart, Viscount Castlereagh, as secretary for war and the colonies, and George Canning as foreign secretary. Seconding them were Charles Jenkinson, Lord Hawkesbury (later Earl of Liverpool) as home secretary; Henry Phipps, Earl of Mulgrave, as first lord of the admiralty, and John

Pitt, Earl of Chatham, as master general of ordnance. Finally, politics much more than merit made Spencer Perceval the exchequer chancellor and Speaker of the House of Commons; George III wanted his fellow outspoken opponent of Catholic emancipation in both those posts. Percival made a good enough Speaker but knew little of finance. Fortunately, William Huskisson, the treasury secretary, was a first-rate bookkeeper. Of this inner cabinet, Castlereagh and Canning might have been a dynamic policy duo had not each disdainfully viewed the other as an upstart rival.

Castlereagh was among the handful of aloof, uptight introverts who rise to power in a profession naturally dominated by extroverts.[13] He was born into a prominent Anglo-Irish family that held vast lands, a safe seat in Ireland's parliament, and marriage ties with other elite families on both sides of the Irish Sea. Armed with his pedigree and a Cambridge University degree, he won election to Ireland's parliament in 1790 and took his seat devoted to political reform. Like so many other liberal politicians of the era, he was forced to shelve his ideals after the French Revolution radicalized him and Britain went to war against it. He was increasingly respected for his fine mind, hard work, and meticulously argued if uninspiring speeches. In March 1798 he temporarily replaced Thomas Pelham as Ireland's chief secretary when Pelham fell ill. Castlereagh's reputation soared as word spread of his decisive leadership during the 1798 Irish rebellion, and Prime Minister Pitt tapped him to be among the insiders who brought about Ireland's union with Britain over the next few years, culminating in 1801. For his efforts, Prime Minister Addington appointed him president of the East India Company's Board of Control in June 1802. His tireless administrative skills again earned him a higher step in the power pyramid; Prime Minister Pitt saw a good deal of his own character reflected in Castlereagh and named him to be his secretary of state for war in July 1805. This stint, however, lasted only seven months. When Pitt died in January 1806, Prime Minister Grenville did not share his predecessor's esteem for Castlereagh and dismissed him to rejoin the backbenchers in the House of Commons.

Canning was a rarity among this era's political elite; his origins were as humble as those of virtually all of his colleagues were privileged.[14]

His father was a debt-ridden alcoholic who had failed at practicing law and peddling wine, and who died when Canning was a year old. Thereafter his mother wielded her beauty, wit, and other charms to work her way up through the theater world until she became a renowned actress. Along the way she found a distant rich Canning relative willing to underwrite her precocious son's education at Eton and Oxford. There Canning displayed skills at writing poetry and prose, and an even greater gift for public speaking. He went on to study law at Lincoln's Inn. Pitt tapped him for a political career after Canning impressed him with his erudition and principles during a meeting in August 1792. It was not until June 1793, however, that Pitt found Canning an open borough seat that he could represent, although Parliament did not convene until January 1794. There Canning swiftly became celebrated for his orations, collegiality, and loyalty, and Pitt named him the undersecretary for foreign affairs in October 1795. During the next four years, Canning also served as a member of the India Control Board, as joint-paymaster general of the forces, and as the Alien Office's receiver general. In 1801 he devoted himself full time to the king's Privy Council.

The latest cabinet inherited its predecessor's strategic dilemma. Lacking the power to invade and defeat France, Whitehall could only launch limited attacks around its empire's periphery or allies. For now the weakest link appeared to be Turkey, which had allied with France in 1806. The Portland government sought to knock Turkey out of the war by seizing Egypt and threatening to destroy Constantinople itself.

Whitehall's orders to Admiral John Duckworth were ambitious. He was to "demand the immediate surrender of the Turkish fleet, together with that of a supply of naval stores from the Arsenal . . . and . . . to accompany this demand with a menace in case of refusal of immediately commencing hostilities against . . . Constantinople."[15] Duckworth's flotilla of eight ships of the line reached the mouth of the Dardanelle Strait on February 10, 1807. However, instead of boldly sailing to Constantinople, a few day's journey away, he hesitated and ordered his fleet to drop anchor. This gave the Turks crucial time to prepare their batteries, spiking both sides of the thirty-eight-mile-long, mile-wide strait. Four days later one of Duckworth's ships of the line accidently caught fire and sank. Duckworth waited another five days before he finally acted. He split his fleet in two and sent Captain Sidney Smith with three ships of the line and a frigate to engage the Turkish batteries and warships, while he proceeded eastward with the rest of his flotilla. Smith's warships sank nine Turkish vessels and two gunboats and destroyed a 32-gun battery, then, on February 20, rejoined Duckworth just beyond cannon shot of Constantinople. Duckworth sent the Turks an ultimatum to surrender or face destruction. When the sultan and his court angrily rejected that demand, Duckworth failed to fulfill his threat. Instead, the expedition lingered another ten days before he ordered his captains to sail westward back down the gauntlet of batteries lining the straits.

The Egypt campaign was an even more humiliating and costly failure. General Alexander Fraser invaded Egypt with 6,000 troops and captured Alexandria on March 16, 1807. But when Fraser attempted to move inland, the Turks defeated him at El Hamed, inflicted a thousand casualties, then bottled him up in Alexandria. His only opening lay seaward where a British fleet was anchored. The British evacuated Alexandria in September 1807.

These British debacles contrasted with Napoleon's ultimate triumph over Frederick William III and Alexander. His initial attempt to inflict a knockout blow in early 1807 led to a bloodbath at Eylau in Poland on February 8, in which the French held the field at a cost of 25,000 casualties to the 15,000 suffered by the Russians under General Levin Bennigsen. Both armies went into winter quarters and replenished their ranks. Napoleon reopened his campaign in mid-May. After a two-month siege, Danzig's defenders surrendered to General François Joseph Lefebvre on May 27. Whitehall meanwhile dispatched William, Earl of Cathcart, with 10,000 King's German Legion troops to Stralsund. This was a gesture rather than a serious campaign, and even then typically too little too late. On June 14 Napoleon trapped and decimated the Russian army led by General Levin Bennigsen at Friedland. The emperor accepted the tsar's plea for an armistice.

Napoleon and Alexander conducted their celebrated first meeting aboard a large barge in the Niemen River on June 25. Two weeks of talks, ceremonies, and banquets culminated with the Treaties of Tilsit, the first treaty between France and Russia on July 7, the second between France and Prussia on July 9. Napoleon let Alexander off easy, taking nothing but promises that Russia would join the Continental System, attempt to mediate peace between France and Britain, and join France against Britain if a treaty was not struck by December 1, 1807. In return, Napoleon would approve a Russian war against Sweden if Stockholm did not cede Finland. Napoleon forced Frederick William to agree to pay a huge indemnity to France, recognize all French conquests and the Rhine Confederation, join the Continental System, and reduce his army to 42,000 men. Napoleon followed up his Tilsit triumphs by having ultimatums sent to Copenhagen, Stockholm, and Lisbon, warning them either to sever trade with Britain and join France against Britain or suffer the consequences of being a French enemy. The deadline was September 1, 1807.[16]

Whitehall rejected Alexander's offer to mediate peace with the same rationale that had prompted Britain's leaders to reject every chance for peace except one since 1793. Indeed, the exception justified the prevailing policy. The 1802 treaty of Amiens produced not peace but a brief cease-fire as each side prepared for the next round of war. Peace was impossible as long as a despotic regime ruled in Paris and expanded the French empire across Europe. Britain was locked into a fight to the death against the regime, and if it lacked the power to crush it in one campaign, then it had to impose a slow death by a thousand cuts. Foreign Minister Canning eloquently elaborated that policy: "Our interest is that till there can be a final settlement that shall last, everything should remain as unsettled as possible: That no usurper should feel sure of acknowledgement; no people confident of their new miseries; no kingdom sure of its existence; no spoliator secure of his spoil; and even the plundered not acquiescent in their losses."[17]

Shorn now of viable allies, Whitehall was desperate to tap any force that might eat away at Napoleon's empire. In 1806 Grenville and his inner cabinet held their noses and began massively underwriting France's exile community in hopes of somehow wielding them into a viable exile government and army. The would-be Louis XVIII and his brother Charles began enjoying annual subsidies, courtesy of Britain's taxpayers, of £10,000 and £4000, respectively. This may appear generous but covered only a sliver of living expenses for those extravagant princes and their entourages. It was also parsimonious compared to Whitehall's total budget for secret payments to "emigrants," which soared from £19,325 in 1805 to £100,849 in 1806, before leveling off at £104,262 in 1807. These investments failed to pay off. The exiles gleefully pocketed the cash but did little to advance the royalist cause.[18]

Instead, Louis and his followers appeared packed aboard a Swedish frigate at Yarmouth in October 1807 and begged for refuge. As part of the peace of Tilsit between the emperor and tsar, Alexander had agreed to expel the Bourbons from their palace at Mittau. The Bourbons first went to Stockholm, but Gustavus IV only underwrote their voyage to Britain. When they arrived at Portsmouth, Whitehall refused to permit the refugees even to stretch their legs ashore, but after prolonged negotiations let them reside in England if Louis called himself Count Lille, the humblest of his many titles, and understood that his presence in no way represented official British recognition of his claim to the French throne. After residing in several country estates, the Bourbon exiles finally crammed into Hartwell House, with Louis enjoying a £16,000 annual allowance, courtesy of British taxpayers.[19]

Whitehall reacted to a Russian threat in 1807 as it had in 1801, by attacking Denmark. Home Secretary Hawkesbury justified the Copenhagen campaign eloquently and opaquely: "We must not permit either the strength of one power or the weakness of another to be converted into a weapon for our destruction."[20] Denmark was targeted because it was a minor power that occupied a vital spot on the map and had a navy of eighteen ships of the line and ten frigates. The power distribution would shift sharply if Denmark allied with France and Russia. Envoy Francis Jackson was dispatched to offer Copenhagen a harsh choice—either ally with Britain and enjoy protection with 15,000 troops, a squadron of warships, and subsidies, or else suffer inevitable destruction. The Danes insisted on maintaining their neutrality. This was not good enough for Whitehall.

The armada included 23 ships of the line, 40 smaller warships, and 27,000 redcoats crammed aboard 377 transports. Admiral James Gambier and General William Cathcart led the navy and army forces, respectively. Among the brigadier generals was Arthur Wellesley. The troops began disembarking on the island of Zealand on August 16, with some contingents dispatched to secure the island while most massed around Copenhagen. Over the next few weeks the British siege lines snaked toward the city. Wellesley's troops repelled a Danish attack at Kioge on August 29, and in their counterattack took 1,200 prisoners. By August 31, the batteries were in place. The Danes refused a demand to surrender on September 1, and the next day, Cathcart ordered his gunners to open fire. Three days of shelling killed at least 2,000 civilians and destroyed a quarter of the city. The Danes capitulated on September 5.

The terms were harsh. The Danes had to surrender all their warships, naval stores, and the island of Helgoland at the mouth of the Elbe River. The British sailed away with skeleton crews on fifteen of the finest vessels and burned the rest, while redcoats occupied Helgoland. Having suffered only 230 casualties, Britain had scored a major victory while suffering relatively minor human costs. The British followed up their brutal attack on Copenhagen by seizing Denmark's West Indian colonies of St. Johns, St. Thomas, and St. Croix in December 1807.

Those "victories," however, were controversial in moral terms. The British had attacked a neutral country, killed a couple of thousand civilians, and confiscated its fleet and colonies. Ensign Robert Blakeney of the 28th Regimentexpressed the views of most Britons when he noted that "some indeed exclaimed that their sufferings were the more aggravated as being inflicted contrary to the laws of all civilized nations. The unfortunate sufferers seemed not to reflect that war was will, not law." Foreign Secretary Canning went a step further by asserting a paradoxical way to overcome the mass outrage of Britain's war crimes: "We are hated throughout Europe and that hate must be cured by fear."[21]

As if British power was not stretched thin enough, a war nearly erupted with the United States in the summer of 1807. Since Britain went to war in 1793, the Americans had angrily protested Whitehall's policy of having the Royal Navy halt American ships and confiscate them and their cargoes if they were heading toward an enemy port as well as impressing any sailors suspected of being British subjects.

No blood was shed, however, during the thirteen years before April 25, 1806, when a cannonball fired by the HMS *Leander* killed a sailor aboard an American vessel at the Verrazano Narrows at the entrance to New York Bay. Upon learning of the killing, President Thomas Jefferson sent a protest to London and issued an order banning the *Leander* and its two accompanying warships from American waters, a ban ignored by the captains of those warships. Well aware that the United States was completely unprepared for war, Jefferson did not order the miniscule American navy to enforce his order. He sent James Monroe and William Pinkney to London with the mission to negotiate a deal that completely upheld America's "freedom of the seas," then rejected the treaty they brought back for falling short of that ideal.[22]

The British committed an even worse atrocity on June 22, 1807, when the HMS *Leopard* bombarded the USS *Chesapeake* after its captain refused to let the British search his vessel for deserters. Three broadsides killed six American sailors, wounded twenty-three, and crippled the ship. The American captain had no choice but to strike his colors. A British boarding party searched the vessel and hauled away four suspected deserters. Once again Jefferson protested to Whitehall and ordered all British warships to leave American waters. Although the British eventually expressed regret for what happened and gave a token amount of money as compensation, they refused to abandon their policy of preying on American ships, cargoes, and sailors.

Although Jefferson was determined to prevent a future incident from sparking war with Britain, he did not, however, believe in peace through military strength. Instead, he insisted that Whitehall would only stop its depredations against American vessels if none put to sea. With this "logic," he got congressional majorities to pass a bill on December 22, 1807, that embargoed America's foreign trade. Foreign vessels could enter American ports to sell and buy, but American vessels were confined only to home waters.

The result was an utter disaster for American wealth and power, and a boost to that of Britain as its merchants gleefully captured that carrying trade from their once fierce rivals. America's exports had soared from $33 million in 1794 to $108 million in 1807, then plunged to $22 million in 1808; in 1807, 211 American vessels packed with goods sailed for foreign ports and only 13 the following year.[23]

Thus did Jefferson avert a possible war by demeaning and debilitating acts of appeasement that devastated America's economy. The *Chesapeake* tragedy would have turned out far differently with a president who understood the art of power. Jefferson took a small step toward reality on March 3, 1809, three days before he left office, when he signed the Non-Intercourse Act, which let Americans trade with all nations except Britain and France. Since nearly all American trade was with either Britain or France, this measure had little effect in lifting America's depressed economy.

Whitehall also ultimately failed to heed a fundamental tenet of the art of power in its policies toward the United States. If bullies are too merciless, they can drive even the weakest of victims to strike back. After nearly two decades of being robbed and humiliated by the British, the Americans would declare war in June 1812.

CHAPTER 8

# The Fifth Coalition, 1808–1809

> The British Government is . . . intimately persuaded that the only assurance of success in War, would be found in the general Conviction of its necessity and in the Efforts which such Conviction must command.
>
> George Canning

> In this war we have supplied by turns almost the whole continent with arms—Russia, Prussia, Sweden, Portugal, Sicily, and Spain—while at the same time our own military establishment are sixfold what they formerly were.
>
> George Canning

Napoleon deluded himself into believing that his Continental System would eventually vanquish Britain. This obsession led him to the Iberian Peninsula, which he would one day rue as his "Spanish ulcer." His initial excuse for invasion was Portugal, which refused to join the blockade and instead traded openly with Britain. The emperor issued a fateful order on July 19, 1807. Foreign Minister Talleyrand was to get Spain to join France in pressuring Prince John, the regent for his mad mother, Queen Maria, to sever Portugal's trade and diplomatic ties with Britain, arrest all Britons, confiscate all British goods, and declare war on Britain. On August 12 the French and Spanish ambassadors in Lisbon issued to their host an ultimatum to accept those demands or else face war. The Portuguese reluctantly agreed to end relations with Britain but refused to go to war. The ambassadors left Lisbon on September 30. Anticipating this refusal, Napoleon had massed an army of 25,000 troops under General Andoche Junot at Bayonne near the Spanish frontier. On October 18 he ordered Junot to lead his men on the long march to Lisbon. Under the Treaty of Fontainebleau, signed on October 27, France and Spain would conquer and divide Portugal between them.[1]

With their nation literally under the gun, the Portuguese turned to Whitehall for help. On October 22, 1807, Foreign Secretary Canning signed with Ambassador Pedro de Souza a convention whereby Britain would protect Portugal if it were invaded. This agreement came not a moment too soon. The cabinet sent orders to General William Cathcart at Copenhagen to dispatch 10,000 troops to Lisbon or, if the city fell, to occupy Portugal's island of Madeira six hundred miles southwest. At Gibraltar, Admiral Sidney Smith received orders to sail his squadron of nine ships of the line to Lisbon to rescue the royal family if need be.

After reaching Lisbon on November 16, Smith helped Portugal's government prepare to evacuate. Prince John put off abandoning his homeland until November 29, when Junot's army was reported just a day's march away. After squeezing several hundred members of Portugal's elite, their belongings, and the royal treasure aboard his vessels, Smith ordered his captains to sail for Rio de Janeiro, Brazil. Junot and his footsore troops marched unopposed into Lisbon the next day.

Thereafter the British literally capitalized on Portugal's plight. With the royal family living in exile and dependent on Britain for liberating their country, Prince John had little choice but to yield to Whitehall's pressure to sign decrees permitting British merchants to trade freely with Portugal, Brazil, and colonies elsewhere.

Spain soon suffered a similar fate. In May 1808 Napoleon exploited a Spanish political crisis to make this country his latest victim. King Charles IV had an weak mind, will, and body. Manuel Godoy, the first minister, had risen to power as the queen's lover and sought to expand his influence by taking advantage of the doddering king. Ferdinand, the crown prince, was so ambitious that he was willing to depose his own parents to take the throne. His first attempted coup was in October 1807, but the king got wind of it and had guards lock him in his royal bedchamber until he tearfully repented. Five months later, on March 19, 1808, he succeeded in getting an army faction to back him into pressuring the king to abdicate at Aranjuez Palace. Ferdinand VII asked Napoleon to recognize his takeover and give him a French princess for a bride. Charles, in turn, pleaded with Napoleon to rescue him from his son and restore him to his throne.

Nothing could have better advanced the emperor's ambitions. He summoned Charles and Ferdinand along with the Cortes, or national assembly, to Bayonne, a dozen miles north of Spain's border. Napoleon talked Charles and Ferdinand into respectively signing treaties on May 5 and May 10, whereby they renounced the throne and ceded it to the emperor in return for huge annual stipends and residences at different French chateaus.[2] Napoleon then beckoned his brother Joseph, whom he had installed as the king of Naples to become the king of Spain. Joachim Murat, who was leading Napoleon's swelling army in Spain under the guise of the bilateral alliance, took Joseph's place as the king of Naples. Napoleon decreed Joseph to be Spain's king on June 6, and had the rump Cortes of forty-seven nobles, twenty priests, and eighty-three other delegates accept this dynastic change as part of a liberal constitution its delegates ratified on June 15.[3]

Napoleon's dream of subduing Spain swiftly became a chimera. In a harbinger of the horrors that lay ahead, a revolt erupted on May 2 against the French in Madrid, which Murat crushed with extreme brutality. Although some 90,000 French troops were deployed in Spain, most were in Burgos, Barcelona, and Madrid or in small detachments leading from those cities back to France. After forcing the royal family to abdicate, the emperor ordered his generals to secure the rest of the country. These French forces soon met resistance.[4]

The word that Napoleon had deposed Spain's royal family and had given the throne to his brother Joseph provoked Spain's civil and military leaders to rebel. Spain was well organized to resist. An intendent headed each of the thirty-two provinces and a captain general each of the fourteen military districts. Spain's army numbered 114,000 troops, who were scattered in corps and smaller detachments across the country. The largest Spanish forces were the 30,000 troops of General Francisco Javier de Castanos in the southwest around Seville, the 6,500 troops of Gregorio García de la Cuesta in the west at Zamora, and the 20,000 troops of General Joaquín Blake in the northwest around Lugo. Battles flared between French and Spanish troops. The French suffered a defeat at Zaragoza where General José Palafox massed over 10,000 mostly militia to defend the city. The most decisive event came when Castanos forced General Pierre Dupont to surrender his 18,000 troops at Baylen on July 23.

Joseph Bonaparte arrived at the head of a column of French troops and an entourage of pro-French Spaniards in Madrid on July 20. Five days later the rump Cortes formally declared Joseph to be the king of Spain. Then came word of Dupont's surrender. Joseph had only 23,000 French troops with him at Madrid. Rather than stand and fight, the new king fled with his court and army northward on August 1. He did not stop running until he reached Logrono's citadel.

Whitehall resolved to do everything possible to aid the Spanish resistance. The trouble was that no central Spanish government existed. Instead, each region's junta fought the French and sent its own envoys to London to beg for money and military equipment. Foreign Minister Canning struck a series of deals with the envoys that distributed about £1,100,000 among them, with £500,000 going to Galicia, £200,000 to Asturias, £200,000 to Seville, £100,000 to Leon, and £100,000 to Cadiz. The British did not just give money. By the year's end, they sent over 120,000 muskets, millions of cartridges, and other vital weapons and equipment to the resistance in Spain.[5]

Canning was appalled at how the juntas elbowed each other in their rush for British largess. He pressured them to bridge their differences and setup a national government. They actually did so at Seville on September 25, 1808, when the Supreme Junta convened with two delegates from each of the thirty-four provinces and one from the Canary Islands. The Supreme Junta tried to govern the country; raise money, arms, supplies, and troops; and devise a strategy against the French. However, incompetence, corruption, and jealousy led to failure.

Spanish troops were split into small regional forces that communicated and coordinated little with each other, and antagonisms among the regions prevented them from agreeing on a commander-in-chief.

Spain's army was further weakened because one of its better generals and some of its better regiments were far away from their homeland. Charles IV had agreed to Napoleon's request, in early 1807, to send troops to garrison strategic towns and fortresses in Prussia and northern Germany on the emperor's supply lines to his army in Poland. After fighting erupted in Spain, Napoleon sought to disarm and intern General Pedro Romana and his 20,000 men. Romana escaped with about 9,000 troops and reached the island of Langeland, where a British flotilla rescued them on August 7, 1808. Romana and his men disembarked at Santander on October 11 and were soon fighting the French.

The rebellion in Spain threatened General Junot's supply lines from Lisbon back across the peninsula to France. With only 26,000 troops, he could at best hold the Tagus River valley. Portuguese resistance to the French invaders grew steadily. The strongest was at Oporto in the north, where Luis de Oliveira and Archbishop António de São José de Castro had formed a junta and General Bernardim Freire de Andrade had gathered troops. On April 8, 1808, General Hew Dalrymple, Gibraltar's governor, sent the first of ten letters over the next couple of months urging Whitehall to send a British expedition to drive the French from Portugal.[6]

Portland's cabinet backed this idea but reasoned that no land campaign was viable without naval superiority in the waters around Portugal and nearby Spain. Admiral John Purvis, whose squadron was blockading Cadiz, was authorized to collaborate with Spanish officials to capture French admiral François Rosily and his five ships of the line, a frigate, and a corvette that had been rotting at anchor there since Trafalgar. The result was a significant bloodless victory. Another worry was Admiral Dimitri Siniavin's Russian fleet of nine warships anchored at Lisbon. The ministers concluded that any threat from that fleet was minimal; formally Britain and Russia were not at war, while Siniavin had not kept up the combat readiness of his vessels and crews. All this emboldened the ministers to organize a Portugal campaign.

For Canning, honor above all justified the expedition: "I had rather a bloody battle and a defeat than safety at a price by running away."[7]

Whitehall named Arthur Wellesley to head that army on June 11, 1808. It was his first independent command since his brilliant 1805 Mahratta campaign. He had resigned from Britain's Indian army and sailed away on March 10, 1805. When he set foot on English soil half a year later on September 10, 1805, he had been gone nearly nine years. It took another three years before he began winning fame as a general on the peninsula that eventually far surpassed what he had earned as a "sepoy general" in India. Meanwhile, he won a pocket borough seat in Britain's Parliament and Kitty Pakenham's hand in marriage. In March 1807 he accepted the post of Ireland's chief secretary and moved to Dublin with his new family. This duty was interrupted in the summer of 1807, when he received orders to lead a division in General David Baird's army during the Copenhagen campaign. He earned praise for his tactics that won the Battle of Kioge. He was thirty-nine years old in April 1808 when he was promoted to be the army's youngest lieutenant general.

Wellesley reached Cork on June 30 and prepared the 9,000 troops there for campaign. After landing in Portugal, his army would be reinforced by 6,000 troops under General Brent Spencer from Gibraltar and 3,000 troops under General William Beresford from Madeira.[8] Wellesley's expedition sailed on July 12 and anchored off Oporto, Portugal on July 24. Wellesley went ashore to confer with General Bernardim Freire de Andrade, Portugal's army commander. They agreed to join forces down the coast at Mondego Bay, with the British arriving by sea and the Portuguese by land.

Wellesley and his troops disembarked at Mondego Bay, eighty miles north of Lisbon on August 1. It took days just to get all the men and supplies ashore. He had a proclamation printed in Portuguese and distributed: "People of Portugal: The Time is arrived to rescue your country; and restore the government of your lawful prince."[9] After Spencer's troops arrived on August 8, Wellesley's army totaled 15,663 men, although only 215 were cavalry and the army was short of draft animals and carts. Freire violated their plan by refusing to join Wellesley, insisting that he would march through the mountains on a parallel road a score of miles eastward. For the British army, safety depended on not stretching too far their umbilical cord to the supply fleet. On August 9, Wellesley began his advance south toward Lisbon.

Although the French outgunned the British in Portugal, Junot failed to capitalize on this edge. Of his 26,000 troops, about 19,000 were deployed in and around Lisbon. Believing that the landing was just a raiding party, Junot sent General Henri François de Laborde with 4,300 troops to drive the redcoats into the sea. The channel of history would have changed dramatically had Junot left 1,000 troops to garrison Lisbon and himself marched with 18,000 against Wellesley. With his superior numbers, Junot might have overwhelmed Wellesley, forcing him to retreat or even capitulate.

Instead, Laborde was disabused of the idea that the British were just a small raiding party after the advanced French and British guards skirmished at Obidos on August 15. Laborde withdrew to Rolica, where on August 17 Wellesley launched a flank attack that scattered the French. The victorious general had resumed his march on Lisbon, when, from the French point of view, a miracle happened.

Wellesley received orders that General Hew Dalrymple, with General Harry Burrard serving as the deputy, would supersede him in command. Wellesley naturally was furious that "of all the awkward situations in the world that which is the most so is to serve in subordinate capacity in an army which one has commanded."[10] Burrard arrived first and halted Wellesley's advance at Vimiero.

Meanwhile, Junot finally stirred from his complacency. He left behind 7,000 troops in Lisbon and marched with the rest to join Laborde, bringing the French field army to 13,000 men. Despite being outnumbered, Junot ordered his men to attack on the morning of August 21. The redcoats poured volley after volley into the advancing French, then counterattacked and routed them. The French and British respectively suffered 2,000 and 720 casualties. To Burrard, Wellesley exclaimed: "Sir Harry, now is your chance. The French are completely beaten. . . . We shall be in Lisbon in three days."[11] Burrard rejected that notion and instead deferred a decision to Dalyrmple, who was expected to arrive that evening. Dalyrmple upheld Burrard's decision to stay put, and both of them gratefully accepted Junot's request the next morning for a truce.

What followed were ten days of talks that culminated with the Convention of Cintra, signed on August 31, 1808. Junot may have been a poor tactician and strategist, but he certainly outfoxed his British counterparts at diplomacy. Although Junot ceded Portugal, he talked Dalrymple into not just letting the French army with all their arms, stores, and plunder escape to fight another day but actually give it a lift back to France courtesy of the Royal Navy. Having a killer instinct and unleashing it when appropriate is a vital source of soft power. Clearly Dalrymple and Burrard lacked this crucial gift and kept Wellesley from exercising his.

News of this squandered victory enraged most members of the cabinet, Parliament, and public alike. Whitehall convened a board of inquiry, which opened hearings on November 14 and issued a report on December 22. The result was an acquittal, as the commissioners approved the armistice by six to one and the convention by four to three. Although Wellesley was vindicated, he remained enveloped in a dark cloud in the minds of many. Only a decisive military campaign could dispel this blow to his reputation. He returned to his seat in the House of Commons, wondering whether he would ever get a chance to prove himself.

Having taken Portugal, the British had to hold it. Napoleon would do whatever he could to avenge the defeat. Another French invasion was only a matter of time. Britain's small army in Portugal was in desperate need of more troops and a first-rate commander. It happened that both were available, but only because of a bizarre diplomatic debacle.

The July 7 Treaty of Tilsit shifted the Baltic basin's power balance. Russia was now Sweden's enemy rather than ally. French troops overran Swedish Pomerania and seized Stralsund. Russian troops massed to invade Sweden's province of Finland. In December 1807 Gustavus IV pleaded for help from Britain. Whitehall promised him £100,000 a month and a fleet and troops as soon as the ice melted in spring 1808. For this, Gustavus simply had to promise to keep fighting. Envoys signed these terms into a treaty on February 8, 1808.[12] Two weeks later the Russians attacked Finland, but it wasn't until May 1808 that General John Moore and 10,864 redcoats packed aboard hundreds of transports, and guarded by scores of warships led by Admiral James

Saumarez, reached Stockholm. Although Moore was renowned for his courage on the battlefield, his confrontational personality made him a poor diplomat. He and the king soon got into shouting matches over how to deploy these British troops and who would command them. Whitehall broke the deadlock by ordering Moore to withdraw his expedition and sail for Lisbon, and from there march into Spain.

During the summer and autumn of 1808 Napoleon's armies suffered a series of defeats in Spain, and now French troops clung only to the regions around Barcelona and Vitoria. At a small palace in Vitoria, Joseph Bonaparte morosely awaited his brother's help in regaining his throne. Napoleon intended to journey to Spain and submit the coup de grace to Spanish resistance, but first wanted to ensure that his Continental System and domination of central Europe were secure. To this end, he organized a glittering summit of France's allies, of whom Russian tsar Alexander was the star, at Erfurt from September 27 to October 14.

Satisfied that his diplomacy at Erfurt had succeeded, Napoleon dashed to Spain and reached Vitoria on November 6. He spent four intense days there planning before unleashing his campaign on November 10. His corps routed every Spanish army before them as they spread across northern then central Spain. On December 4 Napoleon reinstalled his hapless brother on the Spanish throne in Madrid and prepared his campaign's next phase, designed to crush the remaining Spanish resistance.

Two British forces were in Spain at this time, General David Baird's 12,000 troops at Coruna and General John Moore's 21,000 troops at Salamanca. Moore had orders to join Baird and any Spanish forces in Galicia and defend that region, but he chose a roundabout way to get there. Marshal Nicolas Soult and his 15,000-man corps were at Burgos. Moore called on Baird to join him in attacking Soult before Napoleon could march from Madrid to his rescue. British and Spanish morale would soar if Soult was defeated before withdrawing to safety. After launching his campaign in late December, Moore soon realized that he had lost any chance of a surprise attack. Napoleon had learned of his advance and was racing the corps under his immediate command to cut off Moore as he attacked Soult.

Moore reluctantly withdrew his small army northwest on the long, mountainous road toward Coruna. Along the way, thousands of men dropped, exhausted from the cold, hunger, and exertion. At Villafranca, Moore split his army and sent the Light Division to Vigo while he headed with the rest to Coruna. As Napoleon urged his troops forward to catch and destroy Moore, he was distracted by word of a possible political conspiracy against him in Paris and Vienna's preparations to war against him in the spring. On January 3, 1809, he turned over his army's command to Soult and hurried back to Paris to confront the conspirators and ready France for its latest war against Austria.

When Moore led his army's remnants into Coruna on January 12, he was dismayed to find the port empty of the promised ships that would sail them to safety, but he prepared to defend Coruna for as long as possible. Two days later the flotilla finally dropped anchor, but the next day Soult's advance forces appeared. The redcoats faced the daunting challenge of marching to the wharfs, packing into longboats, and being rowed to the transports while under attack. By January 16 Soult had brought up 16,000 troops and ordered an assault. The British repelled the attack, inflicting 1,400 casualties but losing 800 men, including Moore, who was shot dead. In all, Moore's gamble cost over 7,000 British troops killed or captured. This was bad enough, but it could have been much worse—about 15,000 British troops escaped for future campaigns against the French.

Within a month after taking Coruna, Soult's troops had seized northwestern Spain's major ports and cities, including Ferrol, where a Spanish fleet of eight ships of the line and three frigates fell into French hands. French armies elsewhere were just as successful. By the summer of 1809, over 250,000 French troops had overrun most of Spain, with the Spanish clinging to the region around Seville in the southwest and the Mediterranean coast up to Alicante.

Once again Britain was grasping to retain or gain any ally. With Britain's subsidy treaty with Sweden due to expire in December 1808, Canning hoped to renew it but faced a likely stormy diplomatic path in doing so. Gustavus IV had declared Britain's minister, Edward Thornton, persona non grata when he had insisted that the king fulfill his treaty obligations. Canning sent Anthony Merry to Stockholm to replace Thornton and renew the subsidy treaty. Gustavus angrily rejected the £1.2 million subsidy that Merry offered and demanded £2 million instead. He flew into a tantrum when Merry patiently explained that he was not authorized to raise the offer and warned Merry that if he did not receive £300,000 instantly, he would sever relations with Britain and join the Continental System. Merry succumbed to the blackmail and handed over £300,000 in treasury bonds.[13] Canning was enraged when he learned that Gustavus had extorted that money from his minister and informed the king that the money would be considered the first payment of not more than £1.2 million for the next year. Gustavus finally agreed to sign a treaty to this effect on March 1, 1809.[14] Shortly thereafter, on March 13, 1809, a coup overthrew and replaced him with Charles XIII. So for now Britain had both a stable treaty and ruler upon which to ground its alliance with Sweden.

During this era, Captain Thomas Cochrane equaled Horatio Nelson in courage and guile but never rose to command a fleet. He was part of Admiral James Gambier's expedition ordered to destroy the French fleet anchored at Basque Roads, a huge bay protected by Ile d'Oléron and Ile d'Aix off Rochefort to the south and Ile de Ré off La Rochelle to the north. This fleet had recently expanded when Admiral Jean-Baptiste Willaumez led eight ships of the line and seven frigates past Gambier's blockade at Brest, then past Admiral Robert Stepford's blockade at Basque Roads. Spies revealed that Willaumez's ultimate mission was to lead an armada across the Atlantic to reinforce Martinique and Guadeloupe.

After their warships dropped anchor off Basque Roads on March 7, 1809, Gambier and his captains spent weeks debating just how to attack the French fleet protected by forts and batteries. They finally decided that a fireboat attack was the least risky strategy. Gambier assigned Cochrane the task of preparing and leading a fireboat flotilla against the French fleet. On the night of April 11, Cochrane had twenty-one small vessels packed with explosives, manned each with a skeleton crew, and led them toward the French fleet. Cochrane ordered his crews to, at the last minute, ignite and abandon their vessels as the tide and wind pushed them toward the enemy. The attack appeared to fizzle when the fireboats ran ashore or drifted far from any French warship, then exploded spectacularly one by one against the black sky. Yet the following morning, the British were astonished to see eight of the ten French ships of the line and many smaller warships grounded helplessly on mud flats around the bay. The previous night the French captains had panicked as the fireboats approached and cut their cables.

Cochrane signaled Gambier to lead the fleet to attack the stranded French vessels. When Gambier refused, Cochrane sailed his frigate, the HMS *Imperieuse,* toward the two French ships of the line still anchored in deep water. The captains of those warships cut their cables and ran aground, after which the *Imperieuse* bombarded them and other beached vessels. Eventually two other British warships joined the *Imperieuse* in the battle, but Gambier held back the rest of his fleet. By that evening, these unrelenting attacks had blown up three French warships and forced two others to surrender. When darkness ended the fighting, Cochrane was determined to square off with the rest of the enemy fleet the next morning and grudgingly obeyed Gambier's order to return to the fleet.

Gambier gave Cochrane the honor of returning to London with an account of the victory. Parliament, however, voted thanks not to Cochrane, whose courage had almost single-handedly won the victory, but to Gambier, who had refused to fight. This enraged Cochrane, who publicly revealed Gambier's cowardice. Gambier demanded to be court martialed on charges of dereliction of duty and duly received an acquittal from his brother officers. He then submitted a new account of the battle that removed Cochrane's name from the action. Cochrane resigned in disgust. Thus did a toxic mix of incompetence and corruption among the navy's top command drive off a brilliant fighting commander with the potential to become Nelson's successor.

Four years after the traumatic blows of Ulm, Vienna, Austerlitz, and Pressburg, the shock and awe of Napoleon's devastating campaign had worn off for most Austrians, leaving behind a fierce desire for vengeance. By October 1808, most of Francis's ministers and advisers favored war. This, of course, raised the usual conundrum of a surfeit of will and a lack of money to wage war. So, as usual, Vienna turned to London to fill the gap. The request was £2.5 million in preparation money and £5 million for the year in return for fielding 400,000 troops.[15]

This request stunned Whitehall. Britain certainly needed Austria as an ally, but at what cost? For two months the ministers debated how to respond. On December 24 Foreign Minister Canning sent a polite refusal without a counteroffer. His message peaked with a line as powerful as it was diplomatic: "The British Government is . . . intimately persuaded that the only assurance of success in War, would be found in the general Conviction of its necessity and in the Efforts which such Conviction must command."[16]

Vienna was prepared for the rejection of its opening bid and sent a new proposal that promised more troops and demanded less money. Austria would launch 443,000 men against France in return for £2 million in preparation money and £400,000 a month thereafter. Around the same time, Canning received a letter from Ludwig von Kleist, who represented the war faction in Prussia that was conspiring to provoke revolts against French garrisons across Germany. Kleist asked Britain to set up an arms depot at Helgoland for the rebels and launch a campaign that recaptured Hanover.[17]

Canning and his fellow ministers once again bent heads a long time before agreeing on a response. Austria would receive £250,000 up front but thereafter no more than £1 million in cash. Instead, Whitehall would sell as much as £4 million of Exchequer bills discounted at 5 percent in Vienna for Austria's treasury. The Austrians agreed, and a treaty was signed on April 24. As for Kleist's plot, Canning agreed to the arms depot, gave him a letter of credit for £20,000, and sent a liaison officer with him but did not commit to a Hanover campaign. Neither of those gambles would pay off. By the time Whitehall terminated its subsidies after Austria's armistice in late July, Vienna had taken £1,187,500 in cash and bonds.[18] All this money had to catch up with the vast expenditures that Austria was racking up.

The war began on April 9, when 200,000 Austrian troops led by Archduke Charles invaded Bavaria without warning and for the next week pushed back the Bavarian army and an advanced French corps. On April 17 Napoleon reached the front with reinforcements and launched a series of counterattacks that trounced the Austrians at

Abensburg, Eckmuhl, Rastibon, Landshut, and Ebersberg and captured Vienna on May 13. Meanwhile, in northeastern Italy, an Austrian army led by Archduke John attacked and initially pushed back Viceroy Eugene's imperial forces. Eugene pivoted his army and routed the Austrians at Caldiero, then pursued them into Carinthia. The war appeared to be heading toward a repeat of 1805, when Charles defeated Napoleon at Aspern-Esling, twin villages just east of the Danube River, on May 21 and 22 forced the French back across the Danube into Vienna. After swelling his army's ranks, Napoleon recrossed the Danube six weeks later and defeated Charles at the Battle of Wagram on July 5 and 6, then at Znaim on July 10. Charles asked for and received an armistice two days later.

The subsequent peace talks dragged on longer than the fighting. Under the Treaty of Schönbrunn, signed on October 14, Austria yielded Illyria to France, Salzburg to Bavaria, and Galicia to the Duchy of Warsaw. Napoleon was more powerful than ever in Central Europe.

As it had twice before, Whitehall tried to aid Vienna by launching a diversionary attack into the Low Countries. In doing so, Portland and his colleagues either failed to recall recent history or thought they could improve on the dismal work of their predecessors. On June 21, 1809, they authorized an expedition to invade the islands of Walcheren and South Beveland near the mouth of the Scheldt River with the goal of capturing Antwerp and destroying the enemy fleet of ten ships of the line anchored there.[19]

The armada—Britain's largest before the twentieth century—set sail on July 28, and included twenty-seven ships of the line, 225 smaller warships, and 400 transports led by Admiral Richard Strachan; General John Pitt, Earl of Chatham, commanded the 44,000 redcoats packed aboard. The troops landed unopposed. On South Beveland the British marched into the small fortress of Blatz, which the Dutch had abandoned. On Walcheren the British opened a siege of Flushing, defended by 5,800 troops, on August 1; the French surrendered on August 15.

The British were a mere fifteen miles from Antwerp, but they got no further. Napoleon sent Marshal Jean-Baptiste Bernadotte to command the French army. Bernadotte quickly massed and dug in 35,000 troops before the British lines and opened the sluice gates on the dykes holding back the sea. The result was a deadlock with neither side foolish enough to launch a human wave attack on the other side's entrenchments. For the next three months, nature dominated the campaign. Malaria, known there as "Walcheren fever," eventually sickened 14,000 British troops and killed 4,000 of them. In stark contrast, only 106 redcoats died in battle.

Chatham faced a dilemma. He could not advance. If he stayed, disease would steadily whittle his army's strength. If he retreated to the flotilla, the French could pursue and strike as his army tried to escape from the beach. He finally implemented a phased, month-long evacuation on November 4 that was not completed until December 9. In doing so, he was lucky to face an inept enemy commander like Bernadotte, who was content to let the British pack up and leave rather than destroy them.

British victories in the Iberian Peninsula partly obscured the debacle in Holland. Foreign Minister George Canning was determined to undermine Napoleon's empire by empowering Spain and Portugal, and in early 1809 he initiated a series of acts to that end. On January 14 he and ambassador Juan Ruiz de Apodaca, signed a treaty of peace, friendship, and alliance between Britain and Spain. However, his choice of John Frere to be Britain's minister to the Supreme Junta soon ran into trouble when that abrasive man clashed with the proud Spaniards; in July, the accomplished diplomat Richard Colley, Marquess of Wellesley, arrived to replace Frere.[20] Canning's most important act was to set up in Lisbon the British Aid Office, a department of the British Military Commissary, to funnel subsidies both to Portugal's Council of Regency and Spain's Supreme Junta. In 1809 alone, the Aid Office supplied the Portuguese with £270,538, mostly in goods. In July laborers unloaded 30,000 muskets and several hundred thousand cartridges from three vessels at Lisbon. Another flotilla of vessels soon arrived filled with £109,082 worth of uniforms, caps, shoes, blankets, and greatcoats. Britain was even more generous with Spain, committing £465,667 in cash, £2,174,097 worth of treasury bills, 155 cannons, 200,000 muskets, and 90,000 uniforms and other accoutrements to equip as many men.[21]

In return for committing what would be a half dozen years of vast expenditures of British blood and treasure to liberate Portugal and Spain, Whitehall naturally hoped for something in return. British envoys asked Spain for a bilateral free trade treaty, arguing that it was mutually beneficial by "opening to British commerce the Ports of Spanish America; and thereby enabling this Country [Britain] to recruit the Stock of Specie which has been exhausted in the service of Spain."[22] Some of those revenues would return to Spain as subsidies for its war effort, such as it was.

The Spaniards not only rejected free trade but displayed little gratitude and much resentment that the British had not given more aid. Canning expressed the paradoxes and frustrations of trying to nurture a working alliance with the Spaniards: "At present they are sure of us; and that they have a right to us; and that instead of every assistance that we afford them being another matter of fresh acknowledgement, every point of which we hesitate is an injury, and a breach of Engagement. This tone of theirs is offensive, and becomes irksome."[23] This offensive behavior assailed not just him but everyone unfortunate enough to have to deal with such a proud, ungrateful, and corrupt people. Even worse, the Spanish were utterly inept at every dimension of warfare. Augustus von Schaumann, a British commissary with the Spanish, voiced the prevailing disillusionment for their "allies":

> The more one sees of the Spaniards, the more discouraged one gets. Everything that has been so blatantly trumpeted in the papers about their enthusiasm, their great armies, and the stampede to join them is simply lies. It often looks as if Spain were not even willing to defend herself . . . [as] the inhabitants lounge about . . . completely apathetic, indifferent and gloomy, sunk in their idleness."[24] Ambassador Wellesley found the evil's source in the Supreme Junta, which "is neither an adequate representation of the crown, nor of the aristocracy, nor of the people, nor does it comprise any useful quality either of an executive council or of a deliberative assembly. . . . It is not an instrument of sufficient power to accomplish

> the purposes for which it was formed, nor can it ever acquire sufficient force or influence to bring into action the resources of the country and the spirit of the people . . . which might repel a foreign invader.[25]

The Junta did have one power, the power to deny—the Spaniards adamantly rejected every British request to anchor a fleet or disembark an army at Cadiz.

This refusal made Lisbon the only other viable safe base of operations. Portugal's Regency Council not only welcomed as many redcoats as possible to secure the country but even asked for a British general to organize and command its army. Whitehall tapped General William Beresford to the post on February 15, 1809.[26]

Although the Cintra controversy had sidelined General Arthur Wellesley, he remained intensely interested in the Peninsula's fate. On March 7, 1809, he submitted to Whitehall a plan whereby a British army secured Portugal, set up a Portuguese army, and then invaded Spain to drive the French from that country. The plan so impressed the ministers that on April 6 they appointed him to realize it.[27]

Wellesley stepped ashore at Lisbon on April 22, 1809, to command all British forces in the peninsula. Regent John enhanced his power on July 27 by naming him Portugal's generalissimo.[28] Yet Wellesley lacked two vital weapons of war, money and reliable soldiers. He complained that "we are terribly distressed for money. . . . I suspect the Ministers in England are very indifferent to our operations in this country."[29] He also worried that while his army "was excellent . . . on parade, an excellent one to fight . . . we are worse than an enemy in a country; and . . . either defeat or success would dissolve us."[30] With little that he could do about money, Wellesley devoted himself to transforming the Portuguese into professional soldiers. He formed his divisions with two British brigades and one Portuguese, thus forcing the allies to work together and get the Portuguese to emulate the more experienced British. He also established a Light Division composed of British and Portuguese troops trained both in mass infantry and skirmish tactics, of which the green-coated Ninety-fifth Rifle Regiment became the most renowned.

Two French armies menaced Lisbon in the spring of 1809, Marshal Nicolas Soult, with 23,000 troops deployed around Oporto, and Marshal Claude Victor, with 25,000 troops at Talavera, with 6,000 troops under General Pierre Lapisse between them at Ciudad Rodrigo. These forces were just the westernmost spearheads of over 250,000 French troops deployed across most of Spain.

The French threat was less ominous than it appeared. With 39,000 troops, including 20,000 British, 3,000 Hanoverians known as the King's German Legion, and 16,000 Portuguese, Wellesley's army outgunned either French army. The allied forces were deployed in a strategic arc to shield Lisbon. If all three French forces converged on the capital, Wellesley could exploit interior lines to rapidly mass troops against one of the enemy columns and overwhelm it with superior numbers of troops before the others came to its aid. The French would have to concentrate their forces to outgun the British. Logistics and jealousies, however, rendered a juncture between Soult and Victor unlikely. The armies were separated by a couple hundred miles of rugged terrain that would yield little food and water. As important, neither marshal wanted to march to the other's aid and thus put himself temporarily under the other's command.

Wellesley devised a plan to drive Soult from northern Portugal and blunt any offensive by Victor or Lapisse. In April he led 10,000 British and 2,400 Portuguese north, while General William Beresford marched north with his 6,000 Portuguese on a parallel road eastward. He left behind at Abrantes on the Tagus River 4,500 British and 7,000 Portuguese commanded by General Alexander Mackenzie to thwart an advance by Victor and Lapisse. After reaching Coimbra on May 1, Wellesley halted for a week to mass supplies and rest his men, resuming his advance on May 7. His troops scattered an advanced French guard of 4,500 troops at Grijon on May 11, and that night reached the heights overlooking the Douro River and Oporto beyond on the north bank.

Wellesley's strategy for May 12 was ingenious. While his massed cannons bombarded Soult's army in Oporto, most of his troops marched several miles upstream, crossed the river in wine barges, and assaulted Oporto's east side. That surprise attack routed the French, who suffered 300 dead and 1,500 prisoners to 23 British dead, 98 wounded, and 2 missing. Beresford meanwhile crossed the Douro farther east and routed a French force at Lamego. The British advance netted a thousand or so more French stragglers. Soult did not halt his retreat until his battered army reached Orense in northwestern Spain.[31]

After deploying forces to guard Portugal's northern frontier, Wellesley led 20,000 troops against Victor, who was marching toward Lisbon. He hoped to join General Cuesta and his 33,000 Spanish troops, who had advanced to Medellin to cut off Victor. Learning of Wellesley's rout of Soult and the twin advances against himself, Victor about-faced his army near Castelo Branco in the Tagus valley and withdrew into Spain.

Wellesley chased but could not catch Victor. On July 8 he called a halt at Plascenia, where he rested and resupplied his footsore troops, and tried to contact Cuesta. It was not until July 11 that he finally met Cuesta at Alamaraz and convinced him to join forces against Victor. On July 21 their armies met at Oropesa, only to halt the next day at Talavera to allow their supply trains to catch up. The allies were just seventy miles from Madrid.

Meanwhile, with reinforcements, Victor was emboldened to turn his 46,138 troops and march down the Tagus valley against Wellesley and Cuesta. On July 27 he launched his army against the 20,641 British and Portuguese and 34,800 Spanish troops lined along a ridge above a shallow valley, with the Tagus River anchoring their right flank and mountains their left flank. The British and Spanish troops repelled a series of French onslaughts this day and the next. Victor finally gave up and treated back up the Tagus valley. The Battle of Talavera was a bloodbath, with the British suffering 5,365 casualties, including 800 killed, and Cuesta 1,200 casualties, while inflicting over 7,268 dead, wounded, and captured on the French.[32]

Although the allies won a tactical victory by holding their ground during those two days of savage fighting, they did not tarry. Soult was advancing south with 50,000 men to trap the allies against Victor. During August's first week, Wellesley withdrew toward Portugal while Cuesta headed south toward Arzobispo. Victor's army was still too battered to advance further than Talavera which it entered on August 5. Soult, however, hurried after Cuesta and mauled the Spanish army on

August 8, capturing thirty cannons, of which most had been taken by the allies at Talavera. Cuesta led his army's remnant to the Spanish fortress of Badajoz near Portugal's frontier.

The campaign against Victor bitterly disappointed Wellesley. At Talavera he might have won a resounding victory had Cuesta fully cooperated. He vented his frustration in a letter to his brother Richard: "The Spanish troops will not fight; they are indisciplined, they have no officers, no provisions, no magazines . . . If we enter into a co-operation with them the burthen of the war must fall on us, and . . . will rest the disgrace of its certain and unavoidable failure."[33] While the Spanish "allies" seemed as much a curse as a blessing, Wellesley could be proud of his campaign, which had brilliantly realized his strategic goal of repelling the French forces threatening Portugal. Parliament certainly appreciated Wellesley's achievements and rewarded him with the title of Viscount Wellington of Talavera.

The Royal Navy racked up more victories. Whitehall maintained a large fleet and army in the West Indies that numbered 83 warships and 18,053 troops in late 1808.[34] In December Admiral Sidney Smith led an expedition that invaded French Guiana and forced its surrender on January 14, 1809. In early 1809 an armada with the fleet led by Admiral Alexander Cochrane and 10,000 troops led by General George Beckwith invaded Martinique, defended by 10,000 French troops. Beckwith received Martinique's surrender in February 1809, at the cost of 550 casualties. A year later he captured Guadeloupe, after losing 300 men, then occupied St. Eustatius and St. Martens. France was now stripped of its West Indies colonies.

Elsewhere during 1809 and 1810, British expeditions mopped up French colonies in Africa and the Indian Ocean. It only took a ragtag force of 166 armed sailors and marines to capture French Fort St. Louis, then Gorée, at the mouth of the Senegal River in July 1809. The British turned their guns toward the Indian Ocean, taking in succession Mauritius, Ile de Bourbon, and Ile de France, along with the Dutch islands of Java and Sumatra.

In all, the year 1809 revealed stark contrasts between how Britain's leaders amassed and asserted power. During sixteen years of nearly nonstop war, Whitehall steadily constructed an increasingly formidable military machine. The navy's 141,989 sailors and marines manned 108 ships of the line, 150 frigates, and 424 smaller warships. The army's 234,177 troops included 91,999 troops in Britain, 15,858 in Ireland, 35,796 in the Iberian Peninsula, 39,143 on Walcheren, and scores of smaller contingents scattered elsewhere.[35] Finding, equipping, feeding, and deploying all those soldiers and sailors demanded countless farmers, miners, teamsters, factory workers, stevedores, seamen, entrepreneurs, inventors, and financiers to man all the fields, mines, mills, shops, factories, shipyards, warehouses, offices, and banks. Foreign Minister Canning proudly summed up Britain's war effort for 1809: "In this war we have supplied by turns almost the whole continent with arms—Russia, Prussia, Sweden, Portugal, Sicily, and Spain—while at the same time our own military establishment are six fold what they formerly were."[36]

Alas, deficiencies of soft power undermined all this hard power. Canning can be forgiven his pride—he penned those lines in July before protests erupted over Chatham's debacle on Walcheren and Austria's latest defeat at Napoleon's hands. These two defeats revealed clear deficiencies in the art of British power: viable exit strategies and investments are vital elements of soft power.

The ignominy of British arms and diplomacy abroad was matched by the ignominy of British politics at home. The first scandal erupted in January 1809, shocking countless people beyond the inner recesses of the elite where versions of the story had circulated for years. Edward, Duke of York, was popularly seen as the king's good son, a model of loyalty and propriety, if not generalship, contrasting starkly with his older brother, George, the playboy and spendthrift crown prince. Yet York had a dark secret and one that he was whispered to be willing to pay a lot of money to conceal. For whatever reasons, he defied the ageless wisdom to beware a woman, especially a mistress, scorned. He had dumped his longstanding paramour, Mary Anne Clark, in 1805, and generously bought her silence until late 1808, when he made his last payment. As he might have anticipated, she began talking shortly thereafter, her most damning story being that he had let her take a cut of officer commission sales. This forced the House of Commons to form an investigative committee in January 1809. Although the committee reported in March that it had found no definitive evidence to support the charges, the damage was done, and York resigned anyway. His forced retirement lasted two years, when he was reappointed as the army's commander in chief on May 25, 1811. He would be just as lackluster during his second tenure.[37]

Prime Minister Portland suffered a massive paralytic stroke on August 11, resigned on September 6, and died on October 30, 1809. This led to a tumultuous political transition and the most famous duel in the nation's history.[38] The duel was months in the making.

From January through August 1809, Foreign Secretary George Canning had pressed Portland to fire Secretary for War Robert Stewart, Viscount Castlereagh, as a sacrificial political lamb for General John Moore's failed campaign in Spain. As foreign secretary Canning proposed replacing his political foe with his political ally Richard Wellesley, Earl of Mornington. Canning hinted strongly that if Castlereagh did not resign, he would. This alarmed Portland, who recognized how brilliant and vital to Britain's war effort both Canning and Castlereagh were, especially compared to his own admittedly meager abilities. So Portland hurried to George III and offered to resign. The king valued all three ministers and refused to accept any resignation. Instead he advised Portland to split Castlereagh's duties in two, leaving him in charge of colonial affairs while transferring the war's conduct to Canning. He sought to assuage Castlereagh's probable disappointment by naming him president of India's Board of Control. Portland took the idea back to Canning and all other prominent ministers except Castlereagh. While they agreed that the king's idea was a good one, they hesitated to impose it on Castlereagh. They mulled sweetening the deal by giving him the Lord Presidency of the Council and making him Lord Privy Seal, a post with far more prestige than power. They were still trying to figure out what to do when a stroke dropped Portland.

It was only then that Castlereagh learned of the intrigues against him. He hurried to the king, asked if the story was true, and asked to resign when George III acknowledged its veracity. The king rejected his resignation. Castlereagh withdrew to his home to brood for a dozen days before firing off to Canning a letter condemning him for being Janus faced, for sitting day after day with him in amicable company in the cabinet while plotting to take over his war powers. Castlereagh ended his letter by challenging Canning to a duel. Honor bound, Canning had to accept. Few doubted the duel's outcome if each tried to kill the other: Castlereagh was a crack shot, while Canning was a neophyte with firearms.

They and their seconds met on Putney Heath at dawn on September 21. Britain's foreign secretary and war secretary exchanged a terse if courteous greeting. Then each turned his back to the other, walked twelve paces, twirled, lowered his pistol, and fired. The balls shot wide. This should have satisfied each man's honor, but rage still blinded Castlereagh. He demanded a second round. This time Canning again missed, while Castlereagh's shot ploughed into Canning's thigh, though fortunately the ball did not splinter bone. For now each man's career was lost in political limbo. George III was outraged when he learned about the duel, and he barred them from the new government that he asked Spencer Perceval to form.

Perceval cobbled together a cabinet by October 4, 1809. Like Pitt, he took the posts of first lord of the treasury and chancellor of the exchequer. As an earnest evangelical and morally upright man who spurned the temptations of flesh or mammon, Perceval was a bit of an anomaly in the corridors of power.[39] Political imperatives forced him to pick his polar opposite in character as his foreign secretary. Richard Wellesley had a well-deserved notoriety as a rake, profligate, narcissist, and knife-edged wit who had made his fortune and reputation as India's governor-general.[40] Perceval tapped two other Wellesley brothers for prominent posts, William as Ireland's chief secretary and Henry as ambassador to Spain's junta. For other prominent posts, he talked Robert Jenkinson, Lord Hawkesbury, now Earl of Liverpool, into being the secretary for war; Richard Ryder, later Earl of Harrowby, to be the home secretary; and Charles Yorke, to be the first lord of the admiralty.

These men faced the now thirteen-year-old Sisyphean struggle of putting together the latest and sixth coalition against France. As usual, they did not openly question whether this effort actually enhanced or undercut Britain's national interest. They simply lowered their shoulders to their respective diplomatic, financial, and military duties and pushed.

CHAPTER 9

# The Sixth Coalition, 1810–1814

I must have the power to tell the Spanish government that, unless these troops co-operate strictly with me, the assistance shall be withdrawn from them.

Arthur Wellesley, Viscount Wellington

The British government was entitled to interfere in the management of the resources of Spain by the sacrifice of her own blood and treasure in the Spanish cause.

Arthur Wellesley, Viscount Wellington

If we can maintain ourselves in Portugal the war will not cease in the Peninsula, and if the war lasts in Peninsula, Europe will be saved.

Arthur Wellesley, Duke of Wellington

The British and French fought not just a military war, but an inseparable political war for hearts and minds in the Iberian Peninsula, and both were losing. King Joseph followed Napoleon's directives in how to transform Spain into a modern state. He worked hard to implement the French-style constitution that his brother had largely devised. He at once weakened an anti-French institution and raised revenue on August 18, 1809, when he ordered all religious orders closed and their property confiscated. He nationalized all religious-run primary schools on September 6, 1809. He eliminated all regional and city barriers to trade and created a common market for Spain on October 16, 1809, and on that same day he abolished all local taxes and imposed a national tax system. In December 1809 he appointed a committee to reform Spain's legal system by using the Code Napoleon as its guide.

These measures were designed to modernize Spain's medieval administrative, legal, political, religious, tax, educational, and cultural systems. The trouble was that they alienated far more people to French rule than they endeared. The reforms stripped tens of thousands of influential Spaniards of their privileged positions, wealth, and dignity and gave them yet more reasons to hate the French and do everything possible to drive them from Spain. With time the reforms might have won more converts as more people benefited from them. But the war, martial law, and an empty treasury stymied the reforms from being systematically implemented.

The overwhelming Spanish hatred for France did not translate into love for the British. Most people were sullen rather than exultant when redcoats marched through or bivouacked on their land. Wellington was acutely aware that Britain's military success depended on winning the alliance not just of the Junta and military leaders, but of the common people as well. He issued strict orders against robbery, rape, and murder. He unblinkingly had those accused of crimes tried, and if found guilty, submitted to the harshest punishments.

The word "guerrilla" entered the English lexicon during the Peninsula war. Although hit-and-run wars by common people against an enemy in their midst are undoubtedly as old as humanity, the guerrilla war in Spain reached unprecedented levels of scale and viciousness, vividly captured by artist Francisco de Goya's series of etchings called *Los Caprichos*. What accounts for the sheer savagery of Spain's guerrilla war?[1] Before the French invasion banditry and smuggling were rife across much of Spain, along with a mindset marked by overweening xenophobia, pride, superstition, and brutal vengeance for sullied honor. For ages, most Spaniards suffered being suppressed and exploited by local lords, priests, merchants, and bandits. Napoleon's attempt to conquer and convert Spain into a French-style modern state permitted Spaniards to vent lifetimes of pent-up rage against a hated foreigner. With time the war's nature changed from isolated attacks by small bands to increasingly larger and better-organized, -armed, and -led units of quasi-soldiers. But here too was a hearts-and-minds dilemma. While larger guerrilla groups could attack larger numbers of French troops, they often alienated the local population by exploiting them for food, shelter, clothing, money, and other spoils. They tended to resist the Junta's efforts to integrate and control them within Spain's army. Nonetheless, they proved to be vital British allies by killing, tying down, and isolating ever more French troops. The guerillas obtained their weapons and munitions both by seizing them from the French and receiving them from the British.

No one knew better than Wellington how much Britain's strategy in the Peninsula bled French power: "If we can maintain ourselves in Portugal the war will not cease in the Peninsula, and if the war lasts in Peninsula, Europe will be saved."[2] Yet a moral dilemma accompanied this successful policy. In aiding Spain's armies and guerrillas, Britain inadvertently empowered them to commit the vilest atrocities. Wellington wrote in despair that "the Spanish people are like gunpowder—the least spark inflames them; and, when inflamed there is no violence or outrage they do not commit and nothing can stop their violence. The Spaniard is an undisciplined savage who obeys no law." He searched in vain for an alternative, only to conclude that "we cannot with honor withdraw from [the peninsula] till we shall be obliged to do so."[3] The "honor" that Wellington referred to meant battling the French to the demise of one or the other. The volatility and false pride of Spain's people and leaders were self-defeating. Wellington vainly tried to convince the Junta to withdraw the armies into winter camp and slowly build their strength so that, in spring 1810, the allies could launch a well-coordinated offensive designed to drive the French from the peninsula. But to his despair, the Junta rejected his sound advice.

Instead the Junta ordered all Spanish armies to attack their nearest enemy. Catastrophe was the predictable result. In western Spain, General Don Lorenzo de Pozuela, Duque del Parque brushed aside a small French force at Tamames and marched his 40,000 troops into

Salamanca on October 18. As French forces under General François Kellermann swelled before him, Parque withdrew. Kellermann caught up to him at Alba de Mormes on November 28 and inflicted 3,000 casualties. But Spain suffered a worse defeat in the southwest. There the Junta took a positive step when it retired General Cuesta for all his failures, but unfortunately his replacement, General Carlos Areizaga, was no improvement. On November 19 Marshal Soult's 34,000-man army routed Areizaga's 55,000 troops at the Battle of Ocana, inflicting 4,000 dead and wounded and taking 14,000 prisoners. Soult followed up his victory by invading Andalusia. The Supreme Junta fled to Cadiz just ahead of Soult's army, which marched into Seville on January 31, 1810. Soult did not stop there but led his troops on to Cadiz, in hopes of delivering the coup de grace to Spain. The Junta was so desperate that for the first time it called for British forces to help defend the city. A redcoat contingent arrived from Gibraltar on February 7, and in the following weeks British forces there swelled to 10,000 troops commanded by General Thomas Graham.

The French conquest of Andalusia and siege of Cadiz drastically shifted the Iberian Peninsula's balance of military power. For the next two years, the allies would mostly fight on the defensive. Meanwhile the Junta tried to organize an efficient, representative national government. The first step came on January 1, 1810, when the Junta announced elections to be held for the Cortes on March 1, 1810. The empire was divided into electoral districts, with roughly one representative for every 50,000 people in Spain and one for every 300,000 people in the colonies, in which all males aged twenty-five and over could vote. Of course, holding an election across a country mostly occupied by a foreign invader was an imperfect process. Nonetheless, elections did take place in many regions, and the Cortes opened on September 24, 1810, although with less than half of its seats filled. High on the agenda was crafting a constitution that included the Cortes and a king, whenever Ferdinand VII might escape Napoleon's velvet prison and return to reign over his people and empire. The Supreme Junta renamed itself the Regency Council. For Wellington the institutional reforms were futile as long as the political culture remained unchanged: "The Cortes appears to . . . suffer under the national disease to as great a degree as the other authorities, that is, boasting of the strength and power of the Spanish nation till they are seriously convinced they are in no danger, and then sitting down quietly and indulging in their national indolence."[4]

This was hardly the only deficiency. The Regency Council offended a vital constituency—Spain's colonial subjects or "criollos." Inspired by American and French revolutionary ideals, they demanded equal representation with the "peninsules" in the Cortes and the redress of a long list of grievances. When the Junta rejected their demands, revolts erupted across swathes of Mexico, Venezuela, Columbia, Ecuador, Argentina, Paraguay, and Uruguay from April to October 1810. The rebel groups split between demanding reforms or independence.

This posed a quandary for Whitehall. British strategic interests depended on nurturing a strong Spanish state and army against the French. At the same time, British economic interests would profit if Spain's colonies were opened to bilateral free trade. The Spaniards had repeatedly rejected Whitehall's requests for open markets in return for all the military and financial aid that they received. Should the British wield the threat of assisting the colonial rebels to pressure Spain's government into opening its markets? Doing so could shatter the fragile relationship between London and Cadiz, and cripple the allied war against the French in the Peninsula. The ministers shelved this option for now and instead redoubled the pressure on Spain to open its national and colonial markets to British goods or else face a cutback of British aid.[5]

The Regency Council angrily protested this threat. In response, Whitehall rewarded Lisbon, which had agreed to free trade, and punished Cadiz by adjusting its aid figures. In 1810 the British nearly quadrupled the Portuguese subsidy, distributing £1 million worth of cash, bonds, and goods, including 51,200 muskets, 7.5 million cartridges, 30,000 uniforms, 40,000 shirts, 42,000 knapsacks, and two pairs of shoes for each soldier. In stark contrast, the £445,000 that they gave Cadiz was pointedly lower than the previous year's; they also distributed £291,991 in subsidies to the regional councils. Regardless, over the next year Britain doubled its total aid to both countries, with transfers of £465,667 in cash and £2,174,097 in paper in 1809 rising to £679,069 in cash and £5,382,166 in paper, respectively, in 1810.[6]

The council reacted to Whitehall's largely symbolic aid cutback by more vociferously declaring that the empire would remain firmly closed to British merchants. On August 17, 1811, Charles Stuart, Wellington's envoy at Cadiz, informed the regents that Britain would suspend subsidies until reforms were enacted.[7] The warning was a bluff. Military necessity soon forced Whitehall to transfer vast arsenals from British factories to Spain's armies. By February 1811 Britain had shipped to Spain 342 cannons, 128,040 cannonballs, 222,141 muskets, 99,000 accoutrements, and 43,358,455 cartridges. That far surpassed Portugal's receipt of 6 cannons, 2,000 cannonballs, 114,116 muskets, 50,000 accoutrements, and 16,607,200 cartridges.[8]

For Wellington all this aid should at the very least be exchanged for granting him the same authority over Spain's military that he held over Portugal's. To his brother Richard Wellesley, now the foreign secretary, he wrote that "I must have the power to tell the Spanish government that, unless these troops co-operate strictly with me, the assistance shall be withdrawn from them."[9] To Prime Minister Liverpool, he explained the demand's logic:

> That no permanent advantage could be expected unless the military and financial resources of Spain could be rendered available in nearly the same proportion with those of Portugal. That no real improvement could be looked for in the government of Spain without the active interference of the British government. That the British government was entitled to interfere in the management of the resources of Spain by the sacrifice of her own blood and treasure in the Spanish cause. But that to render the inference of the British minister palatable and effectual, it would be necessary to give some pecuniary aid to the Spaniards.

He called for enlisting 30,000 Spaniards in regiments with British officers and reckoned the annual cost at £3 million.[10]

Spanish pride could definitely be bought, but at what price? Liverpool did not flatly reject Wellington's proposal but noted the dilemma. The present strategy was costly enough and might well end in defeat by massive French offensives that overwhelmed the allies. Yet, if Whitehall spent enough to mobilize Spain for total war, this might pay off with victory or simply spike the cost of ultimate defeat.[11] Despite Whitehall's tepid support, Wellington got his younger brother, Henry Wellesley, now ambassador at Cadiz, to keep pressuring the Regency Council to name his brother generalissimo of Spain's armies. Although the Spaniards angrily rejected his entreaties, their pride could not resist demanding ever more British aid.[12]

As if the bitter relations with Cadiz were not stressful enough, Wellington faced two crises with Lisbon in 1810. As with countless Spaniards, many Portuguese resented rather than appreciated Britain's rescue of their country. Powerful voices called for retaking control over their nation's fate. First, Portugal's Council of Regency debated replacing General William Beresford with Ferdinand Duke Brunswick to command the Portuguese army. Wellington warned the council that he and his army would abandon Portugal if it interfered with his powers as generalissimo, which included naming Portugal's military commanders.[13] Then José de Souza Coutinho, backed by Oporto's bishop, tried to rescind Wellington's title of generalissimo. As the oldest of three powerful brothers, José was known as "the Principal." Domingos was the minister to Britain, and Rodrigo served with the regent in Rio de Janeiro. Charles Stuart represented Wellington on the council and eventually staved off this power play. But it was a "near run thing," a Wellington phrase that summed up any number of military, political, and diplomatic battles in his life.[14]

As Wellington fought these political battles in his rear, he was instructed to stay on the defensive within Portugal this year and build up his forces. He likely noted the rare event when he and Whitehall were in accord. The devastating defeats of Spain's armies opened Portugal to invasion. In the shadow of huge French armies, Wellington asked Liverpool whether he was expected to stand and fight or evacuate. The reply was predictable: "His Majesty would be unwilling that His Army should evacuate Portugal before circumstances should render it absolutely necessary."[15]

These were not idle worries. Having once again vanquished Austria, Napoleon massed troops for a knockout blow in the Iberian

Peninsula. He ordered 100,000 troops to march from Germany to join the 250,000 already there. But he failed either to appoint a marshal to command all those widely dispersed forces or to return to assume this vital role. Instead, he tried to micromanage the war from Paris. This destroyed the ability of his generals to respond swiftly to opportunities or threats, and weeks passed before the emperor reacted to intelligence and requests. Then, more often than not his commands were either irrelevant or self-defeating once they reached a distant headquarters. The result was to aggravate what he called his "Spanish ulcer" into an ultimately deadly cancer rotting his empire.

Napoleon recognized that Wellington's army in Portugal was the keystone of allied power in the Peninsula. If Wellington were destroyed, Spanish resistance would swiftly collapse. To that end, Napoleon appointed André Masséna, on April 16, to command 130,000 troops scattered across western and central Spain and then ordered him to conquer Portugal. On May 15 Masséna established his headquarters at Salamanca. He could only cull 86,000 troops for his offensive; the rest were needed to guard supply lines and cities and to scour the countryside for provisions and guerrillas.

Wellington prepared for the onslaught. Reinforcements swelled his army from 31,000 troops in January to 51,000 troops in September. These, however, were his paper strengths. Disease laid low anywhere from 1 in 10 to 1 in 5 of his soldiers; the worst rate was 23 percent, with 9,405 in hospitals on the eve of Masséna's invasion.[16]

Wellington's strategy was simple. Four formidable defenses blocked Masséna's advance from Salamanca to Lisbon. He let local forces handle the first two, the Spanish fortress of Cuidad Rodrigo and the Portuguese fortress of Almeida. If those capitulated, Wellington would stand first in the mountains, then, if necessary, withdraw within the Lines of Torres Vedras, a twenty-nine-mile double chain of forts and redoubts running from the Tagus River east of Lisbon to the Atlantic Ocean. This defense in depth exploited the dilemma entangling the French in the peninsula: strategic consumption. Armies weakened as they advanced by shedding troops to guard their lengthening supply lines.

Masséna implemented a methodical campaign. The 5,000 defenders of Ciudad Rodrigo held up his advance for six weeks until they surrendered, on July 10. He marched his men a score of miles into Portugal to Almeida, whose 5,000 Portuguese defenders held out until August 26. In all, Masséna's victorious sieges of Cuidad Rodrigo and Almeida cost him precious amounts of time, troops, and supplies. He led 65,000 men from Almeida on September 15.

Wellington and his 51,000 troops—half British and half Portuguese—awaited the enemy on the Sierra do Bussaco mountain range, split by a 1,800-foot pass, just eight miles east of Coimbra and the coastal lowlands. The position nullified Masséna's edge in numbers, especially of cavalry. Rather than seek a way around, Masséna ordered his army to go over the top on September 25. The French were slaughtered as they slowly trudged up the mountain slopes in the face of a hail of bullets. The allies killed 515, wounded 3,800, and captured 300 French, while suffering about 200 dead, 1,000 wounded, and 50 missing.[17]

Masséna did find a way around Bussaco, but by the time he took it the enemy was long gone, Wellington's troops having withdrawn to the Lines of Torres Vedras, looting anything edible from homes, barns, and fields along the way. Massena's army numbered only 55,000 men when it arrived hungry and exhausted before the Torres Vedras lines on October 14. The rains had began on October 2 and rarely let up for the next several months.

Although his army now outnumbered Masséna's, Wellington did not order an attack then or for the next month that the French remained just beyond cannon shot. Instead, he let nature take its course as French supplies dwindled to the vanishing point. Even after Masséna withdrew his army to Santarem on the Tagus River, Wellington waited several days before leading his army cautiously in pursuit. At Santarem Masséna had his 46,000 troops entrench themselves in the surrounding hills for a British assault that never came, and sent pleas to Napoleon for reinforcements. The emperor had none to spare that could reach Masséna in time. Instead, he ordered Soult, whose army was besieging Cadiz, to launch a diversion against the Spanish frontier fortresses of Olivenza and Badajoz.

Leaving Marshal Claude Victor with 11,000 men to carry on Cadiz's siege, Soult marched north with 19,500 men on December 31, 1810. After a short siege, he forced Olivenza's 4,000-man garrison to surrender on January 22 of the following year. He marched on to Badajoz and opened a siege on January 26. General Gabriel Mendizabal advanced with his army to the rescue, but Soult routed him at the Battle of Gebora on February 19. Wellington responded to word of Soult's campaign by dispatching Beresford with his Portuguese division to relieve the siege at Badajoz, but Beresford did not get there in time: the 8,000-man garrison capitulated on March 10, and Beresford halted when he learned of the loss. Leaving behind a 4,500-man garrison at Badajoz, Soult withdrew to Seville. In all, he fought a model campaign by capturing two fortresses, routing an enemy army, and bagging 20,000 prisoners.

Meanwhile, at Cadiz, General Thomas Graham envisioned a way to break the French siege. He talked his colleague General Manuel La Peña into packing 9,500 Spanish, 4,900 British, and 300 Portuguese into transports, sailing down the coast to Algeciras, then marching sixty miles north to strike Victor in the rear. The allies sailed on February 21, landed on February 28, and advanced as far as the Barossa ridge on March 5. Awaiting them there were Victor and 10,000 French troops. Victor ordered an attack that routed the Spanish and forced the redcoats to withdraw with them. The victory came at a high cost, 2,400 French casualties compared to the allied loss of 1,740 killed and wounded.[18]

With no chance of reinforcements, Masséna ordered his army to withdraw from Santarem on March 3, 1811. Over the preceding ten months he had lost over 25,000 troops, with 2,000 killed in action, 8,000 captured, and the rest dead from disease and starvation. Wellington's prudence kept his own army's losses to about 4,000, or one-sixth that of the French.[19]

Wellington cautiously followed Masséna, then halted his advance to besiege Almeida. After replenishing his ranks and supplies, Masséna marched with 42,000 infantry and 4,500 cavalry to Almeida's relief. Wellington blocked his way at Fuentes de Oro with 34,000 infantry and 1,800 cavalry. Masséna ordered an attack on May 3, and the result was the latest bloodbath, with Masséna's army suffering 2,844 casualties to Wellington's 2,453. Massena withdrew with his army to Salamanca; along the way he was relieved of his army's command by Marshal Auguste Marmont. Once again victory humbled Wellington, who admitted: "If Boney had been there we should have been beaten."[20]

In early May, Beresford surrounded Badajoz with 29,000 troops, half British, half Portuguese, but a lack of heavy guns and savvy engineers handicapped the siege. After suffering 700 casualties, he withdrew to the fortress of Elvas, where Generals Joachim Blake and Francisco Xavier Castanos, with 15,000 Spanish troops, joined him. Learning that Soult was advancing against them, the allied generals agreed to take a stand on the hills outside Albuera on the main east-west road. Although outnumbered by three to two, Soult launched his army at the enemy on May 16. The carnage was horrific. The allies lost 5,916 dead and wounded among their 35,284 troops; the British contingent suffered the worst, with 4,407 casualties, or two-thirds of the 6,500 who fought. The French lost 7,000 dead and wounded of their 24,260 troops.[21] The following day Soult withdrew toward Mérida.

Wellington marched his army south and encircled Badajoz, but, like Beresford, he lacked enough heavy guns and engineers for an effective siege. At Mérida, after Marmont and his 40,000 troops joined forces with Soult and his 23,000 troops on June 18, they marched westward to relieve Badajoz. Although Wellington now commanded 54,000 allied troops, he avoided risking his army in the open before superior numbers of French cavalry; instead he withdrew to the highlands around Elvas. After reaching Badajoz on June 20, Soult did not pursue. He replenished the garrison's supplies and sent Marmont north to Salamanca before withdrawing south with his own troops to Seville.

Wellington headed to Ciudad Rodrigo and opened a siege there on August 11. Marmont waited until he massed 58,000 troops, then marched to that fortress's relief in late September. Wellington once again chose to withdraw rather than risk a battle. The fighting on this front ended in 1811, with the two fortresses guarding the western invasion route into Spain in French hands. The strategic balance in the Iberian Peninsula still favored France, but the seesaw would tip decisively toward Britain the next year.

Whitehall traditionally viewed Sicily as the Mediterranean basin's fulcrum of power because that triangle of an island split the sea into western and eastern halves. Whoever controlled Sicily was poised to assert itself in either direction. Yet Sicily's importance to Britain's grand strategy dwindled as that of the Iberian Peninsula swelled. This in turn enhanced British power over the exiled king and queen in Palermo. British officials there certainly needed all the power they could muster: the spineless, vacillating King Ferdinand IV and the hateful, paranoid, backstabbing Queen Marie Caroline were a diplomatic handful. But the royal couple was just the top of the pyramid of frustrations, the court, bureaucracy, army, and navy being corrupt, inept, and often brutal. Little of the £300,000 in annual British subsidies promised by a bilateral treaty signed on March 23, 1807, was actually invested to improve the realm's civil or military institutions. Despite this, the king, queen, and their underlings talked the British into raising the annual handout to £400,000 in a treaty signed on March 30, 1808.[22]

Fed up with all the intrigues, deceit, and venality, Ambassador William Amherst and General John Stuart, who commanded British forces in Sicily, resigned their posts in late 1810. Facing far more pressing priorities at home and abroad, Whitehall did not get around to filling these posts for more than half a year but then gave the diplomatic and military powers to one person, as much for economy as for efficiency.

William Bentinck, the Duke of Portland's second son, stepped ashore as Britain's man in Palermo in July 1811.[23] He owed his rank of major general mostly to nepotism; his military experience was confined to serving as a liaison officer with the Austrian army in Italy from 1799 to 1801 and with the Spanish Junta in 1808. Although he had a reputation for being bright, imaginative, and energetic, he could also be aloof and headstrong. He had actually declined the offer to be the secretary at war in 1809 and Wellington's second-in-command in 1810.

Having let the war pass him by, Bentinck had impulsively grabbed a post at a military and diplomatic backwater, making him all the more determined to make the most of his position. He worked hard to build up a 10,000-man Sicilian division trained and led by British officers for service in eastern Spain. But only a portion of these troops eventually saw action abroad; most were held back to quell worsening outbreaks of violence within Sicily itself. But in November 1812 Bentinck was able to send 4,500 troops to join a British force at Alicante.[24]

A chance directly to undermine the French empire arose when Count Laval von Nugent arrived at Palermo in 1811 with a request from Archduke Francis d'Este, the Austrian emperor's nephew, for money to recruit an army in the Ionian Islands, from which he would attack the French in Dalmatia. Bentinck eagerly latched onto this scheme and asked Whitehall for money. The cabinet appropriated £100,000 for Bentinck to underwrite the scheme. The money disappeared into various hands with nothing to show for it.[25]

This same year a similar scam tempted a British envoy on a neighboring island at another court exiled from the Italian mainland. William Hill was Britain's man in Caligari, Sardinia, where the House of Savoy, which had reigned in Turin, had refuged. One Alessandro Turr approached Hill for money to raise an insurrection against the French in northern Italy. Hill was skeptical and insisted that the Italians would have to revolt before they got any cash, and the scam was foiled.

Bentinck, unable to stir up trouble against the French, turned his attention to foisting a political revolution upon Sicily. On December 7, 1811, he presented Ferdinand IV and Marie Caroline with a reform plan that united their military forces under British command, released all political prisoners, and implemented a constitution that set up a British-style parliament. If they refused, Whitehall would end its subsides, withdraw its troops from Sicily, and leave the realm to Napoleon's mercy. His trump cards were letters intercepted from Marie Caroline to Napoleon whereby she begged forgiveness for the double game she and her husband had played in 1805 and pledged to align with France if he let them return to Naples. Of course, Napoleon would never give up southern Italy, where his brother-in-law, King Joachim Murat, reigned.

Bentinck's ultimatum actually yielded results. In June 1812 Ferdinand IV resigned in favor of his son, Francis, and convened a Sicilian parliament to write a constitution as its first priority. Alas, the constitutional monarchy was just as corrupt and inept as the absolute monarchy it replaced. Bentinck set aside his dream of liberalizing Sicily for a far grander dream of unifying the Italian peninsula. But to realize this he needed to wait for the French empire to suffer some decisive defeats. That time would come.

Britain, meanwhile, experienced its own political changes, one superficial, the other profound. In October 1810 George III began slipping back into madness, a decline hastened by his beloved daughter

Amelia's death on November 2. Prime Minister Perceval introduced a regency bill in Parliament on December 10. Each house hesitated to act, hoping that the king would again recover. This time, however, his madness worsened far beyond previous levels, with no sign of relenting. Parliament passed the regency bill on February 5, 1811, and the following day the crown prince took the oath as prince regent. George III remained officially the king until he died on January 20, 1820. Along the way, like many people who were free spirits and liberals in their younger decades, the man who would replace him as George IV grew more conservative as he aged.

Britain's fate depended little on who reigned and much on who governed. One of the most brilliant diplomats in British history returned to assert the art of power. Robert Stewart, Viscount Castlereagh, spent a couple of years in the political wilderness after blasting a ball into George Canning's thigh during their notorious duel in 1809. In 1812 he finally felt ready to make his political comeback. To this end, he carefully worked behind the scenes with parliament's power brokers to ensure that he not only won an uncontested seat but was elected Speaker of the House of Commons, then was tapped to replace Richard Wellesley as foreign secretary.

For the next decade, Castlereagh dominated British foreign policy.[26] This long reign came not just from his dogged work, political, and diplomatic skills but also because his colleagues in the cabinet were noted chiefly for their mediocrity. Spencer Perceval, for instance, won lasting fame solely as the only prime minister who was assassinated; John Bellingham, incensed that the war had ruined his business, fired a pistol point-blank into Perceval's chest in the antechamber of the House of Commons on May 11, 1812. After the usual intense rounds of political horse trading, Robert Jenkinson, Lord Hawkesbury, Earl of Liverpool, took over as prime minister and rewarded Nicolas Vansittart and Henry Addington, Viscount Sidmouth, to be chancellor of the exchequer and home secretary, respectively, for their loyalty above all. The most important reason why Castlereagh endured as foreign secretary was that his policies notably advanced Britain's national interests. He deftly worked first to destroy Napoleon's empire, then to restore and manipulate in Britain's favor Europe's balance of power.

The Iberian Peninsula's strategic seesaw tipped from France to Britain in 1812. In January Napoleon withdrew 27,000 Imperial Guard troops from Spain, and during the rest of the year summoned there another 50,000 regular troops. Wellington, meanwhile, launched an offensive that eventually took him all the way to Madrid, although his stay was brief.

On New Year's Day, Wellington led his army across the frontier and a week later besieged Cuidad Rodrigo. His batteries opened fire on January 14 and had blasted two breaches in the walls by January 19. That night Wellington ordered an assault. As his troops battled their way over the rubble and into the town, 449 were killed or wounded, including Light Division commander General Robert Crauford, who was shot dead, but the British killed 500 French and took 1,300 prisoners and the fortress. This victory earned Wellington's his latest promotion, from viscount to earl, and a doubling of his stipend to £4,000. Wellington then led his army south to the much more powerful frontier Spanish fortress of Badajoz, defended by 5,000 troops.

Learning of the invasion, Napoleon ordered General Auguste Marmont to retake Ciudad Rodrigo and then Almeida in the vain hope of drawing Wellington back. The ploy did not just fail, it sealed Badajoz's fate. Wellington and his army deployed around Badajoz on January 28, but heavy rains prevented any digging of siege works for weeks, and the first guns did not open fire until March 25. This should have given Marmont enough time to march to the rescue, but instead he was fruitlessly besieging Cuidad Rodrigo. By April 5, Wellington's guns had finally battered three breaches in the walls, and during the assault the next night, the carnage was horrific. The British suffered 3,713 casualties, including over 800 dead, atop 957 casualties during the siege, bringing their total losses to 4,670 troops. But the defenders and the civilians trapped with them suffered far worse. For three days after the surrender, Wellington turned a blind eye and deaf ear as his soldiers looted, burned, raped, and murdered their way through a city of their Spanish ally.[27]

It took nearly two months for Wellington to replenish his army's ranks and supplies for his campaign's next stage. His confidence swelled with his army's strength and intelligence reports of the enemy's weaknesses. For once he was openly optimistic in a report he sent to Whitehall: "Strong as the enemy are at present . . . they are weaker than they have ever been during the war . . . We have a better chance of success now . . . than we have ever had; and success obtained now would produce results not to be expected from any success over any single French army in the Peninsula upon any other occasion."[28]

Leaving behind General Rowland Hill and 20,000 British and Portuguese troops to thwart a possible advance of Soult and his army from Seville, Wellington led 28,500 British, 18,000 Portuguese, and 3,000 Spanish troops northeast to Salamanca to cut off Marmont at Ciudad Rodrigo. Marmont quickly withdrew his 30,000 men beyond the allied army's relentless pursuit, and on June 17 Wellington and his men marched into Salamanca.

Reinforcements swelled the French army to 50,000 troops, a number that could have risen to 65,000 had Marmont awaited King Joseph and Marshal Jean-Baptiste Jourdan, who were hurrying to join him from Madrid. But Marmont appears to have been bitten with that deadly bug plaguing French commanders in the peninsula, jealousy. Unwilling to cede both command and glory to Jourdan, his senior, Marmont marched his army westward for what he believed would be a decisive victory over Wellington.

Like two nimble-footed prizefighters, the two armies maneuvered across the plains east and south of Salamanca, each trying to sidestep the other for a knockout punch. Wellington grimly noted that "I shan't fight him without an advantage, nor he me."[29] This is a risky strategy, as one has to thin the troops in one's front to hook most of one's army around the enemy. On July 22 Wellington ordered his army to attack when Marmont's regiments were stretched in a long line marching west toward his rear. The result was one of Wellington's quickest and most decisive victories. His troops routed the French and killed or captured nearly 13,000 of them, while suffering only 4,800 casualties. With Marmont among the seriously wounded, General Bertrand Clausel replaced him as the army's commander. French general Maximilien Foy paid tribute to Wellington's military prowess: "Hitherto we had been aware of his prudence, his eye for choosing a position and his skill in utilizing it. At Salamanca he has shown himself a great and able master of maneuver."[30] Parliament once again generously rewarded

Britain's greatest general since Marlborough, this time by promoting him from viscount to marquess and giving him £100,000 to enjoy a lifestyle appropriate to the title.

Wellington might have bagged much of the French army but had only 3,000 cavalry to spearhead his advance and mop up stragglers. As Clausel withdrew his army's remnants toward Burgos, in Madrid King Joseph had a harsh choice to make. With only 15,000 troops and lacking munitions, provisions, and, above all, morale, he withdrew south to join Marshal Louis Suchet at Valencia.

Wellington and his men marched into Madrid on August 12. Their stay was fleeting. Strategic attrition reduced his immediate army to 40,000 troops, a paltry number compared to the over 260,000 French troops in Spain, although most were far away fighting guerrillas and guarding supply lines. The closest allied force was Hill's 19,000 troops in Estremadura, blocking any advance by Soult against Wellington's rear.

To recapture Spain's center, Joseph ordered French troops to evacuate the southwest. Soult ended Cadiz's siege on August 25, and two days later he led his army east from Seville. Along the way he amassed French field forces and garrisons until he had 45,000 troops when he joined Joseph in Valencia on September 25, bringing their combined forces to 60,000 troops. However, from there to Madrid was another long march of several weeks.

Two British expeditions elsewhere in Spain forced the French to spread their forces thinner. Admiral Home Popham commanded the flotilla operating along Spain's northern coast. This year he aided General Gabriel Mendizabal's 10,000-man army and guerilla bands with not just supplies but troops against French forces. The allies conducted a series of attacks on French positions along the coast, culminating with Santander's capture on August 2. Popham and Mendizabal then led their troops eastward to take Bilbao. General Marie Caffarelli du Falga, the region's French commander, led part of his army north to attack the allies on August 13 and finally expelled them after two days of fighting, although he lacked enough men to march on and retake Santander. As for Wellington, during his 1813 campaign, he would shift his supply center from Lisbon to Santander, thus greatly alleviating his army's strategic attrition problem, but British operations along Spain's Mediterranean coast were far less successful. General Frederick Maitland disembarked with a force of 11,000 British and Sicilian troops at Alicante on August 7, in hopes of joining General José O'Donnell's 12,000 troops against Suchet's forces in the region. O'Donnell, however, met with disaster en route to their rendezvous when General Jean Harispe with 5,000 men routed him at Castalla. After learning of this defeat and other French forces marching against him, Maitland hurried his army back to the safety of Alicante.

With word that Soult had evacuated southwestern Spain, Wellington summoned Hill and his army to Madrid. Although his army now numbered 72,000 troops, Wellington felt isolated and vulnerable. If he tried to hold Madrid, he risked being trapped between Joseph's 65,000 troops marching from the south and Clausel's 30,000 man marching from the north. So on September 1 he left General Charles Alten with 18,000 at Madrid and sent Hill with his 19,000 to Toledo, while he led his army of 24,000 British and Portuguese and 11,000 Spaniards north against the weaker of the two French armies. Clausel withdrew his army beyond Burgos after garrisoning that city's castle with 2,000 troops. Rather than bypass Burgos and try to catch up to Clausel, Wellington encircled that city on September 19. The trouble was that he lacked enough tools and heavy guns for a proper siege. The garrison was still defiant after a month that cost the allies 2,000 casualties.

Meanwhile, French forces converged against Wellington at Burgos and Hill and Alten in central Spain. In the north, Napoleon replaced the lackluster Clausel with the more aggressive General Joseph Souham, who advanced with 50,000 troops. With only about 35,000 British, Portuguese, and Spanish troops, Wellington was severely outgunned, and as if that were not dire enough, his supplies were dwindling steadily. On October 22 he ordered his army to abandon the siege and march westward, and he sent instructions to Hill and Alten to join him at Salamanca. Years later he noted that among a great general's attributes was the ability "to know when to retreat and to dare to do it."[31]

Souham and Soult respectively pursued Wellington and Hill but never caught up. By early November Wellington's now reunited army at Salamanca numbered 75,000, including 30,000 British, 20,000

Portuguese, and 25,000 Spanish. Although the combined French armies numbered 100,000 soldiers, Soult, the senior commander, did not dare to attack. Wellington slowly reversed his army's stepson his overstretched supply lines to Ciudad Rodrigo, where his army wintered. The French army split, with Soult marching back to Madrid and General Jean-Baptiste Drouet d'Erlon, the latest northern army commander, remaining at Salamanca.

Although Wellington and his army ended 1812 near where they had started it, they could take ample pride in most of what they had done in between. They had captured the fortresses of Cuidad Rodrigo and Badajoz, routed Marmont at Salamanca, marched into Madrid, chased Clausel from Burgos, then withdrew in good order to Portugal. In all, they inflicted on the French nearly 25,000 killed and wounded, and they had captured over 20,000 troops. These triumphs, however, came at a high cost. In all, 10,207 of Wellington's troops died, 1,720 suffered wounds so severe that they were discharged, and 1,092 deserted, for a total loss of over 13,000 men. Troops on the sick list varied from 13,000 to 20,000 each month, leaving his regiments an average 40 percent under strength.[32]

Meanwhile, Spain took an important political step at home darkened by worsening rebellions in its empire. On March 19, 1812, the Cortes promulgated a constitution that divided powers between the king and parliament and granted limited political rights to Spanish subjects. The American rebellions provoked an economic crisis. The "king's fifth" was the 20 percent cut the government took of the gold and silver mined in the Americas, but revenues plummeted as rebels seized mines or shipments, from 40.7 million reales when the uprisings began in 1810, to 201 million reales in 1811, and a mere 138 million reales in 1812. The widening gap between the Regency Council's income and expenses made it increasingly dependent upon and demanding of British largess.[33]

Foreign Minister Castlereagh talked the cabinet into boosting Spain's cash subsidy from £600,000 to £1 million for 1812, while having Ambassador Wellesley pressure Cadiz to name Wellington generalissimo. This influx of cash followed by Wellington's brilliant 1812 campaign persuaded most Cortes delegates to do so. Castlereagh responded by increasing Spain's aid to £1.2 million in 1813. Thereafter, as the allies drove the French from Spain and invaded France itself, he cut back the subsidies.[34]

The Cortes voted on September 25, 1812, to name Wellington generalissimo and clarified on October 11 that as such he commanded all Spanish forces. Wellington assumed that role on November 22, when he met with the council and Cortes at Cadiz. This series of events deeply offended the pride and provoked enraged protests from countless Spanish officers and soldiers, and no one was more bitterly outspoken than General Francisco Ballesteros who refused to operate under Wellington's command. Spain's war minister had him arrested.

Wellington soon discovered, not to his complete surprise, that his powers as generalissimo were more symbolic than real. The foot-dragging of Spain's generals and ministers exasperated him. Wellington warned the Spaniards that "unless some measures can be adopted to prevail upon the government to force [them] to perform . . . with me, I must resign."[35] Although this threat elicited nothing more than promises of greater cooperation that would largely be unfulfilled, Wellington retained his empty title. He increasingly wondered if the Cortes had named him generalissimo to scapegoat him for any defeats and hog the credit for any victories. Despite the accolades bestowed upon him by parliament, Wellington felt he was underappreciated: "From what I see in the newspapers I am afraid that the public will be much disappointed at the result of the last campaign notwithstanding that it . . . has produced more important results than any campaign in which a British army has been engaged for the last century."[36]

Although no blood was shed, the official state of war between Britain and Russia kept Whitehall from capitalizing on the deteriorating relationship between Alexander and Napoleon. The tsar first requested British help in November 1810, when he secretly sent Carlo Andrea Pozzo di Borgo, a Corsican nobleman and Napoleon hater, for talks with Prime Minister Perceval and Foreign Secretary Wellesley over a possible alliance and subsidy. Before reaching into the government's coffers, the ministers asked for some sign that Alexander might actually break with Napoleon. The sign came on December 31, 1810, when the tsar banned French manufactured and luxury goods and heavily taxed French wine. Although they lauded this as a first step, Perceval and Wellesley asked for a Russian invasion of the Duchy of Warsaw, to force Napoleon to divert forces from the Iberian Peninsula. Alexander drew the line at launching a war against the French empire that most likely would end in another humiliating defeat. For now, neither London nor St. Petersburg was willing to commit anything of substance to the other.

Whitehall received Napoleon's latest peace offering in 1811. He proposed that each side would keep its conquests; accept the Braganza family's rule over Portugal; confine Ferdinand IV's reign to the island of Sicily; confirm Murat's rule over southern Italy; and recognize the "dynasty" currently enthroned in Madrid. In other words, Napoleon wanted Britain to acquiesce in his direct or indirect control over most of the continent, including his satellite kingdoms. Castlereagh replied that if Napoleon was willing to accept Ferdinand VII as Spain's rightful ruler, then talks could begin. Napoleon insisted that his brother Joseph I would kept his throne. This ended any chance of peace as Castlereagh severed communications with Napoleon.

A viable coalition could not arise until potential members resolved their conflicts with each other. In 1808 Alexander declared war on Sweden to fulfill a long-standing Russian ambition to conquer Finland. The Russians won. A 1809 treaty forced Sweden to cede Finland to Russia, join the Continental System, and declare war against Britain. Sweden's link with France appeared to strengthen when, in August 1810, Sweden's national assembly voted to name Jean-Baptiste Bernadotte, an inept and disloyal but nonetheless French marshal, to be their nation's crown prince to childless Charles XIII, the last of the royal family's line. To help cement relations between Paris and Stockholm, the emperor withdrew his troops from Pomerania and restored the province to Sweden. But then, in January 1812, Napoleon wrecked the relationship when he ordered his troops to march back into Pomerania when Bernadotte refused to ally with France against Russia. Bernadotte promptly dispatched an envoy to St. Petersburg to forge an alliance between Sweden and Russia.

Castlereagh sent Edward Thornton to Sweden in March 1812 to bring that realm into the Coalition. Bernadotte requested £1.2 million in British subsidies to do what he was willing to do free with Russia. Thornton explained that the request was far too much. Bernadotte dropped his price to £1 million. Thornton referred it to Whitehall. Castlereagh offered £500,000 to underwrite war goods for Stockholm. Bernadotte agreed and sent agents with a shopping list, which included another £500,000 of subsidies.[37]

Amidst Whitehall's attempts to build the latest coalition came the stunning word that the United States Congress had declared war against Britain, by votes of 70 to 49 in the House of Representatives on June 4 and 19 to 13 in the Senate on June 17; President James Madison signed the declaration on June 18, 1812. The Americans had finally reached a breaking point after enduring nineteen years of British seizures of over 900 of their ships and cargos and thousands of their sailors. How many Americans the British impressed will never be known, but in 1811, Castlereagh admitted that over 3,300 were serving against their will in the Royal Navy and the United States State Department recorded 6,257 formal protests and pleas by Americans to be rescued from British warships. The actual figure may have been as high as 20,000 from 1793 to 1815.[38]

Madison could have ended the war before the human and financial costs truly began to soar. Whitehall had actually suspended the Orders in Council toward the United States on June 16, as Congress was in the process of declaring war. But Madison, pressured by congressional war hawks, did not declare peace when he learned of this concession in August. After getting that same news, General George Prevost, the British commander in Canada, offered General Henry Dearborn, the Lake Champlain front's commander, an armistice. Dearborn accepted. Madison denounced the armistice and insisted that the war would continue until the British stopped kidnapping sailors off American ships. Foreign Secretary Castlereagh explained that "no administration could expect to remain in power that should consent to renounce the right of impressment, or to suspend the practice."[39]

The 1812 War would be a disaster for both America and Britain.[40] At sea the United States was locked into a David versus Goliath struggle, with the American navy numbering only 17 warships, of which the largest were 6 frigates, while the Royal Navy had more than 640 warships, including 124 ships of the line and 116 frigates. On land, however, the odds were roughly even. Although America's 7.5 million people dwarfed Canada's 500,000, the total of the American army's 6,744 regular troops and potential 80,000 volunteers was comparable to around 7,000 British regulars and 86,000 militia in Canada.[41]

Britain's greatest advantage was in the soft power of army leadership, training, and morale. The British inflicted a series of defeats on the Americans by capturing 800 troops at Detroit, 958 troops at Queenstown Heights, and repelling repeated American invasions on the Niagara River, Lake Ontario, St. Lawrence River valley, and Lake Champlain fronts. The most humiliating American defeat came in August 1814, when 4,500 redcoats led by General Robert Ross routed a horde of militia at Bladensburg, Maryland, then marched into the city of Washington to sack and burn the White House, Congress, and other public buildings along with their documents. America's most important victories were against the Indians; in 1813 General William Henry Harrison decisively defeated a coalition of Northwest tribes at the Battle of the Thames, while General Andrew Jackson crushed a rebellious Creek Indian faction known as the Red Sticks in a brutal campaign.

The British burning of Washington was their worst atrocity of many. Secretary of War Henry, Earl of Bathurst, authorized his officers to "take such position as to threaten the inhabitants with the destruction of their property, you are hereby authorize[d] to levy upon them contributions in return for your forbearance." During his Chesapeake campaign, Admiral Alexander Cochrane ordered his captains "to destroy and lay waste such towns and cites upon the coast as may be found assailable . . . and . . . spare merely the lives of the unarmed inhabitants of the United States."[42]

Despite the overwhelming odds against them, the Americans won far more battles than they lost at sea. Most American frigates excelled not just in the hard power of being better designed and built, but more importantly their captains and crew were superior sailors, gunners, and tacticians. During the war, the Americans sank or captured seventeen British warships, most notably the frigate-versus-frigate duels of Captain Isaac Hull's USS *Constitution* against Captain James Dacres's HMS

*Guerriere*; Captain Stephen Decatur's USS *United States* against Captain John Carden's HMS *Macedonian*; and the USS *Constitution* against Captain Henry Lambert's HMS *Java*. America's greatest naval victory was on Lake Erie, hundreds of miles from the nearest salt water. Captain Oliver Perry led nine small warships against Captain Robert Barclay's six warships, which packed more guns, and captured all of them after a ferocious battle near Put-in-Bay on September 10, 1813.[43]

Eventually, the British only gained the upper hand by deploying massive fleets that blockaded the home ports of the frigates and other American warships. The one significant British victory was that of Captain Philip Brooke's HMS *Shannon* over Captain James Lawrence's USS *Chesapeake*, and only after Lawrence succumbed to Brooke's taunts and sailed forth from Boston when his vessel was unready for a voyage, let alone battle.

The greatest American victory came after diplomats signed the Treaty of Ghent, ending the war. A British armada with 4,000 troops led by General Edward Pakenham aboard the flotilla and warships led by Admiral Alexander Cochrane sailed in November 1814. Cochrane explained the expedition's related military and diplomatic goals: "I have it much at heart to give them a complete drubbing before peace is made, when I trust their northern limits will be circumscribed and the command of the Mississippi wrested from them."[44] The armada dropped anchor in Lake Borgne, a bay of the Gulf of Mexico. It took from then until December 23 for the troops and supplies to be conveyed by boats through the bayous and emerge a dozen miles south of New Orleans. General Andrew Jackson, the American commander, responded by ordering an attack on the British camp the night of the twenty-third; the Americans inflicted 46 dead, 167 wounded, and 64 captured on the British, while suffering 24 dead, 115 wounded, and 74 missing. For the next two weeks, the armies sniped and shelled at each other, while the American ranks swelled beyond 5,000 troops.

On January 8, 1815, Pakenham ordered his army to assault the American breastworks behind a shallow canal. The result was among history's most lopsided victories as the British were routed, having lost 291 killed, 1,262 wounded, and 484 captured, while the Americans suffered only 13 killed, 39 wounded, and 19 missing; Pakenham was among the dead. The British, now commanded by General John Lambert, slipped away on January 19. Rather than pursue and destroy the British army, Jackson rather uncharacteristically let them go without a fight. The British finished embarking their troops and supplies and sailed away on January 28, 1815. The New Orleans campaign was among Britain's worst defeats between 1793 to 1815.[45]

Relations between Napoleon and Alexander peaked during the two weeks from their first meeting on that raft in the Nieman River on June 25, 1807, to the signature of the Treaty of Tilsit on July 7, 1807. Alexander bound Russia to France, first in the Continental System, then in war against Britain. The emperor's shock and awe over the tsar soon wore off, and the alliance steadily deteriorated until June 23, 1812, when Napoleon led his army into Russia. Many reasons fed that decline, but underlying them all were Napoleon's insensitivities and Alexander's insecurities. The two locked themselves in a vicious cycle whereby each retaliated against what he perceived as the other's deliberate offenses.

Although tensions had worsened for years, the downward spiral steepened in December 1810, when each ruler committed an act designed to promote his realm's interests regardless of its effect on the other. On December 13 Napoleon annexed Holland, Oldenburg, Hamburg, and Lubeck, and the coastline between those realms, to France. His goal was to tighten the blockade and squeeze smuggling to the vanishing point. Alexander, naturally, saw as a threat the French empire's expansion to the shores of the Baltic Sea and was especially insulted that Napoleon had dethroned the Duke of Oldenburg, his sister's father-in-law. However, Alexander was unaware of this annexation when, on December 31, he decreed that Russian duties on imports arriving over land would rise and those by sea would fall. This hurt French exports that evaded British warships and privateers by being conveyed by land and helped British exports arriving on vessels flying neutral flags. Napoleon was naturally angry when he learned of Alexander's act, designed to hurt the Continental System and French exports. In 1811 he rejected the tsar's demand that he compensate Oldenburg with a swatch of the Duchy of Warsaw and promise in writing that he would not resurrect the Kingdom of Poland. Both monarchs prepared for war and pointed to the other's buildup to justify accelerating his own. Napoleon's annexation of Swedish Pomerania in January 1812 pushed the Swedes to ally with the Russians, and when the Treaty of Bucharest in May 1812 ended Russia's war with the Ottoman Empire, those armies were freed to march north. Napoleon hoped to intimidate Alexander by massing an army of over 600,000 men, half French and half foreign, including 20,000 Prussians and 30,000 Austrians. He threw a glittering summit for his allies at Dresden in May 1812. When the tsar rejected his appeal for negotiations, Napoleon reasoned that he had no choice but to bring Alexander to his knees.

Napoleon invaded Russia with 450,000 troops split among three armies and personally led the 250,000-man center army; another 150,000 troops were deployed either to guard supply lines or feed reinforcements to the front. The lead armies rapidly pursued the smaller Russian armies but failed to circle and destroy them. As in Spain, Napoleon's armies suffered from strategic consumption, with ever more troops lost to desertion, disease, battle, and garrisons along the lengthening supply lines. On September 7, Napoleon might have trapped General Mikhail Kutuzov's 125,000 troops with his 135,000 troops at Borodino had he tried to outflank, rather than directly attack the Russians, and ordered forward his Imperial Guard when the rest of his men had battered the enemy to the breaking point. Instead Kutuzov withdrew most of his army in good order seventy-five miles east through Moscow to safety beyond. Napoleon marched his remaining 95,000 troops into Moscow on September 15 and lingered there for five weeks vainly hoping that Alexander would open peace talks.

All along, despite their common enemy, relations between Britain and Russia remained frosty. Foreign Minister Castlereagh tried to break the ice in July 1812 by dispatching William, Earl of Cathcart, with £500,000 in cash to meet the tsar's immediate needs and the power to seize any chances to advance the allied war effort: "Whatever scheme of policy can most immediately combine the greatest number of powers and the greatest military force against France . . . before she can recruit her armies and recover her ascendancy, is that which we must . . . promote. . . . Whatever plan can be devised for ensuring success in this main point will not meet any opposition here."[46] In August Cathcart journeyed to Abo, Finland, where Alexander and Bernadotte were forging their alliance. There, to Cathcart's relief, the tsar appeared disinterested in shaking down Britain for huge amounts of money—an appearance that proved to be false.[47]

Napoleon finally ordered his army to withdrew from Moscow on October 19. Russian forces converged with some pursuing and others paralleling his retreat. Napoleon always drove off or evaded any Russian forces that got ahead of him, but starvation, disease, frost, and battle steadily devoured his ranks. Napoleon had only 7,000 troops with him when he reached Smogorni west of the Niemen River on December 5. There he gave the command to Marshal Joachim Murat, hurried nonstop west by sleigh and carriage, and finally strode into the Tuileries Palace in Paris near midnight on December 18. The next morning he was a whirlwind of action in reasserting his power over France and rebuilding his decimated army to fight the inevitable allied onslaught the following spring.

How devastating were Napoleon's losses? The highest Russian estimate was that they had buried or cremated 308,000 enemy dead, and captured 6,000 officers and 130,000 troops, along with 900 cannons, 100,000 muskets, and 25,000 vehicles. Stunning as those figures are, they may be an underestimate. Renowned historian David Chandler calculated that Napoleon had lost as many as 570,000 men, of which 370,000 died in the field and 100,000 of the 200,000 prisoners may have died in captivity. At least 150,000 Russians perished, while frostbite and disease crippled perhaps 300,000 more.[48]

Russia rather than Britain largely created the latest coalition. Step one came on December 30, 1812, when Prussian General Johann von Yorck signed the Treaty of Tauroggen, whereby he withdrew his corps into neutrality and allowed the Russian army to advance westward unhindered. With their northern flank open, the French abandoned their position behind the Vistula River and withdrew beyond the Elbe River.

The news of Yorck's act provoked an outburst of mingled pride and trepidation in Berlin. The king and his advisers longed to escape Napoleon's domination and avenge Prussia's humiliating defeats of

1806 and 1807, culminating with the Treaty of Tilsit of July 9, 1807, but still feared provoking the emperor's crushing retaliation. They reluctantly agreed that the time was not yet ripe to do so. Chancellor Karl August von Hardenberg explained: "It is of the utmost importance to show for the present the greatest devotion to Napoleon's system and alliances and to give to all our measures the appearance that they are being taken to support France."[49]

So Frederick William III publically denounced and privately lauded Yorck's treaty, and his confidence rose as Russian armies marched closer and eventually into his realm. The turning point came when Marshal Pierre Augereau abandoned Berlin and withdrew to Hamburg. On February 28, 1813, Frederick William joined Alexander and they secretly signed the Treaty of Kalisch, whereby Russia and Prussia would field 150,000 and 80,000 troops, respectively, against Napoleon and fight until they destroyed his empire and regime. But it was not until March 27 that Frederick William publicly declared war against France.

Austria lagged far behind Prussia in shifting from alliance with France to neutrality to alliance against France. Two reasons explained the slower process. First, the Austrians knew well that if they launched yet another war against France and lost, Napoleon would depose the Hapsburgs and eviscerate Austria to a rump state. Reinforcing this reason was both Francis's sensitivity to being the emperor's father-in-law and genuinely wanting to avoid a war between the two of them.

The transition began on January 30, 1813, when General Karl von Schwarzenberg signed the Convention of Zeyes, which declared an armistice and let him withdraw his corps into Austrian territory. Unlike Yorck, Schwarzenberg did so with his government's full approval. Chancellor Clement von Metternich wrote a series of letters, signed by Francis, to Napoleon explaining that Austrian interests had changed with the debacle in Russia and urging the emperor to negotiate a peace with Alexander by making significant concessions of territory. In April Metternich sent Schwarzenberg to Paris to explain this directly to the emperor. As he did with everyone, Napoleon rejected Schwarzenberg's plea to accept the realities of his devastating defeat in Russia when they met on April 9. Instead, he called on Austria to mass 100,000 troops on its northern frontier. Vienna was happy to comply. This huge army would overshadow the fast approaching campaign and would determine the winner by allying with one side against the other. The Austrian price for alliance would be stiff for either side.

As he learned of these developments, Castlereagh sought to assert a powerful British hand over the rapidly evolving coalition. For this he glittered the promise of British gold. Alexander was just as eager as any leader to enjoy as much British largess as possible, but he left the distasteful begging to his underlings. He had Count Christoph Heinrich von Lieven, his ambassador in London, ask Castlereagh for Britain to assume Russia's £4.5 million debt to Dutch bankers and give Russia £4 million to help fund its war against Napoleon. Castlereagh rejected both requests, but eventually the men reached a compromise that was signed into a treaty on July 6, 1813. Vienna would give St. Petersburg crucial military aid immediately, while deferring talks on any cash subsidies. By late 1813, 50,000 British muskets, 54 cannons, and munitions for both weapons ended up in Russian hands.[50]

Castlereagh dispatched his half-brother, Charles Stewart, to serve as ambassador to Prussia. In doing so, he put blood before merit: Stewart was a hotheaded, boisterous soldier void of the subtleties, patience, knowledge, and psychology vital for diplomacy. Stewart reached Berlin on April 22, only to learn that the king and his key ministers were at the allied headquarters at Dresden. Three days later, Stewart reached Dresden, where he joined Cathcart, who had followed Alexander and his entourage. The allied monarchs were working feverishly with their generals to prepare for Napoleon's latest onslaught.

Castlereagh read the reports of his ambassador to Sweden, Edward Thornton, with increasing concern. His man in Stockholm appeared to have "gone native." Beguiled by Crown Prince Bernadotte's charm, Thornton supported rather than resisted his demands for more money. Since this was unacceptable to Castlereagh, Thornton was then superseded by General Alexander Hope. Yet Hope was just as successfully swayed by Bernadotte, with the result that under the alliance treaty signed on March 3, 1813, Britain paid Sweden £1 million for 30,000 troops; no government during that era ever got so much money for supplying so few soldiers. And Bernadotte wielded his army more to intimidate Denmark, in hopes of forcing its government to yield the province of Norway to Sweden, than to defeat France.[51]

Napoleon left Paris on April 15 and reached Erfurt, his initial headquarters, on April 25. As had been true in his 1812 Russian campaign, hubris was the primary reason for the devastating defeat he was to experience in 1813, his ambitions wildly exceeding his abilities. Just in terms of manpower, the allied armies eventually fielded nearly twice as many troops as his own: he opened his offensive with only about 121,000 troops. Of these, only 10,000 were cavalry. In all his campaigns he never had a smaller ratio of cavalry to infantry. If wielded properly, the side with more cavalry could garner better intelligence and could encircle and destroy the enemy on the battlefield and in retreat, thus turning marginal into decisive victories. Napoleon's crucial void, however, was the loss of his once brilliant ability carefully to calculate and manipulate the ends and means of himself, his enemies, and his potential allies and enemies. Contrary to all evidence before him, he believed that Alexander was eager for peace and that Francis would not war against him.

Napoleon defeated the allies at Lutzen on May 2, entered Dresden on May 11, and trounced them again at Bautzen on May 20 and 21. These victories were not only indecisive but cost him more casualties than his troops inflicted. The allies withdrew beyond his sight and grasp behind thick, impenetrable cavalry screens. The result of all this was that Napoleon agreed to a six-week truce, signed at Plasewitz on June 4 and to expire on July 20. Like his enemies, he used the breathing space to rebuild his army rather than sincerely negotiate.

The allies steadily bolstered the coalition. At Reichenbach, the allies' latest headquarters, Stewart signed an alliance treaty with Prussia on June 14, and Cathcart with Russia on June 15.[52] In a treaty signed on June 27, Austria agreed to join the coalition if Napoleon rejected Vienna's peace terms, which included restoring conquered lands to Austria and Prussia, dissolving the Duchy of Warsaw and Rhine Confederation, and returning independence to Hamburg and Lubeck.

Napoleon pushed Austria into the coalition's eager arms as he contemptuously rejected making compromises vital for peace and saving his crown. Indeed, he seemed driven to be as arrogant, provocative, and insulting as possible. During a stormy meeting with Metternich at Dresden on June 26, he adamantly refused to make any substantive concessions. He did, however, agree to extend the armistice from July 26 to August 10 and let Vienna mediate peace at a conference to open at Prague on July 5. He then squandered this opportunity when he reneged on Austrian mediation and did not send his ambassador, Armand Caulaincourt, to Prague until July 25.

During the intervening month, the rage, demands, and unity against Napoleon swelled. At Trachtenberg from July 9 to 12, the allies forged a common strategy of avoiding battle with Napoleon while defeating his detached subordinates and encircling him with ever larger armies until they converged and destroyed him. They bolstered Bernadotte's army of 30,000 Swedes and 10,000 Germans with 40,000 Prussians and 22,000 Russians. Bernadotte would descend on Napoleon from the north while Generals Robert Barclay and Gerhard von Blucher with 90,000 troops advanced against him from the east. And soon, if Napoleon continued to spurn diplomacy, Schwarzenberg would lead 230,000 Austrian troops against him from the south.

Yet even then, if Napoleon had offered a France reduced to its "natural frontiers," the allies and Austria would have grabbed it. The great powers split over what peace terms they wanted. Britain and Russia were determined to fight until Napoleon was forced to turn the geopolitical clock back to 1789, while Prussia and Austria would have been content to reset it at 1792. At this point, however, they did not openly speak of deposing the emperor himself, knowing that doing so would only provoke a total war to an uncertain finish. Only after the battle of Leipzig did they confidently call for ending Napoleon's rule.

Spain's strategic outlook differed strikingly in early 1813 from a year earlier. The power balance had seesawed decisively from France to Britain and its allies. Napoleon had ordered his brother Joseph to abandon Madrid and concentrate his forces at Salamanca, with his supply line stretching northeastward across Spain through Valladolid, Burgos, and Vitoria to Bayonne in France. Suchet held northeastern

Spain with 68,000 troops deployed across the provinces of Valencia and Catalonia. Beyond those clusters and chains of French forces, Spanish armies and guerrillas prevailed.

Wellington planned a strategy intended to end at the Pyrenees. He massed enough provisions, munitions, and transport to sustain for months 52,000 British and 29,000 Portuguese troops, or 81,000 altogether. No detail was too small. In a campaign where footwear was as vital as cartridges, he insisted that each soldier began that journey with three pairs of shoes. To quicken their paces, he lightened their loads by shedding them of tents and winter coats, and replacing their cast-iron kettles with sheet metal versions. To sustain his army's advance, he would shift his supply center from Lisbon to Santander.

As his troops crossed the frontier into Spain in mid-May, Wellington sought to boost their spirits and fire their imagination by raising his hat and loudly proclaiming: "Farewell Portugal, I shall never see you again!"[53] He then led his men in a series of rapid flanking maneuvers that forced Joseph to abandon Salamanca and rapidly withdraw on his supply line. Joseph did not garrison Valladolid and Burgos but had the citadels blown up behind his retreating army.

Wellington finally caught up to Joseph at Vitoria on June 21 1813. For once he enjoyed a huge edge in numbers, with 78,000 troops to 57,000 French. Still, he took meticulous care in devising tactics to crush the enemy while minimizing his own losses. He aimed at that holy grail of generals, the double envelopment, and nearly pulled it off, but two forces beyond his control thwarted him. General Thomas Graham failed to push his advance all the way around the French left to sever the road to France, and his victorious troops scattered to loot the enemy's baggage train— shortcomings that enabled Joseph to escape with 49,000 troops. In lines that became infamous, Wellington vented his anger that his troops had failed to cut off and destroy Joseph's army: "It is quite impossible for me or any other man to command a British army under the existing system. We have in the service the scum of the earth as common soldiers. . . . The officers of the lower ranks will not perform their duty required from them for the purpose of keeping their soldiers in order. . . . As to the non-commissioned officers . . . they are as bad as their men."[54]

Nonetheless, Wellington and his army won decisively at Vitoria. His troops inflicted 5,460 casualties and took 2,829 prisoners and 151 cannons, while suffering 5,186 killed and wounded.[55] Strategically, Spain was essentially liberated except for San Sebastian, Pamplona, and a stretch of Catalonia's coast held by Suchet. Indeed, all that lay ahead on the hundred or so miles of road to France was a demoralized mob of enemy soldiers, shorn of most of their cannons, munitions, provisions, and pride.

Yet here Wellington faltered. After spending a couple of days restoring order to his army, he could have launched an offensive that relentlessly hounded the French army, snapping at and devouring ever more of its exhausted regiments until none remained. But Wellington lacked the killer instinct of Napoleon, who ruthlessly ran his fleeing enemies into the ground, most decisively during his 1806 campaign against Prussia. The prudence that made Wellington an outstanding tactician inhibited him from inflicting a knockout blow.

Instead, Wellington pointed to San Sebastian and Pamplona, declared that he did not want those fortress cities in his rear, and split his army to besiege them. Yet the garrisons, which numbered only 3,500 and 4,000 second-rate troops, respectively, posed no threat to his communication and supply line, let alone his army. He could have bottled up both towns with Spanish troops while he led his army into France.

San Sebastian was a natural fortress augmented by thick, high stone walls atop a steep headland surrounded by deep seawater and connected by a narrow neck to the mainland. On June 28 allied troops reached the port's outskirts. Weeks of pounding by siege guns finally opened a small breach on July 25. General Thomas Graham, who commanded the siege, impatiently ordered an assault. The defenders killed or wounded over 600 attackers and routed the rest. Graham resumed the bombardment.

Meanwhile, the window of opportunity for a rapid, decisive advance that carried the war into southwestern France shut firmly. The longer Wellington tarried in Spain, the more casualties his troops would suffer when they finally invaded France. Upon learning of the Vitoria debacle, Napoleon dispatched Soult to that front to rally the army's remnants. Soult reached Bayonne on July 11, massed 65,000 troops, and led them over the Pyrenees passes of Roncesvalles and Maya to relieve Pamplona.

Wellington pushed part of his army forward to block Soult before his army could descend from the steep foothills. His troops repelled massive French attacks over nine days, with the fiercest fighting at Sorauren on July 28 and 30, and enjoyed their latest lopsided victory as they inflicted nearly twice as many casualties as they endured, 13,500 to 7,000. Wellington tried to sever Soult's retreat, but the French slipped back over the Pyrenees after leaving powerful garrisons at forts atop the passes. Yet, once again, Wellington did not follow up his victory with a rapid advance. After deploying powerful forces to block another French descent, he could have quick-marched the bulk of his army toward Bayonne and got there before Soult. Instead, he returned to the sieges of Pamplona and San Sebastian.

Week after week the heavy siege guns battered San Sebastian until they knocked out every French cannon and crumbled a three-hundred-yard stretch of wall. Graham ordered an assault on August 31. This time the allies fought their way into the citadel and captured it, but at a horrific cost of 2,400 casualties, including 856 dead. This same day Soult launched his army against Spanish troops defending San Marcial on the coast road to San Sebastian. After severe fighting, the French withdrew, having suffered 4,000 casualties to 2,500 Spaniard dead, wounded, and captured. Wellington's reply during the battle to the Spanish commander's plea for British troops offers insights into his command skills: "Look . . . if I send you the English troops you ask for, they will win the battle; but as the French are already in retreat you may as well win it for yourselves."[56]

Pamplona's siege was more prolonged but nearly bloodless. Crowning a steep, high plateau, Pamplona could not be blasted out, only starved out, and this would take a long time. Allied troops encircled the city on June 25, and four months later, on October 31, the garrison capitulated.

Meanwhile during 1813, the French receded rather than collapsed in northeastern Spain. Although on paper Generals Louis Suchet and Charles Decean commanded 35,000 and 25,000 troops, respectively, neither could field more than a third of their totals, as the rest garrisoned major and minor fortresses in a chain leading back to France. The converging armies of Generals John Murray, Francisco Xavier Elio, and Don Lorenzo Del Parque, along with clouds of guerrillas, forced Suchet to withdrew from Valencia, while General Francisco Copons bedeviled Decean in Catalonia.

Suchet was down but not out. He was adept at swiftly striking an exposed enemy army, and he usually inflicted a sharp if indecisive defeat. His confidence, however, swelled with his victories, and that led to his first serious repulse. On April 13 he launched his 13,000 troops against Murray's 18,000 mostly British, Sicilian, and Spanish troops at Castalla but was driven back with 1,000 casualties. Murray did not follow up his victory. Instead, in June, he embarked his army on transports and sailed to besiege Tarragona, the most powerful fortress along the coast from there to Barcelona. Murray was joined by Copons, while Del Parque and Elio deployed their troops more distantly on roads leading to Tarragona. Then, on June 13, Murray broke off the siege when General Harispe routed Del Parque at Cartagena, inflicting 1,300 casualties. Word of Joseph's debacle at Vitoria forced Suchet to abandon this region and join forces with Decean in Catalonia. There the French were beset by allied forces, including 10,000 British and Sicilian troops led by General William Bentinck. Suchet and Decean launched an attack at a combined force of Spaniards and part of Bentinck's army at Villafranca on September 13, inflicted 600 casualties, and drove them from the field. Thereafter the fighting in northeastern Spain diminished to scattered skirmishes as neither side had enough troops and supplies to march overwhelmingly against the other.

Wellington learned that Whitehall and the allies in Germany expected him to invade France to divert enemy troops from their front. His response was an exercise in dissimulation: "That the Allies are very anxious that we should enter France, and that our government has promised that we should, as soon as the enemy should be finally expelled from Spain; and I think I ought, and will bend a little to the views of the Allies, if it can be done with safety to the army, notwithstanding that I should prefer to turn my attention to Catalonia as soon as I shall have secured this frontier."[57]

What explains Wellington's caution at the gates of France? Experience reinforced his natural prudence and methodical approach to problems. The seesaw Peninsula War had devoured five years of his life. True, he had made steady progress, but in a two-steps-forward, one-step-backward pattern. Although he had staved off the latest pushback by defeating Soult in the nine-day Battle of the Pyrenees, he expected eventually to have to withdraw again sooner or later, as his army was straining at the end of its supply tether in the face of formidable enemy forces. And this was especially worrisome, since he viewed the alliance with Spain as near the breaking point. He wrote Whitehall that "I think I should experience great difficulty in retiring through Spain and Portugal, the Spanish people being hostile."[58] Spain's government, too, was becoming as hostile as its people. The Spanish generals not only rarely obeyed his orders but often did the opposite seemingly, just to undercut him. On top of this, the Regency Council and Cortes in Cadiz failed adequately to cloth, arm, pay, and feed Spanish troops even when the British supplied much of these vital needs. Getting Spanish officials to do anything, however ineptly, cost huge bribes.

In deep despair, Wellington submitted his resignation as generalissimo on October 5. He hoped that his letter would shake up Spain's government and force the genuine progressives to get their more rapacious colleagues to curb their greed. But if they actually accepted his resignation, then good riddance to that mostly empty title. He received a flowery letter from the Council asking him not to resign and promising to rectify problems. Although Wellington questioned the sincerity of those words, he agreed to carry on.

The situation at Lisbon was not as dismal. Portugal's Council of Regency was less corrupt and inept than its Spanish counterpart, and it garnered precious revenues as trade revived. Yet government spending still exceeded income, forcing Whitehall to fill that gap with £2.3 million in 1812 and £2.5 million in 1813.[59] Fortunately, the Portuguese troops under Wellington's command partly offset those deficiencies by being as adept in fighting prowess as British redcoats. Wellington prided himself in being Portugal's generalissimo.

Pamplona's capture psychologically freed Wellington to yield to Whitehall's pressure to invade France. On November 10 he launched his 82,000 troops in a pincer movement against Soult's 62,000 troops defending the Nivelle River, and routed them, inflicting 4,300 killed and wounded while losing 3,400. Soult withdrew his battered army across the Nive River that flowed through Bayonne and into the Adour River valley. Wellington massed his army and carefully planned and executed an attack at St. Pierre on December 13, and again drove off Soult, who lost 2,400 men to 1,800 allied casualties. Wellington was now poised to smash through Soult's last line of defense along the Adour River and march deep into southwestern France in the New Year.

The armistice's expiration on August 10, finally jolted Napoleon awake to the reality that he faced overwhelming military odds that would sooner or later crush him. He raced a courier to Caulaincourt with orders for him to accept the coalition's terms. That opportunity was now dead. Austria dutifully declared war against France on August 12. The allied forces against Napoleon now outgunned him across the entire region by 500,000 to 300,000 troops.

When Vienna joined the coalition, Castlereagh tapped an ambassador to coordinate military and diplomatic efforts with the Austrians. George Gordon, Earl of Aberdeen, was yet another of Castlereagh's puzzling choices as an envoy. He was only twenty-nine years old and a neophyte at diplomacy assigned to haggle with Metternich, among history's most brilliant diplomats. Indeed Metternich dismissed Aberdeen as a "dear simpleton of diplomacy."[60] Nonetheless, Aberdeen soon showed his potential. At Teplitz on October 3, Aberdeen and Metternich signed a treaty by which Britain would underwrite 150,000 troops with £1 million.[61]

Britain's role as the banker and arsenal of monarchy peaked in 1813. That year Whitehall subsidized its allies with £11 million, including Russia with £3,666,666, Prussia with £1,333,332, Sweden with £2,200,000, Portugal with £2 million, Spain with £2 million, Austria with £1 million, Spain with £1 million, and Sicily with £400,000. It also distributed over 1 million muskets to its allies across Europe. Berlin alone got 100,000 muskets, along with 116 cannons and 1,200 tons of munitions.[62]

Four armies of mixed nationalities converged on Napoleon's forces: General Karl von Schwarzenberg from the south with 230,000 troops;

General Gerhard von Blucher from the east with 95,000 troops, and behind him 60,000 troops under General Levin Bennigsen; and General Jean-Baptiste Bernadotte from the north with 40,000 troops. The allied strategy was to evade battles with Napoleon and pounce with overwhelming force against his detached subordinates. Napoleon quick-marched his army to catch up and rout Schwarzenberg at Dresden in a seesaw battle on August 26 and 27. But Napoleon could not be everywhere at once: Friedrich von Bülow beat Nicolas Oudinot's corps at Gross Beren on August 21; Blucher beat Etienne MacDonald's corps at Katzbach on August 23; Ivan Osterman-Tolstoi beat Dominique Vandamme's corps at Klum on August 30; and Bernadotte beat Michel Ney's corps at Dennewitz on September 6. These allied victories encouraged Bavarian king Maximilen Joseph to defect with his 36,000-man army from Napoleon to the coalition with the Treaty of Ried of October 8.

Rather than withdraw from the converging allied armies west to safety, Napoleon stood defiant with 225,000 at Leipzig. From October 16 and 19, the allies massed 340,000 troops and repeatedly attacked the contracting French lines and finally routed them. In the era's largest battle, Napoleon inflicted 54,000 casualties on the allies but lost 73,000 troops killed or captured, and with them any chance of saving his crown if he did not immediately sue for peace. The losses kept mounting. Laurent de St. Cyr surrendered his corps at Dresden on November 11, while smaller garrisons capitulated at Stettin and Modlin. Napoleon finally withdrew west of the Rhine with only 70,000 or so troops.

The remnants of Napoleon's empire collapsed rapidly in Leipzig's wake. Facing overwhelming odds, the French abandoned Amsterdam on November 15. The Dutch reasserted control and summoned Prince William of Orange to return from exile to rule their country as the stadtholder. William, accompanied by British ambassador Richard Trench, Earl of Clancarty, arrived on November 30, followed within a week by 1,500 redcoats and 20,000 muskets. On December 17 General Thomas Graham appeared with 5,500 redcoats, spending the next several months beseiging Antwerp, which was still held by the French. In March 1814 reinforcements swelled Graham's army to 11,200 troops.. Ideally, Graham would have blocked Antwerp with Dutch troops while he led his redcoats into France in liaison with the other allied armies, which certainly would have strengthened Britain's diplomatic hand at Vienna.

Antwerp's siege was a diversion from Napoleon's final defeat. Napoleon's demise would also have happened sooner had Bernadotte not invaded Denmark rather than France. Two very good reasons motivated that assault. The Swedes were seeking to take Norway from Denmark, best done by defeating the Danes and imposing a treaty to this effect. Besides, Bernadotte was hardly eager to war against his homeland. But in failing to join the invasion of France, he angered his coalition partners, especially the British, who had paid a princely sum for him to help crush Napoleon. But it all worked out as Bernadotte and his adopted countrymen desired. The Danes gave up on January 14, 1814, and in the Treaty of Kiel they signed away Norway to Sweden in return for Pomerania and the island of Rugen. Bernadotte then dallied in Denmark for nearly two months, ignoring all entreaties from his allies to hurry to their support. When he finally started his army toward France, the war was over.

Ambassador William Bentinck was British diplomacy's proverbial loose cannon. He dismissed the foreign secretary's instructions as mere suggestions and instead devoted himself to realizing his liberal visions. He was determined to transform the Kingdom of Sicily from a feudal, poverty-stricken, corrupt, violent realm into a constitutional monarchy with a working parliament, powerful army, and flourishing economy. In the first step to these related ends, he signed a treaty with Ferdinand IV on September 12, 1813, that committed Britain to finance, recruit, train, and lead a 7,314-man Sicilian division.[63] Soon, however, Bentinck's ambitions ran into insurmountable Sicilian and international obstacles.

Vienna launched a diplomatic effort that denied Ferdinand IV half of his realm. On January 11, 1814, its ambassador to King Joachim Murat I, at Naples, signed with him a treaty that split most of Italy between them. The Austrians recognized Murat's hold over southern Italy and promised him gains in the Papal States. Murat recognized Austria's claims to northern Italy and agreed to ally with Vienna against his brother-in-law, Napoleon.

This conflicted with British policy. Whitehall remained committed to returning Ferdinand IV from his Palermo palace to his Naples palace. At most, Castlereagh was willing to grant Murat a small principality elsewhere in Italy if he vacated the throne at Naples, to be restored to its rightful king.[64]

Bentinck reacted to the deal between Vienna and Naples with a halfway measure. On February 3, 1814, he signed an armistice that pointedly did not recognize Murat as the king of Naples. Meanwhile, he led his British and Sicilian forces to invade northern Italy. He and his small army disembarked at Livorno, Tuscany's port, on March 9. There, on March 14, he called on all Italians to reclaim their heritage from foreign rule, which got him in heated quarrels with the liaisons from both Vienna and Naples, after which he reembarked his troops and sailed to Genoa, Here, on April 18, he proclaimed the restoration of the Republic of Genoa. The "liberators" soon wore out their presence there as well.

As Metternich so aptly put it, Italy was indeed a geographic expression, and hard experience finally awakened Bentinck to this reality. His Sicilian troops provoked fear rather than presenting a model to emulate, even then having a well-deserved reputation not just for being clannish, greedy, corrupt, and vengeful, characteristics not unknown in the rest of Italy, but also for being outright larcenous and murderous. Atop this, they spoke an unintelligible dialect. In all, northern Italians viewed Sicilians as barbarians from an alien culture and prayed they would disappear back to their realm as soon as possible.

Bentinck and his peripatetic expedition finally returned rather sheepishly to Palermo on June 8. He had made an utter diplomatic mess of things in northwestern Italy. His attempts to liberate Tuscany enraged Vienna, which sought to retake it, and his attempts to reestablish the Republic of Genoa enraged Whitehall, which sought to include it in a reconstituted Kingdom of Savoy, Piedmont, and Sardinia that would serve as a buffer between France and Austria's Italian possessions.

The Austrians and Russians hoped to avoid the bloodbath of invading France and trying to crush Napoleon in his homeland. To this end, Metternich and Foreign Minister Karl von Nesselrode sent Nicolas St. Aignan, a captured French general, to Napoleon with the offer of peace for a France reduced to its natural frontiers of the Rhine, Alps, and Pyrenees. When he learned of it, Castlereagh protested as unacceptable this offer that left the Low Countries and the Scheldt River mouth in French hands. On December 2 Napoleon grudgingly told Caulaincourt to accept the deal. But Metternich and Nesselrode yielded to Britain's demands and ignored Caulaincourt's message. This prompted Napoleon to accuse the allies of negotiating in bad faith.

This nearly catastrophic allied concession prompted Liverpool's government to agree, on December 20, 1813, for Castlereagh to come to the coalition headquarters, and armed with £5 million in credit, assert British interests. Castlereagh took a week to tidy his affairs and draft his own diplomatic instructions. His strategy had two inseparable elements, one for winning the war and another for winning the peace. Whitehall would persist in playing a crucial role in the fight to crush Napoleon, break up his empire, and reduce France to its 1789 borders by underwriting the coalition and Wellington. The diplomacy of peace was a more complex challenge than that of war. A final treaty would restore the power balance by strengthening Austria and Prussia in central Europe to counter France westward and Russia eastward. Also crucial was reconstituting the Netherlands and ensuring that Antwerp and the region around the mouth of the Scheldt River was free from French power. As long as this power balance was maintained, Britain would thereafter avoid getting entangled in the minutia of each great and minor power's demands from one another.[65]

With his "Memorandum of Cabinet" in hand, Castlereagh finally left London on December 28, 1813. Rough seas kept him from The Hague until January 7. His most pressing business there was to secure an engagement between the son of Prince William and Princess Charlotte, the sole child of the crown prince and princess, and thus the potential heir to the British throne. The key prenuptial deal was that the crowns of Britain and the Netherlands would always be worn by separate monarchs. Castlereagh also got the Dutch to cede the Cape of Good Hope, which a British expedition had captured in 1807, in return for money to construct or reinforce fortresses on the French frontier.

Castlereagh headed up the Rhine River, reaching Basel, Switzerland, on January 18, 1814. After several days of talks, he, Metternich, and Prussian Foreign Minister Karl von Hardenberg agreed to shear France's territory back to that of 1789, but they failed to decide who should rule France. Castlereagh was flexible on the question, proposing a descending order of possibilities starting with Napoleon, then some other French general, preferably Bernadotte, and, finally, the Bourbons. Europe's peace and security depended on the stability and legitimacy of France's government and the contentment of its people.[66] The three foreign ministers then journeyed to Schwarzenberg's headquarters at Langres, France, where they hoped to get Alexander to join their agreement. He insisted that they resolve all outstanding diplomatic issues at a postwar congress at Vienna. The four allies pledged themselves to do so by signing the Langres Protocol on January 29, 1814.

Napoleon's diplomacy mirrored his military prospects during the 1814 campaign in eastern France. When he was winning, he sent couriers galloping to Caulaincourt with orders not to compromise, and when he was losing, the messages were to get what he could. The campaign opened in late January as the allied armies of Blucher and Schwarzenberg marched against the nearest French forces. Napoleon's first two battles typified the seesaw pattern of victory and defeat that persisted for the next seven weeks as the emperor was edged westward in the face of ever larger allied forces trying to outflank him. He beat Blucher at Brienne on January 29, and was beaten by Blucher's reinforced army at La Rothière on February 1.

The coalition formally opened a conference at Chatillon on February 3, with Cathcart, Aberdeen, and Stewart representing Britain; Philipp, Count von Stadion, Austria; Wilhelm, Baron von Humboldt, Prussia; and Andrei, Count Razumovsky, Russia. Castlereagh would have preferred to sit down with his fellow foreign ministers and horse trade for a comprehensive deal, but he finally succumbed to Metternich's argument that letting the second-stringers prevail potentially saved face for the principals when the inevitable sticky issues arose.

Although Caulaincourt was there at the conference's opening, he had actually appeared with his credentials at Luneville, France, on January 28. Learning of his arrival, the allies agreed to let him cool his heels in that forlorn town to impress upon him their belief that their allied armies would soon crush Napoleon and impose a peace on France. It was not until February 7 that they offered Caulaincourt a peace grounded on France reduced to its 1789 frontiers. Two days later Caulaincourt accepted that deal, only to have Napoleon reject it. The delegates suspended their conference on February 10 for a week, during which Napoleon won a series of battles and drove back the allied armies, capped by his letter to Francis asking for a separate peace based on France's natural frontiers. Francis ignored this request. Caulaincourt renounced French sovereignty of all non-French lands on March 10, and on March 15 he offered to give up all French conquests except Lucca and Neuchâtel. The allies ignored those gestures, and the Chatillon Conference ended without a peace treaty on March 19.

During this time, the allies did resolve one diplomatic issue. They transformed the coalition from a hodgepodge of bilateral alliances into one quadruple alliance. The Treaty of Chaumont, signed on March 9 but backdated to March 1, 1814, bound the four great powers each to war with 150,000 troops until they won all of their objectives, and thereafter for twenty years to uphold a defensive alliance whereby each would send 60,000 troops to whoever was attacked—although Britain could pay £1.3 million instead of supplying its full contingent.[67]

This hard line was justified. Napoleon admitted to his brother Joseph that "had I before the last operation concluded a peace with the old frontiers, I would have taken up arms in two years' time and have told the nation that it was not a peace but a capitulation." He told Caulaincourt that what "they tried to force on you at Chatillon could have been nothing more than a truce, for no one ever subscribes to his own disgrace, nor would I have been willing to do so."[68]

Napoleon tried to throw a diplomatic and political monkey wrench into the gears of Wellington's military machine preparing to invade southwestern France. Hoping to poison the already frayed ties between Britain and Spain, the emperor grabbed the scepter from his brother Joseph and dangled it before the would-be Ferdinand VII, still luxuriously interned at Talleyrand's Château de Valençay. Ferdinand was free to hurry back to Spain and take the throne if he immediately signed a peace treaty with France, expelled all British and Portuguese forces from his kingdom, pardoned all Spaniards who had collaborated with the French, and joined the Continental Blockade. Ferdinand eagerly signed the Treaty of Valençay on December 11, 1813, and a courier dashed it to Madrid. Had the Cortes ratified the treaty, Napoleon dreamed of quick-marching the 60,000 battle-hardened troops from the Spanish frontier to eastern France, and not just save his throne but let him reconquer his empire.

Napoleon's latest delusion was in for a rude shock. The Cortes unanimously rejected the treaty, and the Regency Council, decreed on February 2, 1814, that Ferdinand was unwelcome in Spain unless he repudiated the disgraceful document that he had signed and instead swore allegiance to the liberal 1812 constitution that made him and his successors constitutional monarchs. Regardless of the Spanish government's decision, Napoleon's defeat was inevitable. Over 250,000 Russian, Prussian, and Austrian troops were then invading eastern France, while Wellington launched 80,000 troops into southwestern France. Upon learning of Napoleon's ploy, Wellington remarked: "I have long suspected that Bonaparte would adopt this expedient; and if he had had less pride and more common sense, it would have succeeded."[69]

Wellington was nearly always sensitive to the hearts-and-minds dilemma of commanding a foreign army in an allied or enemy country. Among his worst worries, as he readied his army to invade France, was that his troops would provoke uprisings among the French, and he was determined to prevent this from happening He insisted that his soldiers respect the local people and had any troops caught committing crimes severely punished. A hard practical reality governed this concern—the worse one treated the locals, the more likely they would rise against oneself. He was well aware that his victorious campaigns depended on the devastating attacks of Spanish guerrillas against French supply and communications lines, diverting tens of thousands of French troops that might otherwise be deployed against the allies, and the likely vengeful and rapacious behavior of his Spanish allies in France especially worried him: "Our success and everything depends upon our moderation and justice, and upon the good discipline of our troops. I despair of the Spaniards. They are in such a miserable state that it hardly fair to expect that they will restrain from plundering . . . and if they plunder, they will ruin us all."[70] He sidestepped this nightmare by taking only 4,000 of the best Spanish troops with him into France, leaving the rest behind in their own country.

Wellington opened his 1814 campaign on February 24. While General John Hope with 30,000 troops besieged Bayonne, Wellington led 45,500 troops northeastward up the Adour River valley. On February 26, Hope's engineers completed a pontoon bridge that let 15,000 British troops march across, deploy on Bayonne's north side, and trap that city's 17,000 defenders; the French held out until April 26. Meanwhile Wellington ordered his army, on February 27, to outflank Soult's 36,000 troops at Orthez. Wellington's latest victory inflicted 4,000 casualties, including 1,350 prisoners, at a cost of 2,164 of his own men.[71]

Wellington then split his army. He sent Beresford north to capture Bordeaux, while he pursued Soult. An insurrection championing the Bourbons cleared Bordeaux of imperial troops, so Beresford and his troops were cheered when they marched into the port on March 12. Wellington, meanwhile, fought a war of maneuver against Soult by quick-marching a column of troops around his flank whenever he stopped to hold a position. Soult's last stand was at Toulouse, where Wellington again sought to encircle and destroy him. On April 10 Wellington launched his 49,000 troops against Soult's 42,000 troops and routed them. The victory was costly, with 4,568 British to 3,236 French casualties.[72] The Battle of Toulouse was also tragically unnecessary, because that night a courier galloped up to Wellington's headquarters with word that Napoleon had abdicated.

In eastern France an intelligence coup precipitated a dramatic shift in allied strategy. In late March, Russian cossacks captured a courier galloping from France's minister of police to Napoleon with this dire message: "The treasury, arsenals, and powder stores are empty. We have no resources left. The population is discouraged and discontented. It wants peace at any price. Enemies of the imperial government are sustaining and fomenting popular agitation. Still latent, it becomes impossible to suppress unless the Emperor succeeds in keeping the Allies away from Paris."[73]

The coalition leaders agreed to dash their armies to Paris for a decisive battle. The end came swiftly: the allied troops reached Paris and routed its defenders on March 30. Vice Grand Elector Talleyrand stayed behind in Paris while the rest of the government fled westward. On March 31 he wielded his authority to negotiate and sign, a capitulation that opened Paris to allied occupation. Later that day, Alexander led a procession of allied troops into the city and accepted Talleyrand's offer of his home as his headquarters. On April 1 Talleyrand convened the Senate and got a majority to approve a provisional government headed by himself, with four of his coterie as his deputies. On April 2 the Senate voted to depose Napoleon and call on Louis XVIII to take the empty throne. Talleyrand then worked with other political leaders to draft France's latest constitution, known as the Charter, that established a constitutional monarchy in which the king and national assembly shared power and guaranteed the political rights of citizens. The Senate ratified the Charter on April 6.

Napoleon meanwhile reached Fontainebleau, thirty-five miles south of Paris, on March 31. With him were only 25,000 troops to the 250,000 allied troops then deployed across eastern France. On April 2 Caulaincourt joined the emperor and informed him of all that had happened in Paris. After two anguished days, Napoleon abdicated in favor of his son on April 4. The allies rejected the gesture. Napoleon abdicated unconditionally on April 6, an act that became official on April 11, when he signed the Treaty of Fontainebleau whereby, in return for renouncing the throne, he was entitled to rule the island of Elba off Italy's western coast and annually receive 2 million francs from France; his wife, Marie Louise,was granted the Duchies of Parma and Gastalla, to be inherited by his son; the rest of the Bonaparte clan would receive generous pensions from the French government.

That night Napoleon swallowed a vial of poison that had dangled from a chain around his neck since the Russian campaign. For better or for worse, the poison had lost its deadly potency. He got violently sick but soon recovered. On April 16 he greeted the allied commissioners who would accompany him to Elba. The emperor and his entourage packed into fourteen carriages and departed Fontainebleau on April 20, reached Fréjus on April 27, boarded the HMS *Undaunted* the next day, and stepped ashore at Portoferrio, Elba's capital on May 4, 1814. Napoleon's exile would not last long.

CHAPTER 10

# The Seventh Coalition, 1814–1815

To give . . . the longest interval of peace with such a character, I should say that it would lie in never suffering him for a moment to doubt your readiness to support the continental Powers against his ambitious encroachments.

Robert Stewart, Viscount Castlereagh

The best security for Europe was the restoration of the King, and that the establishment of any other government than the King's in France must inevitably lead to new and endless wars.

Arthur Wellesley, Duke of Wellington

Tis done—but yesterday a king!
And armed with kings to strive—
And now thou art a nameless thing
So abject—yet alive!

Lord Byron, *Ode to Bonaparte*

If pecuniary difficulties press upon him much longer so as to prevent his vanity from being satisfied by his ridiculous establishment of a Court . . . and if his doubts are not removed, I think he is capable of crossing over with his troops.

Colonel Neil Campbell, on Napoleon at Elba

A cavalcade of carriages brought Louis XVIII and his entourage into Paris on May 3. Most of those who noticed viewed the sight with curiosity, fear, or anger rather than enthusiasm. Tsar Alexander pointedly neither went out to greet the monarch nor invited him to his residence. He harbored nothing but contempt for Louis and the entire Bourbon clan, whom he dismissed as corrupt, inept, and effete, an opinion shared by countless others in France and beyond.

The following day Wellington inspired a far greater stir as he and his staff on horseback clattered into Paris to join the victory parades and balls and add luster to Britain's diplomatic mission. He soon learned that on May 3 parliament had unanimously ennobled him as the Duke of Wellington and granted him £400,000 to live up to the title. All the adulation and honors did not swell the duke's head. When someone remarked that he had never fought Napoleon, Wellington replied: "No, and I am very glad. . . . I would at any time rather have heard that a reinforcement of forty thousand men had joined the French army than that he had arrived to take the command."[1] Although then unimaginable, Wellington would fight a decisive battle with Napoleon just thirteen months later. Wellington departed for London on May 17, but by a route that could not have been more roundabout, he having been instructed to honor Spain's contributions to the coalition by meeting with newly installed King Ferdinand VII at Madrid. He then returned to Bordeaux for a fast ship to England.

The Treaty of Paris, signed by the allied leaders and Louis XVIII on May 30, 1814, mildly punished France. Louis renounced all of France's conquests; ceded Tobago, St. Lucia, and Ile de France (Mauritius) to Britain; ceded Santo Domingo to Spain; agreed to withdraw from the international slave trade five years hence; and acquiesced in his realm's frontiers being returned to those of November 1, 1792. Astonishingly, the victors demanded no monetary spoils in the form of reparations. As important, the treaty committed Britain, Austria, Prussia, and Russia to convene a congress of all European states at Vienna, where they would forge "a real and permanent balance of power in Europe . . . upon principles determined by the Allied Powers amongst themselves."[2]

The coalition's peripatetic diplomacy then shifted to London, as the allied leaders accepted Whitehall's invitation to visit. When

Alexander disembarked at Dover, he could not have uttered words better designed to endear himself to the British people: "God be praised! I have set my foot upon the land which has saved us all."[3] A hero's welcome greeted him and Frederick William when they arrived with their huge entourages in London on June 7. Crowds lined the streets to cheer as the royal processions of carriages slowly clattered past. At some point the two sovereigns parted as Frederick William's cavalcade headed to the York Hotel. In retrospect, Alexander might have saved ample embarrassment had he stayed at the residence of his ambassador, Christoph Lieven. Instead, his carriage disgorged him before the Pulteney Hotel near Piccadilly Square, where he resided for the next three weeks with his younger sister Catherine.

Alexander adored Catherine, whom he affectionately called the "delicious lunatic" for her biting candor and brazen antics. Recently widowed, she was reveling in her newfound freedom as a rich, powerful, twenty-six-year-old single woman. Ever more Londoners, especially the influential ones, did not share the tsar's mirth. They found her obnoxious and petulant. Although Catherine had only been in London since March 31, 1814, she soon fouled a delicate mission of British diplomacy, the official announcement the previous day of the engagement between Charlotte, the only daughter of George and Caroline, the prince regent and princess, and William, the son of William of Orange, the Dutch stadtholder.

It wasn't just William's appearance, manners, and personality that made Charlotte's thought of marrying him repulsive. She secretly loved Prussian Prince Leopold, the king's dashing nephew. Catherine talked Charlotte into breaking her engagement with William after a deplorable incident in which he got drunk and vulgar. Catherine was genuinely opposed to the match, but not for the excuses she poured into Charlotte's ear. Reasons of state rather than female solidarity determined her outlook. Catherine spearheaded St. Petersburg's policies of trying to fix Charlotte up with either Russian grand duke Constantine or Nicholas, while preserving the odious William for marriage with her younger sister Anne, whose nuptials took place a year later. The eventual revelation of Catherine's machinations enraged Charlotte, along with the British government and public. Until then, Charlotte remained Catherine's confidante, not just on potential spouses but on her love-hate relationship with her father. Catherine was unremitting in blistering George for how strictly he tried to govern Charlotte. She also loudly proclaimed her support for Caroline in the battles between her and her estranged husband. Finally, she dallied with opposition leaders like Lords Grey and Holland.[4]

Even had Catherine not poisoned her brother's mind against the prince regent, the tsar would have found much in him to despise. George was loud, vulgar, boastful, perennially hours late for meetings, and often deep in his cups when he arrived. Above all, George was no hero. Unlike Alexander, the prince regent had never visited a war front, let alone campaigned with his troops.

Alexander gave in to his sister's demand that she accompany him to a male-only banquet at the Guildhall, where seven hundred influential Britons gathered to feast, drink, and toast the allied victories. There she shared the table of honor with not just the tsar, but Cossack general Matvei Platov, Prussian generals Blucher, Yorck, and Bülow, and foreign ministers Nesselrode, Hardenberg, and Metternich. Atop this affront, the tsar and grand duchess tarried to chat and laugh with opposition leaders at their table. Prime Minister Liverpool expressed the outraged feelings to Ambassador Lieven: "When folks don't know how to behave, they would do better to stay at home and our Duchess has chosen against all usage to go to men's dinners."[5] It was through such gross insensitivities that in a mere three weeks the tsar went from being the adored toast of the town to the butt of scurrilous aspersions. It was with enormous relief that most informed Britons learned of the departure on June 27 of Alexander and Catherine for Dover and a vessel to the continent.

It was Castlereagh's job to sweep up the diplomatic wreckage from the tsar's sojourn. The settlement of Europe's outstanding problems depended to a great extent on how well the British and Russians got along after the Congress of Vienna convened later that year.

Meanwhile, Wellington returned Odysseus-like to London to an ecstatic welcome on June 23. He had been away five years. His private homecoming was awkward. He was emotionally distant from his wife and two young sons, having begot his family from duty rather than desire. When he took his seat to thunderous applause in the House of Lords on June 28, he surely must have wondered if he would pass the rest of what time lay before him in mere ceremonial duties. He eagerly grabbed Castlereagh's offer to be ambassador to France. Once again, he left his family behind to bury himself in work and relieve himself with pleasures, including a succession of mistresses, overseas.

When Wellington returned to Paris on August 22, his primary mission was to convince Louis XVIII to abandon the international slave trade now rather than five years later, as required by the Treaty of Paris. In this the duke could not pry a commitment from the king. Nonetheless, his diplomatic skills impressed Talleyrand, who remarked: "He never indulged in that parade of mystification which is generally employed by Ambassadors: watchfulness, prudence, and experience of human nature were the only means he employed; and it is not surprising that, by use of these simple agencies, he acquired great influence."[6] Wellington's most enduring achievement during his diplomatic sojourn in Paris, however, had to do with real estate rather than realpolitik. He purchased from Pauline Borghese, Napoleon's sister, her magnificent mansion on the Rue du Faubourg St.-Honoré. It has housed Britain's embassy ever since.

Napoleon destroyed Europe's old international order. Had prudence rather than hubris governed him, he could have won legitimacy for his new order of French acquisitions, spheres of influence, and law after a decade or so of peace. But he squandered the chance, chronically through five years of war in the Iberian Peninsula, and spectacularly through his devastating defeat in Russia. This empowered the statesmen of Britain, Russia, Prussia, Austria, and, eventually, France to construct a version of the world that existed before 1789.

At the Congress of Vienna, Castlereagh dedicated himself to consolidating Britain's roles as the continent's power broker and the world's maritime hegemon. The odds of this happening swelled with the number of understandings he nurtured and deals he cut beforehand with the other great powers. He had prolonged candid talks with Metternich and Hardenberg during their visit to London in June 1814. He then journeyed to Paris in August for talks with Talleyrand. Finally, he headed to Vienna, arriving to head Britain's nineteen-man delegation on September 13. There he grew more frustrated, as for weeks he struggled to buttonhole anyone important to talk about anything serious. He was able to ensure, however, that his delegation was a model of efficiency and probity with its own courier service and "the only delegation never to be penetrated by Austria's secret service."[7]

Diplomacy was on indefinite hold as the cream of European nobility partied day and night to celebrate the end of nearly a quarter century of wars and revolutions that threatened their privileged way of life. For months Castlereagh exchanged bows and chitchat with five monarchs and the noble heads of 216 lesser realms, along with hundreds of diplomats and even more party crashers. Orchestrating the seemingly endless progression of dinners, balls, hunts, Beethoven concerts, sight-seeing excursions, teas, salons, strolls, and dalliances was Prince Clement von Metternich, now Austria's chancellor. Against his will, Castlereagh was sucked into the vortex of this dizzying social whirl. He complained wearily: "We are . . . impeded by the succession of fetes and private Balls—they waste a great deal of valuable time, and prevent . . . Metternich from giving his mind to subjects that ought to engross him."[8] Yet the virtually nonstop orgy benefited Castlereagh in at least one way. Seeing his counterparts at uninhibited play provided insights into how to play them at the negotiating table.

For now the only consensus among Britain, Russia, Austria, and Prussia was that they would decide all major issues as the Council of Four and permit the token presence of second-tier states France, Spain, Sweden, and Portugal and third tier states only on committees where they had a direct stake. The committee with the broadest representation, which initially included Austria, Prussia, Bavaria, Hanover, and Wurttemberg, was on Germany's future; the delegates soon reached a impasse that persisted for five months and was broken only when they agreed to include Bavaria, Saxony, Hesse-Darmstadt, Denmark, and the Netherlands. The four great powers were either the sole members or shared seats with a few other states on the nine other committees eventually formed, including ones for the slave trade, Switzerland,

Tuscany, Sardinia and Genoa, the Duchy of Bouillon, international rivers, diplomatic protocol, statistics, and treaty drafting.

The Congress of Vienna was originally supposed to open on October 1, 1814, but Metternich kept the social calendar so packed that the date was delayed till November 1. Then, on October 30, the eight powers agreed to postpone the official opening until they had resolved all conflicts among them and could present a comprehensive treaty for each state's signature. The actual signing ceremony, known as the Final Act, would not take place until June 9, 1815.

The Council of Four did not regularly begin their behind-the scene-talks until early November. They debated critical conflicts of national interests that could spark the next round of war, this time among two or more of the coalition partners. No one's ambitions worried Castlereagh more than those of Alexander. The tsar made no secret of his intention to reconstitute Russia's existing share of Poland with its 10 million inhabitants as a constitutional monarchy with himself as its king. If the tsar did so and brought genuine economic and political reforms to that realm, he would threaten the security of Prussia and Austria, who each held about 5 million repressed and restless Poles as subjects. The tsar's next logical step would be to liberate those Poles and join them to his own kingdom.

Castlereagh informed Prime Minister Liverpool that it was essential

> to watch him [Alexander], and to resist him, if necessary as another Buonaparte . . . acquiescence will not keep him back, nor will opposition accelerate his march. His Imperial Majesty is never more condescending than to those who speak plainly but respectfully to him, and . . . to give . . . the longest interval of peace with such a character, I should say that it would lie in never suffering him for a moment to doubt your readiness to support the continental Powers against his ambitious encroachments. . . . With such a personage at the head of between forty and fifty millions of people prone to, and adapted to war, you cannot afford to dissolve your continental relations unless you are prepared to acquiesce in a domination that would very soon assume the character of that from which we have escaped.[9]

Castlereagh soon found that Metternich shared his fear and desire to contain the tsar's ambitions. But from Vienna's point of view, Berlin posed a far more immediate threat. Frederick William III demanded all of Saxony and the fortress of Mainz; if he got them, Prussia would dominate Germany. Alexander backed Frederick William's acquisition of Saxony to divert his attention from Poland and to strengthen their friendship and the alliance between their realms. Here too Castlereagh shared a profound common interest with Metternich. They would work to uphold the power balance between the two giants, Austria and Prussia, and the descending order among the other German states. But they had to do so delicately to avoid pushing Frederick William more tightly into Alexander's welcoming arms.

Castlereagh's warnings about Russia and, less so, Prussia alarmed Liverpool and the cabinet, but not how he intended. His colleagues feared that he might get the nation into a war over distant lands and peoples that did not directly threaten British national security. Liverpool cautioned Castlereagh to tolerate rather than resist the tsar's ambitions in Poland and elsewhere in eastern Europe. Secretary for War Bathurst explicitly instructed him not "to involve this country in hostilities at this time for any of the objects which have been hitherto under discussion at Vienna."[10]

Liverpool bore no delusions over the potential threats that could arise from Europe. From London, however, he could view British interests far more broadly than could his man in Vienna, not just across the continent but around the world. He cannily assessed the challenges the nation faced:

> The more I hear and see of the different Courts of Europe, the more convinced I am that the King of France is (amongst the Great Powers) the only sovereign in whom we can have any confidence. The Emperor of Russia is profligate from vanity and self-sufficiency, if not from principle. The King of Prussia may be a well-meaning man, but he is the dupe of the Emperor of Russia. The Emperor of Austria I believe to be an honest man, but he has a Minister [Metternich] in whom no one can trust; who considers all policy as consisting in finesse and trick;

> and who has got his government and himself into more difficulties by his devices than could have occurred from a plain course of dealing.[11]

He explicitly warned Castlereagh not to take the nation to war over any issue in Vienna.

Although he accepted this policy, Castlereagh was quite willing to take the nation to war's brink if it protected or enhanced British security. This risky strategy was simply a practical means to a far more crucial interest that he insisted that Britain shared with Europe's other great and lesser powers: "I consider that in the question now at issue in France is involved the more vital question whether Europe can return to that moral system by which . . . the interests of mankind are to be upheld or whether we shall remain, as we have been during the last twenty years, under the necessity of maintaining a system of military policy; whether Europe shall in the future present the spectacle of an assemblage of free or of armed nations."[12]

While the talks unrolled in Vienna, diplomacy ended a war that most Britons agreed should never have been fought.[13] The war the United States had launched against Britain in June 1812 soon stalemated. In November 1813 Foreign Secretary Castlereagh sent Secretary of State James Monroe a letter asking if he was interested in discussing peace. After gaining the approval of President Madison and the other cabinet secretaries, Monroe replied affirmatively. They eventually chose the city of Ghent in Flanders as a neutral ground for talks. Although Madison soon appointed a delegation, Castlereagh did not do so until May 1814. In June the Madison administration actually dropped its demand that Britain end its impressment policy, a key reason for declaring war in June 1812. The talks finally began on August 8, 1814, then swiftly deadlocked as the British asserted demands unacceptable to the Americans. Castlereagh instructed his three-man diplomatic team to insist on uti possidetis, or that each side could keep what it had taken, an arrangement that then favored the British, and that the Americans create an Indian buffer state in their own territory that could never be violated by settlers or taken away by force or treaty. The Americans adamantly rejected these demands.[14]

It was not until November 18 that the Liverpool government decided on peace without conquest. Wellington was the most important reason for this shift. Liverpool asked him to take charge of Britain's war against the United States, and while he reluctantly agreed to do so, he admitted that he did not expect to win "much success there." He also insisted that Britain had "no right . . . to demand any concession of territory from America."[15]

Ideally, this would have let Britain's envoys at Ghent quickly wrap up a treaty with the Americans. Instead, the haggling persisted for another six weeks before they struck a deal. On Christmas Eve the delegations signed a peace treaty grounded on the status quo ante bellum, or return to the territory that each possessed before the war. All prisoners would be released and no property could be taken from occupied territory. Any prizes taken after 12 days off America's coast to after 120 days in the world's far seas must be returned. The British would compensate the owners of any slaves that were liberated. Each side would make a just peace with the Indians in its territory. A joint commission would delineate the boundary between the United States and Canada. The Treaty of Ghent was ratified by Prince Regent George on December 28, and by the United States Senate with a vote of 35 to zero on February 16, 1815.

The 1812 War was among history's more senseless. Yet, although the British did not win any new territory, the war greatly enhanced Britain's trade and thus its economy as its merchants, bankers, shippers, and manufacturers capitalized on American losses. American exports plummeted from $61 million in 1811 to $6.9 million in 1814, while federal revenues from trade fell from $13.3 million to $6 million. The tonnage of American ships dropped just as precipitously, from 948,000 to 60,000. Hard money fled the United States for safe havens aboard, mostly in the British empire, with $2 million and $1.8 million in gold moving to Canada alone in 1814 and 1815, respectively. The national debt soared from $45 million in 1812 to $127 million in 1815. In all, the 1812 war may have stunted and warped America's economy for a generation or so, all to Britain's advantage.[16] As for the war's financial costs, they are impossible to untangle from Whitehall's budget. The immediate effect of the Ghent treaty was to strengthen Britain's diplomatic hand in Vienna.

There Frederick William provoked a crisis on December 29, when he angrily equated those who opposed Prussia's acquisition of Saxony with warring against Prussia. After calming the enraged monarch with platitudes, Castlereagh and Metternich met secretly and agreed that they needed France to counter Russia and Prussia. After Talleyrand, who headed France's delegation, eagerly accepted their offer, they formally asked Hardenberg and Nesselrode, the respective heads of the Prussian and Russian delegations, on December 31, to add France to the Council's ranks. Hardenberg and Nesselrode adamantly rejected the notion.

This prompted Castlereagh, Metternich, and Talleyrand to sign, on January 3, 1815, a secret defensive alliance binding Britain, Austria, and France. The rumor of this alliance was enough to convince Alexander and Frederick William to compromise. First, on January 9, they agreed to accept France as an equal partner in the now Council of Five. On February 3 Wellington arrived to relieve Castlereagh, and his mega-star power prompted everyone to be more conciliatory. On February 8 the Council of Five bowed to Britain's obsession and condemned the international slave trade. The vital breakthrough came on February 11; Frederick William agreed to take only two-fifths of Saxony and let Augustus rule the rest from his Dresden palace, in return for Luxembourg. The German states would retain their sovereignty but organize into a federation with a diet at Frankfort and directory shared by Vienna and Berlin. As for Poland, Austria kept Galicia and Tarnopol, Prussia kept Posen and Thorn, and Cracow would be a free city. The rest of Poland was designated a kingdom under Russian control. Prussia also got Westphalia and Swedish Pomerania. Sweden was compensated with Norway, taken from Denmark. Austria directly got Venetia, Lombardy, and Illyria, while Hapsburgs would rule Tuscany and Parma. Victor Emmanuel, the king of Sardinia, got not just the return of Piedmont with his capital at Turin but the bonus of Genoa.

For now the Council of Five tolerated Murat as the king of Naples and southern Italy, while Ferdinand IV remained confined to Sicily. The Netherlands got the southern Netherlands and William's promotion from prince to king. Pius VII got back the Papal States. Britain retained the Cape of Good Hope and Guiana. And for now, Napoleon could continue to rule his tiny island of Elba. The treaty drafting committee was busy crafting an ever expanding document. The hope was that the Council of Five needed no more than a few more weeks to tie up any diplomatic loose ends, then, after an elaborate signing ceremony, everyone could go home. Castlereagh left Vienna on February 14, joyful that British interests were secure.

Horrifying news shattered the optimism in Vienna on March 7, and London on March 10; Napoleon had escaped with a thousand troops crammed aboard a small flotilla bound for an unknown destination.

What prompted Napoleon's flight? He eventually reasoned that he had nothing to lose. Shortly after stepping ashore at Elba on May 4, 1814, he typically engaged in a frenzy of reform to that realm's administration, laws, taxes, military, roads, port, and economy. This effort was short lived, as he soon emptied his treasury. Louis XVIII refused to honor his commitment in signing the Treaty of Paris to uphold the Treaty of Fontainebleau that required France annually to give Napoleon 2 million francs and smaller stipends to the rest of his family. As for Napoleon's wife and child, he soon learned that not only were they forbidden to see or even write him, but that Marie Louise had taken a dashing Austria colonel, Alfred von Neipperg, as her lover. Then there were the rumors seeping from the Congress of Vienna that the great powers were plotting to depose and send him to some remote island like St. Helena as a prisoner for the rest of his days.

Whitehall had assigned Colonel Neil Campbell to sharply eye Napoleon. At first he was diligent in fulfilling his duties, warning Castlereagh that "if pecuniary difficulties press upon him much longer so as to prevent his vanity from being satisfied by his ridiculous establishment of a Court . . . and if his doubts are not removed, I think he is capable of crossing over with his troops."[17] But with time Campbell grew more complacent and bored. On February 16, 1815, he took leave of Napoleon for a couple of weeks' sojourn at Livorno, ostensibly for a meeting with Austria's envoy there but most importantly to be with his mistress.

Napoleon packed 1,026 Old Guard grenadiers and Polish lancers into a flotilla of small vessels, set sail on February 26, 1815, and stepped ashore near Fréjus on March 1. His triumphant bloodless return to power in Paris is legendary. Upon learning of his landing, Louis XVIII mobilized his army to crush him, but Napoleon's magic won over the troops sent against him, and his army's ranks swelled joyfully as he marched toward the capital. The king and his court fled Paris on March 19, and the next day Napoleon exuberantly restored himself to his throne in the Tuileries Palace.

Napoleon owed his return to power, not just to his extraordinary charisma and luck, but as much to the contempt and anger with which most people viewed the man he replaced. Louis XVIII had little legitimacy after the coalition placed him on the throne, despite the peace that accompanied his reign. Most people accepted with sullen fatalism the full turn of the political wheel over a quarter century from an absolute monarch to a constitutional monarch to a republic to a consulate to an emperor to an absolute monarch and, most recently, back to an emperor. They bitterly lamented that first the revolutionaries, then Napoleon, had taken power with dazzling promises of political, economic, and social progress but soon led France into worsening death, destruction, and despair. Were the sacrifices of a million French lives and vast treasure on the altar of revolutionary ideals and genuine accomplishments all in vain? So when Napoleon returned with his promise to dedicate his rule to peace, prosperity, and liberty, most people were willing to wait and see. The spectacle of Napoleon's last sojourn in power did not last long—less than three months—and he was the most to blame for its brevity.

Napoleon's hope that the great powers would fatalistically accept his resumption of power and pledge to war no more was soon shattered. On March 13 the Council of Eight at Vienna unanimously declared him an international outlaw subject to extralegal and extraordinary justice: "Napoleon Bonaparte, again appearing in France with projects of confusion and disorder, has placed himself beyond the protection of the law and rendered himself subject to public vengeance." The great powers pledged themselves to a total war that destroyed Napoleon and all he represented. On March 25, 1815, they renewed the Treaty of Chaumont, whereby each would field 150,000 troops against France, and opened their alliance to all other European states.[18] The Low Countries were at once the closest staging area for an allied offensive into France and the primary target for a French offensive. There Wellington would command an allied army of British and Dutch troops. Blucher would march to join him with the Prussian army. Schwarzenberg would lead the Austrian army into eastern France. Mikhail Barclay de Tolly would lead a Russian army on the long march westward from Poland. Ideally, Wellington and Blucher would defeat Napoleon on their own but by all means had to hold the line until Schwarzenberg and Barclay de Tolly arrived.

Castlereagh instructed Wellington to spare no expense at Vienna to finance the latest coalition: "If we are to undertake the job, we must leave nothing to chance. It must be done upon the largest scale."[19] As always, Austria, Prussia, and Russia looked to Britain for money, at the very least the £5 million to be split among them as required by the 1814 Treaty of Chaumont. Britain eventually contributed not just this but an additional £9 million to underwrite nearly 1 million troops against Napoleon, although the war ended before most of them could get to the front.[20]

The money was easier to muster than the men. Over the previous ten months since Napoleon's first abdication, the great powers had called home and cut back their armies to enjoy a peace dividend after nearly a quarter century of ruinously expensive warfare. Now they had to recall the depleted regiments and fill them with new recruits. The forces that Russia, Prussia, and Austria still posted outside their respective kingdoms occupied realms that each wanted to keep: Russian troops in Poland, Austrian troops in northern Italy, and Prussian troops in Saxony. In contrast, the few British regiments bivouacked in the Netherlands were there not to assert any territorial claim but to back King William's reassertion of power and intimidate any lingering Bonapartist or radical groups. Whitehall dispatched Richard Trench, Earl of Clancarty, to replace Wellington in Vienna. On March

29 Wellington headed to Brussels to assume his latest command. The tsar's parting words to the duke at once conferred a great trust and burden: "It is for you to save the world again."[21]

Britain's leaders and their allies knew clearly what they were fighting against, but the old haunting question returned over just what they were fighting for. Once again a French Bourbon king had proved incapable of retaining power. Was Louis XVIII's restoration worth the vast expenditure of blood and treasure? Castlereagh worried that not just the king but his entire clan had squandered what little legitimacy they had. If so, then what was the alternative? Britain seemingly had "no cause to support, except an undisguised dictation to France as to her monarchy." If so, then it was better not to back any contender. Castlereagh amended the Coalition treaty so that it did not bind "his Britannic Majesty to prosecute the war with a view of imposing upon France any particular Government." After ridding the world of Napoleon, permanently this time, Britain would let the French decide their own political fate. At Vienna, Clancarty talked the Council of Eight into embracing this policy, which they announced on May 12.[22]

The coalition received a huge boost when Neapolitan king Joachim Murat declared war on Austria on March 15 and marched north from Naples. His campaign peaked at Rimini on March 30, when he declared Italy's liberation from Austria and unification under his rule. An Austrian army under General Friedrich von Bianchi routed Murat at the Battle of Tolentino on May 2 and 3, then pursued the remnants all the way to Naples, which they entered on May 23. Murat escaped disguised as a sailor aboard a ship bound for France. The Austrians now dominated most of the Italian peninsula. As important, with Murat deposed they could concentrate their troops against Napoleon.

The Congress of Vienna finally climaxed when six of the Council of Eight signed a treaty known as the Final Act, with 121 articles, on June 9, 1815; Spain and Sweden held off in hopes of resolving minor issues in their favor. The six great powers then invited the other states to sign. Eventually all did, including Spain and Sweden; the Papal States and the Ottoman Empire were the only holdouts. Of course, the longevity of the new order that the great powers had painstakingly constructed over the previous eight months depended on whether the coalition destroyed Napoleon once and for all.

To this end, British strategy was shaped by its ally and assets in the Netherlands, where around 24,000 British and 12,000 Hanoverian, or King's German Legion, troops were then deployed. King William reacted to Napoleon's return by mobilizing his army, asking for more British troops and money, and urging the rapid joint takeover of France's border fortresses. Whitehall replied by asking William to sit tight and await reinforcements.[23]

Upon reaching Brussels on April 4, Wellington got to work forging an army from the regiments already scattered across the Low Countries and others that slowly arrived, while trying to coordinate efforts with Dutch King William I and Prussian King Frederick William III. The Dutch monarch was a troublesome ally. Many of William's leading army officers had attained power under French rule and remained Bonapartists who sought to undermine the coalition by every possible covert means. Napoleon himself assured William of his peaceful intentions and asked him to expel Wellington and all British forces. Being torn between Paris and London made William sullen and prone to outbursts. He angrily rejected Wellington's request to reduce the Dutch garrisons at the fortresses of Mons, Ath, Tournai, Enghien, Hal, Grammont, Oudenarde, and Ghent, and send him those extra troops. Yet William finally made a major concession that boosted the alliance on May 3, when he authorized Wellington to command all Dutch forces. Alas, there was a catch. This depended on Prince William, the king's twenty-three year-old son, serving as the deputy commander in chief and the immediate Dutch commander. Wellington did not mind all that much. The prince had served competently as one of his aides for three years in the Iberian Peninsula, and the duke kept him on a short leash during the Waterloo campaign.

When asked if he could defeat Napoleon, Wellington pointed to a nearby British soldier and replied: "There it all depends on that article whether we do the business or not. Give me enough of it, and I am sure."[24] Of course, victory rested on much more than how many redcoats Whitehall dispatched to the front. Together Wellington's

93,000 troops and Blucher's 117,000 troops numbered 210,000, vastly outgunning Napoleon's 125,000-man army. The trouble was that the allied armies were far apart and scattered across a hundred-mile front. Napoleon commanded more and better troops than Wellington and would easily overwhelm him if Blucher's Prussian army did not arrive in time. Fortunately, Wellington and Blucher swiftly forged a common strategy during a meeting at Tirlemont on May 3. Napoleon's obvious strategy was to smash between those two enemy armies and rout each on its divergent supply line. Wellington and Blucher planned to close that gap and march quickly wherever Napoleon attacked. On May 8 Wellington confidently wrote that "I believe Blucher and I are so well united, and so strong, that the enemy cannot do us much mischief."[25]

The duke's optimism was not completely warranted. The allied armies were still literally and figuratively far apart. Forty-eight miles then separated the headquarters of Wellington and Blucher at Brussels and Namur, respectively. This was a very hard half day's gallop for a courier atop a successions of fast horses. Wellington's line of communication and supply was short, just several score miles north to the ports of Antwerp and Ostend, and then by ship to England. Blucher's stretched several hundred miles eastward through Liège and Aachen back to faraway Berlin.

Napoleon's campaign plan was simple. He massed his army at Charleroi and split it in two wings, the left under Marshal Michel Ney to march north against Wellington and the right under Marshal Emanuel Grouchy to march northeast against Blucher. Having driven the two allied armies apart, Napoleon would concentrate his troops to destroy whichever army was more vulnerable before turning against the other.

Napoleon was so effective in sealing off the frontier from any infiltration by spies that Wellington believed that any French offensive would most likely start on July 1. When Charlotte, Duchess of Richmond, asked him if she should cancel a ball she had planned, Wellington replied: "Duchess, you may give your ball with the greatest safety, without fear of interruption."[26] Indeed, Wellington was planning to host his own ball on June 21 to help bolster the morale and solidarity of the allied officers and the elite. He attended the Duchess's ball at her mansion in Brussels that began on the evening of June 14 and carried on nearly until sunrise. At three o'clock in the morning of June 15, a courier dashed in with word that the French army had invaded. Wellington's reaction to this startling news is celebrated. He called for the music and dancing to continue, then issued terse orders to the courier, who hurried back to the front. He and Charles Lennox, Duke of Richmond, retired briefly to a study, where they spread a map. "Napoleon has humbugged me, by God!" Wellington declared. "He has gained twenty-four hours march on me." He reassured Richmond that "I have ordered the army to concentrate at Quatre Bras; but we shall not stop him there, and if so, I must fight him there." He pointed at Waterloo. He then left the ball to spend a couple of hours at his headquarters before heading for his army with the dawn.[27]

To succeed, Napoleon's plan depended on his subordinates marching swiftly, massing their troops, and launching overwhelming attacks. Ney, known for his impetuous courage, was strangely cautious on June 16, and this may have lost the campaign for Napoleon. When his advanced guard encountered enemy troops at Quatre Bras, he ordered them to wait until he brought up the rest of his men. This gave Wellington time to hurry regiments there and repel Ney's attacks when they finally began. Meanwhile, Napoleon accompanied Grouchy's wing against Blucher at Ligny. The emperor ordered a series of attacks that battered the Prussians to the breaking point. To administer the coup de grace, he summoned General Jean-Baptiste Drouet d'Erlon's corps, which was stretched along a road linking Quatre Bras and Ligny. Those troops appeared on Prussia's right flank and were just about to smash through it when they withdrew. D'Erlon had obeyed an order from Ney to join him at Quatre Bras, but he did not arrive until dark. The result was that Napoleon routed but failed to crush Blucher at Ligny, while Wellington blunted Ney's attacks at Quatre Bras.

The next morning the allied armies withdrew north on parallel roads, although Blucher dispatched a corps east to guard his supply depot at Namur. Napoleon split Grouchy's wing in two, ordered the marshal to hound Blucher away from Wellington, and marched with the rest to join Ney. Believing that he was trailing the main Prussian army, Grouchy pushed his men toward Namur, a fatal mistake that let

Blucher join Wellington at Waterloo. The emperor tried to hurry Ney in pursuit of Wellington, but a rainstorm turned the roads to quagmires.

The night of June 17 Wellington halted his army and deployed it along a low ridge at Mont St. Jean, a mile south of Waterloo village and a dozen miles south of Brussels. Blucher's corps were clumped a dozen or so miles east. Wellington's forces numbered 67,000, including 25,000 British and 42,000 Dutch and German troops, and 156 cannons. Perhaps only one in five of those troops were veterans; the rest were experiencing the horrors of war for the first time. By the time all of Napoleon's available troops arrived the next day, the emperor had a slightly larger army of 74,000 troops and, with 246 cannons, far more artillery.

The Battle of Waterloo began in early afternoon on June 18, after all the French batteries and divisions were finally into line. The deep mud and lack of time forced Napoleon to attack directly rather than march around an enemy flank. Wellington withdrew his men behind the low ridgeline to shelter them from the French artillery barrage that preceded the assault. He then deployed his troops along the ridge top to pour in volley after volley that decimated and routed the French infantry. The French cavalry then galloped forward. The duke ordered his regiments into squares, which repelled the horsemen with heavy losses. Meanwhile, Blucher's lead corps arrived and attacked the French right flank, forcing Napoleon to divert ever more of his reserves to hold them at bay. The emperor ordered renewed infantry attacks against Wellington.

The two commanders contrasted sharply in how they handled the battle. While Napoleon issued a half dozen broad instructions and let Ney implement the details, Wellington took charge of the tactics like a chess master, issuing terse orders to move troops that checked each French move. At one point a gunner called out to Wellington that he had a good shot at Napoleon and asked permission to fire. "No," the duke replied. "Generals commanding armies have something else to do than to shoot at one another."[28] During the battle's height, he received a message from one of his brigade commanders, informing him that he had lost two-thirds of his men and urging a withdrawal. Wellington replied: "Tell him what he asks is impossible. He and I and every Englishman on the field must die on the spot which we occupy."[29]

As the day stretched into evening and ever more Prussians attacked his right, Napoleon played his last card by sending his Imperial Guard forward to attack. Wellington ordered the decisive volley and charge that broke and routed Napoleon's vaunted Old Guard: "Now Maitland," he shouted, "now's your time. Stand up, Guards! Make ready! Fire!"[30]

The combined armies of Wellington and Blucher routed Napoleon, inflicting 43,656 French dead, wounded, and captured to 24,143 allied losses, including 8,454 British, 8,687 Germans and Dutch, and 6,998 Prussians.[31] Victory as much humbled as elated Wellington. He grimly noted that "Blucher and I have lost 30,000 men. It has been . . . the nearest run thing you ever saw in your life."[32] Having said that, Wellington was unimpressed with Napoleon's tactics that "did not manoeuvre at all" but "just moved forward in the old style."[33] Nonetheless, he had no doubt over who was most responsible for the allied victory: "I don't think it would have done if I had not been there."[34] But he was also generous in sharing credit with the Prussians, attributing "the successful result of this arduous day to the . . . timely . . . operation of General Bulow upon the enemy's flank."[35] He was anything but elated: "Nothing except a battle lost can be half so melancholy as a battle won."[36]

The four-day campaign cost the French and allies nearly identical numbers of losses of 64,602 and 62,818, respectively.[37] Although Napoleon abandoned his army and fled to Paris, the war continued. It took several days for the allied armies to recover and pursue. Grouchy took over the French army's remnants and fought a skilled withdrawal. As the allied armies closely trailed Grouchy, Blucher ordered his cavalry to range far behind the French lines to hunt down and execute Napoleon. When he asked Wellington to support that plan, the duke demurred diplomatically to the allied leader but informed diplomat Charles Stuart that "I will have nothing to do with so foul a transaction."[38]

By the time Napoleon slipped into the Tuileries Palace on June 21, police minister Joseph Fouche and a coterie of other political leaders had overthrown him and formed a provisional government. They forced Napoleon to abdicate the next morning. At a loss over what to do, Napoleon rode a half dozen miles north of Paris to the château of Malmaison, which went to Josephine as part of their divorce settlement and where she had died the previous year. There he tarried to savor memories of happier times. Word that the Prussians were dead set on capturing and executing him roused Napoleon from his reveries. On June 29 he fled to Rochefort, where he hoped to board a frigate and sail to exile in America, but a British flotilla blockaded the bay so thoroughly that no French captain dared set sail. Word reached Napoleon that the government had signed an armistice on July 3. Fearing that it was only a matter of time before Prussian cavalry caught him, he surrendered to Captain Frederick Maitland of the HMS *Bellerophon* on July 15. Maitland sailed with his prize to Britain, reaching Torbay on July 24.

Napoleon sent a typically grandiloquent message to the British monarch: "Exposed to the factions which distract my country and to the enmity of the greatest powers of Europe, I have closed my political career, and I come, like Themistocles, to throw myself upon the hospitality of the British people. I put myself under the protection of their laws, which I claim from your Royal Highness, as the most powerful, the most constant, and the most generous of my enemies."[39]

Just as typically the monarch, this time Prince Regent George, insulted him by refusing to reply. Britain had never recognized Napoleon's title as emperor and was not about to start now. He would be officially referred to as General Bonaparte, and unofficially by any number of insults and expletives.

Yet Napoleon's appearance and plea for mercy entangled the British government in a quandary. Before he knew Napoleon's stunning whereabouts, Prime Minister Liverpool expressed the not-so-secret longing among himself and most of his colleagues that "we wish that the King of France would hang or shoot Bonaparte as the best termination of the business."[40] As he had done the previous year, Louis XVIII returned to Paris with an allied baggage train. His latest exile had filled him not with humility but a rage for vengeance. On July 24, he ordered fifty-seven civilian and military leaders in Napoleon's latest government arrested on the capital charges of treason.

So, while turning Napoleon over to Louis was one option, Liverpool and his colleagues soon had moral qualms about acquiescing in

Napoleon's execution. They finally decided to exile Napoleon to the remote Atlantic Ocean island of St. Helena, roughly midway between Capetown, Buenos Aires, and Antarctica. Castlereagh got the allies to sign, on August 2, a treaty designating Napoleon the coalition's prisoner who would spend his life's remainder in British custody. Meanwhile, Napoleon was transferred to the HMS *Northumberland,* which sailed on August 7, 1815, and arrived at St. Helena on October 17. There Napoleon would pass his life's last years, dictating his memoirs, protesting cruel treatment from Governor Hudson Lowe, and mulling a lifetime of stunning successes and blunders. He died on May 5, 1821. Nonetheless, not just in exile but long after his death, Napoleon cast a long shadow over Europe's great power relations and British foreign policy.

CHAPTER 11

# Legacies

"The statesman lives in time; his test is the permanence of his structure under stress."

Henry Kissinger

Few epochs have ended as decisively as did the Age of Revolution and Napoleon with Waterloo. Britain emerged from twenty-two years of nearly nonstop war with its economy, empire, navy, and prestige more powerful than ever.[1] Its number of colonies alone nearly doubled, from twenty-six in 1792 to forty-three in 1816. The British kept their conquests of Ceylon, Mauritius, and the Seychelles in the Indian Ocean; Cape Colony, Sierra Leone, and Gambia in Africa; Tobago, St. Lucia, Trinidad, and Deemara in the Caribbean basin; and Malta in the Mediterranean, while consolidating the patchwork of colonies and protectorates across most of the Indian subcontinent. Britain won such astonishing spoils for many reasons, but the most vital was that its leaders had mastered the art of smart power, or asserting key elements of hard and soft power to prevail.

Hard cash was literally British power's crucial bottom line. The more revenues that Whitehall garnered, the larger the navy and army that it could muster and the more allies, both overt and covert, that it could entice into the field. The world's most dynamic, diversified, rapidly industrializing economy generated all the cash that let Whitehall be the era's arsenal and banker of monarchy. The British had mastered a virtuous cycle of economic power that included increasingly efficient ways to make, invent, transport, sell, and buy ever more things at home and abroad. The culture celebrated and the market rewarded entrepreneurs and inventers willing to invest in agriculture, manufacturing, finance, and trade.[2]

The war accelerated Britain's industrial revolution, and the industrial revolution was critical to eventually crushing France. The economy more than doubled in size, from £153,920,000 in 1791 to £358,980,000 in 1821. Trade led this growth, with exports more than tripling from £20,390,000 in 1793 to £68,400,000 in 1815. Although Napoleon's Continental System or blockade drastically reduced British exports to Europe, widespread smuggling kept this market alive, while British merchants compensated by developing markets elsewhere.[3]

Twenty-two years of global war did not come cheap. Whitehall's direct costs to wage war from 1793 to 1815 were £1,657,854,518.[4] The budget soared from £19,623,000, with the army's share £4,829,000, the navy's £2,464,000, and ordnance's £844,000 in 1793, to, in 1815, £177,587,979, with the army's £33,795,556, the navy's £21,961,566, and ordnance's £4,480,729.[5] Subsidies to allies amounted to about 8 percent of Britain's total war expenses. In all, more than thirty great, medium, and small states received £65,830,228 from 1793 to 1815, with more than half distributed during the last five years.[6] The British sent not just money overseas but also enormous amounts of firearms, munitions, cannons, swords, bayonets, blankets, backpacks, shovels, uniforms, and other essential tools of war. For instance, from 1808 to 1811 alone Whitehall sent to Portugal and Spain 336,000 muskets, 60 million cartridges, 12,000 pistols, 100,000 swords, and 348 artillery pieces.[7]

Britain was more effective than the other great powers at taxing its subjects and borrowing money; certainly no nation, including France, had a higher tax rate. And while the array of British taxes accounted for about 35 percent of the economy, revenues only covered a portion of the swelling costs. Whitehall had to borrow the rest. The national debt soared from £242.9 million in 1793 to £744.9 million in 1815.[8] In all, Whitehall financed its swelling budgets and interest on the national debt with twenty-six loans from 1793 to 1815.

Indeed, Britain's related industrial, mercantile, and fiscal powers were so great that loans were a smaller proportion, or only about a

**Table 2. British Wartime Expenditures and Revenues, 1688–1815**

| | Total Expenditures (£) | Total Income (£) | Balance Raised by Loans (£) | Loans as Percentage of Expenditures |
|---|---|---|---|---|
| 1688–97 | 49,320,145 | 32,766,754 | 16,553,391 | 33.6 |
| 1702–13 | 93,644,560 | 64,239,477 | 29,405,083 | 31.4 |
| 1739–48 | 95,628,159 | 65,903,964 | 29,724,195 | 31.1 |
| 1756–63 | 160,573,366 | 100,555,123 | 60,018,242 | 37.4 |
| 1776–83 | 236,462,689 | 141,902,620 | 94,560,069 | 39.9 |
| 1793–1815 | 1,657,854,518 | 1,217,556,439 | 400,298,079 | 26.6 |
| **Totals** | **2,293,483,437** | **1,622,924,377** | **670,559,060** | **33.3** |

Source: Kennedy, *Rise and Fall of the Great Powers*, 81.

quarter, of Whitehall's expenditure compared to the one-third average for its five previous prolonged European wars (see table 2).

A key element of Britain's virtuous cycle of power was paying others to do much of the actual fighting on land. For reasons of geography and culture, the British army was small compared to the continent's behemoths. As island dwellers with a large navy, the British did not need many troops to protect themselves. Atop this, British notions of liberty and rights objected to a large standing army.

France's revolutionaries initiated total war, or mobilizing all the nation's human and material resources against one's enemies. The British rose to that challenge. Whitehall expanded the British army from 38,945 men, including 34,262 infantry and 4,681 cavalry in 1793, to 230,469 men, including 201,469 infantry and 28,931 cavalry in 1813.[9] In the Iberian Peninsula, Wellington's army swelled each year, with the largest rise from around 34,7000 troops in 1812 to 42,700 in 1813. His Portuguese and Spanish contingents also increased, reaching about 30,000 and 25,000, respectively, in 1813. A similar troop buildup spearheaded the British empire's expansion across much of India. From 1792 to 1815, the number of troops mobilized by the East India Company soared from 90,000 to 250,000 troops, of whom 31,000 were Europeans. Those figures are even more impressive given the

**Table 3. Size of Armies by Troop Numbers**

| | 1789 | 1812–14 |
|---|---|---|
| Britain | 40,000 | 250,000 |
| France | 180,000 | 600,000 |
| Austria | 300,000 | 250,000 |
| Prussia | 190,000 | 270,000 |
| Russia | 300,000 | 500,000 |

Source: Kennedy, *Rise and Fall of the Great Powers*, 99.

attrition rates from death, disease, discharge, and desertion. In just a decade from 1803 to 1813 alone, the army lost 225,000 men, of whom 188,000 were British and the rest foreigners.[10]

It cost three times more to field a regiment overseas than in Britain, and these were just the paper costs. While Britons would accept a note for payment, foreigners demanded hard coin for requisitions of provisions, laborers, and other goods and services. For instance, in 1813 alone Wellington's army needed 1,300 carts to transport all its munitions, provisions, and other needs. The troops daily devoured an average 100,000 pounds of biscuits, 200,000 pounds of forage corn, and 300 cattle.[11]

War's human costs were as exorbitant as its the financial costs. No campaigns killed more Britons than those in the West Indies. British expeditions captured most of the French and Dutch colonies, at once depriving these imperial rivals and enriching Britain with their markets, products, and revenues. But these relatively easy victories came at an enormous cost. Death, largely from malaria, yellow fever, typhus, and dysentery, killed 43,747 of the 90,000 British soldiers and 24,000 of the 100,000 sailors who served in the West Indies from 1793 to 1801; with desertions and discharges added, the army's attrition rate for the Caribbean was 70 percent.[12] William Grenville offered a requiem of sorts on British operations against Spain's New World colonies: "I always felt a great reluctance to embarking on South American projects because I knew it was much easier to get into them than out again."[13] After the Caribbean and until Waterloo, the Low Countries of the Netherlands and Flanders proved to be the figurative graveyard for the reputations of British generals and the literal graveyard for tens of thousands of British soldiers who died of fever.

The scale, pace, and intensity of warfare expanded during this era. No general then surpassed Napoleon in his strategy of rapid, relentless movements to encircle and annihilate the enemy. Yet the military genius of Arthur Wellesley, the eventual Duke of Wellington, was far less controversial and far more successful than Napoleon's.[14] Unlike Napoleon, Wellington never lost a major battle. He won brilliant victories at Assaye, Vimeiro, Talavera, Busaco, Salamanca, Vitoria, Sorauren, Orthez, Toulouse, and Waterloo. Every battle that Wellington fought against the French weakened Napoleon's empire, although the impact varied. He offered this succinct and unassailable assessment: "I look upon Salamanca, Vittoria, and Waterloo as my three best battles—those which had great and permanent consequences. Salamanca relieved the whole south of Spain, changed all the prospects of the war, and was felt even in Prussia. Vittoria freed the Peninsula altogether, broke off the armistice at Dresden, and thus led to Leipzig and the deliverance of Europe; and Waterloo did more than any other battle I know towards the true object of all battles—the peace of the world."[15]

Wellington mastered defense and offense, strategy and tactics, logistics and intelligence. He excelled Napoleon as a tactician, as he micromanaged battles when the emperor mostly issued broad instructions to his generals. He had a keen eye for adapting terrain to his advantage. For defense, he always sought long steep ridgelines, and during artillery bombardments, he withdrew his troops behind the crest beyond the sight of the enemy gunners. When the enemy attacked, his troops would reappear, pour devastating volleys into the enemy struggling up the slope, then charge with lowered bayonets. In offense, he advanced steadily and methodically like a chess master, forcing the enemy back by arching part of his army toward the enemy rear. He made excellent use of light troops, especially riflemen, whose marksmanship wore down enemy battalions long before they could launch an attack or defend a position.

The Iberian Peninsula was the British army's decisive theater from 1808 to 1813. Napoleon later reckoned that the Peninsula War "overthrew me" and that "all my disasters can be traced back to this fatal knot."[16] Indeed this front was not merely an ulcer but a cancer eating away at Napoleon's empire. And Wellington stands above all others for inflicting it.

Wellington was the era's only great British army commander. Generals Charles Grey, Ralph Abercromby, John Moore, William Beresford, John Hope, and Rowland Hill were rarely more than competent in their independent commands. Being in his own class made the burdens of command increasingly onerous for Wellington: "I certainly feel every day more and more the difficulty of the situation in which I am placed. I am obliged to be everywhere, and if absent from any operation, something goes wrong."[17]

Britain could never have warred for twenty-two years, let alone ultimately triumphed, without vanquishing its enemies at sea, and outstanding fleet commanders won these victories.[18] Decisive naval battles were as dramatic as they were rare. The British won all six of the era's largest engagements: Richard Howe at the First of June (1794); John Jervis at St. Vincent (1797); Adam Duncan at Camperdown (1797); Horatio Nelson at the Nile (1799), Copenhagen (1801), and Trafalgar (1805); and Thomas Cochrane at Basque Roads (1809). The Royal Navy also scored some brilliant victories by capturing or destroying enemy warships in their home ports, as at Toulon (1793), Helder (1799), and Copenhagen (1807).

A killer instinct is among a great commander's vital virtues, best illustrated in an exchange between Nelson and Admiral William Hotham. After winning a limited victory by taking two enemy warships at the 1795 Battle of Hyeres, Hotham tried to sooth Nelson's disappointment by insisting, "We must be contented; we have done very well." To that Nelson retorted: "Had we taken ten sail, and allowed the eleventh to escape, being to get at her, I could never have called it well done."[19] Nelson exemplified the strategy of total war at sea, arguing that it was "annihilation that the country wants, and not merely a splendid victory. . . . Numbers only can annihilate."[20] Nelson's obsession with battles of annihilation was exacerbated by the rarity of such opportunities.

Britain warred at sea against France and its allies mostly through the monotony of blockade than the terror of battle. There were two blockade strategies, close and distant. A close blockade just beyond cannon shot of fortresses protecting a port virtually ensured an engagement with any enemy warships that sailed forth. This effectively plugged the port if the enemy warships were inferior in number. For this reason Nelson preferred a distant blockade by which he posted a few frigates in sight of the port while his ships of the line hovered beyond the horizon in hopes of enticing the enemy to sortie. After the frigates brought word of the enemy numbers and direction, Nelson then pursued with his fleet for a decisive battle. This was a risky strategy. Napoleon snookered Nelson twice, in 1798 and 1805, when French fleets sailed and Nelson spent agonizing months trying to find them. Of course, Nelson finally did catch up at the Nile and Trafalgar.

The British partly excelled at sea because they outspent their enemies. The attrition rates for vessels were stunning. The Royal Navy lost 317 vessels from 1803 to 1815, of which storms and shipwrecks destroyed 223, or more than two-thirds, and battle the rest. Britain got new warships in two ways, building them and capturing them. British naval and mercantile power were inseparable, with each feeding the other. The quickest way to augment the naval and merchant fleets was courtesy of Britain's enemies. Of the 134 warships captured from 1803 to 1815, 33 ships of the line and 68 frigates were baptized into the Royal Navy. From 1793 to 1801 alone, the number of British merchant ships soared from 15,000 to 18,000 while those of France plummeted from 2,000 to a hundred or so. In addition to captures, the convoy system, which the Admiralty introduced in 1793 and made mandatory in 1798, was a major reason why the merchant fleet swelled.[21]

British naval supremacy, of course, flowed as much from soft as hard power. Vigorous training empowered British gunners to fire twice as fast as their human targets. A refined flag system let fleet commanders direct their warships. Innovations in the quality of cannons, gunpowder, ramrods, and rigging sharpened Britain's edge at sea. Most vital were Britain's sea captains, who excelled in handling their ships and men and sailing boldly against the enemy.[22] Nelson was more than just an extraordinarily gutsy and aggressive leader, always on the prowl for battles of annihilation. Although he ensured that his ships and sailors were prepared for battle, he valued one source of naval power

**Table 4. Size of Navies by Number of Ships of the Line**

| | 1789 | 1815 |
|---|---|---|
| Britain | 195 | 214 |
| France | 81 | 80 |
| Spain | 72 | 25 |
| Russia | 67 | 40 |
| Netherlands | 44 | 0 |

Source: Kennedy, *Rise and Fall of the Great Powers*, 99.

even above seamanship, gunnery, and discipline: "The great thing in all military service is health . . . it is easier for an officer to keep men healthy than for a physician to cure them."[23]

Mustering all this hard army and navy power was challenging enough. Tougher still was wielding it decisively against the enemy. A debate raged throughout the era over whether a "continental" or "colonial" strategy, championed respectively and most famously by William Grenville and Henry Dundas, better empowered Britain to win the war. This, however, was a false choice, since every British campaign was essentially an expedition in which navy and army forces worked closely together.[24] The colonial strategy prevailed from 1793 to 1808, the continental strategy thereafter through Wellington on the Iberian Peninsula.

Napoleon once famously said that he would rather fight than join a coalition. Whether or not they were aware of this axiom, Britain's leaders must have muttered similar sentiments. From 1793 to 1815 Whitehall knit together seven coalitions against France, only to witness all but the last two unravel. British diplomats struggled endlessly to assert their nation's interests with often Janus-faced allies. Perhaps the most crucial divide was between the global oceanic interests of the British Isles and the claustrophobic overlapping continental interests of Austria, Prussia, and Russia. But of course the essential reason why the first five coalitions failed was because the French decisively defeated them.

Henry, Lord Petty, the chancellor of the exchequer, explained the dilemma of Britain's coalition strategies: "It was ridiculous to talk of saving Europe if Europe could not save itself. It was not in the desperate affairs of the continent that England could step in and save her. No, she had only to look to better times. She could be more useful in following up victory, not in remedying defeat; and therefore was a government wise in keeping up and refusing to exhaust the resources of the country until they could be useful."[25]

In this Sisyphean labor, Whitehall usually got plenty of bang for its bucks, but not much else. No government agreed to complete free trade with Britain. What the British got instead was a torrent of complaints from its "allies" that whatever money they pocketed was not enough and that much more was essential.

Portugal was the sole notable success. In 1808 Regent John not only agreed to lower Portugal's domestic and colonial trade barriers to British merchants but named Arthur Wellesley to be Portugal's generalissimo, who then assigned General William Beresford to remake Portugal's army with British officers, equipment, and training. Beresford brilliantly fulfilled that task; by 1810, Portuguese regiments were just as adept at marching and fighting as British regiments. This was partly due to Wellesley's apprenticing a Portuguese brigade to two British brigades in a division.

In stark contrast, having Spain as an "ally" was a double-edged sword for Britain. The quality of the Spanish officers and troops was generally abysmal. Spanish generals bickered incessantly, uniting only to reject the efforts of British generals to forge a common strategy with them. Wellington lamented that in battle the Spaniards "would fire a volley while the enemy was out of reach, and then run away."[26] But he blamed this mostly on their wretched officers, who "would ruin any soldiers—and how should the Spaniards have confidence in officers such as theirs."[27] Spanish guerrillas more than made up for the regular Spanish army's deficiencies. From 1808 to 1814 they killed tens of thousands of French soldiers, pinned down hundreds of thousands more, and destroyed or captured hundreds of thousands of tons of French provisions and munitions. The guerillas could be just as brutal toward any Spaniards who collaborated with the French.[28]

Covert actions during this era make for intriguing reading but scored few clear successes. Certainly all of the attempts to stir counterrevolution within France or murder Napoleon failed. Time after time the Alien Office infiltrated agents and spent small fortunes to foment coups only to learn that the police had arrested and often executed the conspirators. These activities were expensive: The covert action budget for the Foreign Office alone rose from £76,759 from 1790 to 1794 to £665,222 from 1795 to 1799. About 80 percent of that was spent by the Berne station, first under William Wickham and then James Talbot.[29] Yet these efforts diverted enormous amounts of French men and money to internal security from where they might otherwise have been more usefully deployed.[30] Atop this the only alternative was to do nothing. Grenville summed up the moral dilemmas entangled with covert actions, especially the unsavory methods and people that often accompany them: "Our business is . . . to combat the evil in its present and tangible form. . . . I fear as you do that the persons concerned in those plans want many of the quantities necessary for success, but they are the only instruments we have and we must work with them."[31]

Great leaders are masters of smart power or selecting, nurturing, combining, and asserting appropriate measures of physical and psychological or hard and soft power to prevail in a conflict. This art is so daunting that even the greatest leaders at times fumble. Soft power is clearly the more difficult source to master, since it resides in the labyrinths of individual and collective minds. Take just one ageless emotion, pride. Inspiring just the right amount in oneself and one's group can be a tremendous source of soft power, but too little or too much can be self-defeating. An excess of pride propelled General John Moore in 1808 to launch his David versus Goliath campaign against Napoleon's armies in Spain: "I was aware that I was risking infinitely too much, but something must be risked for the honour of the Service, and to make it apparent that we stuck to the Spaniards long after they themselves had given up their cause as lost."[32] The campaign ended in near disaster, as the French army chased the British across northern Spain to Corunna, where the army's remnants barely escaped aboard a flotilla; Moore was among the dead.

In the modern era, nationalism has been pride's largest and most volatile vehicle. Napoleon certainly discovered the paradox to his deep regret. He was brilliant at mobilizing France for war, partly by forging a more powerful collective identity among its diverse peoples. Yet he inadvertently inspired nationalism in his enemies when he warred against them. In exile on St. Helena, he lamented that the "system I pursued in Spain . . . would have eventually been for the good of that country, yet it was contrary to the opinion of the people, and therefore I failed."[33]

The Achilles' heel of man is, of course, himself. Humankind is at once the most calculating and emotional of animals, and these defining characteristics as much conflict with as complement each other. Speaking from experience, British diplomat Harold Nicolson offered penetrating insights into the relationship among diplomacy, politics, and human nature: "Nobody who has not actually watched statesmen dealing with each other can have any real idea of the immense part played in human affairs by such unavowable and often unrecognizable causes as lassitude, affability, personal affection or dislike, misunderstanding, deafness or incomplete command of a foreign language, vanity, social engagements, interruptions and momentary health."[34] Nicolson issued a timeless warning to historians about the pitfalls of research: "Most documents are composed after the event and all too frequently they are designed, and even falsified, in the hope of giving to what was a chance or empirical decision the appearance of prescience, wisdom, and intent."[35] Only rare individuals muster the strength to transcend such crippling limitations as hubris, greed, and ignorance.

Regardless of just how well or poorly British leaders fulfilled their duties, the epoch was hard on them. Unrelenting stress aggravated by heavy drinking and eating led to an array of afflictions, including cirrhosis of the liver, obesity, diabetes, gout, and ultimately failures of hearts, livers, kidneys, and brains. Bad health killed Pitt, Fox, and Grenville in their forties or fifties. Defending one's "honor" could also be deadly. Had they been better shots, the celebrated duels between Pitt and Tierney and between Castlereagh and Canning might have ended with the death of either or both combatants. For whatever tragic reasons, nineteen parliamentarians killed themselves and another twenty went insane from 1790 to 1820. And, of course, topping the list of notable tragedies was "King George's madness."[36]

The erratic distribution of gifted individuals across the frontiers of humanity can be as capricious as those of geography. What mix of nature, nurture, and chance brings great leaders to power? How many countless other individuals who might have been as or more outstanding than those we recall resided in the wings of history without ever striding onto its stage? As for Britain, how important were its political leaders in determining when and how France was finally defeated? Did it really matter who ran the country?

Leadership certainly matters anytime in determining what to do and then getting it done. Yet in international relations the art of power is never wielded alone. National leaders are surrounded by advisers and ministers who are extensions of complex political systems, which in turn are embedded in nation-states packed with rival interest groups, mass medias, and public opinions. Nonetheless, at times an especially brilliant or inept individual has indeed changed the course of history for better or worse.

The era is split between political continuity and turnover. William Pitt was the prime minister for the war's first decade, and he along with Henry Dundas and William Grenville dominated foreign policy. Then, for the next dozen years there were six prime ministers (including a brief return of Pitt himself), nine foreign secretaries, and seven secretaries of war.

Although Pitt died nearly a decade before Waterloo, he became popularly known thereafter as "the savior of Europe" and more recently as "Britain's greatest prime minister."[37] Does he merit this status? He certainly does by at least two measures. He was prime minister for eighteen years; only Horace Walpole served longer, nosing ahead by eleven months. Even more astonishing was Pitt's assumption of that power when he was only twenty-three years old. Not only was he Britain's youngest prime minister, but only two of his successors—Liverpool and Blair—were younger when they took office than Pitt was when he died in office.

William Pitt was arguably a greater peace than war leader. His peacetime policies were progressive. He championed reforms for parliament and Ireland that promoted political equality and rights for all men. He got a bill passed that increased the oversight and curbed some of the excesses of the East India Company. Despite this legacy, posterity tends to remember him as a conservative or Tory, mostly due to his government's harsh security measures during the 1790s. Pitt was conservative only in contrast to his most persistent opponent, Charles Fox, although they differed more in style than substance. He called himself a "parliamentary Whig," meaning that he sought to maintain the dynamic balance of power between the king and Parliament.

Pitt's greatest triumph during his first nine years in power was to impose fiscal sanity on Britain. He arrested and eventually reversed the national debt by a bill in 1786 that raised taxes, largely on the rich, and streamlined government so that it did more and cost less. Thereafter he asserted an eagle-eyed vigilance over what money went where and pared any wasteful spending that he found. From 1784 to 1792 he kept the annual government budget steady, with about £1.5 million in civil expenses and £4 million in military expenses. Meanwhile, revenues steadily rose until the budget deficit was eliminated in 1788 and surpluses annually appeared until they dissolved with war in 1793. History thereafter would have differed drastically had Pitt not revolutionized the government's fiscal system. Instead of teetering at default's brink like its allies, Whitehall was empowered to underwrite seven coalitions against France.[38] Atop all that, Pitt increased the navy's budget, with its core the building and launching of thirty-three ships of the line from 1783 to 1790. This allowed the Royal Navy to sail with ninety ships of the line in 1793.[39] Yet the longer Pitt held power, the more his policies and character were criticized. Perhaps his key flaw was that he learned the art of geopolitics on the job and never quite mastered it. Critics lambasted Pitt's strategy that dispersed rather than massed Britain's army and navy.

Robert Stewart, Viscount Castlereagh, was that age's other great British statesman. If Pitt's policies were crucial for eventually crushing France, Castlereagh's diplomacy was just as crucial for winning an enduring peace. After Waterloo the center of European diplomacy shifted from Vienna to Paris. Castlereagh and his staff were the first to arrive, reaching Paris on July 6, and there the foreign secretary conducted negotiations on an array of vital issues until November 23; for much of that time Wellington acted as his deputy. Louis XVIII and his entourage, packed into a cavalcade of coaches, clattered into Paris on July 8. Alexander was the first allied monarch to reach Paris, on July 15, with Frederick William and Francis appearing a couple of days later.

Having again crushed France, the coalition partners had to decide its fate in a way that best preserved the continent's peace and stability. Wellington expressed the prevailing view that "the best security for Europe was the restoration of the King, and that the establishment of any other government than the King's in France must inevitably lead to new and endless wars."[40] But this posed a dilemma, as Prime Minister Liverpool put it, that if the allies restored "Louis XVIII on the throne, he will be able to maintain himself there?"[41] The dismay—and, for some, outright contempt—among the allied leaders for such a feckless king and royal family was worse than ever. But French foreign minister Talleyrand and Austrian chancellor Metternich joined Wellington in countering such misgivings by demanding what other choice there was to rule France. In the end the allies held their noses and conceded that the Bourbons were the best of a bad lot.

Alexander insisted that the future of France and thus Europe depended on more than just the inept Bourbons. The French Revolution and Napoleonic empire would never be truly destroyed while liberalism and nationalism, the root of those evils, persisted. Only the revival and collective assertion of fundamentalist Christianity could counter and repress those godless modern ideologies. The tsar envisioned a holy alliance that united the great Christian powers, starting with Orthodox Russia, Protestant Prussia, and Catholic Austria. Although the tsar had harbored such a vision for years, a woman with apparent mystical powers named Julie von Krudener had recently convinced him to realize his dream. Psychologically, what became known as the Holy Alliance was as much about redeeming himself as redeeming Europe. It was an antidote to a midlife crisis brought on by chronic depression and years of brutal warfare in which he was a key participant, exacerbated by his diminishing physical powers and appearance, fading eyesight and hearing, balder dome, and worsening limp.

Frederick William typically was fawning in support of Alexander's vision. Metternich heartily agreed with Alexander that the great powers should work together to crush liberal and nationalist revolutions but sneered at the tsar's mysticism behind his back. He crusaded against liberalism and nationalism for very practical reasons: these forces threatened to destroy Austria's polyglot ethnic and religious empire. The

Russian, Prussian, and Austrian monarchs signed the Holy Alliance Treaty on September 26, 1815.

Castlereagh treated the tsar and his vision with diplomatic kid gloves, but privately he was scathing: "Foreseeing the awkwardness of this piece of sublime mysticism and nonsense, especially to a British Sovereign, I examined with Prince Metternich every practical expedient to stop it. . . . [But] the deed was done, and no other course remained than to do homage to the sentiment upon which it was founded, and to the advantages Europe might hope to derive from three such powerful Sovereigns directing all their influence to the preservation of peace."[42]

Castlereagh worked as assiduously as Alexander for a moral issue that was as heartfelt for most Britons as the Holy Alliance was for the tsar, and he raised as many diplomatic eyebrows. Britain had outlawed itself from the international slave trade in 1807, and the foreign secretary argued that all other true Christian peoples should follow its lead. When puzzled statesmen asked him why the issue meant so much to him, among the many reasons he cited was a unanimous House of Commons resolution on May 2, 1815, that all other states should end that trade, and that Britain would not return any captured colonies unless the original owner state agreed to do so.

This was a powerful diplomatic weapon to wield, but it was still a hard sell. As in Britain, those who profited from the trade pressured their respective governments not to surrender it. It took Castlereagh half a year just to rack up promises from such relatively minor traders as the Netherlands, Denmark, and Sweden, and more than a year before he enlisted France, Portugal, and Spain in that cause. Indeed, the French initially rejected Castlereagh's offer of Trinidad or a huge subsidy to do so; they eventually pledged to abolish slavery north of the equator within five years and without any British reward. Castlereagh then dangled the promise of £800,000 in front of Spain to do the same. Desperate for cash, the Spanish finally succumbed, as later did the Portuguese for £300,000 each.

The conflicting diplomatic crusades of Alexander and Castlereagh combined with the very mixed feelings about the Bourbon restoration to delay a peace settlement for four months. The Treaty of

Paris, signed on November 20, 1815, was far tougher on France than the one eighteen months earlier. Fearing that a harsh peace would not last long, Whitehall resisted but finally gave in to the demands of Austria, Prussia, and Russia that France pay a very heavy price for its latest aggressive war. The indemnity came to 1,905,950,000 francs; allied troops would occupy France for five years to ensure the money was paid and to help crush any threat to Louis XVIII's regime. The French government, eager to rid itself of foreign occupation, paid off the penalty within three years, and the allies steadily withdrew their forces until late 1818, when none were left.[43]

The Bourbons could extract that vast sum of money from the French people and pay off the coalition partners as swiftly as they did because they ruled with an iron fist. First Louis XVIII until his death in 1824, then his brother Charles X until he was deposed in 1830, wielded a "White Terror" that crushed any dissent. Whitehall backed that policy with the Machiavellian truism that if the Bourbons could not inspire love, then they had to provoke fear to stay in power. The Bourbons did so, however, with mass arrests and imprisonments rather than executions. Prime Minister Liverpool observed: "It is a curious circumstance that after the sanguinary scenes which we recollect at the beginning of the French Revolution, all parties appear now to have an insuperable repugnance to executions. This arises not from mercy, but from fear."[44]

Liverpool, Castlereagh, and their colleagues were just as Machiavellian toward the Holy Alliance. They at once gingerly backed most of its initiatives while sidestepping any commitments that would drag Britain into expensive and prolonged conflicts across the continent at odds with British interests. Let the Russians, Prussians, and Austrians dissipate their power by acting like Europe's firemen, racing to extinguish one liberal or nationalist uprising after another. Rebellions would periodically flare as long as the rulers of the realms where they took place refused or failed to eliminate the underlying causes.

The result was the Concert of Europe among the five great powers and the overlapping Holy Alliance among Russia, Prussia, and Austria, with mostly rhetorical differences between them. During the subsequent congresses at Aix-la-Chapelle (Aachen) in 1818, Carlsbad in 1819, Troppau in 1820, Laibach (Ljubljana) in 1821, and Verona in

1822, British statesmen worked assiduously to ensure that pragmatism prevailed over idealism. Castlereagh expressed at Laibach his confidence that "each state . . . adhering to its peculiar habits of action, will nevertheless remain unalterably true to the fundamental obligation of the Alliance, and that the present European system . . . will long continue to subsist for the safety and the repose of Europe."[45]

In all, Castlereagh brilliantly secured British interests at Vienna and subsequent congresses. He won not only acceptance of the vast extension of Britain's commercial and territorial empire since 1793 but its largely unchallenged expansion for the indefinite future. In Europe, Britain and Russia emerged as polar opposites in power and interests, overshadowing and sandwiching between them France, Austria, and Prussia. For nearly four decades, Britain and Russia worked together with their lesser partners to resolve problems through the Concert of Europe, while London and St. Petersburg steadily expanded their respective empires without worrying about the other until they discovered their collision course in Central Asia. Castlereagh's success was partly due to his skill in masking his assertion of British interests behind constant exhortations to his great power colleagues on the vital need for them to maintain their hegemony of power to manage conflicts and keep the peace. Metternich played tribute to this skill when he lauded Castlereagh for being "the most European and the least insular of all the foreign ministers."[46]

The ultimate proof of power is whether its assertion not just gains but keeps what was sought, a challenge succinctly expressed by Henry Kissinger: "The statesmen lives in time; his test is the permanence of his structure under stress."[47] By this measure, the Concert of Europe was an outstanding success. Although the near-yearly great power congresses lasted less than a decade after its founding, the Concert's legacy of cooperation, compromise, self-restraint, limited intervention, and respect for each other's spheres of influence endured and tempered European diplomacy for nearly a century until Sarajevo. During this time, wars among the great powers were few and limited in time and players involved. This is a tribute to how well not just Britain's statesmen but their European colleagues mastered the art of power.[48]

# Notes

### Abbreviations

**Addington Correspondence** G. Pellew, ed., *The Life and Correspondence of the Right Hon. Henry Addington, 1st Viscount Sidmouth,* 3 vols. (London: John Murray, 1897).

***British Diplomacy*** C. K. Webster, ed., *British Diplomacy: Select Documents dealing with the Reconstruction of Europe, 1813–15* (London: G. Bell, 1921).

**British Foreign Policy** Harold Temperley and Lillian Penson, eds., *The Foundations of British Foreign Policy* (Cambridge: Cambridge University Press, 1938).

**BL** British Library

**British Statistics** B. R. Mitchell and Phyllis Deane, *Abstract of British Historical Statistics* (Cambridge: Cambridge University Press, 1962).Castlereagh Correspondence Charles William Vane, Marquis of Londonderry, ed., *The Correspondence, Despatches, and Other Papers of Viscount Castlereagh, Second Marquis of Londonderry,* 12 vols. (London: John Murray, 1848–53).

**Chad Conversations** Gerald Wellington, ed., *The Conversations of the First Duke of Wellington with George William Chad* (Cambridge: Cambridge University Press, 1956).

**Cornwallis Correspondence** Charles Ross, ed., *The Correspondence of Charles, First Marquis, Cornwallis,* 3 vols. (London: John Murray, 1859).

| | |
|---|---|
| ***Creevey Papers*** | John Gore, ed., *The Thomas Creevey Papers* (New York: Macmillan, 1904). |
| ***Croker Papers*** | Louis J. Jennings, ed., *The Croker Papers: The Correspondence and Diaries of John Wilson Croker, Secretary to the Admiralty from 1809 to 1830,* 3 vols. (London: John Murray, 1885). |
| **Dropmore** | Report on the Manuscripts of J. B. Fortescue, esq., preserved at Dropmore (Dublin: John Falconer, 1908). |
| **FO** | Foreign Office. |
| **HO** | Home Office. |
| **George III Correspondence** | Arthur Aspinall, ed., *The Later Correspondence of George III,* 5 vols. (Cambridge: Cambridge University Press, 1962–70). |
| ***Life of Pitt*** | Philip Henry Stanhope, Lord Stanhope, *Life of the Right Honorable William Pitt,* 4 vols. (London: John Murray, 1867). |
| **Malmesbury Correspondence** | James Harris, *Earl Malmesbury, The Diaries and Correspondence of James Harris, the First Earl of Malmesbury,* 4 vols. (London: Richard Bentley, 1845). |
| ***Memoirs of the Courts*** | Duke of Buckingham and Chandos, ed., *Memoirs of the Courts and Cabinets of George the Third,* 2 vols. (London: Hurst & Blackett, 1853–55). |
| **Napoleon Correspondence** | Thierry Lentz et al., ed., *Napoleon Bonaparte Correspondance Generale,* vols. 1–9 (Paris: Fayard, 2004–12). |
| **Nelson Dispatches** | Nicolas Harris, ed., *The Dispatches and Letters of Vice-Admiral Lord Viscount Nelson,* 7 vols. (Cambridge: Cambridge University Press, 2011). |
| **Parliamentary Debates** | William Cobbett, ed., *Parliamentary Debates,* 22 vols. (London: R. Bagshaw, 1804–12). |
| ***Parliamentary History*** | William Cobbett, ed., *The Parliamentary History of England from the Earliest Times to 1803,* 36 vols. (London: R. Bagshaw, 1806–20). |

| | |
|---|---|
| ***Parliamentary Register*** | John Debrett, ed., *The Parliamentary Register, or, History of the Proceedings and Debates of the House of Commons,* 2nd ser., 45 vols. (London: R. Spottiswoode, 1781–96); 3rd ser., 18 vols. (London: R.Spottiwoode,, 1797–1802). |
| **Pitt-Rutland Correspondence** | Rutland, Duke of, *Correspondence between the Right Hon. William Pitt and Charles, Duke of Rutland* (London: R. Spottiswoode, 1842). |
| **Pitt Speeches** | *The Speeches of the Right Hon. William Pitt in the House of Commons,* 3 vols. (London: Longman, Hurst, and Orne, 1817). |
| **PRO** | Public Record Office (National Archives) |
| **Stanhope Conversations** | Philip Henry Stanhope, fifth earl of Stanhope, *Notes of Conversations with the Duke of Wellington, 1831–1851* (London: John Murray, 1885). |
| **WO** | War Office. |
| **Wellesley-Pole** | Charles Webster, ed., *Some Letters of the Duke of Wellington to his Brother, William Wellesley Pole* (Camden Miscellany, Royal Historical Society, vol. 18, 1948). |
| **Wellington Dispatches** | Colonel Gurwood, ed., *The Dispatches of Field Marshall the Duke of Wellington,* 8 vols. (London: Park, Furnivall, and Parker, 1944). |
| **Wellington Supplements** | Duke of Wellington, *The Supplementary Despatches, Correspondence, and Memoranda of Field Marshall Arthur, Duke of Wellington,* 15 vols. (London: John Murray, 1858–72). |
| **Wraxall Memoir** | Nathaniel Wraxall, ed., *The Historical and Posthumous Memoirs of Sir Nathaniel William Wraxall, 1772–1784* (London: Bickers and Sons, 1884). |

## Preface

1. For the most comprehensive overview, see Schroeder, *Transformation of European Politics.*
2. William Pitt speech, February 1790, *Parliamentary History,* 28:351.
3. Ralph Waldo Emerson, "History" and "Napoleon, or the Man of the World." in Oliver, *Essential Writings of Ralph Waldo Emerson,* , 113–31, 449–66; Tolstoy, *War and Peace,* 1603–6, 821–23, 943–44, 1031–35, 1133–36, 1178–1215.

4. There is no literature to review to justify *The Art of British Power.* Although there are hundreds of books on Britain and this era, this book is unique in two crucial ways: (1) I have clearly defined and applied the concept of power to analyzing a nation's policies during an epoch of history; (2) I have comprehensively and systematically analyzed British policy during the age of revolution and Napoleon.

*The Art of British Power* provides an empirical rather than theoretical analysis. I spurn theories because they provide nothing more than gross caricatures of reality. For a brilliant demolition of the deterministic and ahistorical pretensions of theories, especially neorealism, to explain or predict international relations, power, and history, see Paul Schroeder, "Historical Reality vs. Neo-Realists Theory." See also, Robert Keohane, ed., *Neo-Realism and Its Critics* (New York: Columbia University Press, 1986); Keohane, *International Institutions and State Power.*

## Chapter 1

1. For other explorations of the nature and application of power, see Nester, *Globalization: A Short History*; Nester, *Globalization, Wealth, and Power*; Nester, *Globalization, War, and Peace*; Nester, *Revolutionary Years*; Nester, *Hamiltonian Vision, 1789–1800*; Nester, *Jeffersonian Vision, 1800–1815*; Nester, *Age of Jackson*; Nester, *Age of Lincoln.*
2. Sun Tzu, *Art of War.*
3. Tilley, *Formation of Nation States in Western Europe*, 42.
4. Downing, *Military Revolution and Political Change*; Stone, *Imperial State at War*; Bonney, *Rise of the Fiscal State in Europe.*
5. Brewer, *Sinews of Power*).
6. Smith, *Theories of Nationalism*; Gellner, *Nations and Nationalism*; Boerner, *Concepts of National Identity*; Anderson, *Imagined Communities*; Greenfeld, *Nationalism*; Hobsbawm, *Nations and Nationalism*; Schulze, *States, Nations, and Nationalism*; Hastings, *Construction of Nationhood.*
7. Hobsbawm, *Nations and Nationalism*, 91.
8. For some excellent studies of the origin and development of the modern and especially European state-nation, see Evans, Rusechemeyer, and Skocpol, *Bringing the State Back In*; Hellmuth, *Transformation of Political Culture*; Erbman, *Birth of the Leviathan*; Brewer and Hellmuth, *Rethinking Leviathan*; Blanning, *Culture of Power.*
9. Kissinger, "Congress of Vienna."
10. For in depth, diverse analyses of the complexities of early modern British and European relations and power, seeMahan, *Influence of Sea Power Upon History*; Langford, *Modern British Foreign Policy*; McKay and Scott, *Rise of the Great Powers*; Kennedy, *Rise and Fall of the Great Powers*; Bayley, *Imperial Meridian*;

Schroeder, *Transformation of European Politics*; Black, *A System of Ambition?*; Colley, *Captives: Britain, Europe, and the World*; Ferguson, *Empire: How Britain Made the Modern World*; Sims, *Three Victories and a Defeat*; Ward and Gooch, *Cambridge History of British Foreign Policy.*

11. George Canning, December 11, 1798, *Parliamentary History,* 34:67.
12. George Canning, June 5, 1805, *Parliamentary Debates,* 11:889–90.
13. For some excellent studies on the origins and development of the British state, see Brewer, *Sinews of Power*; Braddick, *Nerves of State*; Claydon and McBride, *Protestantism and National Identity*; Clark, *English Society*; Turner, *Age of Unease*; Harling, *Modern British State*; Evans, *Forging of the Modern State*; Dickinson, *Companion to Eighteenth Century Britain.*
14. Wilson, *Sense of the People*; Newman, *Rise of English Nationalism*; Brockliss and Eastwood, *A Union of Multiple Identities*; Claydon and McBride, *Protestantism and National Identity*; Bradshaw and Roberts, *British Consciousness and Identity*; Kidd, *British Identities before Nationalism*; Langford, *Englishness Identified*; Hoppit, *Parliaments, Nations, and Identities*; Colley, *Britons.*

    For the dynamic between war and identity, see Emsley, *British Society and the French Wars*; Wilson, *Sense of the People*; Macleod, *A War of Ideas?.*
15. Gunn, *Beyond Liberty and Property*; Clark, *Language of Liberty*; Porter, *Enlightenment.*
16. William Grenville to George III, October 12, 1789, George III Correspondence, 1:555.
17. For the House of Lords, see Turberville, *House of Lords*; Jones and Jones, *Politics and Power*; McCahill, *Order and Equipoise: Peerage and the House of Lords.* For the House of Commons, see Namier and Brooke, *House of Commons, 1754–1790*; Thorne, *History of Parliament.*
18. Naumier, *Structure of Politics*; Ford, *His Majesty's Opposition*; Mitchell, *Charles James Fox*; O'Gorman, *Emergence of the Two Party System*; Hill, *British Parliamentary Parties*; Burrow, *Whigs and Liberals.*
19. Rose, *William Pitt and National Revival,* 617.
20. Clark, *British Clubs and Societies.*
21. Phillips, *Electoral Behavior in Unreformed England*; O'Gorman, *Voters, Patrons, and Parties.*
22. Lee, "Parliament, Parties, and Elections, 1760–1815," Eighteenth Century Britain, 70.
23. Phillips, *Electoral Behavior in Unreformed England.*
24. Malmesbury Correspondence, 4:119.
25. Pares, *King George III*
26. Gibson, *Church of England.*
27. Bourne, *Patronage and Society*; Harling, *Waning of the "Old Corruption."*
28. Henry, "The Making of Elite Culture," H.T. Dickinson, ed., *A Companion to Eighteenth Century Britain* (Oxford: Blackwell Publishing, 2006), 312.

29. Mingay, *English Landed Society*; Cannon, *Aristocratic Century*; Beckett, *Aristocracy in England*; Langford, *Public Life*; Habakkuk, *Marriage, Debt, and the Estates System.*
30. Foot and Kramnick, *Thomas Paine Reader*, 249.
31. Morris, *British Monarchy and the French Revolution.*
32. Sainty, *Peerage Creations*; Lowe, "George III, Peerage Creations and Politics"; A.P.W. Malcolmson, "The Irish Peers and the Union, 1800–1971," *Transactions of the Royal Historical Society,* 6th ser., vol. 10 (2000), 300.
33. George III to William Grenville, July 24, 1798, BL add. ms. 58860.
34. For the best biography, see Black, *George III,* especially chapters 19 and 20 for an excellent literature review on how historians have evaluated George III. See also Pares, *King George III.*
35. George III coronation speech draft, October 26, 1760, BL, add. ms. 32684.
36. George III to William Grenville, January 31, 1796, BL add. ms. 58859.
37. George III to William Grenville, June 28, 1800, BL add. ms. 58861.
38. Black, *George III,* 233.
39. George III to William Grenville, February 3, 1806, BL add. ms. 58863.
40. Rohl, Warren, and Warren, *Purple Secret, Genes, "Madness."*
41. Hibbert, *George IV*; Smith, *George IV*; Parissien, *George IV.*
42. Reilly, *William Pitt the Younger,* 176–77.
43. Morris, *British Monarchy and the French Revolution.*
44. For the power of the press, see Aspinall, *Politics and the Press*; George, *English Political Caricature*; Bolton, *Language of Politics*; Smith, *Politics of Language*; Duffy, *English Satirical Print*; Black, *English Press*; Carretta, *George III and the Satirists*; Harris, *Politics and the Rise of the Press*; Donald, *English Political Caricature*; Barker, *Newspapers, Politics, and Public Opinion*; Raymond, *News, Newspapers in Early Modern Britain*; Barker, *Newspapers, Politics, and English Society*; Barker and Burrows, *Press, Politics, and the Public Sphere.*

    For the links between politics and civil society, see Thompson, *Making of the English Working Class*; Perkins, *Origins of Modern English Society*; Porter, *English Society in the Eighteenth Century* (New York: Penguin, 1982); Clark, *English Society*; Kramnick, *Republicanism and Bourgeois Radicalism*; Clark, *Language of Liberty*; Daunton, *Progress and Poverty*; Dickinson, *Politics of the People*; Wilson, *Sense of the People*; Tilly, *Popular Contention in Great Britain*; Wahrman, *Imagining the Middle Class*; Rule, *Albion's People*; Rogers, *Crowds, Culture, and Politics*; Roberts, *Making English Morals*; Wahrman, *Making of the Modern Self*; Hinton, *A Mad, Bad, and Dangerous People.*
45. Christie, *Wilkes, Wyvill, and Reform*; Black, *The Association.*
46. William Grenville to Marguess of Buckingham, April 28, 1797, *Memoirs of the Courts,* 2:376.
47. Butterfield, *George III, Lord North, and the People*; S. Conway, The British Isles and the War of American Independence (New York: Oxford University Press, 2000).

48. For comparative studies, see Crouzet, *Britain*; Crafts, *British Economic Growth*; Pomeranz, *Great Divergence*. For financial power, see Hidy, *House of Baring*; Pressnell, *Country Banking*; O'Brien, "Political Economy of British Taxation"; O'Brien and Hunt, "Rise of a Fiscal State in England; Brewer, *Sinews of Power*; O'Brien, *Power with Profit*; Stone, *Imperial State at War*; Braddick, *Nerves of State*; Ferguson, *World's Banker*.

49. For overviews of the industrial revolution, see Crouzet, *First Industrialists*; Clarkson, *Proto-Industrialization*; Crafts, *British Economic Growth*; Wrighley, *Continuity, Chance, and Change*; Hudson, *Regions and Industries*; Hudson, *Industrial Revolution*; Mathias, *First Industrial Nation*; Floud and Johnson, *Cambridge Economic History*.

For the agrarian revolutions, see: Chambers and Mingay, *Agricultural Revolution*; Kerridge, *Agricultural Revolution*; Overton, *Agricultural Revolution in England*; Mingay, *Parliamentary Enclosure in England*.

For the related trade and industrial revolutions, see Parkinson, *Trade Winds*; Semmel, *Rise of Free Trade Imperialism*; Williams, *British Commercial Policy*; Davis, *Industrial Revolution and British Overseas Trade*; Hobsbawm, *Industry and Empire*; Ashworth, *Customs and Excise*.

For the transportation revolution, see Ward, *Finance of Canal Building*; Pawson, *Transport and Economy*.

For the technological and scientific revolutions, see Munsen and Robinson, *Science and Technology*; Tunzelman, *Steam Power and British Industrialization*; Berg, *Age of Manufacturers*.

For the entrepreneurship and business revolution, see Pollack, *Genesis of Modern Management*; McKendrick, Brewer, and Plumb, *Birth of a Consumer Society*; Hoppit, *Rise and Failures of English Business*; Corfield, *Power and the Professions in Britain*; Thompson, *Gentrification and the Enterprise Culture*.

For the cultural and social revolution, see Wolfe and Seed, *Culture of Capital*; Earle, *Making of the English Middle Class*; Langford, *A Polite and Commercial People*; Kidd and Nicolls, *Making of the British Middle Class?*.

50. William Pitt, February 17, 1792, *Parliamentary Register*, 29:833–34.

51. Ehrman, *Younger Pitt*, 2:501.

52. Henry Dundas report, March 31, 1798, PRO 30/8/243.

53. John Rule, "Manufacturing and Commerce," in H. T. Dickinson, ed., *A Companion to Eighteenth Century Britain*, 129–30.

54. George, *London Life in the Eighteenth Century*, 319; Corfield, *Impact of English Towns*; Vries, *European Urbanization*, table 3.6; Borsay, *English Urban Renaissance*; Williamson, *Coping with City Growth*; Clark, *Cambridge Urban History of Britain*.

55. Wrigley and Schofield, *Population History of England*, appendices 5, 6.

56. Henry Dundas to William Pitt, July 9, 1794, HMC, 412.

57. Hellmuth, "The British State," in *Eighteenth Century Britain*, 21; Cookson, *British Armed Nation*.

58. For an excellent overview, see Black, *Britain as a Military Power.*
59. Life of Pitt, 1:122.
60. Brewer, *Sinews of Power,* 54.
61. Hall, *British Strategy,* 46.
62. Mackesy, *War without Victory.*
63. Unless otherwise indicated, the information for the following section on the army came from Guy, *Road to Waterloo*; Haythornthwaite, *Armies of Wellington.*
64. Stanhope Conversations, 14, 18.
65. Western, *English Militia in the Eighteenth Century*; Cookson, *British Armed Nation*; Gee, *British Volunteer Movement*.
66. Glover, *Peninsular Preparation*; Houlding, Fit for Service.
67. Haythornthwaite, *Armies of Wellington,* 21.
68. Wellington to Rowland Hill, June 18, 1812, Wellington Dispatches, 9:240. For a firstrate analysis, see Fletcher, *Galloping at Everything.*
69. For the relationship between Britain's naval and national power, see Harding, *Evolution of the Sailing Navy*; Black and Woodfine, *British Navy and the Use of Naval Power*; Harding, *Seapower and Naval Warfare,* 1650–1830; Lincoln, *Representing the Royal Navy*; Padfield, *Maritime Power and the Struggle for Freedom*; Wilkinson, *British Navy and the State*; Harding, *British Admirals of the Napoleonic Wars*; Rodger, *Command of the Ocean.*

    For naval histories from 1793 to 1815, see Parkinson, *Britannia Rules*; Adkins and Adkins, *War for All the Oceans*; Mostert, *Line upon a Wind.*

    For naval shipbuilding and resources, see Albion, *Forests and Sea Power*; Morriss, *Royal Dockyards*; Coad, *Royal Dockyards.*

    For naval administration, see Lavery, *Nelson's Navy.* For manpower and ship life, see Lewis, *A Social History of the Navy*; Rodgers, *Wooden World.*
70. Mostert, *Line upon a Wind,* 64.
71. Adkins and Adkins, *War for all the Oceans,* 82.
72. For the best account, see Sparrow, *Secret Service.* See also Mitchell, *Underground War against Revolutionary France*; Nelson, *Home Office*; Urban, *Man Who Broke Napoleon's Codes*; Pocock, *Terror Before Trafalgar.*
73. Ehrman, *Younger Pitt,* 3:469.
74. Dozier, *For King, Constitution, and Country,* 51.
75. Aspinall, *Politics and the Press*; Werkmeister, *A Newspaper History of England*; Jones, *Britain and Revolutionary France.*
76. Ehrman, *Younger Pitt,* 3:469–70.
77. Henry Dundas to William Grenville, October 4, 1800, Dropmore, 6:236.
78. Harlow, *Founding of the Second British Empire*; Cain and Hopkins, *British Imperialism*; James, *Rise and Fall of the British Empire*; Marshall, *Oxford History of the British Empire*; Armitage, *Ideological Origins of the British Empire.*
79. Johnston, *Ireland in the Eighteenth Century*; O'Connell, *Irish Politics and Social Conflict*; McDowell, *Ireland in the Age of Imperialism*; Moody and Vaughan, *A New History of Ireland*; Bartlett, *Fall and Rise of the Irish Nation.*

80. Duffy, "War, Revolution, and the Crisis," in Mark Philp, ed., *The French Revolution and British Popular Politics*, 121. Bartlett, *Fall and Rise of the Irish Nation.*
81. For a classic work on the West Indies and British strategy during this era, see Duffy, *Soldiers, Sugar, and Seapower.*
82. Duffy, *Soldiers, Sugar, and Seapower*, 385.
83. Mitchell and Deane, *Abstract of British Historical Statistics,* 312, 276–337; Armytage, *Free Port System.*
84. Marshall, *Problems of Empire.*
85. McKay and Scott, *Rise of the Great Powers*; Kennedy, *Rise and Fall of the Great Powers*; Schroeder, *Transformation of European Politics.*
86. George Canning to Castlereagh, October 20, 1818, Castlereagh Correspondence, 12:56.
87. For British foreign policy, see Langford, *Modern British Foreign Policy*; Black, *Natural and Necessary Enemies*; Black, *Knight Errant and True Englishmen*; Clarke, *British Diplomacy and Foreign Policy*; Scott, *British Foreign Policy*; Black, *A System of Ambition*; Black, *British Foreign Policy.*
88. William Pitt, February 3, 1800, *Parliamentary History,* 34:2443–46; Temperley and Penson, *The Foundations of British Foreign Policy.*
89. George Tieney, February 3, 1800, *Parliamentary History,* 34:1528–29.

## Chapter 2

1. For nineteenth-century accounts by people who either themselves or their descendents knew Pitt, see Pretyman, *Memoirs of the Life of the Right Hon. William Pitt*; *Life of Pitt.*

   For the most detailed and lengthy biography, see John Ehrman's trilogy *The Younger Pitt: The Years of Acclaim* (vol. 1), *The Younger Pitt: The Reluctant Transition* (vol. 2) and *The Younger Pitt: The Consuming Struggle* (vol. 3). For good one volume biographies, see Reilly, *William Pitt the Younger*; Hague, *William Pitt the Younger.*
2. Ehrman, *Younger Pitt,* 1:4–5.
3. Reilly, *William Pitt the Younger*, 6.
4. William Pitt speech, February 26, 1781, *Parliamentary Register*, 1781, 2:17.
5. Wraxall Memoir, 3:217.
6. Wilberforce and Wilberforce, *Life of William Wilberforce*, 1:18.
7. Hague, *Willliam Pitt the Younger*, 220–21.
8. Hague, *William Pitt the Younger*, 214–16.
9. Ehrman, *Younger Pitt,* 1:582.
10. Ehrman, *Younger Pitt,* 1:108–10; Reilly, *William Pitt the Younger*, 328–33; Hague, *William Pitt the Younger*, 201–204.
11. Cannon, *Fox-North Coalition*; Mitchell, *Charles James Fox*; P. D. G., *Lord North.*
12. George III to William Pitt, March 25, 1783, PRO 30/8/103.
13. George III to Carmarthen, July 6, 1784, BL add. mss. 27914.

14. William Pitt to Charles, Duke of Rutland, August 8, 1785, Pitt-Rutland Correspondence, 102.
15. Spencer Perceval to William Huskisson, August 21, 1809, Bentley, *English Historical Documents.*
16. Greig, *Farington Diary,* May 17, 1809, 5:162.
17. Wraxall Memoir, 3:217.
18. Butler, *Reminiscences of Charles Butler*1:161.
19. Reilly, *William Pitt the Younger,* 123.
20. Wilberforce and Wilberforce, *Life of William Wilberforce,* 95.
21. Hague, *William Pitt the Younger,* 150–52.
22. Patrick O'Brien, "Political Biography and Pitt the Younger"; J. Torrance, "Social Class and Bureaucratic Innovation: The Commissioners for Examining the Public Accounts, 1780–1787," *Past and Present,* 56–81; Breihan, "William Pitt and the Commission on Fees"; Binney, *British Public Finance and Administration.*
23. William Pitt to Edward Thurlow, July 20, 1784, Stanhope, *Miscellanies,* 23–26.
24. William Pitt to Rutland, September 19, 1784, Pitt-Rutland Correspondence, 43–44.
25. William Pitt to Rutland, September 19, 1784, Pitt-Rutland Correspondence, 43–44.
26. *Life of Pitt,* 1:337.
27. Ehrman, *Younger Pitt,* 1:373.
28. Hague, *William Pitt the Younger,* 235; Wraxall Memoir, 5:98.
29. Ehrman, *British Government and Commercial Negotiations* .
30. William Pitt to James Harris, December 5, 1786, Malmesbury Correspondence, 2:211.
31. James Harris to Carmarthen, February 23, 1787, Malmesbury Correspondence, 2:256.
32. Cabinet to George III, February 26, 1787, George III Correspondence, 1:367.
33. Derry, *Regency Crisis and the Whigs.*
34. Thomas Moore, *Memoirs of the Life of the Right Honorable Richard Brinsley Sheridan* (1825), 2:38. Pollock, *Wilberforce.*
35. Journal, October 28, 1787, Wilberforce and Wilberforce, *Life of William Wilberforce,* 1:149.
36. Anstey, *Atlantic Slave Trade and British Abolition*; Drescher, *Capitalism and Antislavery*; Turley, *Culture of English Antislavery*; Davis, *Problem of Slavery*; Blackburn, *Overthrow of Colonial Slavery*; Oldfield, *Popular Politics and British Anti-Slavery.*

## Chapter 3

1. O'Gorman, *Whig Party and the French Revolution*; Dickinson, *Britain and the French Revolution*; Jarrett, *Three Faces of Revolution.*

2. William Pitt speech, February 1790, *Parliamentary History*, 28:351.
3. Charles James Fox speech, April 15, 1791, *Parliamentary History*, 29:248–49.
4. Thompson, *Making of the English Working Class*; Goodwin, *Friends of Liberty*; Cookson, *Friends of Peace*; Deane, *French Revolution and Enlightenment*; Williams, *Artisans and Sans Culottes*; Credel, *Origins of War Prevention*; Graham, *Nation, the Law, and the King.*
5. Maccoby, *English Radical Tradition*; Kennedy, *Jacobin Clubs in the French Revolution*; Hone, *For the Cause of Truth*; Stafford, *Socialism, Radicalism, and Nostalgia*; Dickinson, *British Radicalism*; Spencer, *Birth of Romantic Radicalism.*
6. Philp, *French Revolution and British Popular Politics*, 2.
7. Edmund Burke, February 9, 1790, *Parliamentary History*, 28:332–54.
8. Burke, *Reflections on the Revolution.* For an excellent overview of Burke's political philosophy, see Byrne, *Edmund Burke for Our Time.*
9. Gregory Claeys, Thomas Paine: Social and Political Thought (Boston: Unwin Hyman, 1989); John Keane, Thomas Paine: A Political Life (New York: Grove Press, 1989); Jack Fruchtman, Thomas Paine: Apostle of Freedom (New York: Four Walls, Eight Windows, 1994).
10. Foot and Kramnick, *Thomas Paine Reader*, 359, 207.
11. Cobban, *Debate on the French Revolution*; Butler, *Burke, Paine, Godwin*; Hole, *Pulpits, Politics, and Public Order*; Philp, *French Revolution and British Popular Politics*; Sack, *From Jacobite to Conservative*; Morris, *British Monarchy and the French Revolution.*
12. Dozier, *For King, Constitution, and Country.*
13. Mori, *William Pitt and the French Revolution*, 82.
14. Duffy, "War, Revolution, and the Crisis in the British Empire," in Philp, *French Revolution and British Popular Politics*, 122.

For the United Irishmen and the revolutionary movement, see Eliot, *Partners in Revolution*; Eliot, *Wolf Tone*; Smyth, *Men of No Property*; Stewart, *A Deeper Silence*; Curtain, *The United Irishmen.*

For the broader political situation, see McDowell, *Ireland in the Age of Imperialism*; O'Brien, *Anglo-Irish Politics*; Kelly, *Prelude to Union.*

15. William Pitt, April 19, 1791, *Parliamentary History*, 29:342.
16. Hague, *William Pitt the Younger*, 300–304.
17. Francis, Carmarthen, Duke of Leeds, to Anthony Merry, February 2, 1790, FO 72/16; Francis, Carmarthen, Duke of Leeds, to Marquis del Campo, February 7, 1790, FO 72/16; Francis, Carmarthen, Duke of Leeds, to Marquis del Campo, February 23, 1790, FO 72/16; William Pitt to Francis, Carmarthen, Duke of Leeds, February 23, 1790, FO 72/16; Francis, Carmarthen, duke of Leeds to William Pitt, February 23, 1790, PRO 30/8/151.
18. William Pitt to William Grenville, May 2, 1790, Dropmore, 1:580.
19. William Pitt speech, May 5, 1790, *Parliamentary Register*, 27:562–65.
20. William Pitt to Alleyne Fitzherbert, July 5, 1790; Declaration and Counter-Declaration, July 5, 1790, FO 72/18.

21. Ehrman, *Younger Pitt,* 1:566; Hague, *William Pitt the Younger,* 282.
22. Joseph Ewart to William Pitt, December 13, 1790, January 15, 1791, PRO 30/8/133. For a few other key reports, see Daniel Hailes to Francis Leeds, December 1, 1790, PRO, FO 62/3; Joseph Ewart to William Auckland, December 18, 1789, January 5, 1791, BL add. ms. 34434, 34435; Francis Jackson [charge d'affaires in Berlin] to Francis Leeds, January 23, February 6, March 11, 1791, PRO, FO 64/20. In addition to Ewart in Berlin, Charles Whitworth was in St. Petersburg, Daniel Hailes was in Warsaw, Robert Liston was in Stockholm, Francis Drake was in Copenhagen, Robert Keith was in Vienna, William Auckland was in The Hague, and Robert Ainsle was in Constantinople.
23. Janis, *Group Think.*
24. William Auckland to Morton Eden, January 11, 1791, BL add. ms. 34435.
25. Francis Jackson to Francis Leeds, March 11, 1791, PRO, FO 64/20.
26. Charles James Fox speech, March 29, 1791, *Parliamentary Register,* 29:48–49; Browning, *Political Memoranda,* 152–59; Samuel Hood to Charles Cornwallis, April 4, 1791, George III Correspondence, Various Collections, 369.
27. William Grenville to Leveson Gower, July 13, 1792, Dropmore, 2:294.
28. Ehrman, *Younger Pitt,* 2:42.

## Chapter 4

1. William Pitt speech, February 17, 1792, Pitt Speeches, 2:36.
2. Ross, *Quest for Victory*; Blanning, *French Revolutionary Wars*; Griffith, *Art of War of Revolutionary France.*
3. William Grenville to Robert Keith, September 19, 1791, PRO, FO 7/28. See also William Grenville to Joseph Ewart, August 26, 1791, PRO, FO 64/22; William Grenville to Charles Whitworth, September, 27, 1791, PRO, FO 65/22.
4. Ehrman, *Younger Pitt,* 2:56.
5. Ross, *Quest for Victory,* 26, 28.
6. Henry Dundas to George III, August 17, 1792, BL add. ms. 58968.
7. Doyle, *Oxford History of the French Revolution,* 193.
8. Blanning, *French Revolutionary Wars,* 82–88; Doyle, *Oxford History of the French Revolution,* 197–200.
9. William Grenville to William Auckland, November 13, 1792, PRO, FO 37/41.
10. William Grenville to Simon Vorontsov, December 28, 1792, PRO, FO 65/23.
11. William Grenville to Charles Whitworth, December 29, PRO, FO 65/23; William Grenville to William Auckland, December 29, 1792, PRO, FO 37/42.
12. William Pitt speech, February 1793, *Parliamentary History,* 30:283.
13. Ehrman, *Younger Pitt,* 2:250.
14. William Pitt speech, February 1, 1793, *Parliamentary Register* 2:88–93.
15. William Miles to William Pitt, February 6, 1793, PRO, FO 30/8/159.
16. George III to William Grenville, February 9, 1793, BL add. ms. 58857.

17. William Pitt speech, February 12, 1793, *Parliamentary Register,* 34:459.
18. William Pitt speech, April 23, 1793, *Parliamentary Register,* 35:686–87.
19. Treaty with Russia, March 25, 1793, PRO, FO 97/342; Treaty with Hesse-Cassel, April 10, 1793, PRO, FO 93/43; Treaty with Sardinia, April 25, 1793, PRO, FO 93/87; Treaty with Spain, May 25, 1793, PRO, FO 93/99; Treaty with the Two Sicilies, July 12, 1793, PRO, FO 93/96; Treaty with Prussia, July 14, 1793,PRO, FO 93/78; Treaty with Hesse-Cassel, August 23, 1793, PRO, FO 93/43; Treaty with Austria, August 30, 1793, PRO, FO 93/11; Treaty with Baden, September 21, 1793, PRO, FO 93/12; Treaty with Portugal, September 10, 1793, PRO, FO 93/77; Treaty of Hesse-Darmstadt, October 5, 1793, PRO, FO 93/44.
20. Sherwig, *Guineas and Gunpowder,* 18–19.
21. William Grenville to Charles Whitworth, June 14, 1793, PRO, FO 65/24.
22. James Harris, Earl of Malmesbury to William Grenville, December 26, 1793, Malmesbury Correspondence, 3:28–31.
23. William Grenville to James Harris, Earl of Malmesbury, March 7, 1793, PRO, FO 64/32; Treaty with Prussia, April 19, 1794, PRO, FO 94/183; Treaty with Holland, April 19, 1794, PRO, FO 93/46.
24. Helleiner, *The Imperial Loans.*
25. William Grenville to Henry, Earl of Spencer, July 19, August 26, 1794; Henry, Earl of Spencer, and Thomas Grenville to William Grenville, August 12, 1794, PRO, FO 7/38.
26. William Grenville to Henry, Earl of Spencer, and Thomas Grenville, August 29, 1794; Henry, Earl of Spencer, and Thomas Grenville to William Grenville, September 22, 1794; William Grenville to Morton Eden, December 18, 1794, PRO, FO 7/38; January 13, 1795, PRO, FO 7/39; 7/40.
27. Charles Whitworth to William Grenville, April 19/29, 1793, PRO FO 65/24; William Grenville to Charles Whitworth, June 14, 1793, PRO, FO 65/24.
28. Hutt, *Chouanarie and Counter-Revolution.*
29. Treaty with Hanover, January 7,1794, *Journal of the House of Commons,* 49:197–98.
30. Morriss, *Royal Dockyards,* tables 2–3, 12, 16–17; Acerra and Meyer, *Marines et Révolution,* 115; Parkinson, *Britannia Rules,* 9; Blanning, *French Revolutionary Wars,* 208.
31. Turner, *Gallant Gentlemen,* 118–19.
32. Henry Dundas to James Murray, April 16, 1793, PRO, WO 6/7.
33. Ehrman, *Younger Pitt,* 2:267–68.
34. Charles, Duke of Richmond, to Henry Dundas, July 1, 1793; Henry Dundas to Charles, Duke of Richmond, July 8, 1793, BL loan ms. 57 (Bathurst), vol. 107. See Rose, "Duke of Richmond on the Conduct of the War," , 554–55.
35. William Auckland to William Grenville, February 12, 14, 15, 20, 1793, William Grenville to William Auckland, February 13, 19, 1793, PRO FO, 37/44; William Pitt to William Auckland, March 2, 1793, BL add. ms. 464519.

36. Frederick, Duke of York, to George III, January 19, 1793, George III Correspondence, 1:826; Instructions for Duke of York and Major General Gerard Lake, February 23, 1793, PRO, WO 6/10.
37. William Pitt speech, June 17, 1793, *Parliamentary Register,* 35:675.
38. Ehrman, *Younger Pitt,* 2:303.
39. Banning, *French Revolutionary Wars,* 200.
40. Samuel Hood to Henry Dundas, October 27, 1793, PRO, HO, 28/14.
41. King George III declaration, October 29, 1793, *Parliamentary History,* 30:1060.
42. William Pitt to Grenville, October 5, 1793, Dropmore, 2:438–99.
43. William Grenville to Francis Drake, October 22, 1793, PRO, FO, 28/6.
44. Samuel Hood to Henry Dundas, October 28, 1793, PRO, HO 28/14.
45. Mostert, *Line upon a Wind,* 116–17; Parkinson, *Britannia Rules,* 15.
46. Ehrman, *Younger Pitt,* 2:318.
47. Blanning, *French Revolutionary Wars,* 100–101.
48. Ross, *Quest for Victory,* 61–62, 65.
49. Henry Dundas to William Pitt, July 9, 1784, PRO 30/8/157.
50. William Pitt speech, January 21, 1794, Pitt Speeches, 2:174.
51. Dozier, *For King, Constitution, and Country*; Wells, *Insurrection*; Porter, *Plots and Paranoia*; Worrall, *Radical Culture*; Royle, *Revolutionary Britain?.*
52. George III to Henry Dundas, July 17, 1791, BL add. ms. 40100.
53. Rude, *Crowd in History*; Bohstedt, *Riots and Community Politics*; Royle, *Revolutionary Britain?*; Shoemaker, *London Mob.*
54. George III to Henry Dundas, July 16, 1791, BL add. ms. 40100.
55. Cookson, *Friends of Peace*; Hone, *For the Cause of Truth*; Wells, *Insurrection*; Wells, *Wretched Faces*; Bindman, *Shadow of the Guillotine.*
56. Wharam, *Treason Trials*; Barrell, *Imagining the King's Death.*
57. Ehrman, *Younger Pitt,* 2:459.
58. Charles James Fox speech, November 9, 1795, *Parliamentary History,* 32:279.
59. Pasquale Paoli to George III, September 1, 1793, PRO, FO, 79/9; Pasquale Paoli to Samuel Hood, January 4, 1794, PRO, HO 28/15; Gilbert Eliot to Henry Dundas, February 4, 21,22, 1794; Henry Dundas to Gilbert Eliot, March 31, 1794, PRO, WO 6/54; Henry Dundas to Pasquale Paoli, March 7, 1794, BL add. ms. 22688.
60. Bennett, *Nelson the Commander*; Coleman, *Nelson Touch.*
61. Mostert, *Line upon a Wind,* 131–53.
62. Unless otherwise noted, the information for this section comes from Duffy, *Soldiers, Sugar, and Seapower.*
63. William Grenville to James Harris, Lord Malmesbury, September 30, 1794, PRO, FO 64/35, Sherwig, *Guineas and Gunpowder,* n52.
64. Morton Eden to William Grenville, May 4, 1795, PRO, FO 7/41; Loan Convention with Austria, May 4, 1795; Treaty with Austria, May 20, 1795, PRO, FO 93/11; Morton Eden to William Grenville, October 10, 1795; William Grenville to Morton Eden, December 22, 1795, PRO, FO 7/43.

65. Treaty with Russia, February 18, 1795, PRO, FO 65/30; Charles Whitworth to William Grenville, February 19,1795; William Grenville to Charles Whitworth, March 9, 1795, PRO, FO 65/29; Charles Whitworth to William Grenville, June 14, 23, 1795, PRO, FO 65/30.
66. Gallet, *Les paysans en guerre,* 132.
67. Sherwig, *Guineas and Gunpowder,* 77.
68. Mostert, *Line upon a Wind,* 163.
69. Mahan, *Influence of Sea,* 2:232.
70. Prince of Wales Correspondence, 3:9.
71. Malmesbury Correspondence, 3:259–60.
72. Malmesbury Correspondence, 3:219–20.
73. William Pitt speech, December 8, 1795, *Parliamentary History,* 32:570.
74. William Pitt speech, December 8, 1795, *Parliamentary History,* 32:572.
75. For a recent analysis, see Nester, *Napoleon and the Art of Diplomacy.*
76. Banning, *French Revolutionary Wars,* 151.
77. Banning, *French Revolutionary Wars,* 160.
78. Banning, *French Revolutionary Wars,* 161.
79. Elliot, *Partners in Revolution*; Eliot, *Wolf Tone*; Gough and Dickson, *Ireland and the French Revolution*; Dickson, Keogh, and Whelan, *United Irishmen*; Keogh, *French Disease*; Curtin, *United Irishmen.*
80. Stuart Jones, *An Invasion that Failed*; Acerra and Meyer, *Marine et Révolution,* 195–97.
81. Cox, *Free Coloreds in the Slave Societies*; Duffy, *Soldiers, Sugar, and Seapower,* 136–56, 195, 244.
82. William Pitt to Henry Dundas, December [n.d.], 1796, *Life of Pitt,* 2:351.
83. For good books on Paul that explain his volatile character and relationship with Whitehall, see Hugh Ragsdale, *Paul I: A Reassessment of His Life and Reign* (Pittsburgh: University of Pittsburgh Press, 1979); Hugh Ragsdale, *Tsar Paul and the Question of Madness: An Essay in History and Psychology* (New York: Praeger, 1988); Angelo Rappoport, *The Curse of the Romanovs: A Study of the Lives and Reigns of Two Tsars, Paul I and Alexander I of Russia* (New York: Forgotten Books, 2012).
84. Mostert, *Line upon a Wind,* 194.
85. Coleman, *Nelson Touch,* 137.
86. Mitchell and Deane, *Abstract of British Historical Statistics,* chap. 14, tables 2, 5, chap. 15, table 2.
87. Morton Eden to William Grenville, January 22, February 19, April 27, 1796, PRO, FO 7/44; William Grenville to Charles Craufurd, April 29, 1796, PRO, FO 29/9; William Grenville to Morton Eden, May 20, June 10, 17, 1796, PRO, FO 7/45.
88. Sherwig, *Guineas and Gunpowder,* 83–85; William Grenville to Morton Eden, January 3, 1797, PRO, FO 7/48; William Grenville to Morton Eden, May 2, 1797, PRO, FO 7/49.

89. Sherwig, *Guineas and Gunpowder,* 93; William Grenville to Morton Eden, September 26, 1797, PRO, FO 7/50.
90. Mainwaring and Dobree, *Mutiny: The Floating Republic,* 9.
91. George III Correspondence, 2:xxiv.
92. Parkinson, *Britannia Rules,* 40–45; Mostert, *Line upon a Wind,* 202–16.
93. George III to William Grenville, June 1, 1797, HMC., 3:327.
94. Malmesbury Correspondence, 3:355.

## Chapter 5

1. William Grenville to Morton Eden, April 20 and 27, 1798, PRO, FO 7/51; Morton Eden to William Grenville, April 10, 1798, PRO, FO 7/54.
2. William Grenville to Charles Whitworth, August 29, 1798; Charles Whitworth to William Grenville, September 5, 1798, PRO, FO 65/40; Morton Eden to William Grenville, September 1, 1798, PRO, FO 7/53; Charles Whitworth to William Grenville, October 4, December 4, 1798; William Grenville to Charles Whitworth, October 23, November 16, December 13, 1798, Treaty with Austria, December 13 1798, PRO, FO 65/41; Treaty with Russia, December 29, 1798, PRO, FO 94/206; William Grenville to Charles Whitworth, January 25, 1799, PRO, FO 65/42.
3. William Grenville to Charles Whitworth, March 15, 27, May 3, 7, 23,1799; Charles Whitworth to William Grenville, April 30, 1799, PRO, FO 65/42; William Grenville to Charles Whitworth, June 26, 29, 1799, PRO, FO 65/43; Treaty with Russia, June 22, 1799, PRO, FO 93/81.
4. William Grenville to Charles Whitworth, August 1, 1799; Charles Whitworth to William Grenville, September 24, 1799, PRO, FO 65/44; Charles Whitworth to William Grenville, November 13, 1799, William Grenville to Charles Whitworth, December [n.d.], 1799, PRO, FO 65/45.
5. Reilly, *William Pitt the Younger,* 358–60.
6. William Pitt to Lady Chatham, May 28, 1798, PRO 30/8/12, fol. 482.
7. Hague, *William Pitt the Younger,* 427.
8. George III to William Pitt, May 30, 1798, *Life of Pitt,* 3:xiv.
9. Pakenham, *Year of Liberty*; Elliot, *Partners in Revolution*; Gough and Dickson, *Ireland and the French Revolution.*
10. William Pitt speech, February 3, 1800, Pitt Speeches, 3:257.
11. Madden, *United Irishmen,* 1:360–61; Doyle, *Oxford History of the French Revolution,* 258–59.
12. Cole, *Napoleon's Egypt,* 8.
13. George, Earl of Spencer, to John Jervis, Earl of St. Vincent, April 29, 1798, Nelson's Dispatches, 3:24–27.
14. Adkins and Adkins, *War for all the Oceans,* 37–38.
15. Coleman, *Nelson Touch,* 187–215.

16. William Sidney Smith to Napoleon Bonaparte, May 9, 1798, Barrow, *Life and Correspondence,* 1:293–94.
17. Bourrienne, *Memoirs of Napoleon Bonaparte,* 2:304–305.
18. Napoleon Bonaparte to Francis II, December 25, 1799; Napoleon Bonaparte to George III, both in Napoleon Correspondence, 2:4815; 4816.
19. William Grenville to George III, December 31, 1799, George III Correspondence, 3:2095.
20. Ehrman, *Younger Pitt,* 335.
21. William Pitt to Henry Dundas, December 31, 1799, Stanford, *Life of the Right Honorable William Pitt,* 3:207.
22. George III to William Grenville, January 3, 1800, George III Correspondence, 3:2095; George III to William Grenville, June 28, 1800, Dropmore, 6:256.
23. Grenville to Talleyrand, January 4, 1800; Talleyrand to Grenville, January 14, 1800, *Parliamentary History,* 34:1200–1204.
24. J. Holland Rose, *Pitt and the Great War,* 384.
25. William Pitt speech, February 3, 1800, Pitt Speeches, 4:26.
26. William Grenville, points for the Cabinet, March 24, 1800, George III Correspondence, 3:2120; Henry Dundas to William Grenville, April 9, 1800, George III Correspondence, 4:193; Henry Dundas to William Pitt, April 10, PRO, 30/8/157; Henry Dundas to William Grenville, April 10, 1800, PRO, 30/8/140; William Grenville to William Pitt, April 11, 1800, PRO, 30/8/140; Henry Dundas to William Grenville, April 20, 1800; William Grenville to Henry Dundas, April 23, 1800, George III Correspondence, 4:199, 200.
27. Charles Grey to Henry Dundas, January 16, 1800, Dropmore, 6:98–99.
28. Mackesy, *War without Victory,* 33.
29. Charles Cornwallis to Alexander Ross, November 6, 1800, Cornwallis Correspondence, 3:300–301.
30. William Grenville to Charles Whitworth, October 27, November 1, 12, 23, 28, December 5, 1799, PRO, FO 65/45; William Grenville to Gilbert Elliot, Lord Minto, February 8, 1800, PRO, FO 7/58.
31. Charles Whitworth to William Grenville, October 27, 1799; November 28, December 5, 1799, PRO, FO 64/44; 64–45.
32. William Huskisson to Henry Dundas, December 25, 1799, HMC, Dropmore, 4:71.
33. Treaties with Austria, June 20, 1800, PRO, FO 94/14; 94/15; 94/16. Although the treaties were dated June 20, they were actually signed on June 23.
34. Cabinet meeting, September 4, 1799, BL, add. ms. 59306.
35. William Grenville to Charles Elliot, Lord Minto, January 13, 1801, PRO, FO 7/62.
36. William Pitt speech, February 2, 1801, *Parliamentary Register,* 3rd ser., 14:52–55.
37. Thomas Grenville to Buckingham, January 13, 1801, *Memoirs of the Courts,* 3:117.

38. George III to William Grenville, November 27, 1800, George III Correspondence, 3:442.
39. William Grenville to Earl Carysfort, December 16, 1800, PRO, FO 7/61.
40. Mostert, *Line upon a Wind,* 390, 389.
41. Harrison, *Life of Nelson,* 2:295.
42. For acceptance of the story, see Bennett, *Nelson the Commander,* 195–96. For a flat rejection, see Coleman, *Nelson Touch,* 257–61.
43. Horatio Nelson to Henry Addington, April 4, 1801, Nelson Dispatches, 4:332.
44. Bolton, *Passing of the Act of Union*; Geoghegan, *Irish Act of Union.*
45. William Pitt speech, January 31, 1798, Pitt Speeches, 3:387.
46. Wilkinson, *Duke of Portland,* 152.
47. John Watson, *The Reign of George III* (Oxford: Clarendon Press, 1960), 399.
48. George III to William Pitt, February 6, 1795, PRO 30/8/103.
49. Rose, *Pitt and Napoleon,* 243–44.
50. Ehrman, *Younger Pitt,* 3:503.
51. Barnes, *George III and William Pitt,* 373–79.
52. Ziegler, *Addington*); Fedorak, *Henry Addington, Prime Minister.*
53. Addington Correspondence, 1:285–86
54. Addington Correspondence, 1:183.
55. Addington Correspondence, 1:287.
56. Malmesbury Correspondence, 4:78.
57. Reilly, *William Pitt the Younger,* 393.
58. Fedorak, *Henry Addington: Prime* .
59. Ehrman, *Younger Pitt,* 3:47–48.
60. Ehrman, *Younger Pitt,* 3:572.
61. Mackesy, *British Victory in Egypt.*
62. Sherwig, *Guineas and Gunpowder,* 136–39.
63. Mostert, *Line upon a Wind,* 421, 413.

## Chapter 6

1. Grainger, *Amiens Truce.*
2. Thomas Jefferson to Robert Livingston, April 18, 1802, Paul Leicester Ford, ed., *The Writings of Thomas Jefferson,* 10 vols. (New York: G. P. Putnam, 1892–99), 8:143–47.
3. Napoleon to Talleyrand, March 24, 1803, Napoleon Correspondence, 4:7535.
4. Whitworth to Hawkesbury, February 21, March 14, 1803, *Papers Relative to the Discussions with France in 1802 and 1830* (London: A. Strahan, 1803), 38:102–11; 43:133–34. Bonaparte to Talleyrand, May 1, 10, 13, 1803, Napoleon General Correspondence, 4:7617; 7629; 7638.
5. For overviews of this era, see Glover, *Britain at Bay*; Hall, *British Strategy*; and Kagan, *End of the Old Order.*

6. Parkinson, *Britannia Rules*, 87–88; Ward, Protheero, and Leathes, *Cambridge Modern History: Napoleon*, 210.
7. Hall, *British Strategy*, 104.
8. Yapp, *Strategies of British India*; Ingram, *Commitment to Empire.*
9. For the best books on Wellington as a military commander, see Longford, *Wellington*; Bryant, *Great Duke*; Hibbert, *Wellington*; Huw Davies, *Wellington's Wars* (New Haven, Conn.: Yale University Press, 2013); Muir, *Wellington.*
10. Hibbert, *Wellington,* 7.
11. Bryant, *Great Duke,* 92.
12. Longford, *Wellington,* 122.
13. Windham Papers, 1:224.
14. Glover, *Wellington as Military Commander*; Bryant, *Great Duke*; Weller, *Wellington in the Peninsula.*
15. Arthur Wellesley to General Stuart, July 3, 1804, Chad Conversations, 19; Croker to Hertford, September 22, 1825, *Croker Papers,* 1:337.
16. Bryant, *Great Duke,* 3342.
17. Diary, June 14, 1808, *Croker Papers,* 1:12–13.
18. Wellesley orders, July 31, 1808, Wellington Supplements, 6:91–92.
19. Bryant, *Great Duke,* 29.
20. Chad Conversations, 20.
21. First quote combined from two letters, Arthur Wellesley to Scott Waring, 12,1804, Arthur Wellesley to Lieutenant Colonel Close, January 22, 1804, Wellington Dispatches, 2:997. Second quote from Arthur Wellesley to Major Malcolm, April 13, 1804, Wellington Dispatches, 2:1141.
22. William Grenville to William Pitt, January 31, 1803, *Life of Pitt,* 4:116.
23. Harcourt, *Diaries and Correspondence,* 2:122.
24. Life of Pitt, 4:225.
25. Sparrow, *Secret Service,* 303.
26. Schom, *Trafalgar,* 139–41.
27. Parkinson, *Britannia Rules,* 97.
28. Simms, *Impact of Napoleon,* 164.
29. Napoleon to George III, January 1, 1805, Napoleon Correspondence, 5:9484.
30. Mulgrave to Talleyrand, January 14, 1805, PRO, FO 27/71.
31. "At the Restoration of Peace, a general Agreement and Guarantee for the mutual protection and security of the different Powers, and for reestablishing a general System of Public Law in Europe," State Papers, PRO, FO 65/60.
32. Sack, *Grenvillites.*
33. *Morning Chronicle,* November 19, 1801, New York Public Library.
34. Life of Pitt,4:234.
35. Ehrman, *Younger Pitt,* 760–775.

36. Lord Mulgrave's Proposals for the Reconstruction of Europe in 1804, December 15, 1804; Mulgrave to William Pitt, December 15, 1804, PRO 30/58/5; Mulgrave to Leveson Gower, January 21, April 17, 1805, FO 65/57.
37. Leveson Gower to William Pitt, February 16, March 7, 22, 1805, PRO 30/58/6; Treaty with Russia, April 11, 1805, PRO, FO 93/81.
38. Declaration with Austria, August 9, 1805, PRO, FO 65/59.
39. Treaty with Sweden, December 3, 1804, PRO, FO 93/101; Treaty with Sweden, August 31, 1805, PRO, FO 93/101; Treaty with Sweden, October 3, 1805, PRO, FO 94/306; Henry Pierrepont to Henry Phipps, Earl of Mulgrave, September 1, October 23, 1805; Henry Phipps, Earl of Mulgrave, to Henry Pierrepont, September 3, 1805, FO 73/34.
40. Henry Phipps, Earl of Mulgrave to Francis Jackson, September 10, 1805, Francis Jackson to Henry Phipps, Earl of Mulgrave, September 20, 1805, PRO, FO 64/68; Francis Jackson to Henry Phipps, Earl of Mulgrave, October 7, 1805, PRO, FO 64/69; Henry Phipps, Earl of Mulgrave to Dudley Rider, Earl Harrowby, October 27, 1805; Dudley Rider, Earl of Harrowby to Henry Phipps, Earl of Mulgrave, November 10, 1805, PRO, FO 64/70.
41. For the best overviews, see Schom, *Trafalgar*; Mark Adkin, *Trafalgar Companion*; Adkins, *Nelson's Trafalgar*; Nicolson, *Seize the Fire*).
42. Arthur Bryant, *Years of Victory, 1802–1812* (London: Collins, 1944), 77.
43. Napoleon to Villeneuve, December 12, 1804, Napoleon Correspondence, 4:9441; Napoleon to Decres, December 14, 1804, Napoleon Correspondence, 4:9445; Napoleon to Missiessy, December 23, 1804, Napoleon Correspondence, 4:9465; Napoleon to Ganteaume, March 2 (2 letters), April 7, 11, 23, 1805, Napoleon Correspondence, 5:9619, 9620, 9792, 9821, 9886; Napoleon to Villeneuve, March 2, 22, 1805, Napoleon Correspondence, 5:9623, 9726.
44. Napoleon to Villeneuve, May 8, 1805, Napoleon Correspondence, 5:10006.
45. Napoleon to Villeneuve, July 26, August 13, 23, 1805, Napoleon Correspondence, 5:10468, 10562, 10631; Napoleon to Ganteaume, July 20, August 22, 1805, Napoleon Correspondence, 5:10429, 10626.
46. Diary, October 1, 1834, *Croker Papers*, 2:233–34.
47. Napoleon to Decres, September 4, 8, 15, 1805, Napoleon Correspondence, 5:10742, 10761, 10803; Napoleon to Villeneuve, September 14, 1805, Napoleon Correspondence, 5:10797.
48. Schom, *Trafalgar*, 304, 315.
49. Schom, *Trafalgar*, 355; Bennett, *Nelson the Commander*, 276.
50. Life of Pitt, 4:346.
51. Schneid, *Napoleon's Italian Campaigns*, 47–49.
52. Original quote from Life of Pitt, 4:269. For discussions of its veracity, see Ehrman, Younger Pitt, 3:822; Reilly, *William Pitt the Younger*, 435–36; Hague, *William Pitt the Younger*, 572.
53. *Life of Pitt*, 4:381.

## Chapter 7

1. Jupp, *Lord Grenville.*
2. George Canning to Granville Leveson Gower, August 12, 1807, PRO, FO 30/29.
3. Schneid, *Napoleon's Italian Campaigns,* 49–55.
4. Drescher, *Econocide*; Eltis, *Economic Growth*; Anstey, *Atlantic Slave Trade.*
5. Napoleon to Joseph Bonaparte, June 21, July 4, July 28, July 30, August 12, 1806, Napoleon Correspondence, 6:12347, 12427, 12589, 12612, 12702; Napoleon to Talleyrand, August 18; August 22, 1806, Napoleon Correspondence, 6:12748, 12775.
6. Robert Stewart, Viscount Castlereagh to George Canning, May 16, 1807, PRO, FO 64/74; Treaty with Prussia, June 27, 1806, PRO, FO 93/78.
7. Napoleon to Frederick William III, September 12, October 12, October 19, 1806, Napoleon Correspondence, 6:12908, 13259, 13288; Napoleon to Joseph Bonaparte, September 12, 1806, Napoleon Correspondence, 6:12913; Napoleon to Talleyrand, September 12 (2 letters), 1806, Napoleon Correspondence, 6:12914, 12915; Napoleon to Maximilen Joseph, September 21, 1806, Napoleon Correspondence, 6:13051.
8. Chandler, *Campaigns of Napoleon,* 443–506.
9. Napoleon to Hugues Maret, December 17, 1807, Napoleon Correspondence, 7:16899.
10. Hecksher, *Continental System,* 245; Mitchell and Deane, *Abstract of British Historical Statistics,* 282.
11. Jupp, *Lord Grenville,* 387–412.
12. Wilkinson, *Duke of Portland.*
13. For the best biography, see Bew, *Castlereagh.* See also Bartlett, *Castlereagh.*
14. Dixon, *George Canning.*
15. *British Strategy.*
16. Napoleon to Talleyrand, June 20, 24, 25, July 9, 1807, Napoleon Correspondence, 7:15889, 15923, 15927, 15997; Napoleon to Alexander, July 3, 4, 6 (2 letters), 1807, Napoleon Correspondence, 7:15941, 15946, 15965, 15966, 15993; Napoleon to Josephine, July 7, 1807, Napoleon Correspondence, 7;15982.
17. George Canning to Granville Leveson Gower, October 2, 1807, PRO, FO 30/29.
18. Sparrow, *Secret Service,* 325.
19. Philip Mansel, *Louis XVI* (London: John Murray, 2005), 137–69.
20. Charles Jenkinson, Lord Hawkesbury, speech, February 11, 1805, *Parliamentary Debates,* 3:364.
21. Adkins and Adkins, *War for All the Oceans,* 214; Hinton, *A Mad, Bad, and Dangerous People.*
22. Hickey, "Monroe-Pinkney Treaty of 1806."
23. Nettels, *Emergence of a National Economy,* 396.

**Chapter 8**

1. Napoleon to Talleyrand, July 19, 1807, Napoleon Correspondence, 7:16042; Napoleon to Jean Baptiste Champagny, September 4, 7, 1807, Napoleon Correspondence, 7:16285, 16311; Napoleon to Christophe Duroc, September 25, 1807, Napoleon Correspondence, 7:16414; Napoleon to Jean Junot, November 8, 12, December 20, 23, 1807. January 7, 28, May 15, 18, 1808, Napoleon Correspondence, 7:16739, 16772, 16908, 16925 8:16963, 17094, 17914, 17980; Napoleon to Henri Clarke, December 6, 23, 1807, Napoleon Correspondence, 7:16858, 16917; Napoleon to Jean Savary, December 7, 1807, Napoleon Correspondence, 7:16871.
2. Napoleon to Jean Baptiste Champagny, October 7, 1807, March 9, 1808, Napoleon Correspondence, 7:16848, 8:17350; Napoleon to Charles IV, September 8, November 13, 1807, January 10 (2 letters), February 25, 1808, Napoleon Correspondence, 7:16336, 16776 8:16973, 16974, 17279; Napoleon to Joachim Murat, March 30, April 1, 5, 10, 24, 25, 29, 30, May 1, 2 (2 letters), 5 (2 letters), 6, 8, 1808, Napoleon Correspondence, 8:17523, 17545, 17557, 17582, 17680, 17698, 17734, 17743, 17750, 17758, 17759, 17778, 17779, 17788, 17815; Napoleon to Fernando, Prince of Asturias, April 16, 1808, Napoleon Correspondence, 8:17624; Napoleon to Talleyrand, April 25, May 1, 6, 9, 1808, Napoleon Correspondence, 8:17699, 17751, 17789, 17826.
3. Napoleon to Louis Bonaparte, March 27, 1808, Napoleon Correspondance, 8:17510; Napoleon to Joseph, April 18, May 10, 1808, Napoleon Correspondance, 8:17654, 17829.
4. Napoleon to Joachim Murat, February 20 (2 letters), March 5, 8, 9, 14, 26, 27, April 9, 17, 26, 28, May 13, 15, 19 (2 letters), 21, 22, 30, 1808, Napoleon Correspondence, 8:17250, 17251, 17339, 17347, 17356, 17401, 17505, 17514, 17581, 17641, 17715, 17723, 17888, 17921, 17996, 17997, 18028, 18050, 18168; Napoleon to Bertrand Bessieres, March 26, 30, May 13, 1808, Napoleon Correspondence, 8:17486, 17522, 17890; Napoleon to Denis Decres, May 21, 1808, Napoleon Correspondence, 8:18018.
5. Sherwig, *Guineas and Gunpowder*, 198.
6. Dalrymple, *Memoir Written by Sir Hew Dalrymple Bart.*, 10–11.
7. Dixon, *George Canning*, 121.
8. Robert Stewart, Earl Castlereagh to Brent Spencer, January 16, May 17, 1808, PRO, FO 6/185.
9. Longford, *Wellington*, 148.
10. Arthur Wellesley to William Wellesley-Pole, August 19, 1808, Wellesley-Pole, 5.
11. Wellington to Temple, October 19, 1808, Wellington Supplements, 6:162.
12. Treaty with Sweden, February 8, 1808, PRO, FO 93/101; Edward Thornton to George Canning, February 9, 1808, PRO, FO 74/46.

13. George Canning to Anthony Merry, November 10, December 23, 1808; Anthony Merry to George Canning, December 6, 1808, PRO, FO 73/50.
14. Anthony Merry to George Canning, February 23, 1809, PRO, FO 73/54; Treaty with Sweden, March 1, 1809, PRO, FO 93/101.
15. Communication from the Austrian Government, October 11, 1808, PRO, FO, 7/89.
16. George Canning reply to Austrian Government, December 24, 1808, PRO, FO 7/98.
17. August Wagner to George Canning, March 12, 1809; Ludwig von Wallmoden to George Canning, March 29, 1809, PRO, FO 7/90; Ludwig von Kleist to George Canning, March 12 and 13; April 11, 1809, PRO, FO 64/80.
18. George Canning to Ludwig von Wallmoden, April 20, 1809 (2 letters), PRO, FO 7/90; Treaty with Austria, April 24, 1809, PRO, FO 93/11; George Canning to Ludwig von Kleist, [undated]; George Canning instructions to Lieutenant Maimburg, April 24, 1809, PRO, FO 64/80; George Canning to Treasury Lords, June 24, 1809, PRO, FO 7/91; George Canning to Louis Starhemberg, July 29, 1809, PRO, FO 7/90.
19. Bond, *Grand Expedition.*
20. For good books on Richard Wellesley along with his brothers in Spain and elsewhere, see Severn, *A Wellesley Affair: Richard Marquess Wellesley and the Conduct of Anglo-Spanish Diplomacy, 1809–1812* (Tallahassee: University of Florida Press, 1981); John Severn, *Architects of Empire: The Duke of Wellington and His Brothers* (Norman: University of Oklahoma Press, 2007).
21. Sherwig, *Guineas and Gunpowder,* 219–23; Esdaile, *Peninsula War,* 175–76.
22. George Canning to Richard Wellesley, September 16, 1809, PRO, FO 72/75.
23. George Canning to Richard Wellesley, August 12, 1809, Wellesley Papers, BM add. mss. 37286:253–56.
24. A. Ludovici, ed., *On the Road with Wellington: The Diary of a War Commissary in the Peninsula Campaigns* (London: Greenhill Books, 1999), 79–80.
25. Richard, Marquess Wellesley to George Canning, September 15, 1809, BL add. mss. 37289.
26. Treaty with Portugal, April 21, 1809, PRO, FO 93/77.
27. "Memorandum on the Defense of Portugal, March 7, 1809, Wellington Dispatches, 3:181–83; Castlereagh to George III, March 26, 1809, George III to Castlereagh, March 27, 1809, George III Correspondence, 5:3844.
28. Percy Strangford to John Villiers, July 10, PRO, FO 63/77.
29. Wellington to Berghersh, September 1, 1809, Wellington Supplements, 6:343.
30. Wellington to Castlereagh, June 17, 1809, Wellington Dispatches, 4:407.
31. Weller, *Wellington in the Peninsula,* 79.
32. Weller, *Wellington in the Peninsula,* 105–107, 104.
33. Arthur Wellesley to William Wellesley-Pole, August 29, 1809, Wellesley-Pole, 22.
34. Hall, *British Strategy,* 184.

35. Hall, *British Strategy*, 1, 8–9.
36. George Canning to de Garay, July 20, 1809, Wellesley Papers, BM add. mss. 37286.
37. Berry, *By Royal Appointment*, 48–52; Harling, "Duke of York Affair."
38. Bartlett, 91–98; Dixon, *George Canning*, 129–56.
39. D. Gray, *Spencer Perceval.*
40. Iris Butler, *The Eldest Brother: The Marquess Wellesley, 1760–1842* (London: Hodder and Stoughton, 1972).

## Chapter 9

1. Esdaile, *Fighting Napoleon.*
2. Roberts, *Napoleon and Wellington*, 72.
3. Wellington to Lord Burghersh, December 17, 1809, Weigall, *Correspondence of Lord Burghersh*, 39.
4. Esdaile, *Peninsula War*, 307.
5. Kaufman, *British Policy.*
6. Sherwig, *Guineas and Gunpowder*, 228–30, 232.
7. Charles Stuart to Richard Wellesley, August 17 and 24, 1811; October 12, 1811, PRO, FO 63/112; 63/113.
8. Spain and Portugal Accounts, February 28, 1811, PRO, FO 63/120.
9. Wellington to Richard Wellesley, January 26, 1811, Wellington Dispatches, 7:194.
10. Muir, *Britain and the Defeat of Napoleon*, 120.
11. Liverpool to Wellington, September 10, 1810, Wellington Supplements, 6:591–93.
12. Henry Wellesley to Richard Wellesley, January 12; March 25 and 30, 1811, PRO, FO 72/109; 72/110.
13. Wellington to Charles Stuart, September 7, 1810, Wellington Dispatches, 4:263–64.
14. Charles Stuart to Richard Wellesley, February 2, 1811, PRO, FO 63/106. Wellington to Charles Stuart, October 6, 1810; Wellington to Robert, Lord Liverpool, October 27, 1810, Wellington Dispatches, 6:494–95; 545–46.
15. Liverpool to Wellington, January 2,1810, Wellington Supplements, 6:464; Wellington to Liverpool, January 31, February 9, 1810, Wellington Dispatches, 3:719–22, 729–31; Liverpool to Wellington, February 27, 1810, PRO, WO 6/50.
16. Muir, *Britain and the Defeat of Napoleon,* 129–30.
17. Howard, *Battle of Bussaco,* 140.
18. Gates, *Spanish Ulcer*, 252.
19. Bryant, *Great Duke,* 242.
20. Wellington to Liverpool, July 2, 18111, Wellington Despatches, 7:177.
21. Bryant, *Great Duke,* 263.

22. Charles Gray, Viscount Howick, to William Drummond, October 3, 1806; William Drummond to Charles Gray, Viscount Howick, March 11, 1807; William Drummond to George Canning, October 29, 1807; George Canning to William Drummond, December 26, 1807, PRO, FO 70/30; George Canning to William Drummond, June 25,1808, PRO, FO 70.32; Treaty with Sicily, March 23, 1807; Treaty with Sicily, March 30, 1808, PRO, FO 93/96.
23. John Rosselli, *Lord William Bentinck, 1774–1839* (London: Chatto and Windus, 1974).
24. William Bentinck to Liverpool, January 25, 1812; Liverpool to William Bentinck, March 4, 1812; Wellington to William Bentinck, March 24, 1812; William Bentinck to Henry Wellesley, April 11, 1812, Wellington Dispatches, 7: 289–91, 300–301, 556–67, 588–89.
25. Nugent memorandum (3 documents), n.d. [March 1811], PRO, FO 7.100; William Bentinck memorandum on Archduke Francis, n.d. [July? 1811], PRO, FO 70/44; Henry Wellesley to William Bentinck, October 21, 1811, PRO, FO 70/44.
26. Webster, *Foreign Policy of Castlereagh.*
27. Esdaile, *Peninsula War,* 387.
28. Wellington to Liverpool, May 26, 1812, Wellington Despatches, 9:176–77.
29. Hibbert, *Wellington,* 120.
30. Longford, *Wellington,* 288.
31. Bryant, *Great Duke,* 330.
32. Muir, *Britain and the Defeat of Napoleon,* 205–206.
33. Esdaile, *Peninsula War,* 406.
34. Castlereagh to Henry Wellesley, March 30, 1812, PRO, FO 72/127; Henry Wellesley to Castlereagh, March 4, 1814, PRO, FO, 72/159.
35. Esdaile, *Peninsula War,* 438.
36. Wellington to Bathhurst, September 13, 1813, Wellington Dispatches, 11:124.
37. Castlereagh to Edward Thornton, March 13, July 18, 1812, PRO, FO 73/71; Edward Thornton to Castlereagh, April 9, 16, 29, June 23, July 18, 1812, PRO, FO 73/72; 73/73.
38. Parkinson, *Britannia Rules,* 147; Perkins, *Prologue to War,* 399.
39. Jonathan Russell to James Monroe, September 17, 1812, *American States Papers,* 3:594–95.
40. For the best overview, see Hickey, *War of 1812.* Other very good accounts include: Coles, *War of 1812*; Horsman, *War of 1812*; John R. Etling, *Amateurs to Arms!*; Borneman, *1812.* For an excellent literature review, see Hickey, "War of 1812."
41. Etling, *Amateurs to Arms!,* 11, 69.
42. Mostert, *Line upon a Wind,* 670–71.
43. Toll, *Six Frigates*; Dillon, *We Have Met the Enemy.*
44. Mostert, *Line upon a Wind,* 670.

45. For an overview, seeRemini, *Battle of New Orleans*; For casualties, see Etling, *Amateurs to Arms!*, 299, 308.
46. Castlereagh to William, Earl of Cathcart, January 15, 1813, Castlereagh Correspondence, 8:301–305.
47. Castlereagh to William, Earl of Cathcart, July 24, August 30, October 20, 1812, PRO, FO 65/78; William, Earl of Cathcart, to Castlereagh, June 25, September 12, November 20, December 6, 1812, PRO, FO 73/73, 73/74 65/80.
48. A. A. Lobanov-Rostovsky, *Russia and Europe, 1789–1825* (Durham, N.C.: Duke University Press, 1947), 240–41; Chandler, *Campaigns of Napoleon*, 852–53.
49. Muir, *Britain and the Defeat of Napoleon*, 247.
50. Alexander to Christoph Lieven, January 20, 1813, Castlereagh to Christoph Lieven, July 21, 1813, PRO, FO 65/89. Castlereagh to Cathcart, July 6, 1813, Castlereagh Correspondence, 9:30.
51. Castlereagh to Alexander Hope, January 17, 1813, Alexander Hope to Castlereagh, February 24, 1813, PRO, FO 73/79; Treaty with Sweden, March 3, 1813, PRO, FO 93/101.
52. Treaty with Prussia, June 14, 1813; Treaty with Russia, June 15, 1813, PRO, FO 94/184; 93/81.
53. Hibbert, *Wellington*, 133.
54. Wellington to Henry, Earl of Bathurst, July 2, 1813, Wellington Despatches, 10:495–96.
55. Weller, *Wellington in the Peninsula* , 266–69.
56. Wellington, Stanhope Conversations, 22.
57. Wellington to Bathurst, September 19, 1813, Wellington Despatches, 7:10.
58. Wellington to Bathurst, November 27, 1813, Wellington Despatches, 7:166–68.
59. Sherwig, *Guineas and Gunpowder*, 367.
60. Kissinger, *A World Restored*, 100.
61. Castlereagh to George, Earl of Aberdeen, August 6, September 21, October 6, November 5, 1813, PRO, FO 7/101; Treaty with Austria, October 3, 1813, PRO, FO 93/11; George, Earl ofAberdeen, to Castlereagh, October 10, 1813, PRO, FO 7/102.
62. Sherwig, *Guineas and Gunpowder*, 288, 309.
63. Treaty with Sicily, September 12, 1812, PRO, FO 93/96.
64. Castlereagh to Aberdeen, August 6, 1813, Aberdeen to Castlereagh, September 14, 1813, PRO, FO 7/102.
65. Instructions for Castlereagh, December 26, 1813, PRO, FO 139/1.
66. Castlereagh to Liverpool, January 22, 1814, Wellington Supplements, 8:534–35.
67. Treaties with Russia, Austria, and Prussia, March 1, 1814, PRO, FO 93/81, 93/11, 93/78.
68. Muir, *Britain and the Defeat of Napoleon*, 319.
69. Hamilton-Williams, *Fall of Napoleon*, 60.
70. Wellington to Henry, Earl Bathurst, November 21, 1813, BL Add. Mss. 38255, ff. 55–58.

71. Weller, *Wellington in the Peninsula,* 342–50.
72. Weller, *Wellington in the Peninsula,* 350–63.
73. Barbara Norman, *Napoleon and Talleyrand: The Last Two Weeks* (New York: Stein and Day, 1970), 76.

## Chapter 10

1. Stanhope Conversations, 9, 81.
2. Treaty of Paris, May 30, 1814, Wellington Supplements, 9:129.
3. Haythornthwaite, *Armies of Wellington,* 8.
4. Aspinall, "Rupture of the Orange Marriage Negotiations."
5. Nicolson, *Congress of Vienna,* 116.
6. Longford, *Wellington,* 382.
7. Dallas, *Final Act,* 133.
8. Castlereagh to Prince Regent, October 29, 1814, Aspinall, *Letters of George IV,* 1:494.
9. Castlereagh to Liverpool, November [n.d.], 1814, Yonge, *Life and Administration of Robert Banks*
10. Liverpool to Castlereagh, October 28, November 25, 1814, Bathurst to Castlereagh, November 27, 1814, *British Diplomacy,* 219–22, 244–46, 247–48.
11. Liverpool to Wellington, December 23, 1814, Wellington Supplement, 9:494.
12. Castlereagh, March 20, 1815, *Parliamentary Debates,* 30:266–306.
13. For overviews, see Engelman, *Peace of Christmas Eve*; Perkins, *Castlereagh and Adams*; Updyke, *Diplomacy of the War of 1812.*
14. Castlereagh to Liverpool, August 28, 1814, Castlereagh Correspondence, 10:100–1;

Gouldburn to Bathurst, August 21, 1814, Wellington Dispatches, 9:188–89; Liverpool to

Castlereagh, September 2, 1814, Wellington Dispatches, 9:214; Liverpool to Bathurst, September 14, 1814, Bickley, *Report on the Manuscripts,* 287.

15. Liverpool to Castlereagh, November 18, 1814, Wellington Supplements, 9:438–39; Liverpool to Castlereagh, November 4, 1814; Liverpool to Wellington, November 4, 1814, Wellington to Liverpool, November 9, 1814, Wellington Dispatches, 9:405, 406; 425–26.
16. Nettels, *Emergence of a National Economy,* 385–86, 399; Hammond, *Banks and Politics in America,* 182–83; Hickey, *War of 1812,* 303.
17. Campbell, *Napoleon at Fontainebleau and Elba,* 304.
18. Protocol with Austria, Russia, and Prussia, March 25, 1815, PRO, FO 92/14; Wellington to Castlereagh, March 12, 25, 1815, Wellington Supplements, 12:267, 278.
19. Robert Stewart, Vviscount Castlereagh to Wellington, March 26, 1815, Castlereagh Correspondence, 10:285.

20. Sherwig, *Guineas and Gunpowder*, 338.
21. Stanhope Conversations, 25.
22. Castlereagh to Wellington, March 16, 1815, Wellington Supplements, 9:597; Amendment to Protocol with Austria, Russia, and Prussia, March 25, 1815, PRO, FO 92/13.
23. Bathurst to William of Orange, March 21, 1815, PRO, FO 6/16; William of Orange to Bathurst, April 3, 1815, PRO, WO 1/205; Castlereagh to Wellington, March 16, 24, 1815, Wellington Supplements, 9:597, 608–9.
24. Creevey Papers, 228.
25. Wellington to Charles Stewart, May 8, 1815, Wellington Dispatches, 8:66–69.
26. Longford, *Wellington*, 416.
27. Malmesbury Correspondence, 2:445–46.
28. Longford, *Wellington*, 472.
29. Bryant, *Great Duke*, 443.
30. Bryant, *Great Duke*, 447.
31. Bowden, *Armies at Waterloo*, 324–27.
32. Creevey Papers, 142.
33. Hibbert, *Wellington*, 178.
34. Creevey Papers, 142.
35. Wellington to Bathurst, June 19, 1815, Wellington Despatches, 12:484.
36. Edgecumbe, *Diary of Frances, Lady Shelly*, 1:102.
37. Bowden, *Armies at Waterloo*, 324–27.
38. Wellington to Charles Stuart, June 28, 1815, Wellington Despatches, 12:516.
39. Marchand, *Memoires de Marchand* , 1:205.
40. Liverpool to Castlereagh, July 21, 1815, Wellington Supplements, 2:47.

## Chapter 11

1. For the expansion of British hard power, see Bayly, *Imperial Meridian*; Paul Johnson, *Birth of the Modern*; Hyam, *Britain's Imperial Century*; Mori, *Britain in the Age of the French Revolution*; Colley, *Captives: Britain, Empire, and the World*; Bayly, *Birth of the Modern World,*; Porter, *Absent-Minded Imperialists.*

On the expansion of British soft power, see Newman, *Rise of English Nationalism*; Claydon and McBride, *Protestantism and National Identity*; Hoppit, *Parliaments, Nations, and Identities*; Kidd, *British Identities before Nationalism*; Kumar, *Making of English National Identity*; Semmel, *Napoleon and the British*; Colley, *Britons.*

2. Sherwig, *Guineas and Gunpowder*; Brewer, *Sinews of Power.* For fiscal policies, see Fetter, *Development of British Monetary Orthodoxy*; Daunton, *Taxing Leviathan.*
3. Duffy, *Soldiers, Sugar, and Seapower*, 391–92, 424; Mitchell and Deane, *Abstract of British Historical Statistics*, 281–81. For trade, see Hecksher, *Continental System*; O'Brien and Hunt, "Rise of a Fiscal State in England," 175; Parkinson, *Trade Winds*; Williams, *British Commercial Policy.*

4. Kennedy, Rise and Fall of the Great Powers, 105. For other estimates, see P.K. O'Brien, "Public Finance in the Wars with France, 1793–1815," in Dickinson, *Britain and the French Revolution,* 176; Jenks, *Migration of British Capital,* 17.
5. Mitchell and Deane, *Abstract of British Historical Statistics,* 391; Haythornthwaite, *Armies of Wellington,* 9–10.
6. Sherwig, *Guineas and Gunpowder,* 345, 354.
7. Hall, *British Strategy,* 28.
8. Mitchell and Deane, *Abstract of British Historical Statistics,* 402.
9. Haythornthwaite, *Wellington's Armies,* 21.
10. Muir, *Britain and the Defeat of Napoleon,* 276; Fortescue, *County Lieutenancies and the Army,* 291–93.
11. Hall, *British Strategy,* 34–35, 36.
12. For the best estimates and an evaluation of previous ones, see Duffy, *Soldiers, Sugar, and Seapower,* 326–67.
13. Hall, *British Strategy,* 144.
14. Bryant, *Great Duke*; Weller, *Wellington in the Peninsula*; Glover, *Wellington as Military Commander.*
15. Bryant, *Great Duke,* 400.
16. De las Casas, *Memorial de Sainte Helene,* 1:584.
17. Wellington to Liverpool, May 15, 1811, Wellington Despatches, 7:552–53.
18. Parkinson, *Britannia Rules*; Padfield, *Maritime Power and the Struggle for Freedom*; Adkins and Adkins, *War for All the Oceans*; Mostert, Line upon a Wind.
19. Mahan, *Influence of Sea Power,* 361.
20. Nelson Diary, March 14, 1795, Nelson Dispatches, 7:79.
21. Hall, *British Strategy,* 47, 31; Blanning, *French Revolutionary Wars,* 209.
22. Acerra and Myers, *Marine et Révolution,* 252.
23. Mostert, *Line upon a Wind,* 453; Cannadine, *Admiral Lord Nelson.*
24. Christie, *Wars and Revolutions*; Prest, *Albion Ascendant.*
25. Henry, Lord Petty, speech, July 31, 1807, *Parliamentary Debates,* 9:1042.
26. *Croker Papers,* 3:276.
27. Stanhope Conversations, 9.
28. Esdaile, *Peninsula War*; Esdaile, *Fighting Napoleon.*
29. Mitchell, *Underground War,* 256–60.
30. For the best account, see: Sparrow, *Secret Service.* See also Mitchell, *Underground War*; Nelson, *Home Office.*
31. Sparrow, *Secret Service,* 106.
32. Weller, *Wellington in the Peninsula,* 62.
33. Wilson, *A Diary of St. Helena,* 104.
34. Nicolson, *Congress of Vienna,* 19.
35. Nicolson, *Congress of Vienna,* 19.
36. Thorne, *History of Parliament,* 1:331–32.

37. Reilly, *William Pitt the Younger,* vii, ix.

38. Mitchell and Deane, *Abstract of British Historical Statistics,* chap. 14, table 2.

39. Ehrman, *Younger Pitt,* 1:313.

40. Wellington to Bathurst, July 2, 1815, Wellington Dispatches, 8:188–93.

41. Liverpool to George Canning, June 13, 1815, Wellington Supplements, 10:464–65.

42. Castlereagh to Liverpool, September 28, 1815, *British Diplomacy,* 384.

43. Philip Mansel, *Louis XVIII* (London: John Murray, 1981), 354.

44. Liverpool to George Canning, August 4, 1815, Wellington Supplements, 2:94–96.

45. Castlereagh to Tsar Alexander, July 16, 1821, Castlereagh Correspondence, 12:407.

46. Dallas, *Final Act,* 155.

47. Kissinger, *A World Restored,* 187.

48. Holbraad, *Concert of Europe*; Bridge and Bullen, *Great Powers and the European State System*; Schroeder, "Did the Vienna Settlement Rest on a Balance of Power?"

# Bibliography

## Primary Sources

*American States Papers: Foreign Relations: Documents, Legislative and Executive of the Congress of the United States.* 38 vols. Washington, D.C.: Gales and Seaton, 1832–61.

Aspinall, Arthur, ed. *The Correspondence of George Prince of Wales, 1770–1812.* 8 vols. London: Cassell, 1963–71.

———. *The Later Correspondence of George III.* 5 vols. Cambridge: Cambridge University Press, 1962–70.

———. *The Letters of George IV, 1812–30.* Cambridge: Cambridge University Press, 1938.

Barrow, J., ed. *The Life and Correspondence of Admiral Sir William Sidney Smith.* 2 vols. London: Richard Bentley, 1848.

Bentley, J. H., ed. *English Historical Documents, 1783–1832.* London: Routledge, 1967.

Bickley, Richard, ed. *Report on the Manuscripts of Earl Bathurst.* London: T. B. Hart, 1923.

Bishop of Bath and Wells, ed. *The Journal and Correspondence of William, Lord Auckland.* 4 vols. London: R. Bentley, 1861–62.

Bourrienne, Louis Antoine Fauvelet de. *Memoirs of Napoleon Bonaparte.* New York: Scribners, 1889.

Browning, Oscar, ed. *The Political Memoranda of Francis Fifth Duke of Leeds.* London: Nicolas and Sons, 1884.

Burke, Edmund. *Reflections on the Revolution in France* Mineola, N.Y.: Dover, 2006.

Butler, Charles. *Reminiscences of Charles Butler.* London: John Murray, 1822.

Campbell, Neil. *Napoleon at Fontainebleau and Elba, being a Journal of Occurrences in 1814 and 1815, edited by Archibald Neil Campbell MacLachlan.* London: John Murray, 1853.

Cobbett, William, ed. *Parliamentary Debates.* 22 vols. London: R. Bagshaw, 1804–12.

———. *The Parliamentary History of England from the Earliest Times to 1803.* 36 vols. London: R. Bagshaw, 1806–20.

Copeland, Richard, ed. *The War Speeches of William Pitt the Younger.* Oxford: Clarendon, 1918.

Dalrymple, Sir Hew. *Memoir Written by Sir Hew Dalrymple Bart. of his Proceedings as connected with Affairs of Spain and the Commencement of the Peninsula War.* London: John Murray, 1830.

Debrett, John, ed. *The Parliamentary Register, or, History of the Proceedings and Debates of the House of Commons.* 2nd ser. 45 vols. London: R. Spottiswoode, 1781–96; 3rd ser. 18 vols. London: R.Spottiwoode,, 1797–1802.

Duke of Buckingham and Chandos, ed. *Memoirs of the Courts and Cabinets of George the Third.* 2 vols. London: Hurst and Blackett, 1853–55.

Duke of Rutland. *Correspondence between the Right Hon. William Pitt and Charles, Duke of Rutland.* London: R. Spottiswoode, 1842.

Duke of Wellington. *The Supplementary Despatches, Correspondence, and Memoranda of Field Marshall Arthur, Duke of Wellington.* 15 vols. London: John Murray, 1858–72.

Edgecumbe, Richard, ed. *The Diary of Frances, Lady Shelly, 1787–1817.* 2 vols.. New York: Scribners, 1912.

Foot, Michael, and Isaac Kramnick, eds. *The Thomas Paine Reader.* New York: Penguin, 1987.

Ford, Paul Leicester, ed. *The Writings of Thomas Jefferson.* 10 vols. New York: G.P. Putnam, 1892–99.

Gore, John, ed. *The Thomas Creevey Papers.* New York: Macmillan, 1904.

Greig, James, ed. *The Farington Diary.* 8 vols. London: Hutchinson, 1922.

Gurwood, Colonel, ed. *The Dispatches of Field Marshall the Duke of Wellington.* 8 vols. London: Park, Furnivall, and Parker, 1944.

Hansard, T. C., ed. *The Parliamentary Debates from the Year 1803.* London: T. C. Hansard, 1812.

Harcourt, L. V., ed. *The Diaries and Correspondence of the Right Hon. George Rose.* London: Richard Bentley, 1860.

Harris, Nicolas, ed. *The Dispatches and Letters of Vice-Admiral Lord Viscount Nelson.* 7 vols. Cambridge: Cambridge University Press, 2011.

Jennings, Louis J., ed. *The Croker Papers: The Correspondence and Diaries of John Wilson Croker, Secretary to the Admiralty from 1809 to 1830.* 3 vols. London: John Murray, 1885.

*Journal of the House of Commons.* London: His Majesty's Stationery Office, 1803.

Lentz, Thierry et al., ed. *Napoleon Bonaparte Correspondance Generale.* Vols. 1–9. Paris: Fayard, 2004–12.

Malmesbury, James Harris, Earl of. *The Diaries and Correspondence of James Harris, the First Earl of Malmesbury.* 4 vols. London: Richard Bentley, 1845.

Marchand, Louis. *Memoires de Marchand, premier valet de chambre et executeur testamentaire de l'Empereur.* 2 vols. Paris: Plon, 1952–55.

Mitchell, B. R., and Phyllis Deane. *Abstract of British Historical Statistics.* Cambridge: Cambridge University Press, 1962.

Oliver, Mary, ed. *The Essential Writings of Ralph Waldo Emerson.* New York: Modern Library, 2000.

*Papers Relative to the Discussions with France in 1802 and 1830.* London: A Strahan, 1803.

*Parliamentary Register or History of the Proceedings and Debates of the House of Commons.* London: J. Debbrett, 1781.

Pellew, G., ed. *The Life and Correspondence of the Right Hon. Henry Addington, 1st Viscount Sidmouth.* 3 vols. London: John Murray, 1897.*Report on the Manuscripts of J. B. Fortescue, esq., preserved at Dropmore.* Dublin: John Falconer, 1908.

Ross, Charles, ed. *The Correspondence of Charles, First Marquis, Cornwallis.* 3 vols. London: John Murray, 1859.

Sheridan, Richard Brinsley. *Memoirs of the Life of the Right Honorable Richard Brinsley Sheridan.* Ed. Thomas Moore. Philadelphia: H. C. Carey and I. Lea, 1825.

*The Speeches of the Right Hon. William Pitt in the House of Commons.* 3 vols. London: Longman, Hurst, and Orne, 1817.

Stanhope, Philip Henry, First Earl of Stanhope. *Miscellanies: Collected and Edited by Earl Stanhope.* London: John Murray, 1872.

Stanhope, Philip Henry, Fifth Earl of Stanhope. *Notes of Conversations with the Duke of Wellington, 1831–1851.* London: John Murray, 1885.

Stanhope, Philip Henry, Lord Stanhope, *Life of the Right Honorable William Pitt,* 4 vols. (London: John Murray, 1867).

Temperley, Harold, and Lillian Penson, eds. *The Foundations of British Foreign Policy.* Cambridge: Cambridge University Press, 1938.

Vane, Charles William, Marquis of Londonderry, ed. *The Correspondence, Despatches, and Other Papers of Viscount Castlereagh, Second Marquis of Londonderry.* 12 vols. London: John Murray, 1848–53.

Webster, C. K., ed. *British Diplomacy: Select Documents dealing with the Reconstruction of Europe, 1813–15.* London: G. Bell, 1921.

Webster, Charles, ed. *Some Letters of the Duke of Wellington to his Brother, William Wellesley Pole,* Royal Historical Society. Vol. 18, 1948.

Weigall, Lady Rose, ed. *The Correspondence of Lord Burghersh, 1808–1840.* London: John Murray, 1912.

Wellington, Gerald, ed. *The Conversations of the First Duke of Wellington with George William Chad.* Cambridge: Cambridge University Press, 1956.

Wilson, Arthur, ed. *A Diary of St. Helena: The Journal of Lady Malcolm.* London: Allen and Unwin, 1899.

Wraxall, Nathaniel, ed. *The Historical and Posthumous Memoirs of Sir Nathaniel William Wraxall, 1772–1784.* London: Bickers and Sons, 1884.

## Secondary Sources

Acerra, Martine, and Jean Meyer. *Marines et Révolution* (Rennes: Ouest France), 1988.

Adkin, Mark. *The Trafalgar Companion : The Complete Guide to History's Most Famour Sea battle and the Life of Admiral Lord Nelson.* London: Aurum, 2005.

Adkins, Roy. *Nelson's Trafalgar : The Battle That Changed the World.* New York: Penguin, 2005.

Adkins, Roy, and Lesley Adkins. *The War for All the Oceans: From Nelson at the Nile to Napoleon at Waterloo.* New York: Viking, 2006.

Albion, R. G. *Forests and Sea Power.* Cambridge, Mass.: Harvard University Press, 1926.

Anderson, Benedict. *Imagined Communities: Reflections on the Origins and Spread of Nationalism.* New York: Verso Press, 1991.

Anstey, Roger T. *The Atlantic Slave Trade and British Abolition, 1760–1810.* London: Verso, 1975.

Armitage, David. *The Ideological Origins of the British Empire.* Cambridge: Cambridge University Press, 2000.

Armytage, Frances. *The Free Port System in the British West Indies.* London: Longmans, 1953.

Ashworth, William J. *Customs and Excise: Trade, Production, and Consumption in England, 1640–1845.* Oxford: Oxford University Press, 2003.

Aspinall, Arthur. "The Rupture of the Orange Marriage Negotiations, 1814." *History*: 34 (1949): 44–60.

———. *Politics and the Press, 1780–1850.* New York: Barnes and Noble, 1973.

Barker, Hannah. *Newspapers, Politics, and Public Opinion in Late Eighteenth Century England.* Oxford: Oxford University Press, 1998.

———. *Newspapers, Politics, and English Society, 1695–1855.* New York: Routledge, 2002.

Barker, Hannah, and S. Burrows, eds. *Press, Politics, and the Public Sphere in Europe and North America, 1760–1820.* New York: Cambridge University Press, 2002.

Barnes, Donald. *George III and William Pitt.* Palo Alto: Stanford University Press, 1973.

Barrell, John. *Imagining the King's Death: Figurative Treason, Fantasies of Regicide, 1793–1796.* Oxford: Oxford University Press, 2000.

Bartlett, C. J. *Castlereagh.* New York: Scribners, 1966.

Bartlett, Thomas. *The Fall and Rise of the Irish Nation: The Catholic Question, 1690–1830.* New York: Barnes and Noble, 1992.

Bayly, Christopher A. *Imperial Meridian: The British Empire and the World, 1780–1830.* New York: Longman,1989.

———. *The Birth of the Modern World, 1780–1914: Global Connections and Comparisons.* Oxford: Oxford University Press, 2004.

Beckett, J. V. *The Aristocracy in England, 1660–1914.* Oxford: Oxford University Press, 1986.

Bennett, Geoffrey. *Nelson the Commander.* New York: Scribners, 1972.

Berg, Maxine. *The Age of Manufacturers: Industry, Innovation, and Work in Britain, 1700–1820.* Oxford: Oxford University Press, 1985.

Berry, Paul. *By Royal Appointment: A Biography of Mary Ann Clark, Mistress of the Duke of York.* London: Femina, 1970.

Bew, John. *Castlereagh: Enlightenment, War, and Tyranny.* London: Quercus, 2011.

Bindman, David. *The Shadow of the Guillotine: Britain and the French Revolution.* London: British Museum Publications, 1989.

Binney, J. E. D. *British Public Finance and Administration, 1774–92.* Oxford: Oxford University Press, 1958.

Black, E. C. *The Association: British Extra-Parliamentary Organization, 1769–1793.* Cambridge, Mass.: Harvard University Press, 1963.

Black, Jeremy. *Britain as a Military Power, 1688–1815.*

———. *British Foreign Policy in an Age of Revolution, 1783–1793.* New York: Cambridge University Press, 1994.

———. *The English Press in the Eighteenth Century.* London: Croom Helm, 1987.

———. *George III: America's Last King.* New Haven, Conn.: Yale University Press, 2006.

———, ed. *Knight Errant and True Englishmen: British Foreign Policy, 1660–1800.* Edinburgh: University of Edinburgh Press, 1989.

———. *Natural and Necessary Enemies: Anglo-French Relations in the Eighteenth Century.* Athens: University of Georgia Press, 1986.

———. *A System of Ambition: British Foreign Policy, 1660–1793.* New York: Longmans, 1993.

Black, Jeremy, and Philip Woodfine, eds.The British Navy and the Use of Naval Power in the Eighteenth Century. Leicester: Leicester University Press, 1998.

Blackburn, Robin. The Overthrow of Colonial Slavery, 1776–1848. London: Verso, 1988.

Blanning, T. C. W. *The Cûlture of Power and the Power of Culture: Old Regime Europe, 1660–1789.* New York:. Oxford University Press, 2003.

———. *The French Revolutionary Wars, 1787–1802.* London: Arnold, 1996.

Bonney, R., ed. *The Rise of the Fiscal State in Europe, 1200–1815.* Oxford: Clarendon Press, 1999.

Boerner, Peter, ed. *The Concepts of National Identity: An Interdisciplinary Dialogue.* Baden-Baden: Nomos, 1986.

Bolton, G. C. *The Passing of the Act of Union: A Study in Parliamentary Politics.* Oxford: Clarendon Press, 1966.

Bolton, James T. *The Language of Politics in the Age of Wilkes and Burke.* Westport, Conn.: Greeenwood, 1975.

Borsay, Peter. *The English Urban Renaissance: Culture and Society in the Provincial, 1660–1770.* Oxford: Oxford University Press, 1989.

Bohstedt, John. *Riots and Community Politics in England and Wales, 1790–1810.* Cambridge, Mass.: Harvard University Press, 1983.

Bond, Gordon C. *The Grand Expedition: the British Invasion of Holland in 1809.* Athens: University of Georgia Press, 1979.

Borneman, Walter R. *1812: The War That Founded a Nation.* New York: Harper, 2004.

Bourne, J. M. *Patronage and Society in Nineteenth Century England.* London: E. Arnold, 1986.

Bowden, Scott. *The Armies at Waterloo: A Detailed Analysis of the Armies That Fought.* Arlington, Tex.: Empire Games Press, 1983.

Braddick, M. J. *The Nerves of State: Taxation and the Financing of the English State, 1558–1714.* Manchester: Manchester University Press, 1996.

Bradshaw, Brendan, and Peter Roberts, eds. *British Consciousness and Identity: The Making of Britain, 1533–1707.* Cambridge: Cambridge University Press, 1998.

Breihan, John R. "William Pitt and the Commission on Fees, 1785–1801." *History Journal* 27 (1984): 58–81.

Brewer, John. *The Sinews of Power: War, Money, and the English State, 1688–1783.* New York: Alfred A. Knopf, 1989.

Brewer, John, and Eckhart Hellmuth, eds. *Rethinking Leviathan: The Eighteenth Century State in Britain and Germany.* Oxford: Clarendon Press, 1999.

Bridge, F. Roy, and Roger Bullen. *The Great Powers and the European State System, 1815–1914.* London: Longman, 2004.

Brockliss, Laurence, and David Eastwood, eds. *A Union of Multiple Identities: The British Isles 1750–1850.* Manchester: Manchester University Press, 1997.

Bryant, Arthur. *The Great Duke or the Invincible General.* New York: William Morrow, 1972.

———. *Years of Victory, 1802–1812.* London: Collins, 1944.

Burrow, J. W. *Whigs and Liberals: Continuity and Change in England Political Thought.* Oxford: Clarendon Press, 1988.

Butler, Iris. *The Eldest Brother: The Marquess Wellesley, 1760–1842.* London: Hodder and Stoughton, 1972.

Butler, Marilyn, ed. *Burke, Paine, Godwin, and the Revolution Controversy.* Cambridge: Cambridge University Press, 1984.

Butterfield, Herbert. *George III, Lord North, and the People, 1779–1780.* New York: Russell and Russell 1968.

Byrne, William F. *Edmund Burke for Our Time: Moral Imagination, Meaning, and Politics.* DeKalb: Northern Illinois Press, 2011.

Cain, P. J., and A. G. Hopkins. *British Imperialism: Innovation and Expansion, 1688–1914.* New York: Longman, 1993.

Cannadine, David, ed. *Admiral Lord Nelson: Context and Legacy Houndmills,* Basingstoke, England: Palgrave Macmillan, 2005.

Cannon, John. *The Fox-North Coalition: Crisis of the Constitution, 1782–84.* Cambridge: Cambridge University Press, 1969.

Cannon, John. *The Aristocratic Century: the Peerage of Eighteenth Century England.* Cambridge: Cambridge University Press, 1984.

Carretta, Vincent. *George III and the Satirists: From Hogarth to Byron.* Athens: University of Ohio Press, 1990.

Chambers, J. D., and G. E. Mingay. *The Agricultural Revolution, 1750–1880.* London: Batsford, 1966.

Chandler, David C. *The Campaigns of Napoleon: The Mind and Method of History's Greatest Soldier.* New York: Macmillan, 1966.

Christie, Ian R. *Wars and Revolutions: Britain, 1760–1815.* Cambridge, Mass.: Harvard University Press, 1982.

———. *Wilkes, Wyvill, and Reform: The Parliamentary Reform Movement in British Politics, 1760–1785.* London: Macmillan, 1962.

Claeys, Gregory. *Thomas Paine: Social and Political Thought.* Boston: Unwin Hyman, 1989.

Clark, J. C. D. *The Language of Liberty, 1660–1832: Political Discourse and Social Dynamics in the Anglo-American World.* Cambridge: Cambridge University Press, 1994.

———. *English Society, 1688–1832: Ideology, Social Structure, and Political Practice during the Ancient Regime.* Cambridge: Cambridge University Press, 2000.

Clark, Peter. *British Clubs and Societies, 1580–1800: The Origins of an Associational World.* Oxford: Clarendon Press, 2000.

———, ed. *The Cambridge Urban History of Britain, 1540–1840.* New York: Cambridge University Press, 2000.

Clarke, John. *British Diplomacy and Foreign Policy, 1782–1865: The National Interest.* Boston: Unwin, Hymen, 1989.

Clarkson, L. A. *Proto-Industrialization: The First Phase of Industrialization?* London: Macmillan, 1985.

Claydon, Tony, and Ian McBride, eds. *Protestantism and National Identity: Britain and Ireland, 1650–1850.* Cambridge: Cambridge University Press, 1998.

Coad, J. The Royal Dockyards, 1690–1815: Architecture and Engineering Works of the Sailing Navy. Aldershot: Scolar Press, 1989.

Cobban, Alfred, ed. *The Debate on the French Revolution.* London: N. Kaye, 1950.

Cole, Juan. *Napoleon's Egypt: Invading the Middle East.* New York: Palgrave Macmillan, 2008.

Coleman, Terry. *The Nelson Touch: The Life and Legend of Horatio Nelson.* New York: Oxford University Press, 2002.

Coles, Harry L. *The War of 1812.* Chicago: University of Chicago Press, 1965.

Colley, Linda. *Britons: Forging the Nation, 1707–1837.* New Haven, Conn.: Yale University Press, 2009.

———. *Captives: Britain, Empire, and the World, 1600–1850.* New York: Pantheon, 2002.

Conway, S. *The British Isles and the War of American Independence.* New York: Oxford University Press, 2000.

Cookson, J. E. *The British Armed Nation, 1793–1815.* Oxford: Oxford University Press, 1997.

———. *The Friends of Peace: Anti-War Liberalism in England, 1793–1815.* Cambridge: Cambridge University Press, 1982.

Corfield, Penelope J. *The Impact of English Towns, 1700–1800.* Oxford: Oxford University Press, 1982.

———. *Power and the Professions in Britain, 1700–1850.* New York: Routledge, 2000.

Cox, E. L. *The Free Coloreds in the Slave Societies of St. Kitts and Grenada, 1763–1833.* Knoxville: University of Tennessee Press, 1984.

Crafts, N. F. R. *British Economic Growth during the Industrial Revolution.* Oxford: Oxford University Press, 1985.

Credel, Martin. *The Origins of War Prevention: The British Peace Movement and International Relations, 1730–1854.* Oxford: Oxford University Press, 1996.

Crouzet, François. *Britain Ascendant: Comparative Studies in Franco-British Economic History.* New York: University of Cambridge Press, 1985.

———. *The First Industrialists: The Problem of Origins.* Cambridge: Cambridge University Press, 1985.

Curtain, Nancy J. *The United Irishmen: Popular Politics in Ulster and Dublin, 1791–1798.* Oxford: Oxford University Press, 1994.

Dallas, Gregor. *The Final Act: The Roads to Waterloo.* New York: Henry Holt, 1996.

Daunton, Martin. *Progress and Poverty: An Economic and Social History of Britain, 1700–1850.* Oxford: Oxford University Press, 1995.

Daunton, Martin. *Taxing Leviathan: The Politics of Taxation in Britain, 1799–1914.* Cambridge: Cambridge University Press, 2001.

Davies, Huw. *Wellington's Wars.* New Haven, Conn.: Yale University Press, 2013.

Davis, David Brion. *The Problem of Slavery in the Age of Revolution, 1770–1823.* Ithaca, N.Y.: Cornell University Press, 1997.

Davis, Ralph. *The Industrial Revolution and British Overseas Trade.* Leicester: Leicester University Press, 1979.

Deane, Seamus. *The French Revolution and Enlightenment in England, 1789–1832.* Cambridge, Mass.: Harvard University Press, 1988.

de las Casas, Emmanuel. *Memorial de Sainte Helene.* Paris: Editions du Seuil, 1968.

Derry, John W. *The Regency Crisis and the Whigs, 1788–89.* Cambridge: Cambridge University Press, 1963.

Dickinson, H. T. *Britain and the French Revolution.* Basingstoke: Macmillan, 1989.

———. *British Radicalism and the French Revolution, 1789–1815.* Oxford: Oxford University Press, 1985.

———, ed. *A Companion to Eighteenth Century Britain.* Oxford: Blackwell, 2002.

———. *The Politics of the People in Eighteenth Century Britain.* Basingstoke, UK: Palgrave Macmillan, 1995.

Dickson, David, Daire Keogh, and Kevin Whelan, eds. *The United Irishmen: Republicanism, Radicalism, and Rebellion.* Dublin: Irish Academic Press, 1993.

Dillon, Richard. *We Have Met the Enemy: Oliver Hazard Perry, Wilderness Commodore.* New York: Harper and Row, 1965.

Dixon, Peter. *George Canning: Politician and Statesman.* New York: Mason and Charter, 1976.

Donald, Diana. *English Political Caricature: Satirical Prints in the Reign of George III.* New Haven, Conn.: Yale University Press, 1996.

Downing, Brian. *The Military Revolution and Political Change: The Origins of Democracy and Aristocracy in Early Modern Europe.* Princeton, N.J.: Princeton University Press,1992.

Doyle, William. *The Oxford History of the French Revolution.* New York: Oxford University Press, 1989.

Dozier, Rober, *For King, Constitution, and Country: The English Loyalists and the French Revolution.* Lexington: University of Kentucky Press, 1983.

Drescher, Seymour. *Capitalism and Antislavery: British Mobilization in Comparative Perspective.* Basingstoke, UK: Palgrave Macmillan, 1986.

———. *Econocide: British Slavery in the Era of Abolition.* Pittsburgh: University of Pittsburgh, 1977.

Duffy, Michael. *The English Satirical Print, 1660–1832: The Englishman and the Foreigner.* Cambridge: Cambridge University Press, 1986.

———. *Soldiers, Sugar, and Seapower: The British Expeditions to the West Indies and the War against Revolutionary France.* Oxford: Clarendon Press, 1987.

———. "War, Revolution, and the Crisis." In Mark Philp, ed. *The French Revolution and British Popular Politics.* Cambridge, U.K.: Cambridge University Press, 1991.

Earle, Peter. *The Making of the English Middle Class: Business, Society, and Family Life in London, 1660–1730.* Berkeley: University of California Press, 1989.

Ehrman, John. *The British Government and Commercial Negotiations with Europe, 1783–1783.* Cambridge: Cambridge University Press, 1963.

———. *The Younger Pitt: The Consuming Struggle.* Stanford, Calif.: Stanford University Press, 1996.

Ehrman, John. *The Younger Pitt: The Reluctant Transition.* Stanford, Calif.: Stanford University Press, 1983.

Ehrman, John. *The Younger Pitt: The Years of Acclaim.* Stanford, Calif.: Stanford University Press, 1969.

Eliot, Marianne. *Partners in Revolution: The United Irishmen in France.* New Haven, Conn.: Yale University Press, 1982.

———. *Wolf Tone.* New Haven, Conn.: Yale University Press, 1990.

Eltis, David. *Economic Growth and the Ending of the Trans-Atlantic Slave Trade.* Oxford: Oxford University Press, 1987.

Emsley, Clive. *British Society and the French Wars, 1793–1815.* Basingstoke: Macmillan, 1979.

Engelman, Fred L. *The Peace of Christmas Eve.* New York: Harcourt, Brace, 1962.

Erbman, Thomas. *The Birth of the Leviathan: Building States and Regimes in Medieval and Early Modern Europe.* Cambridge: Cambridge University Press, 1997.

Esdaile, Charles. *The Peninsular War: A New History.* New York: Palgrave Macmillan, 2003.

Esdaile, Charles J. *Fighting Napoleon: Guerillas, Bandits, and Adventurers in Spain, 1808–1814.* New Haven, Conn.: Yale University Press, 2004.

Etling, John R. *Amateurs to Arms!: A Military History of the War of 1812.* New York: Da Capo Press, 1995.

Evans, Peter, Dietrich Rusechemeyer, and Theda Skocpol, eds. *Bringing the State Back In.* Cambridge: Cambridge University Press, 1985.

Evans, Eric J. *The Forging of the Modern State: Early Industrial Britain, 1783–1870.* New York: Pearson, 2001.

Fedorak, Charles John. *Henry Addington, Prime Minister, 1801–1804: Peace, War, and Parliamentary Politics.* Akron, Ohio: Akron University Press, 2002.

Ferguson, Niall. *The World's Banker: The History of the House of Rothschild.* London: Weidenfeld and Nicolson, 1998.

Ferguson, Niall. *Empire: How Britain Made the Modern World.* New York: Basic Books, 2004.

Fetter, Frank. *The Development of British Monetary Orthodoxy, 1797–1875.* Cambridge, Mass.: Harvard University Press, 1965.

Fletcher, Ian. *Galloping at Everything: The British Cavalry in the Peninsular War and at Waterloo, 1808–15.* Mechanicsburg, Penn.: Stackpole Books, 1999.

Floud, Roderick, and Paul Johnson, eds. *The Cambridge Economic History of Modern Britain: Industrialization, 1700–1860.* New York: Cambridge University Press, 2004.

Ford, Archibald S. *His Majesty's Opposition, 1714–1830.* Oxford: Clarendon Press, 1964.

Ford, Paul Leicester, ed. *The Writings of Thomas Jefferson.* 10 vols. New York: G. P. Putnam, 1892–1899.

Fortescue, John. *The County Lieutenancies and the Army, 1803–1814.* London: Macmillan, 1909.

Fruchtman, Jack. *Thomas Paine: Apostle of Freedom.* New York: Four Walls, Eight Windows, 1994.

Gallet, Jean. *Les paysans en guerre.* Paris: Editions Ouest-France, 1988.

Gates, David. *The Spanish Ulcer: A History of the Peninsular War.* New York: De Capo, 1986.

Gee, Austin. *The British Volunteer Movement, 1794–1814.* Oxford: Oxford University Press, 2003.

Gellner, Ernest. *Nations and Nationalism.* Oxford: Clarendon, 1985.

George, M. Dorothy. *English Political Caricature, 1793–1832: A Study of Opinion and Propaganda.* Oxford: Oxford University Press, 1959.

———. *London Life in the Eighteenth Century*. Harmondsworth: Penguin, 1966.

Geoghegan, Patrick M. *The Irish Act of Union: A Study in High Politics, 1798–1801*. Dublin: Irish Academic Press, 1999.

Gibson, William. *The Church of England, 1688–1832, Unity and Accord*. London: Routledge, 2001.

Glover, Michael. *Wellingtβon as Military Commander*. New York: Penguin, 2001.

Glover, Richard. *Britain at Bay: Defense against Bonaparte, 1803–14*. London: Allen and Unwin, 1973.

———. *Peninsular Preparation: The Reform of the British Army, 1795–1809*. Cambridge: Cambridge University Press, 1963.

Goodwin, Albert. *The Friends of Liberty: The English Democratic Movement in the Age of the French Revolution*. Cambridge, Mass.: Harvard University Press, 1979.

Gough, Hugh, and David Dickson, eds. *Ireland and the French Revolution*. Dublin: Irish Academic Press, 1990.

Graham, Jenny. *The Nation, the Law, and the King: Reform Politics in England, 1789–1799*. Lanham, Maryland: University Press of America, 2000.

Grainger, John D. *The Amiens Truce: Britain and Bonaparte, 1801–1803*. Rochester, N.Y.: Boydell Press, 2004.

Gray, D. *Spencer Perceval: The Evangelical Prime Minister, 1762–1812*. Manchester: Manchester University, 1963.

Greenfeld, Liah. *Nationalism: Five Roads to Modernity*. Cambridge, Mass.: Harvard University Press, 1992.

Griffith, Paddy. *The Art of War of Revolutionary France, 1789–1802*. Mechanicsburg, Penn.: Stackpole Books, 1998.

Gunn, J. A. W. *Beyond Liberty and Property: The Process of Self-Recognition in Eighteenth Century Political Thought*. Kingston, Ont.: McGill University Press, 1983.

Guy, Alan James. *The Road to Waterloo: The British Army and the Struggle against Revolutionary and Napoleonic France*. London: National Army Museum, 1990.

Habakkuk, John. *Marriage, Debt, and the Estates System: English Land Ownership, 1650–1950*. Oxford: Oxford University Press, 1994.

Hague, William. *William Pitt the Younger*. New York: Harper Perennial, 2004.

Hall, Christopher D. *British Strategy in the Napoleonic War, 1803–1815*. Manchester: Manchester University Press, 1992.

Hamilton-Williams, David. *The Fall of Napoleon*. London: Arms and Armour Press, 1994.

Hammond, Bray. *Banks and Politics in America*. Princeton, N.J.: Princeton University Press, 1957.

Harding, Richard. *The Evolution of the Sailing Navy, 1509–1815*. Basingstoke: Palgrave Macmillan, 1995.

Harding, Richard. *Seapower and Naval Warfare, 1650–1830*. Annapolis, Maryland: Naval University Press, 1999.

Harding, Richard. *British Admirals of the Napoleonic Wars: The Contemporaries of Nelson.* London: Chatham, 2005.

Harling, Philip. "The Duke of York Affair (1809) and the Complexities of War Time Patriotism." *History Journal* 39 (1996): 963–84.

———. *The Modern British State: An Historical Introduction.* Oxford: Clarendon, 2001.

———. *The Waning of the "Old Corruption": The Politics of Economical Reform in Britain, 1779–1840.* Oxford: Oxford University Press, 1996.

Harlow, Vincent T. *The Founding of the Second British Empire, 1763–1793.* London: Longman, 1964.

Harris, Bob. *Politics and the Rise of the Press: Britain and France, 1620–1800.* London: Routledge, 1996.

Harrison, James. *The Life of the Right Honourable Horatio Lord Viscount Nelson.* London: Ranelagh Press, 1806.

Hastings, Adrian. *The Construction of Nationhood: Ethnicity, Religion, and Nationalism.* Cambridge: Cambridge University Press, 1997.

Haythornthwaite, Philip J. *The Armies of Wellington.* London: Brockhampton Press, 1996.

Heckscher, Eli. *The Continental System, an Economic Interpretation.* Oxford: Clarendon Press, 1922.

Helleiner, Karl F. *The Imperial Loans: A Study in Financial and Diplomatic History.* Oxford: Clarendon, 1965.

Hellmuth, Eckhart. "The British State." In H. T. Dickinson, ed. *A Companion to Eighteenth Century Britain.* Oxford: Blackwell, 2006.

———. *The Transformation of Political Culture: England and Germany in the Late Eighteenth Century.* Oxford: Clarendon Press, 1990.

Henry, Maura A. "The Making of Elite Culture." In H. T. Dickinson, ed. *A Companion to Eighteenth Century Britain.* Oxford: Blackwell, 2006.

Hibbert, Christopher. *George IV: Regent and King, 1811–1830.* New York: Penguin, 1973.

———. *Wellington: A Personal History.* Reading, Mass.: Perseus Books, 1997.

Hickey, Donald R. "The Monroe-Pinkney Treaty of 1806: A Reappraisal." William and Mary Quarterly. 44, no. 1 (January 1987): 65–88.

———. *The War of 1812: A Forgotten Conflict.* Urbana: University of Illinois Press, 1990.

———. "The War of 1812: Still a Forgotten Conflict?" *Journal of Military History* 65, no. 3 (July 2001, 741–69.

Hidy, Ralph Willard. *The House of Baring in American Trade and Finance: English Merchant Bankers at Work, 1763–1861.* Cambridge, Mass.: Harvard University Press, 1949.

Hill, B. W. *British Parliamentary Parties, 1742–1832: From the Fall of Walpole to the First Reform Act.* London: Allen and Unwin, 1985.

Hinton, Boyd. *A Mad, Bad, and Dangerous People: England, 1783–1846.* New York: Oxford University Press, 2008.

Hobsbawm, Eric. *Industry and Empire: The Economic History of Britain since 1750.* New York: W. W. Norton, 1999.

———. *Nations and Nationalism since 1780: Program, Myth, Reality.* New York: Cambridge University Press, 1995.

Holbraad, Carsten. *The Concert of Europe: A Study in German and British International Theory, 1815–1914.* New York: Barnes and Noble, 1971.

Hole, Robert. *Pulpits, Politics, and Public Order in England, 1760–1832.* Cambridge: Cambridge University press, 1989.

Hone, J. Ann. *For the Cause of Truth: Radicalism in London, 1796–1821.* Oxford: Oxford University Press, 1982.

Hoppit, Julian, ed. *Parliaments, Nations, and Identities in Britain and Ireland, 1660–1850.* Manchester: Manchester University Press, 2003.

———. *The Rise and Failures of English Business, 1700–1800.* Cambridge: Cambridge University Press, 1987.

Horsman, Reginald. *The War of 1812.* London: Eyre and Spottiswoode, 1969.

Houlding, J. A. *Fit for Service: The Training of the British Army, 1715–1795.* Oxford: Oxford University Press, 1981.

Howard, Donald P. *The Battle of Bussaco: Massena versus Wellington.* Tallahassee: University of Florida Press, 1965.

Hudson, Pat. *The Industrial Revolution.* London: Macmillan, 1992.

———, ed. *Regions and Industries: A Perspective on the Industrial Revolution in Britain.* Cambridge: Cambridge University Press, 1989.

Hutt, Maurice. *Chouanarie and Counter-Revolution: Puisaye, the Princes, and the British Government in the 1790s.* Cambridge: Cambridge University Press, 1983.

Hyam, Ronald. *Britain's Imperial Century, 1815–1914: A Study of Empire and Expansion.* Basingstoke, UK: Palgrave Macmillan, 1993.

Ingram, Edward. *Commitment to Empire: Prophecies of the Great Game for Asia, 1797–1800.* Oxford: Oxford University Press, 1981.

James, Lawrence. *The Rise and Fall of the British Empire.* New York: St. Martin's Griffith Press, 1994.

Janis, Irving. *Group Think: Psychological Studies of Policy Decisions and Fiascos.* New York: Centage Learning, 1982.

Jarrett, Derek. *Three Faces of Revolution: Paris, London, New York in 1789.* London: G. Philip, 1989.

Jenks, Leland H. *The Migration of British Capital to 1875.* New York: Nelson, 1963.

Johnson, Paul. *The Birth of the Modern: World Society, 1815–1830.* New York: HarperCollins, 1991.

Johnston, Edith M. *Ireland in the Eighteenth Century.* Dublin: Gill and Macmillan, 1974.

Jones, Clive, and David Lewis Jones, eds. *Politics and Power: The House of Lords, 1603–1911.* London: Secker and Warburg, 1986.

Jones, Colin, ed. *Britain and Revolutionary France: Conflict, Subversion, and Propaganda.* Exeter, UK: University of Exeter press, 1983.

Jupp, Peter. *Lord Grenville, 1759–1834.* Oxford: Clarendon, 1985.

Kagan, Frederick W. *The End of the Old Order: Napoleon and Europe, 1801–1805.* New York: Da Capo Press, 2006.

Kaufman, William W. *British Policy and the Independence of Latin America, 1804–1814.* New Haven, Conn.: Yale University Press, 1951.

Keane, John. *Thomas Paine: A Political Life.* New York: Grove Press, 1989.

Kelly, James. *Prelude to Union: Anglo-Irish Politics in the 1780s.* Cork: Cork University Press, 1992.

Kennedy, F. *The Jacobin Clubs in the French Revolution: The First Years.* Princeton, N.J.: Princeton University Press, 1982.

Kennedy, Paul. *The Rise and Fall of the Great Powers: Economic Change and Military Conflict from 1500 to 2000.* New York: Vintage, 1988.

Keogh, Diare. *The French Disease: The Catholic Church and Irish Radicalism, 1790–1800.* Dublin: Irish Academic Press,1993.

Keohane, Robert. *International Institutions and State Power.* Boulder, Colo.: Westview, 1989.

———, ed. *Neo-Realism and Its Critics.* New York: Columbia University Press, 1986.

Kerridge, Eric. *The Agricultural Revolution.* New York: A. M. Kelly, 1967.

Kidd, Alan J., and David Nicolls, eds. *The Making of the British Middle Class?: Studies of Regional and Cultural Diversity since the Eighteenth Century.* Stroud, UK: Sutton, 1998.

Kidd, Colin. *British Identities before Nationalism: Ethnicity and Nationhood in the Atlantic World, 1600–1800.* Cambridge: Cambridge University Press, 1999.

Kissinger, Henry A. *A World Restored: Metternich, Castlereagh, and the Problems of Peace, 1812–1822.* New York: Echo Books, 2013.

———. "The Congress of Vienna: A Reappraisal." *World Politics* 8, no. 2 (January 1956): 264.

Kramnick, Isaac. *Republicanism and Bourgeois Radicalism: Political Ideology in Late Eighteenth Century England and America.* Ithaca, N.Y.: Cornell University Press, 1990.

Kumar, Krisham. *The Making of English National Identity.* Cambridge: Cambridge University Press, 2003.

Langford, Paul. *Englishness Identified: Manners and Character, 1650–1850.* Oxford: Oxford University Press, 2000.

———. *Modern British Foreign Policy: The Eighteenth Century, 1688–1815.* New York: Vintage, 1976

———. *A Polite and Commercial People: England, 1727–1783.* Oxford: Oxford University Press, 1989.

———. *Public Life and the Propertied Englishman, 1689–1798.* Oxford: Oxford University Press, 1991.

Lavery, Brian. *Nelson's Navy: The Ships, Men, and Organization, 1793–1815.* Annapolis, Maryland: Naval Institute Press, 1989.

Lee, Stephen D. "Parliament, Parties, and Elections, 1760–1815." In H. T. Dickinson, ed. *Companion to Eighteenth Century Britain.* New York: Blackwell, 2002.

Lewis, Michael. *A Social History of the Navy, 1783–1815.* London: Allen and Unwin, 1960.

Lincoln, Margarette. *Representing the Royal Navy: British Sea Power, 1750–1815.* Burlington, Vermont: Ashgate, 2002.

Lobanov-Rostovsky, A. A. *Russia and Europe, 1789–1825.* Durham, N.C.: Duke University Press, 1947.

Longford, Elizabeth. *Wellington: Years of the Sword.* New York: Harper and Row, 1969.

Lowe, W. C. "George III, Peerage Creations and Politics,1760–1784." *Historical Journal* 35 (1992): 587–609.

Ludovici, A., ed. *On the Road with Wellington: The Diary of a War Commissary in the Peninsula Campaigns.* London: Greenhill Books, 1999.

Maccoby, Simon. *The English Radical Tradition, 1763–1783.* Westport, Conn.: Greenwood, 1978.

Mackesy, Piers. *The British Victory in Egypt, 1801: The End of Napoleon's Conquest.* New York: Routledge, 1995.

———. *War without Victory: The Downfall of Pitt, 1799–1802.* Oxford: Clarendon Press, 1984.

Macleod, Emma Vincent. *A War of Ideas?: British Attitudes to the Wars against Revolutionary France.* New Haven, Conn.: Yale University Press, 1998.

Madden, Richard. *The United Irishmen: Their Lives and Times.* 4 vols. Dublin: J. Madden and Company, 1857–60.

Mahan, Alfred Thayer. *The Influence of Sea Power Upon History: The French Revolution and Empire, 1793–1812.* 2 vols. Boston: Little, Brown, 1892.

Mahan, Alfred Thayer. *The Influence of Sea Power Upon History, 1660–1783.* New York: Barnes and Noble, 2004.

Mainwaring, G. E., and Bonamy Dobree. *Mutiny: The Floating Republic, An Account of the Mutinies at Spithead and Nore in 1797.* New York: Pen and Sword, 2004.

Malcolmson, A. P. W. "The Irish Peers and the Union, 1800–1971." *Transactions of the Royal Historical Society,* 6th ser., vol. 10 (2000), 300.

Mansel, Philip. *Louis XVI.* London: John Murray, 2005.

Marshall, P. J. ed. *The Oxford History of the British Empire: The Eighteenth Century.* Oxford: Oxford University Press, 1998.

———. *The Problems of Empire: Britain and India, 1757–1813.* London: Allen and Unwin, 1968.

Mathias, Peter. *The First Industrial Nation: An Economic History of Britain, 1700–1914.* New York: Routledge, 2001.

McCahill, Michael W. *Order and Equipoise: The Peerage and the House of Lords, 1783–1806.* London: Royal Historical Society, 1978.

McDowell, R. B. *Ireland in the Age of Imperialism and Revolution, 1760–1801.* Oxford: Oxford University Press, 1979.

McKay, Derek, and Hamish M. Scott, *The Rise of the Great Powers, 1648–1815.* London: Longman, 1983.

McKendrick, Neil, John Brewer, and J. H. Plumb. *The Birth of a Consumer Society: The Commercialization of Eighteenth Century England.* Bloomington: University of Indiana Press, 1982.

Mitchell, Harvey. *The Underground War against Revolutionary France: The Missions of William Wickham, 1794–1800.* Oxford: Oxford University Press, 1965.

Mitchell, L. G. *Charles James Fox and the Disintegration of the Whig Party, 1782–1794.* Oxford: Clarendon Press, 1971.

Mingay, G. E. *English Landed Society in the Eighteenth Century.* London: Routledge, 1963.

———. *Parliamentary Enclosure in England: An Introduction to Its Causes, Incidence, and Improvements, 1750–1850.* London: Longman, 1997.

Moody, T. W., and W. E. Vaughan. *A New History of Ireland: Eighteenth Century Ireland, 1691–1800.* Oxford: Oxford University Press, 1986.

Mori, Jennifer. *Britain in the Age of the French Revolution, 1785–1820.* London: Longman, 2000.

———. *William Pitt and the French Revolution, 1785–1795.* New York: St. Martin's Press, 1997.

Morris, Marilyn. *The British Monarchy and the French Revolution.* New Haven, Conn.: Yale University Press, 1998.

Morriss, Roger. *The Royal Dockyards during the Revolutionary and Napoleonic Wars.* Leicester: Leicester University Press, 1983.

Mostert, Noel. *The Line upon a Wind: The Great War at Sea, 1793–1815.* New York: W. W. Norton, 2007.

Muir, Rory. *Britain and the Defeat of Napoleon, 1807–1815.* New Haven, Conn.: Yale University Press, 1996.

———. *Wellington: Waterloo and the Fortunes of Peace, 1814–1852.* New Haven, Conn.: Yale University Press, 2015.

Munsen, A. E., and Eric Robinson. *Science and Technology in the Industrial Revolution.* Manchester: University of Manchester Press, 1969.

Naumier, Lewis. *The Structure of Politics at the Accession of George III.* London: Macmillan, 1957.

Namier, Lewis, and John Brooke, eds. *The House of Commons, 1754–1790.* 3 vols. New York:. Oxford University Press, 1964.

Nelson, R. R. *The Home Office, 1782–1801.* Durham, N.C.: Duke University Press, 1969.

Nester, William R. *The Age of Jackson and the Art of American Power.* Washington, D.C.: Potomac Books, 2013.

———. *The Age of Lincoln and the Art of American Power.* Washington D.C.: Potomac Books, 2013.

———. *Globalization: A Short History of the Modern World.* New York: Palgrave Macmillan, 2010.

———. *Globalization, War, and Peace in the Twenty-First Century.* New York: Palgrave Macmillan, 2010.

———. *Globalization, Wealth, and Power in the Twenty-First Century.* New York: Palgrave Macmillan, 2010.

———. *The Hamiltonian Vision, 1789–1800: The Art of Power in the Early Republic.* Washington D.C.: Potomac Books, 2012.

———. *The Jeffersonian Vision, 1800–1815.* Washington D.C.: Potomac Books, 2012.

———. *Napoleon and the Art of Diplomacy: How War and Hubris Determined the Rise and Fall of the French Empire.* New York: Savas Beattie, 2012.

Nettels, Curtis P. *The Emergence of a National Economy, 1775–1815.* New York: Holt, Rhinehart, and Winston, 1962.

Newman, Gerald. *The Rise of English Nationalism: A Cultural History, 1740–1830.* Houndmills, Basingstoke: Macmillan, 1997.

Nicholson, Adam. *Seize the Fire: Heoism, Duty, and Nelson's Battle of Trafalgar.* New York: HarperCollins, 2006.

Nicolson, Harold. *The Congress of Vienna: A Study in Allied Unity, 1812–1822.* New York: Harcourt, Brace, and Company, 1946.

Norman, Barbara. *Napoleon and Talleyrand: The Last Two Weeks.* New York: Stein and Day, 1970.

O'Brien, Gerard. *Anglo-Irish Politics in the Age of Grattan and Pitt.* Dublin: Irish Academic Press, 1987.

O'Brien, Patrick. "Political Biography and Pitt the Younger as Chancellor of the Exchequer." *History* 83 (1998): 225–33.

O'Brien, Patrick K. "The Political Economy of British Taxation, 1660–1815." *Economic History Review* 41 (1988): 1–32.

———. *Power with Profit: The State and Economy, 1688–1815.* London: Weidenfeld and Nicolson, 1991.

———."Public Finance in the Wars with France, 1793–1815." In Dickinson, *Britain and the French Revolution.* Basingstoke: Macmillan, 1989.

O'Brien, Patrick K., and Philip A. Hunt. "The Rise of a Fiscal State in England, 1485–1815." *Historical Research* 96 (1993): 129–76.

O'Connell, M. R. *Irish Politics and Social Conflict in the Age of the American Revolution.* Westport, Conn.: Greenwood, 1976.

O'Gorman, F. *The Whig Party and the French Revolution.* Basingstoke, UK: Macmillan, 1967.

O'Gorman, Frank. *The Emergence of the Two Party System, 1760–1832.* London: E. Arnold, 1982.

———. *Voters, Patrons, and Parties: The Unreformed Electoral System of Hanoverian England, 1734–1832.* Oxford: Clarendon Press, 1989.

Oldfield, J. R. *Popular Politics and British Anti-Slavery: The Mobilization of Public Opinion against the Slave Trade, 1787–1807.* Manchester: Manchester University Press, 1995.

Overton, Mark. *Agricultural Revolution in England: The Transformation of the Agrarian Economy, 1500–1850.* Cambridge: Cambridge University Press, 1996.

Padfield, Peter. *Maritime Power and the Struggle for Freedom: Naval Campaigns that Shaped the Modern World, 1788–1851.* London: John Murray, 2003.

Pakenham, Thomas. *The Year of Liberty: The Story of the Great Irish Rebellion of 1798.* London: Hodder and Stoughton, 1969.

Pares, Richard. *King George III and the Politicians.* London: Oxford University Press, 1953.

Parissien, Steven. *George IV: Inspiration of the Regency.* New York: St. Martin's Press, 2001.

Parkinson, C. N. *The Trade Winds: A Study of British Overseas Trade during the French Wars, 1793–1815.* London: Allen and Unwin, 1948.

Parkinson, C. Northcote. *Britannia Rules: The Classic Age of Naval History, 1793–1815.* London: Allan Sutton, 1994.

Pawson, E. *Transport and Economy: The Turnpike Roads of Eighteenth Century Britain.* New York: Academic Press, 1977.

Perkins, Bradford. *Castlereagh and Adams: England and the United States, 1812–1823.* Berkeley: University of California Press, 1964.

———. *Prologue to War: England and the United States, 1805–1812.* Berkeley: University of California Press, 1968.

Perkins, Harold. *The Origins of Modern English Society.* New York: Routledge, 1969.

Phillips, John A. *Electoral Behavior in Unreformed England: Plumpers, Splitters, and Straights.* Princeton, N.J.: Princeton University Press, 1982.

Philp, Mark, ed. *The French Revolution and British Popular Politics.* Cambridge: Cambridge University Press, 1991.

Pocock, Tom. *The Terror Before Trafalgar: Nelson, Napoleon, and the Secret War.* Annapolis, Maryland: Naval Institute Press, 2005.

Pollock, John. *Wilberforce.* New York: St. Martin's Press, 1977.

Pollack, Sidney. *The Genesis of Modern Management: A Study of the Industrial Revolution in Great Britain.* New York: Penguin, 1965.

Pomeranz, Kenneth. *The Great Divergence: China, Europe, and the Making of the Modern World.* Princeton, N.J.: Princeton University Press, 2000.

Porter, Bernard. *The Absent-Minded Imperialists: Empire, Society, and Culture in Britain.* Oxford: Oxford University Press, 2004.

———. *Plots and Paranoia: A History of Political Espionage in Britain, 1790–1988.* New York: Routledge, 1992Porter, Roy. *English Society in the Eighteenth Century.* New York: Penguin, 1982.

———. *Enlightenment: Britain and the Creation of the Modern World.* New York: Penguin, 2000.

Pressnell, L. S. *Country Banking in the Industrial Revolution.* Oxford: Oxford University Press, 1956.

Prest, Wilfrid. *Albion Ascendant: English History, 1660–1815.* Oxford: Oxford University Press, 1998.

Pretyman, George Tomline. *Memoirs of the Life of the Right Hon. William Pitt.* 3 vols.. London: John Murray, 1821.

Ragsdale, Hugh. *Paul I: A Reassessment of His Life and Reign.* Pittsburgh: University of Pittsburgh Press, 1979.

———. *Tsar Paul and the Question of Madness: An Essay in History and Psychology.* New York: Praeger, 1988.

Rappoport, Angelo. *The Curse of the Romanovs: A Study of the Lives and Reigns of Two Tsars, Paul I and Alexander I of Russia.* New York: Forgotten Books, 2012.

Raymond, Joad ed. *News, Newspapers in Early Modern Britain.* London: Routledge, 1999.

Reilly, Robin. *William Pitt the Younger: A Biography.* New York: G.P. Putnam's Sons, 1978.

Remini, Robert V. *The Battle of New Orleans.* New York: Penguin Books, 1999.

Roberts, Andrew. *Napoleon and Wellington: The Battle of Waterloo and the Great Commanders Who Fought It.* New York: Simon and Schuster, 2001.

Roberts, M. J. D. *Making English Morals: Voluntary Associations and Moral Reform in England, 1787–1886.* New York: Cambridge University Press, 2004.

Rodger, N. A. M. *The Command of the Ocean: A Naval History of Britain, 1649–1815.* New York: W. W. Norton, 2006.

———. *The Wooden World: An Anatomy of the Georgian Navy.* New York: W. W. Norton, 1986.

Rogers, Nicholas. *Crowds, Culture, and Politics in Georgian Britain.* Oxford: Oxford University Press, 1998.

Rohl, J. C. G., M. Warren, and D. Warren. *Purple Secret, Genes, "Madness," and the Royal House of Europe.* London: Corgi Books, 1999.

Rose, J. Holland. "The Duke of Richmond on the Conduct of the War in 1793." *English Historical Review* 25, no. 99 (July 1910): 554–55.

———. *Pitt and Napoleon: Essays and Letters.* London: Hand Press, 2012.

———. *William Pitt and National Revival.* London: G. Bell and Sons, 1911.

———. *William Pitt and the Great War.* London: G. Bell and Sons, 1911.

Ross, Steven T. *The Quest for Victory: French Military Strategy, 1792–1799.* New York: A.S. Barnes and Company, 1973.

Rosselli, John. *Lord William Bentinck, 1774–1839.* London: Chatto and Windus, 1974.

Royle, Edward. *Revolutionary Britain?: Reflections on the Threat of Revolution in Britain, 1789–1848.* Manchester: Manchester University Press, 2000.

Rude, G. *The Crowd in History: A Study of Popular Disturbances in France and England, 1730–1848.* New York: Wiley, 1964.

Rule, John. *Albion's People: English Society, 1714–1815.* London: Longman, 1997.

———. "Manufacturing and Commerce." In H. T. Dickinson, ed., *A Companion to Eighteenth Century Britain.* Oxford: Blackwell, 2006.

Sack, James J. *From Jacobite to Conservative: Reaction and Orthodoxy in Britain, 1760–1832.* New York: Cambridge University Press, 1993.

———. *The Grenvillites, 1801–1829: Party Politics and Factionalism in the Age of Pitt and Liverpool.* Urbana: University of Illinois Press, 1979.

Sainty, J. C. *Peerage Creations, 1649–1800.* London: Whitey Blackwell, 1998.

Schneid, Frederick C. *Napoleon's Italian Campaigns, 1805–1815.* Westport, Conn.: Praeger, 2002.

Schom, Alan. *Trafalgar: Countdown to Battle, 1803–1805.* New York: Oxford University Press, 1990.

Schroeder, Paul W. "Did the Vienna Settlement Rest on a Balance of Power?" *American Historical Review* 97, no. 3 (June 1992): 683–97.

———. "Historical Reality vs. Neo-Realists Theory." *International Security* 19, no. 1 (Summer 1994,): 108–48.

———. *The Transformation of European Politics, 1763–1848.* Oxford: Clarendon Press, 1994.

Schulze, Hegan. *States, Nations, and Nationalism from the Middle Ages to the Present.* Oxford: Clarendon Press, 1996.

Scott, H. M. *British Foreign Policy in the Age of the American Revolution.* Oxford: Oxford University Press, 1990.

Semmel, Bernard. *The Rise of Free Trade Imperialism: Classical Political Economy, the Empire of Free Trade, and Imperialism, 1750–1850.* Cambridge: Cambridge University Press, 1970.

Semmel, Stuart. *Napoleon and the British.* New Haven, Conn.: Yale University Press, 2004.

Severn, John. *Architects of Empire: The Duke of Wellington and His Brothers.* Norman: University of Oklahoma Press, 2007.

———. *A Wellesley Affair: Richard Marquess Wellesley and the Conduct of Anglo-Spanish Diplomacy, 1809–1812.* Tallahassee: University of Florida Press, 1981.

Shoemaker, Robert. *The London Mob: Violence and Disorder in Eighteenth Century England.* London: Hambledon, 2004.

Simms, Brendan. *The Impact of Napoleon: Prussian High Politics, Foreign Policy, and the Crisis of the Executive, 1797–1806.* New York: Cambridge University Press, 1997.

———. *Three Victories and a Defeat: The Rise and Fall of the First British Empire.* New York: Basic Books, 2007.

Smith, Anthony D. *Theories of Nationalism.* London: Holmes and Mier, 1983.

Smith, E. A. *George IV.* New Haven, Conn.: Yale University Press, 1999.

Smith, Olivia. *The Politics of Language, 1791–1819.* Oxford: Oxford University Press, 1984.

Smyth, Jim. *The Men of No Property: Irish Radicals and Popular Politics in the Late Eighteenth Century.* Basingstoke, UK: Palgrave Macmillan, 1992.

Sparrow, Elizabeth. *Secret Service: British Agents in France, 1792–1815.* London: Boydell Press, 1999.

Spencer, Peter. *The Birth of Romantic Radicalism: War, Popular Politics, and English Radical Reformism, 1800–1815.* Aldershot, UK: Scholar Press, 1996.

Stafford, William. *Socialism, Radicalism, and Nostalgia: Social Criticism in Britain, 1775–1830.* New York: Cambridge University Press, 1987.

Stanhope, Lord Philip Henry. *Life of the Right Honorable William Pitt.* 4 vols.. London: John Murray, 1867.

Stewart, A. T. Q. *A Deeper Silence: The Hidden Origins of the United Irishmen.* Belfast: Blackstaff Press, 1993.

Stone, Lawrence, ed. *An Imperial State at War: Britain from 1689 to 1815.* London: Routledge, 1994.

Stuart Jones, E. H. *An Invasion that Failed: The French Expedition to Ireland, 1796.* Oxford: Oxford University Press, 1950.

Sun Tzu. *The Art of War.* Oxford: Clarendon Press, 1963.

Thompson, E. P. *The Making of the English Working Class.* New York: Penguin, 1969.

Thompson, F. M. L. *Gentrification and the Enterprise Culture: Britain, 1780–1980.* Oxford: Oxford University Press, 2001.

Thorne, R. G., ed. *The History of Parliament: The House of Commons, 1790–1820.* 5 vols. London: Haynes Publishing, 1986.

Tilley, Charles, ed. *The Formation of Nation States in Western Europe.* Princeton, N.J.: Princeton University Press, 1975.

———. *Popular Contention in Great Britain, 1758–1834.* Cambridge, Mass.: Harvard University Press, 1995.

Toll, Ian W. *Six Frigates: The Epic History of the Founding of the U.S. Navy.* New York: W. W. Norton, 2006.

Tolstoy, Leo. *War and Peace.* New York: Vintage Classics, 2007.

Torrance, J. "Social Class and Bureaucratic Innovation: The Commissioners for Examining the Public Accounts, 1780–1787." *Past and Present* 78, 1 (1978), 56–81.

Tunzelman, G. N. *Steam Power and British Industrialization to 1860.* Oxford: Oxford University Press, 1978.

Turberville, A. S. *The House of Lords in the Age of Reform, 1784–1837.* London: Faber and Faber, 1958.

Turley, David. *The Culture of English Antislavery, 1780.* London: Routledge, 1991.

Turner, E. S. *Gallant Gentlemen: A Portrait of the English Officer.* London: M. Joseph, 1956.

Turner, Michael J. *The Age of Unease: Government and Reform in Britain, 1782–1832.* London: Longman, 2000.

Updyke, Frank A. *The Diplomacy of the War of 1812.* Glousceter, Mass.: P. Smith, 1965.

Urban, Mark. *The Man Who Broke Napoleon's Codes: The True Story of a Forgotten Hero in Wellington's Army*. New York: HarperCollins, 2001.

Vries, Jan de. *European Urbanization, 1500–1800.* Cambridge, Mass.: Harvard University Press, 1984.

Wahrman, Dror. *Imagining the Middle Class: The Political Representation of Class in Britain, 1780–1840.* New York: Cambridge University Press, 1995.

———. *The Making of the Modern Self: Identity and Culture in Eighteenth Century England. New Haven, Conn.*: Yale University Press, 2004.

Ward, Adolphus William, and George Peabody Gooch, eds. *The Cambridge History of British Foreign Policy, 1783–1919.* Cambridge: Cambridge University Press, 2011.

Ward, A. W., G. W. Protheero, and Stanley Leathes, eds. *The Cambridge Modern History: Napoleon.* New York: Macmillan, 1909.

Ward, J. R. *The Finance of Canal Building in Eighteenth Century England.* London:. Oxford University Press 1974.

Watson, John. *The Reign of George III.* Oxford: Clarendon Press, 1960.

Webster, C. K. *The Foreign Policy of Castlereagh, 1812–1815: Britain and the Reconstruction of Europe.* London: G. Bell and Sons, 1931.

Weller, Jac. *Wellington in the Peninsula.* Mechanicsburg, Penn.: Stackpole Books, 1992.

Wells, Roger. *Insurrection: The British Experience, 1795–1803.* Gloucester: Sutton, 1983.

———. *Wretched Faces: Famine in Wartime England, 1793–1801.* Gloucester: Sutton, 1988.

Werkmeister, Lucyle. *A Newspaper History of England.* Lincoln: University of Nebraska Press, 1988.

Western, John R. *The English Militia in the Eighteenth Century: The Story of a Political Issue, 1660–1802.* London: Routledge, 1965.

Wharam, Alan. *The Treason Trials, 1794.* Leicester: Leicester University Press, 1992.

Wilberforce, Robert, and Samuel Wilberforce. *The Life of William Wilberforce.* London: John Murray, 1838.

Wilkinson, Clive. *The British Navy and the State in the Eighteenth Century.* London: Boydell Press, 2004.

Wilkinson, David. *The Duke of Portland: Politics and Party in the Age of George III.* Basingstoke, UK.: Palgrave Macmillan, 2003.

Williams, Gwyn A. *Artisans and Sans Culottes: Popular Movements in France and Britain during the French Revolution.* London: Edward Arnold, 1989.

Williams, Judith Blow. *British Commercial Policy and Trade Expansion, 1750–1850.* Oxford: Oxford University Press, 1972.

Williamson, Jeffrey G. *Coping with City Growth during the British Industrial Revolution.* New York: Cambridge University Press, 1990.

Wilson, Kathleen. *The Sense of the People: Politics, Culture, and Imperialism in England, 1715–1785.* Cambridge: Cambridge University Press, 1995.

Wolfe, Janet, and John Seed, eds. *The Culture of Capital: Art, Power, and the Nineteenth Century Middle Class.* Manchester: Manchester University Press, 1988.

Worrall, David. *Radical Culture: Discourse, Resistance, and Surveillance, 1790–1820.* Detroit: Wayne State University Press, 1992.

Wrighley, E. A. *Continuity, Chance, and Change: The Character of the Industrial Revolution in England.* Cambridge: Cambridge University Press, 1988.

Wrigley, F. A., and R. S. Schofield, The Population History of England, 1541–1871. New York: Cambridge University Press, 1989.

Yapp, M. E. *Strategies of British India: Britain, Iran, and Afghanistan, 1798–1850.* Oxford: Oxford University Press, 1980.

Yonge, Duke Charles. *The Life and Administration of Robert Banks, Second Earl of Liverpool, K.G.* 3 vols. London: Macmillan, 1868.

Ziegler, Philip. *Addington: A Life of Henry Addington, First Viscount Sidmouth.* New York: John Day Company, 1965.

# Index